Five Years a Dragoon
('49 to '54)
And Other Adventures on the Great Plains

FIVE YEARS A DRAGOON

('49 to '54)

And Other Adventures on the Great Plains

† † † † † † † † † † †

BY PERCIVAL G. LOWE

With an introduction and notes by Don Russell
Foreword by Jerome A. Greene

†

UNIVERSITY OF OKLAHOMA PRESS
NORMAN AND LONDON

To the Memory

of Major David H. Hastings, U.S.A., who died in retirement at his home in Bath, New York, to whom I owe more than to any other for his kindly guidance in my youth and inexperience while serving under him, and whose friendly care led me through the greatest difficulties, this volume is gratefully dedicated by the author.

Library of Congress Catalog Card Number: 65-11223
ISBN: 0-8061-1089-9

New edition copyright © 1965 by the University of Oklahoma Press, Publishing Division of the University. All rights reserved. Manufactured in the U.S.A. First printing of the new edition, 1965. First paperback printing, 1991.

Contents

† † † † † † † † † † †

	Foreword, by Jerome A. Greene	page ix
	Editor's Introduction	xi
	Editor's Note on Identification	xxix
	Author's Preface	xxxi
Part I	Enlistment and First Assignment	3
Part II	The First Two Years	27
Part III	Campaigns of 1852–53	78
Part IV	From Soldier to Civilian	124
Part V	At Fort Riley	143
Part VI	The Kansas War of 1856	167
Part VII	The Cheyenne Expedition	185
Part VIII	Mule Trains to Utah	229
Part IX	Private Business and Government Service	277
Part X	Freighter and Contractor	312
	Index	324

Illustrations

† † † † † † † † † † †

Percival G. Lowe *following page* 64
Parade ground at Fort Leavenworth, 1865
Fort Kearny, 1858
Fort Laramie, 1855
Soldiers in uniform
Colonel Samuel Cooper
Major General Philip St. George Cooke
Brevet Brigadier General Albert Sidney Johnston

Monument to Major E. A. Ogden *following page* 192
Cavalry stables, Fort Riley
Post exchange, Fort Riley
Post hospital, Fort Riley
Battle of Wounded Knee monument, Fort Riley
Kaw Methodist mission, Council Grove
Pioneer store, Council Grove
Denver in 1859

Sketches

Wagon corral	*page* 210
Six-mule team	287
The camp	294

Foreword
by Jerome A. Greene

☩ ☩ ☩ ☩ ☩ ☩ ☩ ☩ ☩ ☩ ☩

Few military reminiscences stand alone as salient documents for the eras they depict. Most diaries and journals—even personal narratives written years after the events—generally comprise one-dimensional tracts requiring augmentation from additional sources to achieve thoroughness and objectivity. Such is not the case with Percival G. Lowe's *Five Years A Dragoon ('49 to '54) And Other Adventures on the Great Plains*, first published in 1906, more than fifty years after its author enlisted at a Boston recruiting station. In the more than eighty years that have passed since *Five Years a Dragoon* first appeared (including twenty-five since its first republication by the University of Oklahoma Press), Lowe's history of his experiences on the antebellum trans-Mississippi frontier has become a classic. Military descriptions of this period, particularly those written by enlisted men, are rare; Lowe's book, therefore, provides valuable data from that perspective about the role of the U.S. Army during its early operations in the West. In effect, these activities presaged the great post–Civil War Indian campaigns that lasted into the 1890s.

Particularly important was Lowe's participation in, and subsequent descriptions of, several significant episodes in western history as a soldier with the First Regiment U.S. Dragoons and later as a civilian employee of the Quartermaster Department. In 1851 he witnessed the grand councils at Fort Laramie and Fort Atkinson that sought to instill peace among the Indians by defining tribal boundaries and that set the tone for Indian-white (and Indian-Indian) relations for years to come. In 1855, Lowe was at Fort Riley, Kansas, when a highly virulent cholera epidemic struck the post with crippling intensity. Two years later he accompanied Colonel Edwin V. Sumner's famous expedition against the Cheyennes, and a year after that became peripherally involved in Utah Territory's "Mormon War." Throughout his frontier service, Lowe's unit engaged Indians only a few times and—at least by the time he recorded his memoirs—he attained considerable respect for them.

Lowe's account of his adventures in the West offers literate, first-person history that is as important today as when it initially appeared. Complementing the text, Don Russell's introductory discussion about the army's composition between 1848 and 1861 provides military context for Lowe's reminiscences. Moreover, his insightful explanation of the pervasive and perplexing system of brevet rank employed by the nineteenth-century army remains a welcome bonus. Russell's judiciously employed editorial notes further enhance Lowe's narrative with expert information and commentary by one not only familiar with the era, but who personally knew many veterans of the Indian-fighting army. In sum, the combination of Lowe and Russell is too good to pass up. Happily, this latest reprinting of *Five Years a Dragoon* assures continued availability of a worthy contribution to frontier military history.

Editor's Introduction

☩ ☩ ☩ ☩ ☩ ☩ ☩ ☩ ☩ ☩ ☩

This book is unusual first because it was written by an enlisted man of the Regular Army during a time of peace—disturbed only by those police actions we call Indian wars. Of books or long narratives written by enlisted men during the entire period of Indian wars, there are perhaps a score or so. Many officers wrote of their experiences, as did a considerable number of officers' wives. There are a few books by correspondents for newspapers and magazines, and a few by such civilian employees as scouts. However, almost all of these narratives of Indian wars relate to the period following the Civil War. The period covered by Percival G. Lowe, between the Mexican War and the Civil War, received scant attention. Yet it marked the beginning of more than a half century of almost continuous Indian warfare.

That statement will be accepted without question by those who take their ideas of the West from the dramas of television and motion pictures. The warfare was continuous only in that scarcely a month passed without soldiers somewhere having one or two fights with Indians. It was not continuous if that implies that all soldiers in Western garrisons were always fighting Indians. Actually the warfare was sporadic and casual. At no time did all Indians, any considerable part of them, or even an entire tribe unite against white invasion. In few of the 206 fights recorded between 1848 and 1861 were as many as a hundred soldiers engaged. Many were fought by very small detachments. It can be figured, not too accurately, that a soldier would average one Indian fight during a five year enlistment. Lowe about hit the average. Of the two or three minor brushes with Indians that he describes, none resulted in casualties to troops; hence, they are not included in the official list of engagements. Yet the First Dragoons was one of the most active regiments on the frontier. During Lowe's five years his regiment recorded sixteen Indian fights. Nine of them were fought by one company or less; seven by two companies or parts of two companies. Lowe's company had had two fights of record the fall before he joined it.

Lowe's service was typical of the period. It was not devoid of incident or adventure, but it also included many days of hardship on the march and of boredom in garrison. In these marches, however, he saw the Santa Fe Trail and the Oregon Trail in their days of heaviest wagon traffic. The posts he knew include some of the most famous in the history of the Westward Movement—Fort Leavenworth and Fort Riley, still occupied by troops; Fort Laramie and Fort Union, both preserved by the National Park Service; and Fort Kearny, the site of which is a state park.

Historic interest in the things he did and the places he describes is distinctly secondary, however, to that in the persons he met and knew. In his decade as dragoon, quartermaster employee, and freighter of goods, he names, often quite casually, a roster that is a who's who of the Plains.

What Lowe says about Jim Bridger has often been quoted, for facts are few and legends many concerning this dean of the mountain men. Lowe also mentions Tom Fitzpatrick, Andrew Dripps, William Bent, Lucian B. Maxwell, and Kit Carson; Francis X. Aubrey of the famous ride; John M. Hockaday of stagecoach fame; William H. H. Larimer, founder of Denver; John W. Iliff, cattle king; Frank Grouard, scout; Senator David C. Broderick of California, and B. Gratz Brown, who ran for Vice-President. Indians mentioned were Spotted Tail, Man-Afraid-of-His-Horses, Satanta of the Kiowas (or maybe it was Satank), and Fall Leaf, who discovered Pikes Peak gold.

The officers Lowe knew included twenty-two who became major generals and fifteen who became brigadier generals on the Union side in the Civil War, and nine who became general offi-

Editor's Introduction

cers after the war. On the Confederate side were two generals (Samuel Cooper and Albert Sidney Johnston), three lieutenant generals (Simon Bolivar Buckner, T. H. Holmes, and Stephen D. Lee), six major generals, and eleven brigadier generals.

There were not to be that many general officers in the army again until World War II, and one wonders if any enlisted man of that later period knew as many as sixty officers who became generals.

Recognizable names are among those known by Lowe—Hancock, Harney, Sumner, Canby, Carr, Marcy, Cooke, Sturgis, Emory, Marmaduke, Porter.

THE AUTHOR

Little need be added to what Percival G. Lowe tells about himself in his book. He was born in Randolph, Coos County, New Hampshire, September 29, 1828. His father, Clovis Lowe, was merchant, real estate dealer, justice of the peace, and Democratic member of the legislature. Percival's mother was Alpha Abigail, daughter of Thomas Green of Scotch descent. The "G." may stand for Green, his mother's family name, but all references found name him either as "Percival G. Lowe" or "P. G. Lowe."

He had a sister and three brothers. Oscar died in 1898 in Cambridge, Massachusetts. Pembroke C. S. Lowe briefly managed the Box Elder Ranch for Percival at the beginning of the Civil War, went to Leavenworth when the ranch was sold, served in the Quartermaster's Department during the war, and in later years lived in Phillips County, Kansas. The most notable member of the family was Thaddeus Sobieski Constantine Lowe who became a balloonist and headed the army's first air reconnaissance unit (if it can be called a unit) during the Civil War. He also developed water gas and refrigeration and built an electric railway from his home in Pasadena, California, to the summit of Mount Lowe.

Percival, when fourteen- or fifteen-years-old, went to Lowell, Massachusetts, where he worked as a newsboy and a clerk in a dry-goods store. He was a sailor two years in the coastal trade, returned to Lowell and learned the daguerreotype business, and in January, 1849, went to sea again in the whaling ship *Jane Howes*, which voyaged to Puerto Rico, Bermuda, the Azores, and the Gulf of Mexico.

On his return in the fall, he determined to enlist in the mounted service, inspired to seek further adventure by his reading, he says, of the novels of Marryat, Cooper, and Scott, Frémont's reports of his explorations, and Irving's *Adventures of Captain Bonneville*.

Both in background and disposition Lowe may seem an unusual recruit for the peacetime army, and his rapid advancement—to first sergeant during his five-year enlistment—is an indication of outstanding qualities. Yet he tells us of finding others of his own kind in barracks, and at no time does he give any impression of feeling himself set apart from his fellow soldiers. Almost everyone who writes of the Regular Army in the Indian wars tends to downgrade the enlisted men. Officers who served with them over-emphasize the numbers of foreigners, principally Irish and Germans, although at all times native-born Americans were in the majority. Desertion and other crimes were common enough, as Lowe tells us, and heroic fighting men were rarely plaster saints, but men who were misfits in civilian life were not necessarily so in the army. The soldier had many advantages over the unskilled laborer of the nineteenth century, and enlisted men came largely from the ranks of unskilled labor. Few had much education, but even fewer were depraved or vicious.

No doubt remains that this was Lowe's assessment of his fellow soldiers as he tells of his departure at the end of his enlistment. "My last roll call was made at reveille," he says, "and I passed from right to left of the troop and shook hands with every man. I was obliged to nerve myself to the utmost to meet this trial, one of the greatest of my life. My work was done, I had turned my back on my best friends. I would never make better."

Editor's Introduction

Lowe, however, felt that he had learned all he could in the army and saw a better future as civilian employee of the Quartermaster's Department, in which he served five years. In 1855 he was master of transportation of the party sent to build Fort Riley, and there he survived one of the worst cholera epidemics ever to strike an army post. In 1856 he was in charge of supplies for troops sent to quell disorders in "Bleeding Kansas." In 1857 he was master of transportation for Colonel Sumner's campaign against the Cheyennes. In 1858, Lowe was in charge of wagon trains for the army of Utah in the "Mormon War." These years were quite as adventurous as his years of enlistment.

In 1859, Lowe joined the Pikes Peak gold rush and engaged in a mercantile and jobbing business in Denver. At the end of 1860 he organized a freighting business. When the Civil War began he turned down a commission as lieutenant colonel of Colorado Volunteers because he did not think the war would last very long. He had just started his own business, and had been recently married—perhaps the fact that his wife's family owned slaves was a factor. However, through most of the war and for several years afterward he was employed in transporting supplies for the federal army.

In Leavenworth he was president of the city council and police commissioner. He was also sheriff and state senator. He was a life member and director of the Kansas State Historical Society and its president in 1893. He contributed to the *Kansas Historical Collections* and the *United States Cavalry Journal*.

Percival G. Lowe died on March 5, 1908, in San Antonio, Texas, and was buried in the military cemetery at Leavenworth beside his wife, who had died three years before.

Five Years a Dragoon was published by the Franklin Hudson Publishing Company in Kansas City, Missouri, in 1906. It commands no great price as rarity, yet copies are sufficiently scarce that most of them now are to be found in reference libraries, where they are more often quoted than read. It is a book worth reading.

Five Years a Dragoon
United States Army, 1848–61

The army Lowe joined in 1849 was still in the process of being cut back after its expansion for the war with Mexico. Although the Regular Army had a large share in the fighting, it had been expanded by only ten temporary line regiments, actually less than had been employed in the War of 1812. That was possible because of a modification of the militia system called the Volunteer Army. Every male citizen was a member of the militia, liable to service in case of invasion or insurrection. There had been dispute, verging on mutiny, during the War of 1812 whether militia could be ordered to leave its state, and there was considerable doubt whether it could be called to serve in a foreign country (Mexico). These difficulties were solved by asking citizens to volunteer for federal service in regiments organized under state control. The volunteer system worked creakily, but was immensely popular, and was continued through the Civil War and Spanish-American War.

The annexation of Texas in 1845, settlement of the dispute with Great Britain over the Oregon country in 1846, and acquisition of the Southwest after conclusion of the Mexican War in 1848, added two-thirds as much territory as had been the United States in 1844. Putting it another way, the acquisitions of four years totaled two-fifths of the present forty-eight contiguous states. The new territory was inhabited by thousands of Indians, some hostile; others would be. With a lack of logic for which this democracy has frequently been distinguished, the army was cut to its lowest strength since 1838. The authorized figure was 10,317, including 882 officers, organized in fifteen regiments. Even after four more regiments were added in 1855, there was available one soldier to protect 120 square miles west of the Mississippi River, where most of the army was employed. East of the Mississippi there was one soldier to 1,300 square miles.

The peacetime army, when Lowe joined, consisted of eight regiments of infantry, four of artillery, two of dragoons, and one

Editor's Introduction

of mounted riflemen—the same as in 1846, before the war. Each artillery regiment had twelve companies, two of which were light artillery with horse-drawn guns. The rest manned seacoast defenses and other permanent fortifications. During the Mexican War more than half of the artillery companies served as infantry, and frequently they served as infantry in Indian wars.

Dragoons theoretically were troops trained to fight both on foot and on horseback. A dragoon was armed with a musketoon, which was a short, smooth-bore musket, a horse pistol, also smooth-bore, and a sabre. *Cavalry Tactics, 1841*, under which all mounted troops were trained, provided for instruction with the lance, but there is no record of it ever having been employed in battle. The dragoons formed a separate branch of service, with a six-pointed star as an emblem and facing colors of orange.

The First Regiment of United States Dragoons, which Lowe joined, totaled 650 persons. It was commanded by a colonel, assisted by a lieutenant colonel and two majors. Heading the regimental staff was the adjutant, an extra first lieutenant being allotted to the regiment to fill that office. The regimental quartermaster was a lieutenant detailed from one of the companies. Enlisted men of the regimental staff were a sergeant major, a quartermaster sergeant, a principal musician, and two chief buglers.

Each of the ten companies had a captain, a first lieutenant, and a second lieutenant. Enlisted men were four sergeants, four corporals, two buglers, one farrier-and-blacksmith, and fifty privates.

Other regiments were similarly organized, but with some differences. The Regiment of Mounted Riflemen, raised especially to guard the Oregon Trail, also had ten companies, but each of sixty-four privates. Infantry regiments had ten companies, each of forty-two privates. Artillery companies also had forty-two privates. Each artillery regiment was allowed twenty-four musicians for a band, but infantry bands were limited to twenty pieces, augmented usually by the company drums, fifes, and bugles, and the regimental principal and chief musicians. Dragoons and riflemen got along without bands.

The Quartermaster General was a brigadier general; all other departments were headed by colonels, and only two had any enlisted men assigned. The Ordnance Department had 37 officers, 53 sergeants, and 495 enlisted men of ordnance—they were not called privates, and the number was not specifically limited. The Corps of Engineers had 43 officers and a company of 100 enlisted men, including 78 privates, stationed at West Point as an instruction and demonstration company. The Corps of Topographical Engineers, which was a separate service charged with exploring and map making, consisted of 37 officers.

The Adjutant General had thirteen officers as assistants, of whom nine retained commissions in their regiments. There were two inspectors general, and that was all there was in that department. The Judge Advocate was not even a department; that office was held by a brevet major who also retained his regimental commission. The Surgeon General in 1848 headed eighty surgeons and assistant surgeons, but that number was to be cut to seventy. Under the Paymaster General were thirty officers, but he was to cut down to eighteen paymasters. Eight officers made up the Subsistence Department.

As Lowe became a civilian employe of the Quartermaster's Department after 1854, its organization is given in more detail as of that period—although changes were slight. An act of Congress of March 3, 1855, recognized that more soldiers were needed to fight Indians and added two regiments of cavalry and two of infantry to the army. Cavalry was a separate branch of service from dragoons and mounted riflemen, and each had its own promotion list. (The three branches were consolidated at the beginning of the Civil War as cavalry: the First and Second Dragoons becoming the First and Second Cavalry; the Regiment of Mounted Riflemen becoming the Third Cavalry; and the First and Second Cavalry of 1855 were renumbered Fourth and Fifth.)

Editor's Introduction

The Quartermaster General was Thomas Sidney Jesup, who had held that office as brigadier general since 1818. In 1828 he was breveted major general for ten years faithful service in one grade. He died in 1860. There were two assistant quartermaster generals with the rank of colonel; two deputy quartermaster generals with the rank of lieutenant colonel; four quartermasters with the rank of major (there had been eight in 1848); and twenty-eight assistant quartermasters with the rank of captain, of whom six continued to hold rank in line regiments and served in the Quartermaster's Department as brevet captains. (In 1848 there had been thirty-eight assistant quartermasters, of whom twenty were brevet captains detailed from line regiments.)

Heading this army in 1848 were two major generals and four brigadier generals, but Congress provided that no vacancies were to be filled until this was reduced to one major general and two brigadier generals. The reduction was not long in coming. Zachary Taylor resigned as major general in 1849 to become President. Brigadier General Stephen Watts Kearny died in 1848. E. P. Gaines, who had been brigadier general since 1814, died in 1849. J. E. Wool and D. E. Twiggs were the surviving brigadier generals.

The major general was Winfield Scott. In 1855 Congress authorized his promotion to brevet lieutenant general, to date from his victory at Veracruz in 1847. On the day he received that commission Scott filed a claim for back pay and allowances on the ground that as commanding general of the army he had been on duty in his brevet rank. An opinion of the attorney general upheld Scott's claim and he collected. It would have been simpler and less expensive to have promoted him to the lineal rank.

This wariness of high rank, starvation of the staff, and destitution of the line can be understood only in consideration of the tremendous popular prejudice against the very idea of a Regular Army. Typical is a complaint of Horace Greeley in 1859 (in his *An Overland Journey*): "Whenever our people shall have grown wise enough to maintain no standing army whatever but the barest skeleton of one, to be clothed with flesh whenever needed by calling out volunteers, the annual expenditures may be reduced at least one-fourth." Within two years the existing skeleton was to prove wholly inadequate.

Had it not been for Indian wars there probably would have been no Regular Army, yet at no time was it organized and trained to fight Indians. Always the Indian wars were considered a temporary disturbance that would soon be over. However, Congress was unwilling to provide for the army any but fighting men. The appropriation acts set forth in detail the organization of each unit of the army—yet no unit was thus organized. Most of the officers in the staff departments, all officers who were instructors at the Military Academy, all on recruiting service, all who were aides-de-camp, and some who were Indian agents were taken from the officers assigned to regiments and companies. Few companies on the frontier had two officers present for duty; many had only one.

BREVET COMMISSIONS

Footnotes give in some detail the military records of most of the officers known by Lowe, including their brevet commissions. These records reveal much about the army of the 1850's, the slowness of promotion, the variety of duties performed, and the curiosities of the brevet system. No one writing now about the Indian-fighting army understands the brevet system. That is not a presumptuous statement, for no one in the army understood it while it was in use. For example, Generals Scott and Gaines indulged in acrimonious and public argument over relative brevet rank that nearly resulted in courts-martial for both of them and did result in both of them being passed over for promotion to a vacancy as major general commanding the army.

Almost all definitions of brevet rank in dictionaries and other works of reference are in error. The most common definition is a commission that entitles an officer to rank above his pay. We have seen that Scott was paid as lieutenant general by brevet and even collected back pay on a pre-dated commission. It is often defined as an honorary commission, but brevets were used for many purposes that had nothing to do with honors. It has been called a temporary commission, but an honorary brevet had more permanency than a commission in the line. An officer might be employed temporarily in his brevet commission, but that employment might also be permanent, as was Scott's. On the other hand, brevets were sometimes used to give pay in advanced rank for a temporary assignment. Many definitions state that brevets were granted in ranks from first lieutenant to lieutenant general. Actually there were brevets in all ranks from second lieutenant to general.

Brevet Major General James Barnet Fry, in his *The History and Legal Effect of Brevets in the Armies of Great Britain and the United States* (New York, Van Nostrand, 1877), defined the brevet as "a commission conferring upon an officer a grade *in the Army* additional to and higher than that which he holds by virtue of his commission *in a particular corps* [italics mine] of a legally established military organization." That is technical, complicated, and almost tells the story, but the Brevet Major General seems to have made one slip: What was a brevet second lieutenant higher than?

A great many of the officers known to Lowe started their army careers as brevet second lieutenants. This occurred during a long period in which there were more West Point graduates each year than there were vacancies in the army. These officers were attached to and served with a regiment, but did not belong to it. Obviously they were paid in their brevet rank. Some got regular commissions immediately; some not for as much as two years. They were not, as might be supposed, supernumerary shavetails tagging along for instruction and training. Arriving at his company in which there were no vacancies, the brevet second lieutenant perhaps found his captain serving as post quartermaster, his first lieutenant acting as aide to the division commander, and his second lieutenant on recruiting service. There were even cases known of officers sick, or on leave. The responsibility given a brevet second lieutenant without a home to call his own was sometimes appalling.

Warfare with the Sioux might have started had there been no such bungled affair as the Grattan massacre, but it was the first encounter and it was bungled. The victim and detachment commander was a brevet second lieutenant, James Lawrence Grattan, who served in that lowly grade from the day of his graduation from West Point, July 1, 1853, until he was killed, August 19, 1854. A classmate of his, Philip Henry Sheridan, was brevet second lieutenant until November 22 of that year. Grattan was sent on his ill-fated mission from Fort Laramie, one of the most important posts on the Plains, by its commanding officer, Second Lieutenant Hugh Brady Fleming, an officer of two years' service, one of them as brevet second lieutenant.

During the Mexican War there were a few cases of non-commissioned officers becoming brevet second lieutenants for gallant and meritorious service in battle. One so honored was David H. Hastings, to whom Lowe dedicates this book. It is also of record that Private Frederick W. Stowe, First Connecticut Light Artillery, was brevetted second lieutenant for meritorious services in the Civil War to date from June 12, 1865.

There is at least one other bestowal of this grade. The State of Illinois, which seems to be a law unto itself in military titles—the state has commissioned at least three lieutenant generals at times when that rank was a rarity in federal services—has bestowed upon graduates of high school R.O.T.C. courses the rank of brevet second lieutenant in the Illinois National Guard.

Lowe knew several officers who were or had been brevet captains in the Quartermaster's Department. These officers retained their commissions, usually as first lieutenants, in line regiments until in course of time they were promoted to the regular rank of captain quartermaster. Few ever returned from staff to line duty. Similarly four assistant adjutant generals were brevet majors

Editor's Introduction

and eight were brevet captains, although not all of them retained regimental commissions. The judge advocate was a brevet major and captain in the Ordnance Department. All these officers were paid in their brevet ranks. The only saving to the government was in not filling the places of those who retained commissions in their legally established military organization. Of course somewhere down the line the vacancy was eventually occupied by a brevet second lieutenant.

Brevet rank originated in England in 1692 and came to America at the beginning of the Revolution when the Articles of War of the British Army were adopted almost verbatim. The original purpose seems to have been to give regimental officers an additional rank for duty outside his regular assignment. This would not apply to general officers, who had no assignments to organizations. During the Revolution all troops were raised by states and officers were named by governors, including general officers, and neither the Continental Congress nor General Washington had power to promote them. It was dispute over this matter that led to the treason of Benedict Arnold. Brevet commissions were within the power of Congress and seem to have been used principally to employ foreign officers as engineers and in other staff positions.

From 1784 to 1791 the commander of the United States Army was Josiah Harmar, who was lieutenant colonel commandant of its only regiment. In 1787 he was commissioned brevet brigadier general, possibly to give him rank over militia officers called to serve with him in Indian fighting.

The brevet as an award of merit got legal recognition in the act of Congress of July 6, 1812, which authorized the President to confer brevet commissions for gallant actions or meritorious conduct, or to officers who shall have served ten years in any one grade. During the War of 1812 such brevets were conferred on 155 officers, and the army managed to employ and pay most of them in their brevet ranks. Congress clamped down on this in

1818, requiring advice and consent of the Senate for brevet commissions and requiring that officers be paid in brevet rank only while actually on duty in higher command.

Somewhere along the line Senators got the idea that brevets were exclusively for battle honors—quite forgetting that every appropriation act manned the staff departments with brevet officers, the original purpose of brevet rank—and after 1829 refused to confirm brevet commissions "for ten years' faithful service in one grade."

During the Mexican War it became customary to recommend for brevet every officer taking part in battle; eventually it was considered a reflection on an officer's conduct if he were not so recommended. Of course each such brevet was of the next highest rank, so that an officer's brevet rank might be several grades higher than his actual rank. In the Civil War this custom was continued, and a blanket act of March 13, 1865, upped nearly everyone one more rank, many of these brevets being "for gallant and meritorious service during the war" without specifying a battle. During the Civil War, however, officers were seldom employed in their brevet ranks. Temporary promotion was taken care of by commissions in the Volunteers.

This led to further complications. Many an officer's record showed him to have been brevet brigadier general of Volunteers, brigadier general of Volunteers, brevet brigadier general, brigadier general, brevet major general of Volunteers, major general of Volunteers, brevet major general, and, rarely, major general. The two Regular Army ranks (for clarity "U.S.A." was sometimes added) were infrequent. After the war there were only five major generals, ten brigadier generals of the line, and nine of the staff. To complete the line-up, there was one lieutenant general—a rank held successively by Grant, Sherman, and Sheridan—and one general—a rank held by Grant and Sherman, and, after a lapse, conferred on Sheridan on his deathbed.

Many officers boasted four commissions as general officers, two in the Volunteers and two by brevet, not counting the pos-

Editor's Introduction

sibility of two more by brevet in the Regular Army. All such Regular Army officers also retained rank in their regiments, and were promoted in those assignments as vacancies occurred during the war. All of the commissions in Volunteers, by brevet or otherwise, were vacated eventually; some of them lasted a year and more after Lee's surrender. There remained 152 brevet major generals and 187 brevet brigadier generals, many of them captains and majors in regular assignment.

However, many found employment in their brevet commissions. The country was divided into five military divisions (geographical, not tactical, divisions) which took care of the major generals of regular rank. Within the divisions were departments, and under the Reconstruction Act each former Confederate state was made a department. The departments were further subdivided into districts, and each district, department, and military division was an appropriate command for a general officer. Many of them were commanded by brevet major generals acting in their brevet ranks. Also the commanders of expeditions against Indians made up of different corps—infantry and cavalry, for example—served in their brevet ranks.

Congress cracked down on brevets again in 1869. The use of brevet ranks on courts-martial, which had been authorized since 1829, was ended. Officers were not to be employed in their brevet ranks except by direction of the President. Thereafter brevets could be conferred only for "distinguished conduct and public service in the presence of the enemy" in time of war. Until 1890 "in time of war" was interpreted as not including Indian wars, which were considered police actions. After Congress reversed its stand, a backlog of recommendations since 1867 was approved by the Senate in 1894, but many officers having long since been promoted to ranks higher than those now offered by brevet declined the empty honor.

An act of 1870 banned the wearing of uniform of brevet rank while on duty in lineal rank and similarly banned the use of brevet rank in official communications.

It may be noted that almost all of Lowe's references to officers are in their brevet ranks. This was no mere matter of military courtesy; it extended, by necessity, to official correspondence, for who, except perhaps an officer's immediate superior, would know whether he was serving at any particular time in his brevet or his lineal rank. It would have been an absurdity to address a brevet major or brevet captain in the Quartermaster's Department by his regimental rank in which he had not served perhaps for years and, in all probability, would never serve again. Even after 1870 an officer could be employed in his brevet rank, and it must have been quite a problem to keep it straight in official papers. Orally and socially the courtesy of the brevet title was still extended.

A story is told that a senator blocked unanimous consent for the brevets for the Spanish-American War because a name in which he was interested was not on the list, and that army authorities declined to add that name to the list and never again recommended brevet commissions. There were exceptions: for example, Elwell Stephen Otis was commissioned brevet major general as of February 4, 1899, "for military skill and most distinguished service in the Philippine Islands." The date is that of the outbreak of the Philippine Insurrection.

The last brevet rank ever conferred was also the highest ever conferred. During World War I the highest permanent rank in the army was that of major general. An act of Congress authorized the wartime appointment as general of the chief of staff and the commander of United States forces in France. Tasker H. Bliss retired as chief of staff at the end of 1917 and was sent to France as United States representative on the Supreme War Council. When Peyton C. March took over as chief of staff, he would be entitled to the rank as four-star general, and Bliss would automatically revert to his rank as major general. It was of course unthinkable to demote Bliss, especially when all other Allies were represented by higher ranking officers. It was recalled that the brevet law was still on the books, and Bliss was nominated "to be general, by brevet, for distinguished conduct and public

Editor's Introduction

service in the presence of the enemy," adhering to the letter of the act of 1869, but without exaggeration, as Paris and Versailles, in May, 1918, were very much "in the presence of the enemy."

It was customary to address General Bliss in his brevet rank. In fact no one, except assiduous readers of the Congressional Record, knew that it was a brevet rank.

Editor's Note on Identification

† † † † † † † † † † †

THE PRINCIPAL RELIANCE in identifying officers is *Historical Register and Dictionary of the United States Army*, by Francis B. Heitman (2 vols., Washington, Government Printing Office, 1903). This is a compilation of army registers from 1789 to 1903. If an officer's rank, even brevet rank, and organization is given, there are few misses, despite Lowe's frequently variant spellings of names. Some Civil War officers have been identified in *Official Army Register of the Volunteer Force of the United States Army* (Washington, Adjutant General's Office, 1867). There is much useful information on Civil War generals in the tenth volume of *Photographic History of the Civil War*, Francis Trevelyan Miller, editor-in-chief. Most other sources are stated in the notes.

Author's Preface

† † † † † † † † † † †

At the close of a busy life, interspersed with exciting adventures, I find myself living in the past, enjoying the recollections of old comrades and business associates, the scenes in which we mingled in early manhood, the bivouac under the blue sky, the faithful vigil of the weary sentinel for the safety of all.

The living who know of the truthfulness of statements herein made are few, but the records live.

Always blessed with a good memory, it seemed to be renewed—to come to my assistance, as, step by step, I travel the old roads and recount the incidents of long ago.

Fortunately I kept an accurate daily journal of some of the campaigns of which I write, and have only to copy extracts, brief, but comprehensive enough without being too voluminous.

My recollection of Fort Riley were first embodied in an address delivered before the Kansas State Historical Society. Referring to this address I received many letters of congratulation and approval. The *Journal of the United States Cavalry Association* did me the honor to publish it and a number of Army friends signified their approval and urged me to write more, which I did with considerable reluctance, mistrusting my ability; the *Journal* continued to encourage me and publish my articles and the result, with all of its imperfections, is here given to the world. Whatever may be its fate in the hands of civilians, I earnestly hope that it may be read by soldiers, who may find some consolation in comparing their present comfortable homes, pay and emoluments with what soldiers enjoyed fifty years ago.

The stories here told, the scenes and incidents referred to, will never be repeated.

The great plains have been transformed into cultivated fields producing food for millions and sending to the markets of the world the finest animals known to the meat-consuming nations of the earth. The wild herds and savage men have all passed away, never to return. Instead of the wigwam we have the modern home, farm, factory, school and church—instead of savage isolation and war, the railroad, telegraph, telephone, rural mail delivery, and the highest intelligence and refinement known to civilization.

P. G. LOWE, Leavenworth, Kansas

December 25, 1905, the fifty-sixth anniversary of my arrival at Fort Leavenworth.

FIVE YEARS A DRAGOON
('49 to '54)
And Other Adventures on the Great Plains

Part I
Enlistment and First Assignment

† † † † † † † † † † †

I HAD BEEN RAISED ON A FARM until fifteen; had been newsboy and sold papers about the streets of Lowell, Mass.; had been three years a sailor, including a whaling voyage, and learned the daguerreotype business in the gallery of Mr. Plumb on Washington Street, Boston, and became a first-class operator. I was a persistent reader of voyages, travels, campaigns, explorations and history, and novels such as Marryat's, Cooper's, Scott's, etc., and the spirit of adventure was so strong that I determined to enlist in the mounted service, which was sure to place me on the great plains of the West, among Indians, buffaloes, and other big game, and the mountaineers and trappers of whom I had read so much. Frémont's Narrative of 1843–44, and Captain Bonneville's Adventures gave the finishing touches to my inclination. It seemed to me that five years in this kind of field would round out my education, so to speak, and if I lived would then be ready to settle down to something permanently.

Having determined upon this course, I presented myself at the recruiting office in Boston, giving my occupation as a farmer. The recruiting officer, Major Sibley,[1] of the Second Dragoons, thought

[1] This was Henry Hopkins Sibley, who as brigadier general led the Confederate invasion of New Mexico Territory in 1862 that came to grief in the battles of Apache Pass and Glorieta. A native of Louisiana, Sibley was graduated from West Point in 1838, standing thirty-first in his class, and was commissioned second lieutenant in the Second Regiment of United States Dragoons. He became first lieutenant in 1840, served as regimental adjutant, 1841–46, and was promoted to captain on February 16, 1847. He was brevetted major for gallant and meritorious conduct in the affair at Medelin, near Veracruz, Mexico, on March 25, 1847. He became major in lineal rank in the First Dragoons on May 13, 1861, and resigned

that I was not twenty-one, and by my general appearance not a farmer—did not look like one, and did not dress like a young man just off the farm. I told him that I was born on the twenty-ninth of September, 1828, hence, this being the sixteenth of October, 1849, I had a safe margin of eighteen days. The Major assured me this was probably the least funny business I would ever attempt; "And, mark me, young man," said he, "if you take this step you will regret it only once, and that will be from the time you become acquainted with your position until you get out of it; and another thing, a large percentage of men never return to their friends. If you have no friends you ought to have, and if for any reason you want to hide yourself from the world, try something from which you can free yourself if you so desire. You may come back to-morrow."

I was not pleased at the thought of forcing myself into trouble in spite of the admonition given me, and spent an anxious night, but brushed all aside in the morning, and assured the Major that I hoped he would accept me; and by way of recommending myself, informed him that I was not only a farmer, but had been three years at sea, giving him something of my seafaring experience. He admitted that a man who could stand all of that might have some show as a soldier, and I was accepted.

My descriptive roll said twenty-one years, five feet, eleven inches high, dark-complexioned, dark brown hair, gray eyes, weight 175 pounds, and in perfect health.

I gave a large trunk full of clothes to the recruiting sergeant, who was just my size, and in return he had the tailor fit for me two complete suits of fatigue uniform and an overcoat. I retained a large valise, with its contents—books—with which I would not part until compelled to. I was, therefore, well clothed, and had about $125 in money, which no one suspected. It proved a great convenience to be able to buy something good to eat for myself and one or two modest greenhorns who had not learned to

---
the same day to join the Confederate Army. He died August 23, 1886. He was the inventor of the conical Sibley tent and Sibley stove.

Enlistment and First Assignment

quench thirst, subdue hunger, and otherwise obliterate their misery with whisky.

Unlike the recruits of to-day, the fact that a man would get drunk was no bar to his enlistment, and his moral character was of little interest. Once enlisted, the proper authorities would attend to the rest. Being physically all right, his habits cut little figure. Family trouble, disappointment in love, riots and personal difficulties, making one amenable to the law, often caused men to enlist who proved to be the best of soldiers. In my troop there were men isolating themselves from society for all sorts of reasons. A man drunk would not be enlisted; but however tough looking, if he were sober at the time of presenting himself, and physically able, he would pass. Uniformity of size was not considered. In my troop one man weighed 100 pounds, and was five feet, four, while several were above six feet and weighed from 200 to 225 pounds. Endurance was the test; all else was waived.

A few days after enlisting I was sent, with fifteen others, via New York (where as many more joined us) to Carlisle Barracks, Pennsylvania,[2] then a school for mounted service recruits—First and Second Dragoons and Mounted Rifles—all of which were stationed at various points in the Indian Territory, Texas, New Mexico, or on the Pacific Coast.

At Carlisle there were two troops—A and B. I was assigned to A. Colonel Philip St. George Cooke[3] commanded the post; Lieu-

[2] Carlisle Barracks, a prisoner-of-war camp during the American Revolution, was established as a recruit depot in 1838 and was used mainly for that purpose until relinquished by the army in 1879 to become the famous Carlisle Indian School under First Lieutenant Richard H. Pratt. It reverted to army control in 1918 as a hospital for wounded men of World War I and subsequently the Medical Field Service School was set up there.

[3] Cooke, a distinguished cavalry leader and tactician, was author of *Cavalry Tactics* adopted by the army in 1861. Born in Leesburg, Virginia, he was graduated from West Point in 1827 and assigned to the Sixth Infantry. When the First Dragoons was organized in 1833, he was promoted to first lieutenant in that regiment, becoming captain in 1835, and major, Second Dragoons in 1847. During the Mexican War he led the Mormon Battalion in a march across the desert to California, as told in his *Scenes and Adventures in the Army* (1857) and *The Conquest of New Mexico and California* (1878). He was brevetted lieutenant colonel for his Mexican

tenant D. H. Hastings[4] was adjutant. There were several West Point graduates brevet second lieutenants—who were waiting assignment or an opportunity to join the regiment to which already assigned. All of the noncommissioned officers were Mexican War veterans, and at Carlisle because of their supposed special fitness to discipline recruits.

It fell to my lot to drill under Lieutenant Beverly Robertson,[5] late major-general in the Confederate Army. He was, to my fancy, a splendid man; gentle, firm, persistent, never seeming to lose patience, yet never yielding to anything short of the most perfect performance possible of the movement undertaken. Carbine and saber drill came in the forenoon, on foot, and mounted drill in the afternoon. As a boy, I had good horses to ride. The prediction

---

War services, attained the lineal rank in 1853, colonel in 1858 and brigadier general in 1861, and brevet major general in 1865. He died in 1895. Confederate General J. E. B. Stuart was his son-in-law and the writer John Esten Cooke, his nephew. See Otis E. Young, *The West of Philip St. George Cooke* (Glendale, Calif. Arthur H. Clark Co., 1955.)

[4] David H. Hastings, a native of Ireland, rose from the ranks, after enlisting as a private in Company B, Second Infantry in 1837, becoming first sergeant of his company in 1840. In 1845 he was transferred to Company K, Third Artillery, and again passed through the ranks of private, corporal, and sergeant to first sergeant. He was serving in the Company of Engineers in 1848 when he was brevetted second lieutenant in the First Dragoons in 1848, attaining the regular rank six months later and becoming first lieutenant in 1854 and captain in 1860. He was severely injured by the falling of his horse while in pursuit of Indians near Fort Buchanan, New Mexico, on October 7, 1857. In 1861 he returned to Carlisle Barracks, where he was superintendent of the Mounted Recruiting Service and commanded the Cavalry School. He was promoted to major, Fifth Cavalry, on September 23, 1863, and was retired on December 7 for disability resulting from wounds and injuries in line of duty. He died in Baltimore in 1882. Says his regimental history, "He belonged to the old school of soldiers, and was a good and faithful officer." Lowe dedicated his book to Major Hastings.

[5] Beverly Holcombe Robertson, a Virginian, was graduated from West Point in 1849 and was assigned to the Second Dragoons as brevet second lieutenant; he became second lieutenant a year later and first lieutenant in 1855. He served as regimental adjutant, 1860–61, was promoted to captain March 3, 1861, and was dismissed on August 8. He was commissioned brigadier general by the Confederate States on June 9, 1862, and commanded the "Valley" cavalry brigade, made up of the Second, Sixth, Seventh, Eleventh, and Twelfth Regiments of Virginia cavalry, after Brigadier General Turner Ashby was killed.

that I would sooner or later have my neck broken, was believed by most of the careful mothers in my neighborhood, and youngsters were forbidden to ride with that "Lowe boy." This is about the way all boys with energy enough to enjoy life are looked upon.

Horses were kept for use in drilling, and among them a beautiful bay, apparently gentle, bright eyes, long thin neck, fine head, high withers, fine sinewy legs, and standing out by himself a perfect picture of a horse. I chose him when we came to drill, and he was assigned to me. The man in charge of the stable said that he would run away, and had thrown several men, but I thought this an attempt to frighten a recruit. Commencing with mounting bareback, then with saddles and crossed stirrups, and going through the evolutions at a walk, in a few days quite a squad, perhaps twenty, had advanced so that they were, while still riding with crossed stirrups, drilled at a trot, and then at a gentle gallop. At the command "gallop" my horse, in spite of all I could do, ran across the parade ground, and out towards the town. I could turn him, but could not check his speed. Here and there I went, turning at pleasure, but failing to check him. Finally I turned toward a plank fence, thinking I might stop him there, but the fence did not bother him a bit—over he went, and with scarcely a heartbeat, kept on, going over the fence on the other side, and then off like the wind. At last I got headed towards the squad, standing at rest, ran into it and stopped. Lieutenant Robertson had sent the noncommissioned officers to look for me, but they could scarcely keep in sight. An order was issued forbidding the use of this horse ("Murat") by any of the recruits. Of course, everybody at the post talked about it, and a witty Irishman wrote a parody on "John Gilpin's Ride," in which the recruit and his steed were shown up in humorous style.

The following Sunday, having invited two friends—Wagner and O'Shea—to breakfast with me at the "Little Brick House" just out of the post, we had agreed to go direct from the parade-ground when dismissed from inspection. We took no breakfast at mess except a cup of coffee, and saved our appetites for the feast. I had arranged with the man who kept the place to have fried chicken and necessary accompaniments. We looked forward to our ten o'clock breakfast with pleasant anticipations. Wagner was a Kentuckian, about thirty-three years of age and well educated. He had met with business reverses in Louisville, and after going to New York to straighten out his affairs met with so much discouragement he concluded to enlist. He wanted to hide himself from all his friends and have time to think, as he said, without restraint. O'Shea was about twenty-five, came to New York after the Irish riots of 1848. Found himself among strangers, without money, and believing the Army was the place for him, enlisted. I never knew a handsomer man or more perfect gentlemen.

The parade over, we went to breakfast. I sat at the end of the table with my two friends on either side. The breakfast was before us and I about to serve, when in came a noisy band of ruffians, swearing and making themselves generally disagreeable. The leader, or chief bully, six feet two inches high—a giant weighing two hundred and twenty-five pounds—came straight to our table and said: "Here, b'ys, is a foine lay-out; here, Tom, take a leg; here Jimmy, take a wing; here, Slathery, take the breast that ye're so fond of," as he proceeded to take in his dirty fingers the parts named and pass them to his friends. Not a word was spoken by our party, but about the time the dish was nearly empty, seeing my astonished look, the bully said to me, in a sneering sort of tone, "Ye're a foine child, sure." Then I sprang to my feet, drew my saber and went for him with all the venom and fury of which I was possessed—cut and thrust. The fact that the saber had a dull edge, as all sabers had at that time, accounts for his not being killed. His companions tried to save him, and two of them received scars on account of it. My two friends drew their sabers and vowed to kill any one who interfered, and I pounded the howling wretch until he lay prostrate, begging for his life, and I was exhausted. From that day to this I have never ceased to be thankful that I did not kill the poor unfortunate creature, and in

Enlistment and First Assignment

my thankfulness he was fully forgiven. A file of the guard came at "double quick." "The recruits are killing each other," was the cry. The officer of the day, Lieutenant Fields,[6] came just as the guard was about to take all hands to the guard house, and took things coolly. The first move was to send "Big Mit," as he was called, to the hospital, covered from head to foot with cuts and bruises. It took all of his party of ruffians, half-drunk as they were, to carry him off. A file of the guard went along, and when "Mit" was deposited in the hospital his friends were confined in the guard house. Wagner and the man who kept the place explained the affair to Lieutenant Fields, who directed us to stay and get our breakfast and then report to First Sergeant Smart; the sergeant of the guard was to take charge of us until that time, but not to take us to the guard house without further orders. We were too much wrought up to enjoy breakfast, and I told the lieutenant (the first words I had spoken during the whole affair) that we would go now. Under guard we went, and the story was told in full and written down. The ruffians were also interviewed and did not deny the outrage, but said they had not intended to have any trouble, which was doubtless true, for the same gang had terrorized everybody that came in their way. Every new batch of recruits must be hazed and bulldozed; to resist was to be knocked down, kicked and adorned with a black eye. These three innocent-looking fellows were the first real snags they had struck. The doctor reported "Mit" not necessarily dangerously wounded, but that he was badly bruised about the head, hands and arms. The adjutant was present with Lieutenant Fields, and wrote a report of the affair. When the whole matter was explained to the

---

[6] He probably means Charles William Field (not Fields), born in Woodford County, Kentucky, in 1818, who was graduated from West Point in 1849 and assigned to the Second Dragoons as brevet second lieutenant. He became a second lieutenant two years later, served as regimental quartermaster, 1853–55, and was commissioned first lieutenant in the Second Cavalry, a new regiment, in 1855. He became captain January 31, 1861, and resigned on May 30. He was commissioned a Confederate brigadier general in 1862 and major general in 1864, commanding Field's Division, First Army Corps, Army of Northern Virginia. He died in Washington, D.C., on April 9, 1892.

commanding officer, the guard was withdrawn from Wagner, O'Shea and myself, and that ended the matter so far as we were concerned.

But I was getting too much notoriety and it troubled me. I had no taste for the sort of heroism growing out of brawls and fights. I had never made intimates easily, and now I shrank from the curiosity seekers who wanted to [shake the hand that had wielded the saber against the ruffian.]

At Carlisle quite a number of the best behaved men were retained to do regular duty, as in a company. They were called "the permanent party." Of course they were liable to be sent away to join some troop in one of the mounted regiments. A large percentage of them were made "lance" noncommissioned officers—corporals or sergeants. Some men served there for years. The chances seemed good for all of us to stay all winter, in which case a large garrison would accumulate. I grew depressed at this prospect. But finally an order came to send seventy-four men to Fort Leavenworth for the First Dragoons—sixteen for K, then at Fort Leavenworth, thirty-four for F, then at Fort Scott, 120 miles south of Fort Leavenworth, and twenty-four for B, 300 miles west of Fort Leavenworth, at Fort Kearney.[7]

It was the rule at Carlisle to send off all the troublesome characters with each batch going to join troops. This was probably

[7] Fort Leavenworth, Kansas, on the Missouri River near the city of Leavenworth, was established in 1827 and named for Gen. Henry Leavenworth. It was a base for many an expedition to the Far West in its early days. A military prison was authorized there in 1837. General William T. Sherman ordered establishment of a School for Application for Infantry and Cavalry Officers in 1885, since which time the post has been an educational center for the army. Fort Scott, Kansas, named for Winfield Scott, was established in 1842, abandoned in 1853, reoccupied during the Kansas border troubles, 1857–58, reoccupied during the Civil War, 1862–65, and re-established 1869–73. Its headquarters is a museum and several of its buildings are in private use in the city of Fort Scott. Fort Kearny, Nebraska, was established in 1848 to protect the Oregon Trail and was named for Stephen Watts Kearny. The city that grew up across the Platte River is spelled Kearney, and a few official records so spell the fort. Fort Kearny was abandoned in 1876. The site is a state park. Lowe consistently used the spelling "Kearney."

Enlistment and First Assignment

the last chance to unload this class before spring, and a dozen or more of them were booked, including my friend "Big Mit" and his gang. Lieutenant Fields was to go in command of the seventy-four. "Mit" came from the hospital, head bandaged and right hand in a sling. His comrades fell in from the guard house. When the roll was called I found myself, "Big Mit" and one of his comrades of the same name (a smaller but more vicious man) in B Troop. I was not pleased, but said nothing. Wagner, to whom I had become attached (a man so superior that daily association with him was a positive pleasure and a great advantage to me), was assigned to K and O'Shea to B Troop.

We went from Carlisle to Harrisburg by rail, thence by canal boat to a point in the Alleghenies where a railroad ran over the mountain, the motive power being a stationary engine on top of it. We marched from where we left the canal boat, over the mountains to St. Johnsberg on the other side, and there took canal boat to Pittsburg, thence by steamboat to St. Louis, where we transferred to another boat, the *Haidee*, to go up the Missouri River. This, we all hoped, would be our last change, and in a week we should land at Fort Leavenworth.

Not far above St. Louis, after several days of hard struggle with the ice, our boat was frozen in at Portland, Missouri; and now we were told that the way the country roads then ran, we were three hundred miles from Fort Leavenworth. The country was covered with snow and ice. For two weeks we had been on canal and steamboat, with no exercise, and were in no condition to march. From Portland to Fulton was nineteen miles, over rough hills, with no place between the two towns to stop, so that we must walk all of that distance the first day. A couple of wagons were hired to haul our baggage. A few men rode in the wagons. "Mit" was recovering from his injuries rapidly, but he rode. Wagner and I arrived at Fulton at dark, but many did not get in until very late. The icy roads had exhausted me. The long one-story hotel had a long dining-room table with plenty to eat—a whole prairie chicken for each man—but not a mouthful could I eat. I doubled my blanket, spread it on the floor in one corner, took off my shoes and lay down with all my clothes on, including overcoat. I was too fearfully weary to rest well on the hard oak floor, but was astonished at my improved condition in the morning. I really enjoyed the breakfast.

The second day, from Fulton to Millersburg, was twelve miles. Snow fell all day, but the roads were better, weather milder, and we did not suffer so much. We were scattered about the little village, myself and half a dozen others at a comfortable brick house with good fireplaces. I asked the good lady for hot water and some towels, and after a delightful bath, put on clean clothes, ate a good four o'clock dinner, and slept in a good bed, where every time I woke I could see the bright fire. Oh, how I enjoyed that night! In the morning my troubles had vanished; but how I did hate to leave this good home to launch out again on the ice and snow! But there was no more trouble from this point to the end of the journey. I was sometimes cold, and endured many inconveniences, but never complained, and was never tired after the second day. Wagner, O'Shea and I nearly always closed the day's journey ahead of the others. If we wanted a lunch we bought it. We could buy a pair of homemade woolen socks at almost any farm house, and not a day passed that I did not give one or more pairs to some sufferer.

I do not remember all of our route through the grand old State of Missouri, nor every stopping place. Some of them were Fulton, Millersburg, Boonville, Columbia, Marshall, Lexington, Hambrights, Independence and Westport.

At Grinter's Ferry crossing of the Kaw River, the old ferryman and his wife lived on the south side. He was an old soldier and fond of talking, and while we waited until all caught up, he explained that the military road that we had come into between the ferry and Westport, ran south to Fort Scott, about one hundred miles, and thence to Fort Gibson and other points south, and after crossing the ferry ran west of north twenty-two miles to Fort Leavenworth.

Enlistment and First Assignment

We crossed the ferry towards evening, and Mr. Mundy, government blacksmith for the Delaware Indians, furnished us a good supper. And what a managing housekeeper Mrs. Mundy must have been. Seventy-five hungry men were furnished a supper they could never forget, and not one failed to have plenty. To this day I remember how delicious the biscuits were, and then we had honey with them; and the venison, ham and coffee! Just think of it! A lot of rough fellows meeting such a feast. I felt sorry for Mrs. Mundy, but there seemed no end to her supplies. Isaac Mundy and his wife were born in Virginia and married there. He was a great hunter; accidentally shot himself, and was buried with Masonic honors at White Church, in Wyandotte County, Kansas, February 27, 1858. At the request of the Indians he was buried at the foot of the grave of Chief Ketchum. Mrs. Mundy raised a good family of seven children—four daughters and three sons. All except one married and raised families, and they are among the best and most prosperous people of Platte County, Missouri. Mrs. Mundy is living with her daughter and son-in-law, Hon. Lot W. Ringo, of Weston. She is nearly ninety years old.*

The Mundys accommodated all that they could in the house, and a lot of us occupied an old storeroom boarded up and down, wide cracks in sides and floor. We shivered, but did not sleep. It was the twenty-fourth of December and cold, with plenty of snow on the ground—certainly a dreary Christmas Eve—and a hard freezing night. At midnight we came out and huddled around a big fire until breakfast. Some of the men kept it burning all night. The breakfast was a duplicate of the supper, and the Indian girl who waited on me at both meals, wearing a clean calico dress, looked charming.

This was expected to be our last meal until we reached Fort Leavenworth, but we heard such good accounts of the fort that there was no complaint, and the prospect of any kind of a home kept all in good humor.

Interesting incidents of this trip by rail, by canal boats, by

* Mrs. Mundy died a year after this article was published in the *Journal*.

steamboats, and on foot, were numerous, and the opportunity to study human nature excellent. I had a hundred dollars on leaving Carlisle, and do not think there were twenty-five dollars more with the whole party, except what Corporal Wood and Lieutenant Fields had. A few who had been at Carlisle some time and had been paid off, possessed a dollar or two, and as a canteen could be filled with whisky for twenty-five cents, there was enough to make a good deal of noise and get up a fight once in a while. It was fortunate that there was no more money among the tough element (about twenty), who made all the trouble, did nearly all of the complaining, and caused all of the complaints from citizens along the road.

As I look back after long years of experience, I think that no young officer could have managed better than did Lieutenant Fields, with the assistance of Corporal Wood. He had graduated the previous June from West Point and reported at Carlisle in the fall, hence this was his first "campaign," and I venture to say that throughout his active Indian campaigns in Texas and elsewhere, experience as a general in the Confederate army, and in the service of the Khedive of Egypt after the Civil War, he never had a more trying trip than this. Throughout all of it he showed the utmost good judgment and common sense, with which he was abundantly blessed. Corporal Wood had been a pork packer in Louisville, where he failed in business. He enlisted in the First Dragoons and served through the Mexican War. He had but six months to serve, and wanting to be discharged as far west as possible, was sent out with us. He was a fine clerk; understood government accounts, and was fully competent to act as commissary and quartermaster for our detachment. It was all plain sailing on canal boats and steamboats, where he managed to give us fairly good meals for the small government allowance, and no man had just cause to complain. He was a determined, lion-hearted man, who would brook no nonsense, and on two occasions settled rows and insolent complaints with a club, the moral effect of which was to insure quiet, peace and fairly good

Enlistment and First Assignment

order. He was that peculiar type of man who would have commanded as completely as a private as he would as a captain. While gentle and soft of voice, no man could be intimate with him without his consent.

When we took the steamer at St. Louis, Lieutenant Fields said to Wood: "Well, barring accidents, Corporal, we should have little trouble from here to Fort Leavenworth." When we became frozen up at Portland a hard problem was before him. The whole face of the country was covered with snow and ice. As the miserable roads then ran, the distance was estimated to be about three hundred miles to Fort Leavenworth, country thinly settled and towns wide apart. We must be on the road about twenty days, and how was he to subsist us? Corporal Wood had saved his money during his four and one-half years' service, mostly as clerk, and now revealed to Fields the fact that he had considerable, and it was settled that he should furnish the command necessary subsistence, arrange for Lieutenant Fields to give vouchers wherever they would be acceptable, and pay his own money when necessary, taking proper vouchers for his own protection. He bought a cheap horse, rode ahead each day and made arrangements in town or village or on plantation to feed us—dinner at the end of the day's march, and breakfast, and to furnish the best lodging practicable. We had an abundance of everything that the country through which we passed afforded. Our sleeping accommodations were necessarily poor in some places, on plantations where there was not room in the houses, but the people throughout the journey were very kind, and none of us would have gone hungry if there had been no pay in it. After our arrival at Fort Leavenworth, Wood told me that his vouchers were all paid.

Lieutenant Fields bought a fine horse as we came by Cincinnati, but seldom rode him, nearly always giving a ride to some weary straggler. Some men were always riding in the wagon; probably half of them rode more or less during the trip, and it was noticeable that, while a few rode for want of good shoes, the tough gang, from temporary illness, caused by whisky, did the most of the riding, while the fellows who made no noise, walked without complaining. Of course, the noncommissioned officers were "lance," made for the trip, chief among them being the acting first sergeant. He had been at Carlisle some time; was believed to have been a deserter from the British army in Canada; at any rate he had been a British soldier, and was an all-around brute—big, burly and noisy. He was quite efficient among toughs, but could be induced to "let up" for a bottle of whisky. However, I had escaped his special notice, in my quiet way, and had nothing to complain of, but was glad he was going to K instead of B Troop.

And now, on this beautiful Christmas Day, about eight o'clock, we left the ferry, our kind host and his family, on our last day's march—twenty-two miles to Fort Leavenworth. Up over the Wyandotte hills, past a few Indian cabins, out upon the prairie by the military road; and except that it was sloppy, caused by the melting snow in the afternoon, marching was good. We had been cautioned not to stroll on ahead, as we had heretofore been permitted to do, but to keep near together so as to march into the garrison in good order. Edward Brydon was our trumpeter—and perfection in his line—an Irishman by birth, printer by trade, now entering upon his third enlistment, and returning to Troop B, from which he had been twice honorably discharged. He had tried to live out of the army, but his good nature and convivial habits brought him back. He was loyal to his troop, had served under Captain E. V. Sumner,[8] then lieutenant colonel, com-

---

[8] Edwin Vose Sumner, born in Boston, Massachusetts, in 1797, was appointed second lieutenant, Second Infantry from New York in 1819. He was promoted first lieutenant in 1823, captain, First Dragoons in 1833, major, Second Dragoons in 1846, and lieutenant colonel, First Dragoons in 1848. During the Mexican War he was brevetted lieutenant colonel for Cerro Gordo and colonel for Molino del Rey. In 1855 he became colonel of the new First Cavalry and commanded the expedition against the Cheyennes of 1857. He was promoted to brigadier general on March 16, 1861, and major general of Volunteers on July 4, 1862. He had previously, on May 31, been named brevet major general for gallant and meritorious conduct in the Battle of Fair Oaks. He died on March 21, 1863. His son of the same name was appointed second lieutenant, First Cavalry, in 1861, became brevet brigadier gen-

Enlistment and First Assignment

manding Fort Leavenworth, and thought him a great captain; did not know the present captain, and did not expect to find many of his old friends in the troop. I liked "Old Ned," as he was called, always kind and intelligent. He assured me that B was the best troop in the service. I had occasion to do him a few little favors on the trip, which he never forgot, and as we walked along together that day he pointed out the lay of the country, the location of Indian tribes—the Shawnees south of the Kaw River where we crossed, the Wyandottes in the forks of the Kaw and Missouri, the Delawares west of the Wyandottes and the little band of Muncies just below the Fort where is now Mount Muncie Cemetery and the Soldiers' Home, and the Kickapoos west of the Fort in Salt Creek Valley.[9] Pilot Knob, standing out a hundred and fifty feet above the plain, five miles south of the Fort, was in sight early in the day, but it took us a long time to get east of it. Six miles south of the post, on high ground, stood a one-room log cabin, and in the door, completely filling it from side to side and top to bottom, like a picture in a frame, stood a big Delaware Indian woman. She smilingly scanned the ranks for some one she knew, when Brydon said: "By the holy horn

eral of Volunteers in 1865, and brigadier general in the Regular Army in 1899. Another son, Samuel Storrow Sumner was appointed second lieutenant, Second Cavalry in 1861; was captain and brevet major at the end of the Civil War; was brevetted lieutenant colonel for the Indian fight at Summit Springs, Colorado, in 1869; was major general of Volunteers in the Spanish-American War; and brigadier general, Regular Army, in 1901.

[9] A series of treaties, 1829-40, set up reservations in Kansas for a number of eastern tribes; in 1854 efforts began to remove them to the Indian Territory that became Oklahoma. The Shawnee, of Algonquian linguistic stock, ranged from South Carolina to the Ohio River in earlier days. Wyandottes or Wyandots were mainly Hurons of Iroquoian stock, driven from the vicinity of Quebec and Montreal by the Iroquois Confederacy, or Five Nations. The Delawares or Lenni Lenape, were an Algonquian Confederacy, first known in Delaware, New Jersey, and Pennsylvania. The Muncies, or Munsees, were a tribe of the Delaware Confederacy, the only one commonly named separately. The Kickapoos were an Algonquian tribe from Wisconsin and Illinois. A part of the Kickapoos left Kansas and settled eventually in Mexico. Most of the Mexican Kickapoos and some from Kansas accepted a reservation in Indian Territory, but about half the tribe remained on the Kansas Reservation.

spoons, there's Indian Mary!" and he went up and shook hands with her. She had from time to time been a servant in some of the officers' families, had grown old in the service, and was well liked.

And now the flag at the Fort was plainly in sight. We crossed Five Mile Creek (in measuring the military road from Fort Leavenworth the starting-point was the flag staff and the creeks and landmarks were spoken of as so many miles from that point), then Three Mile, and up the hill to what is now the head of Broadway, Leavenworth, and on across Two Mile Creek and up the long grade to the top of the hill, where the flag was near, little more than a mile away, and the buildings plainly in view. Our journey was nearly ended. Half a mile before reaching the post we heard a bugle sounding retreat and Brydon joined in, the ranks were closed up, the roll called, and we marched in good order in front of the commanding officer's quarters, halted, faced the quarters and stood at attention, while Colonel Sumner heard the roll called and saw the names checked off. The men for B Troop stood on the right, Brydon on the extreme right, and the Colonel recognized him, shook hands, and said: "Well, Brydon, you are back again." "Yes, Colonel." "Couldn't keep out?" queried the Colonel. "No, Colonel, I had to come back." "Well," said the Colonel, "I am glad you returned to your old troop."

We were not detained long; marched down to the brick quarters occupied by K Troop and filed into the dining room for supper. On a table bread and boiled pork were cut in slices, a big kettle of coffee was there, and each man passed his tin cup, which was filled. All of us stood and received our rations, fell back as soon as supplied, and ate our supper—not half as much nutriment as we needed. The British deserter had been supplied with whisky since his arrival, and he officiated in handing each man his ration, taking a slice of pork, putting it on a slice of bread and handing it to the nearest man—a Christmas dinner long to be remembered.

We were assigned to the brick quarters south of K Troop, where we found a detachment of six men of I Troop, First Dra-

Enlistment and First Assignment

goons, just in from Riado,[10] New Mexico, with the mail. Wood had reported our approach early in the afternoon, and with these men had our bed sacks filled and the squad room warm. We had to thank the first sergeant of K Troop for our miserable supper. He was making company funds; soon after deserted with horse and equipments and most of the funds.[11] Little more than a year later, when a corporal, with two comrades who had suffered with me, I was sent to Platte City after this man, the commanding officer having heard that he had been seen there. Sure enough, we

---

[10] Riado should be Rayado. A post was established at Rayado, New Mexico, on May 31, 1850; abandoned August 7, 1851; reoccupied July 16 to September 18, 1854. Rayado is in Colfax County, twelve miles south of Cimarron on state route 21 and about thirty-five miles east of Taos. See Francis Paul Prucha, *A Guide to the Military Posts of the United States* (Madison, The State Historical Society of Wisconsin, 1964), and maps, Plates 17 and 20.

[11] Distributions from the post or regimental fund and the savings from the company rations constituted the company fund, to be disbursed by the captain for the benefit of the enlisted men of the company, pursuant to resolves of the company council, consisting of all the company officers present. The post fund was raised by a tax on the sutler, not to exceed 10 cents a month for each officer and soldier, and by the saving on the flour ration, estimated at one-third, by baking bread in the post bakery. The ration—one man's allowance for one day—was three-fourths pound of pork or bacon or one and one-fourth pounds of fresh or salt beef; 18 ounces of bread or flour or 12 ounces of hard bread or one and one-fourth pound of corn meal. To each one hundred rations were added eight quarts of beans or ten pounds of rice, or twice a week 150 ounces of desiccated potatoes and 100 ounces of mixed vegetables; ten pounds of coffee or one and one-half pounds of tea; fifteen pounds of sugar, four quarts of vinegar, two quarts of salt, four pounds of soap, and one pound of sperm candles, or one and one-fourth pound of adamantine candles, or one and one-half pounds of tallow candles. Now it was possible to issue to each man his ration, including a piece of candle weighing 0.16 of an ounce to light him on his way, and he could make the best of it. However, the normal procedure was to issue the rations in bulk to the company, although at this time there was no official provision for mess sergeant or cooks. In K Troop as described by Lowe the first sergeant was handling the mess, presumably with volunteer cooks from among the troopers. Obviously by skimping on the food ("not half as much nutriment as we needed," says Lowe), the first sergeant would be "making company funds," and if the captain were careless enough to leave it in his hands, the sergeant could desert and make off with it. Regulations made the captain responsible, and even he could not spend the fund without approval of the Company Council made up of his officers.

found him, and after a brief struggle, brought him back riding behind one of the men, and placed him in the guard house. I told him that nothing paid better than common humanity and decency, and that but for our miserable reception at the end of a three hundred mile march in cold winter, we might not have felt it incumbent upon us to invade a man's house to capture him. Our duty hardly justified the trouble and risk we took. I am sorry to say that he made his escape from the guard house before he was tried and drummed out, which he surely would have been.

A dozen overcoats had disappeared from as many unfortunates since we left Carlisle—all sold for a mere song, to get money to buy whisky, and this in the face of the cold the losers were exposed to. One mile above the Fort, on the opposite side of the Missouri River, was a place called "Whisky Point," where anything could be sold or traded for whisky, and an enterprising pilot interested a few of the new arrivals, and a couple more overcoats were gone, and a man each from B, F, and K Troops found themselves in the guard house at daylight. The next day transportation was furnished and the detachment for F Troop started for Fort Scott, 120 miles south. The detachment for K Troop had found their places on arrival. And now it was settled that the detachment for B Troop would remain until spring. The detachment of six men of I Troop would also remain until spring. And strange as it may appear, I remember the names of these men fifty-six years later. Jones, a lance sergeant; Privates Talbot, Worrel, McKenzie, Fox and Byrns.[12] Except Byrns, these men had all passed through the Mexican War, and I may as well tell of their end now. Worrel died on a farm in Leavenworth County, Kansas, about 1880; he had served ten years. McKenzie

---

[12] Richard Byrnes (not Byrns), a native of Ireland, served as private, corporal, sergeant, and sergeant major in the First Cavalry, 1856–61; was commissioned second lieutenant, Seventeenth Infantry, May 14, 1861; transferred to the Fifth Cavalry, September 21, 1861; became first lieutenant July 17, 1862, and colonel of the Twenty-eighth Massachusetts Infantry on October 18, 1862. He died on June 12, 1864, of wounds received June 3 in the Battle of Cold Harbor, one of the Wilderness battles.

Enlistment and First Assignment

and Fox were killed by Indians. Jones and Talbot were discharged at Rayado, New Mexico. Byrns, who was then (1849) twenty-one years of age, was killed in the battle of the Wilderness while colonel of a volunteer regiment and commanding a brigade in the Union Army. He served in all the grades of noncommissioned officer, was badly wounded in 1854 in New Mexico by Indians, and secured his commission as second lieutenant in the regular army at the commencement of the Civil War. An Irishman by birth, well educated, and my warm and constant friend from our first meeting to the time of his death.

And now the two detachments were thrown together—B and I—with Sergeant Jones in charge and Lieutenant Fields the detachment commander, and under their management our quarters were made comfortable, and our own mess and food properly prepared. We were paid off in January, 1850, to end of December, 1849—$8 per month, with $1 retained each month. A couple of dollars from each man to buy extras for the mess did wonders. Hucksters from Missouri brought vegetables, and we fared fairly well. Three months we had ahead of us before we could cross the plains to join our troop. Lieutenant Fields or Sergeant Jones drilled us on foot twice a day. We had to do our share of guard and other duty, but had no horses to care for. I took great pride in saber exercise, and practiced much with small swords made of tough hickory with Miller, Byrns, O'Shea and others. Miller was an Englishman, who had seen better days, and enlisted in New York because he was absolutely hungry—"too proud to beg and too honest to steal"—a teacher by profession and master of several languages. O'Shea was a graduate of Dublin College, and a better all around man I never met. He was the champion boxer, and that was a leading branch of our exercises. Rules of good behavior were strict and well observed. I never had more congenial companionship, and that kept us alive and fairly happy. We made the best of everything, and did no growling; found some good books in the post library and did much reading. In fact, I was getting along quite contentedly, until one Saturday I had cleaned up carbine, saber, belts, etc., for Sunday morning inspection,[13] and left them in my "rack." When I came up from supper I found in their place very dirty equipments. At first I thought it a joke, and glanced around quietly. Byrns was lying on his bunk, and told me that he saw "Big Mit" take my "kit" and put his in place of it. I took mine from his rack, and was in the act of adjusting it, when he came in, rushed at me like a roaring maniac, and raised his carbine to strike. In less time than it takes to tell it, I was all over him with my saber. Men came rushing up from supper; word passed that the men of the "detachment," as it was called, were killing each other, and a file of the guard was called; but Jones came first, and made a detail to carry off "Mit." Lieutenant Fields came with the officer of the day, and Byrns told the story in good shape. When they left Lieutenant Fields said to the officer of the day: "I think that brute will leave that young fellow alone hereafter."

A month later "Mit" returned to the squad room and I went over to him and said: "Well, how are you?" He replied, "Sure I'm sore, and will be for some time." "Well," said I, "I am sorry for you and hope you will soon be well again." After an embarrassing pause I said, "And now, 'Mit,' how does it stand between us? Are we to live in peace, or have I to look out for you and be ready to kill you some day—I want to know just what to expect?" "Sure," said he, "don't be too hard on me; sure, only that I was drunk I would have no trouble wid ye." "Well," said I, "you are sure to get drunk again; I expect that; but it won't be any excuse for crossing me; you have had two chances with me, and I don't want to stand guard over myself all the time; I hold no malice toward you; won't do anything about the past, but what of to-morrow or some other day when you feel like breaking some fellow's neck—

---

[13] Army Regulations provided: "Captains will inspect their companies every Sunday morning. No soldier will be excused from Sunday inspection except the guard, the sick, and the necessary attendants at the hospital." Hospitals also were inspected every Sunday. Regiments and post garrisons were inspected on the last day of every month. Sunday inspections continued through most of the nineteenth century. By 1895 the day had been shifted to Saturday.

Enlistment and First Assignment

am I to be the victim? I want it settled." "Sure," said he, "I like ye first rate, and ye'll find me yer friend all the time." "All right," said I, "let's shake," and we did. From that time on he tried to be kind to me.

Leaving out of our squad a few who could find nothing in life worth living unless able to procure whisky, we had a remarkably good set of men, some scholars, some good singers and quite a smattering of theatrical talent, out of which was organized a so-called Thespian Society. Warren Kimball, Rogers, Glennon, Miller, O'Shea, Hill, "Little" Duffy and others made up the actors, and gave a performance once a week during February and March in our dining room. A little assistance came from K, but the "detachment" contained more genius in that line than the balance of the Post. All officers and ladies at the Post came to the performances.

K Troop was commanded by Captain and Brevet Major Caleb Carlton,[14] a fine officer and strict disciplinarian; he had a good troop and fine noncommissioned officers. How he happened to have a thief and all around tough for a first sergeant I never knew. When this sergeant deserted he was succeeded by a fine man, and my friend Wagner was made corporal. Two years later he was made first sergeant, and soon after a relative died in Baltimore, leaving him a large fortune, and the Secretary of War discharged him so that he might look after it. On his return from

[14] Caleb Henry Carlton was not graduated from West Point until 1859, and then became an officer in the Seventh Infantry. Lowe must have confused two officers, and in all probability is referring to James Henry Carleton, who at this time was captain in the First Dragoons and brevet major for Buena Vista. J. H. Carleton, on sick leave in the later months of the Mexican War, took a detachment from Carlisle Barracks to Fort Leavenworth in 1848, and was stationed there, 1848–50, although absent for six months of that period on detached service. During the Civil War he led the "California Column" to New Mexico and as brigadier general of Volunteers directed campaigns against Indians. A brevet major general, he served as lieutenant colonel of the Fourth Cavalry after the war. See Aurora Hunt, *James Henry Carleton, 1814–1873, Western Frontier Dragoon* (Glendale, Calif., Arthur H. Clark Company, 1958), 111–12.

New Mexico, on his way East, he spent one night with me at Fort Leavenworth, where I had become first sergeant of B Troop.

FORT LEAVENWORTH AS I SAW IT IN 1849.

At the corner of what is now Kearney Avenue and Sumner Place, the south end on Kearney Avenue and west front on Sumner Place, stood a two-story brick building with wide front porches above and below, used as dragoon quarters—the building that our detachment occupied. Immediately north of this, fronting the same way, was a similar building—K troop quarters.* Running east from the southeast corner of first mentioned building was a stone wall with portholes looking south. A two-story block house stood a little south of the east end of the wall. Southeast of the block house, about where the chapel now stands, was the sutler's store, kept by Colonel Hiram Rich. There is a marked contrast between an old-time army sutler's store and a church, especially if both be *first-class*. South of the store was the parsonage, in those days occupied by Chaplain Kerr. The house was of logs, and still stands, with several additions, and all covered like a frame house. A little west of the parsonage, across what is now Scott Avenue, was the residence of Colonel Rich. Southeast of that was the home of the veteran Ordnance Sergeant Fleming.

At the northeast corner of what is now Sumner Place stood a one-story and basement building fronting west, used as officers' quarters. It is still standing, with another story added. On the opposite corner, north side, fronting south on Sumner Place and parade ground, was another building used as officers' quarters, since rebuilt and much enlarged. West of that was the best build-

---

* These two buildings were the first permanent structures of the Post occupied by troops, and were built in the early '40's. Later they were used as the headquarters for the Department of the Missouri, where Sheridan, Hancock and Pope commanded. In 1881 the buildings were vacated by the headquarters and fitted up for quarters for student officers for the Infantry and Cavalry School, established the same year. Two years ago these buildings were torn down, and the site has been chosen for the Administration Building of the Post, which is to be erected at an early day.—EDITOR. [From Lowe's original book.]

Enlistment and First Assignment

ing at the Post, then the commanding officer's quarters, very much the same as it now is, though enlarged and improved from time to time. The last three buildings referred to, and the logs in the parsonage, and the wall, are all that is left of the Post of 1849. Between the commanding officer's quarters and the northwest corner of what is now Sumner Place, fronting south toward the parade ground, were four or five buildings used as officers' quarters. West of the parade ground, on what is now a part of McClellan Avenue, fronting east, were four or five one-story and basement buildings generally used as quarters for soldiers' families or citizen employees.

Between the first above mentioned brick building and south end of west row of buildings stood a row of log stables—six, I think—main entrance in end fronting south on what is now Kearney Avenue, which was then a thoroughfare from the steamboat landing west out on to the plains. Each stable was about 36x100 feet. Immediately north of these stables, south of the middle of the parade ground, was a magazine, mostly underground, over which a sentinel was always posted.

I have mentioned all of the buildings around the parade ground as it then was, and all south of the stone wall. West of the line of stables and south end of west line of buildings stood "Bedlam"[15]—correctly named—a large two-story frame, with front and back porches and stone basement. It was the quarters of unmarried officers, with an officers' mess attached. (A lieutenant in those days would be content with one room, and all of his furniture would not be worth $25.) 'Twas here they fought their battles o'er, from West Point and the girls they left behind them, through the swamps of Florida, the wilds of Texas, over the great plains, the mountains, on the Pacific Slope and the fields of Mexico. 'Twas here they met after tedious campaigns, recountered their triumphs, disappointments and hardships; through heat,

---

[15] A famous "Bedlam" is preserved at Fort Laramie, Wyoming. It is the scene of Captain Charles King's novel, *Laramie: or The Queen of Bedlam* (Philadelphia, J. B. Lippincott Company, 1889).

cold, hunger and disease—and now the feast, if not always of reason, at least the flow of soul—and other things.

Southeast of "Bedlam" about one hundred yards stood the guard house, an unmerciful dungeon, stone basement and heavy log superstructure. Southwest of the guard house and south of "Bedlam" stood the hospital, built of brick, with porches all around, and quite comfortable. On the ridge, about where the riding school now is, was a block house similar to the one heretofore mentioned. Where the hop room now is stood a one-story stone building, used as commissary and quartermaster storerooms and offices, about one hundred feet on what is now McPherson Avenue by about fifty feet on what is now Scott Avenue. A little northwest of this a two-story stone building, now embraced in the Military Prison, was built in 1850 and used as quartermaster's stores and offices. Still farther north, covering the ground beyond the buildings now composing the south front of the Military Prison, were a few homes of employees, the wagon, blacksmith, carpenter, saddler, and other shops and quartermaster's stables and corrals. Also scattered here and there were a few small houses; at the steamboat landing a warehouse. The flagstaff and sundial stood just south of the west end of the present hop room. There was generally a sentinel posted there, and it was said that a sergeant of the guard regulated his watch by the dial on his rounds with the midnight relief.

This is as correct an account as I can give from memory of Fort Leavenworth fifty-six years ago.

Part II
The First Two Years

† † † † † † † † † † †

The road from Fort Leavenworth to New Mexico ran through what is now Easton, at the crossing of Stranger Creek; then through what is now Winchester, Ozakee at the crossing of Grasshopper, now Delaware River and Soldier Creek, four miles north of where now stands Topeka. There it crossed the Kaw on Papan's Ferry, about sixty miles from Fort Leavenworth, thence to Council Grove, sixty miles farther, intersecting the main Santa Fé Trail from Independence, Missouri, east of the Grove.

To reach the "Oregon Trail," I quote from General Cooke's "Scenes and Adventures in the Army," page 283:

"We followed for two days the trails of former marches, guiding us through the intricate and broken but picturesque grounds which border the Missouri. The third day we struck out boldly into the almost untrodden prairie, bearing quite to the west. The sixth day, having marched about ninety miles, we turned towards the south, crossing a vast elevated and nearly level plain, extending between two branches of the Blue River. Thus without an obstacle for fifteen miles, we reached and encamped upon its banks. The seventh day, leaving the Blue and turning to the northwest, between two tributaries from that direction, we soon espied on a distant ridge the wagon tops of emigrants; gradually converging, in a few hours we met. Here was a great thoroughfare, broad and well worn, the longest and best natural road perhaps in the world."

The above had reference to the route taken by Colonel Kearny in his campaign to the Rocky Mountains and back in 1845.

Sometimes Government travel crossed the Missouri River at the Fort, went up on north side to about opposite the mouth of the Platte and thence up that stream. St. Joseph, Missouri, had become an important outfitting and starting-point for trips across the plains, and a good road ran southwest from that place, crossing the Big Blue where is now Marysville, Kansas.

Major Ogden,[1] then quartermaster at Fort Leavenworth, was ordered to lay out a road from that point to intersect this St. Joe road. He employed a lot of Kickapoo Indians as guides, with a Negro named Morgan, who lived with them, as interpreter. A detachment of B Troop came in from Fort Kearney with the mail, and with ours, less two men who had deserted, and some infantry recruits en route to Kearney and Laramie, acted as escort to Major Ogden's road surveying party, and a number of officers and their families en route to Kearney and Laramie.

We left Fort Leavenworth on the second of April, 1850. The first night out we camped at the springs near where Lowemont, Kansas, is now located. We followed the military road to Santa Fé about eight miles, and from there to the intersection of the St. Joe road about one hundred and twenty miles; we followed the divides on account of excessive wet weather, heading, or crossing near the head of the streams running northeast into the Missouri and those running southeast into the Kaw, crossing the Delaware where is now Kennekuk, the Nemaha where is now Seneca, intersecting the road from St. Joe between Seneca and Marysville.[2]

Of the officers en route to Kearney and Laramie on this trip, I remember only Colonel Loomis[3] of the Sixth Infantry, Captain Wharton[4] of the Sixth Infantry and family, and Captain Dyer[5]

[1] Edmund Augustus Ogden was commissioned captain and assistant quartermaster in 1838 and brevet major in 1848. He died in 1855.

[2] Lowemont is in Leavenworth County, northwest of the fort; Kennekuk, where Chief Kennekuk is buried, in Atchison County, became a Pony Express station; Seneca is Nemeha County seat; Marysville is Marshall County seat.

[3] Gustavus Loomis, lieutenant colonel of the Sixth Infantry since 1840, was born in Vermont, entered West Point in 1808, and served in artillery in the War of 1812. He became colonel of the Fifth Infantry in 1851, retired in 1863, was brevetted brigadier general, and died in 1872.

[4] Henry W. Wharton was commissioned second lieutenant in the Sixth Infantry in 1837, first lieutenant in 1838, and captain in 1847. In the Civil War he

The First Two Years

of the Artillery, who was Chief of Ordnance during the war between the States.

Major Ogden and the Kickapoos left us at the crossing of the Blue and returned to Fort Leavenworth. We arrived at Fort Kearney and joined our troop in due time.

Captain and Brevet Major R. H. Chilton* commanded the post and troop. Of all troops in the service this, *its members claimed*, was the most distinguished. Its first captain was E. V. Sumner,†

was colonel of the Second Delaware Infantry and retired in 1863 as major, Ninth Infantry. He died in 1868.

5 Alexander Brydie Dyer was first lieutenant in the Ordnance Department since 1847 and brevet captain since 1848, for the battle of Santa Cruz de Rosales. Born in North Carolina, he was graduated from West Point in 1837 and commissioned in the Third Artillery, transferring to Ordnance in 1838. He became captain in 1853, major in 1863, and brigadier general and Chief of Ordnance in 1864, serving in that office until his death in 1874. He was brevetted major general in 1865 for faithful, meritorious, and distinguished service in the Ordnance Department during the Civil War.

* Robert Hall Chilton was a native of Virginia and a graduate of the M.A. in 1837. He was assigned to the First Dragoons, became major and paymaster in 1854 and resigned April 29, 1861, to enter the Confederate States army. He was appointed brigadier-general, serving on the staff of General Robert E. Lee as adjutant general. He died February 18, 1879.

† Edwin Vose Sumner was born in Boston in 1797, and educated at Milton Academy. He was appointed second lieutenant of the Second Infantry in March, 1819, became first lieutenant in 1823, and was promoted to captain First Dragoons (now First Cavalry) at the organization of that regiment in March, 1833. In 1846 he was promoted major Second Dragoons (now Second Cavalry), and in 1848 Lieutenant colonel First Dragoons; and when the First Cavalry (now the Fourth) was created in 1855, he was appointed its colonel. He was appointed brigadier general in March, 1861, and major general of Volunteers in June of the same year. He died in March, 1863.

General Sumner had his share of wars. He distinguished himself in the Black Hawk War, and took part in numerous expeditions against Indians. He participated in every engagement of General Scott's army in its advance from the Vera Cruz [*sic*] to the City of Mexico, was wounded while leading a cavalry charge at Cerro Gordo, and for gallantry in holding back 5,000 Mexican lancers at Molino del Rey, was brevetted colonel.

In the Civil War he commanded the First Corps of the Army of the Potomac, and was in about all the battles that army engaged in, till General Hooker was placed in command of it. Thereupon he asked to be relieved and was ordered to major general during the War of the Rebellion. It had been continually in the Indian country or Mexico since its organization. It had many traditions of hard campaigns, skirmishes, night attacks by Indians, battles, cold, heat, hunger and feasting, from the Missouri River to Old Mexico, through Texas and all of the Indian Territory from Missouri to Utah and from Minnesota to Texas; and now it was located in the heart of the Pawnee country. At that time the Pawnees were the most dangerous of any Indians on the overland trail to California. Its last battle was the fall before on the Little Blue River where a dozen men were wounded, one fatally, and a dozen or more horses killed or wounded. A number of Indians were killed and many wounded.

Soon after the battle above referred to, Major Chilton became aware of the presence of some Pawnees on an island in the Platte about two miles from the post, and took twenty men with him, intending to surround and make them prisoners.[6] His orders were emphatic not to shoot—he wanted prisoners so as to induce the tribe to come in and make terms that would insure peace and safety to the immense emigration sure to move over the trail to California the following spring. After a good deal of skirmishing through tall grass, wild grape vines and willows, Sergeant Martin, Corporals Haff and Cook and Bugler Peel found four Indians on a dry sandy branch of the river and attempted to carry out the Major's instructions by motioning to the Indians to lay down their arms, which they showed a determination not to do. One ran up a dry branch followed by Haff, who soon shot him. Another ran towards a tall cottonwood with Cook after him. At the tree the Indian stopped with his back to it ready to fire. Cook had him so closely covered with cocked pistol, not twenty feet away that the Indian was afraid to lower his gun, and Cook

---

command the Department of Missouri, but he died suddenly while on his way to his station.

He was twice wounded in the Seven Days' Battles before Richmond, and received his fourth battle-wound at Antietam.

[6] The date of this fight of Company B was October 29, 1849.

parleyed with him by signs to induce him to lay it down, but all to no purpose. Finally his robe dropped from his shoulders. Cook knew this meant a desperate condition of the Indian's mind, and as he gave his final war-whoop and dropped the muzzle of his gun, Cook fired. The Indian fell dead, his rifle being discharged so near the same time that but one report was heard. Cook's bullet entered the Indian's mouth without hitting a tooth and came out at the back of his head. Cook was unhurt and sat coolly reloading his pistol when Major Chilton and half a dozen men rode up, and the Major cried out, "Who killed that Indian?" "I did," said Cook, ramming down his cartridge. "Why didn't you make him lay down his arms?" Poor Cook felt terribly outraged; he had risked his life trying to obey orders, and angrily said, "Why, he wouldn't lay down his arms." At this juncture Bugler Peel rode up, and saluting the Major reported that Sergeant Martin had been killed. Martin was the oldest soldier in the troop, had served with the Major in Mexico, and was a great favorite. Peel reported that after Haff and Cook had left him and Martin, one Indian escaped in the brush while Martin was trying to carry out the Major's orders, and Peel seeing that the other Indian was about to fire, shot him near the heart and he fell on his face, immediately raised himself on one elbow, fired, and shot Martin through the heart, and fell dead. Martin fell from his horse and was borne back to the post to a soldier's grave, a victim of obedience to orders. If he had taken Peel's advice all four of the Indians would have been killed and Martin would have lived to aid in the discipline of the troop.

The percentage of good material for mounted service in our squad of recruits was fully equal to that found in the troop when we joined, all the advantage being in experience and discipline, and my sailor experience led me to believe the latter not very complete. A man ordered to do a thing on board of a ship did not stop to think of the reason why, but moved promptly, if he was not waiting for a "rope's end" to catch him, which, or something worse, was sure to follow the slightest hesitation to obey orders.

The life of the ship and all on board might and often does depend on quick obedience. The man who walks the quarter-deck is a prince supreme, and subordinates see that his will is executed—no friction and no questioning authority.

However, the troop as I remember it, was more than equal to any I met afterwards during my enlistment. Two of our detachment transferred to the infantry during the first year because of their inability to ride. There was so much old material in B, that the new was soon moulded into fair shape. The recruits got horses and drilled industriously. One hour mounted drill before breakfast gave us appetites to eat the slice of bread and boiled pork with pepper, vinegar and coffee. Boiled beef and soup (bean or rice) for dinner. Plenty of beef, because the contractor killed buffalo instead of domestic cattle, and gave us all we wanted.

And now it was the middle of May. The road was lined with white wagons, herds of cattle, horses and mules en route to California and Oregon. Some stock had been run off by Pawnees, some robberies committed and a few venturesome hunters said to have been killed. Major Chilton sent old Jeffries, the interpreter, into the Pawnee villages to induce the Indians to come in and have a "talk." Jeffries was a Negro who came into the Pawnee country when a boy with Mr. Sarpie, or Sarpa, of St. Louis, an Indian trader, and had been there more than thirty years. He was very reliable and useful, because the Indians believed what he told them. A number came in, but a strong band that ranged on the Republican River, south of Kearney, did not come. The main villages on Wood River and Loup Fork, north of the Platte, did not show up. The talk with those who did come in lasted several days, during which they feasted, danced and indulged in sham battles. The chiefs made fine promises, and the Major made threats of what he would do if the road was not left clear for emigration.

Then the troop went in search of the band that refused to come in.[7] Southeast to the Little Blue, about forty miles south to the

[7] This was the Skidi Pawnee, according to George E. Hyde, *Pawnee Indians*

Republican, up that river one hundred and fifty miles, several times in hot pursuit of the delinquent Pawnees, the troop marched and finally brought them to a parley. This was a strong band, but had few horses. That is why we caught up with them. Another reason, we were driving them into the Cheyenne and Sioux country, and they were afraid of being caught between two fires. The Sioux and Cheyennes were perfectly friendly with the whites at this time. Major Chilton's movements were with a view of driving the Pawnees in that direction and he succeeded well. Jeffries got the chiefs to come into camp for a talk. The Indians were much frightened, because they were the bad lot, were guilty of outrages, and now they were where the dragoons had the advantage. Finally Major Chilton held the head chief and another and told them to instruct their people to be at Fort Kearney on a certain day and to notify all the other bands to be there for a "big talk," and if they were not there he would "turn loose" on the whole nation and "wipe them off the face of the earth," a favorite expression of his when talking to bad Indians. The next day we saw the Pawnees going northeast at a rapid rate, and a few hours later met a war party of Cheyennes, the finest band I ever saw—about three hundred—well mounted and equipped. One would think them all picked men, from twenty to forty years old—perfect specimens of the finest and handsomest Indians on the plains, in war paint, fierce and confident-looking—coming down to fight the Pawnees, and if we had driven the latter twenty miles farther west these mortal enemies would have met. The Cheyennes had a band of extra horses; but were without women or other encumbrance. Evidently some Pawnee scouts had discovered the Cheyennes without being seen by them, hence the Pawnees' hurry in getting away. Our prisoners and old Jeffries were kept out of sight in a wagon while the Major held a big sign talk with the Cheyenne chief and a few braves, and per-

(Denver, University of Denver Press, 1951), 173. The Skidi only recently (1847) had ended a long feud with their somewhat distantly related kinsmen, the Grand Pawnees (Chauis) because of increasing pressure from Cheyennes and Sioux.

suaded them to go no farther east, but to go north across the Platte to Wood River,[8] where he thought the most of the Pawnees were. This was true, and the Major knew that if worried by the Cheyennes they would be more likely to come in, and seeing their peril from Cheyennes and troops would come down humbly for the sake of Government protection. And thus it worked, the Cheyennes little dreaming of the good they were doing.

Major Chilton's movement on this short campaign had been bold strategy, as I view it after so many years, and the fortunate meeting with the Cheyennes helped his cause very much. We were out about three weeks, during which time we traveled about four hundred miles without forage other than grass. In two wagons we carried tents and half-rations, so that half of our living consisted of fresh meat—mostly buffalo, of which there was an abundance. We had no sickness except a few cases of diarrhea and a little fever. The principal medicines in the Major's "case" were opium, salts and quinine. About seventy men in the party, liable to accidents and casualties of battle, and no doctor. And here I will say, once for all, that with the exception of the trip to Mexico in 1854 and the treaty at mouth of Horse Creek in 1851, in my whole five years of service while on the plains, every summer on a long campaign, liable to battle and always expecting it, we never had a doctor.[9] Let soldiers of to-day congratulate them-

[8] Wood River, along which some groups of Pawnee habitually camped, joins the Platte at Grand Island.

[9] The Medical Department in 1848 consisted of the Surgeon General, 21 surgeons, and 59 assistant surgeons, with the restriction that no vacancies could be filled until the number was reduced to 20 surgeons and 50 assistant surgeons. When the army was increased from 15 to 19 regiments in 1855, there was an increase to 22 surgeons and 72 assistant surgeons. The Surgeon General's Report for 1856 pointed out the impracticability of 94 medical officers serving an army scattered in 89 posts. A resulting reform not only increased the number of medical officers, but also provided, for the first time, for enlisted men in the Medical Department— one hospital steward being authorized for each army post—and as well provided extra-duty pay for enlisted men detailed from the line to be hospital nurses and assistants. See Col. P. M. Ashburn, *A History of the Medical Department of the*

The First Two Years

selves on the liberality of the Government, the humanity and Christianity of the Red Cross, and the universal demand that soldiers have every comfort that our modern civilization affords.

Our horses at the end of this campaign were, with few exceptions, in good condition. The horse of the dead sergeant (Martin), the beautiful chestnut sorrel, trained by a level-headed, painstaking soldier, was mine, and the best in the troop.

According to Major Chilton's calculation, in about ten days nearly all the Pawnees were near Fort Kearney, and the ensuing pow-wow lasted several days, during which the Indians were made to understand the greatness, goodness and power of the white race, and of the Great Father in Washington in particular, and how wicked, ungrateful and foolish the Pawnees were to disturb the white man or interfere with his peaceful travel through the country in any way—all winding up with solemn promises and a grand feast. Of course I took great interest in this new experience and made the most of it as opportunities offered. I learned much from old Jeffries, and sympathized a great deal with these wily devilish fellows, who were at war with all the wild tribes—constantly on guard against the Sioux, Cheyennes, Arapahos, Kiowas and Comanches on the west and south of them. I am sure that Major Chilton's administration of affairs about Kearney settled the Pawnees so far as their hostility to the whites was concerned, with the exception of the lawlessness of small bands of young bucks once in a while along the Little Blue.

And now the road was crowded with emigration west—long trains of wagons, herds of cattle, etc. I got Lieutenant Stanbury's map and list of distances and copied the distances.[10] One day an emigrant inquired about the route and I handed him my list. He insisted upon buying it of me and I let him keep it. I told

United States Army (Boston and New York, Houghton Mifflin Company, 1929), 60–62.

[10] Captain Howard Stansbury of the Topographical Engineers surveyed Great Salt Lake 1849–50. His final report, *Exploration of the Valley of the Great Salt Lake of the Utah* was published in 1853.

Bugler Grant, and we went into partnership. I wrote the guides, he sold them, and we soon divided over $50 between us.

The middle of July three of the best men in the troop—a sergeant, the farrier and a bugler deserted, taking horses and equipments. Corporal Cook and others followed them 150 miles west and brought back the horses, but not the men or equipments. There was much excitement in the troop, and two weeks later another good man deserted, taking two horses. He seemed to have had a citizen confederate. Cook followed and brought back the horses, but nothing else. Up to this time there had been one sentinel at the stable, which was two hundred feet long and forty feet wide, built of sod, with three doors at each end and one in center of building on each side—open windows on both sides about thirty feet apart. Of course no sentinel could get around fast enough to watch all of these openings in this large building, and this fact at last dawned upon the Major, and thereafter the quartermaster sergeant and one company teamster slept in the stable, and two men—both infantry—walked post, showing that the Major was not trusting his troop. He was doing what ought to have been done all the time, for with the California fever then prevailing, the constant stream of emigrants passing, these horses were too much of a temptation to be resisted by men who would, under any circumstances, desert. There were no desertions from the infantry.

In October, 1850, the troop moved to Fort Leavenworth, and occupied the quarters used by our detachment the previous winter. Major Theophilus Holmes,[11] with four companies of the Seventh Infantry, came about the same time that B troop did,

---

[11] Theophilus Hunter Holmes was born in Sampson County, North Carolina, in 1804. On the day of his graduation from West Point in 1829 he was commissioned both as brevet second lieutenant and as second lieutenant, Seventh Infantry. He became first lieutenant in 1835, served as regimental adjutant for a part of 1838, and then was promoted to captain. He was brevetted major for Monterrey. He resigned in 1861 and became a Confederate lieutenant general, holding district and department commands. He led an unsuccessful attack on Helena, Arkansas, in 1863. He died at Fayetteville, North Carolina, in 1880.

and left in the spring. Like all I saw of the Sixth, the Seventh was a well disciplined, well behaved organization.

The Kaw Indians[12] near Council Grove had been committing some depredations—stealing horses and otherwise making themselves troublesome—and in January, 1851, Major Chilton, with about fifty men of his troop went to Council Grove, 120 miles, had a "big talk," took four of the principal chiefs of the Kaw Nation prisoners and brought them to Fort Leavenworth. About half of the men on this trip were more or less frostbitten, several of them severely. It was a horrible trip for men so poorly provided for a 240-mile march in such severe weather. Overshoes, mittens, gloves, leggings or other extra wraps were not then provided by the Government, nor kept for sale, and men made for themselves out of old blankets, skins, pieces of old canvas and cast-off clothing, anything that necessity prompted them to invent for protection from the bitter cold. Not a house between Fort Leavenworth and Papan's Ferry across the Kaw, sixty miles, and none between the ferry and Council Grove—the whole country an expanse of snow. Plenty of fuel in every camp, and fires kept burning all night. The horses were huddled together in best sheltered places and fires built to windward so that the rays of heat would float towards them. Corn was hauled for them, and as there was no hay, cottonwood trees were felled to browse on, the limbs trimmed off and piled before them. Nothing was left undone that could be done under the circumstances for the comfort of men and horses, but with all that there was great suffering.

On the seventeenth of March, 1851, I was promoted to corporal.

About this time Second Lieutenant D. H. Hastings* joined B

---

[12] The Kaw, or Kansa, Indians, for whom the Kansas River and the state of Kansas are named, were one of the Southern Sioux tribes, but rarely were called Sioux. When Lowe mentions Sioux he usually means Teton Sioux.

* David H. Hastings was born in Ireland, and appointed second lieutenant, First Dragoons, in 1848. He had served as an enlisted man in Company B, Second Infantry, Company K, Third Artillery, and Company A, Engineer Corps. He re-

Troop. He brought with him a fine reputation for long and faithful service, and looked every inch an officer to be respected. He served many years as a first sergeant, won his commission in the Mexican War, where one heel was shot off, and he wore a cork one. A man of iron will and nerve, he was all that a good soldier could wish in a good officer.

The April following Major Sackfield Macklin,[13] paymaster U. S. A., left Fort Leavenworth for Forts Kearney and Laramie to pay off troops, and carried with him the money necessary for that purpose. I never knew the amount, but as there were two companies of Sixth Infantry at Kearney, and one of Sixth Infantry and three of mounted rifles (now Third Cavalry) at Laramie, and the average in each company about sixty men, and when we reached them there would be six or eight months' pay due, the amount carried must have been quite large, though soldiers then averaged but about half as much pay as they get now—$8 per month for mounted privates, $7 for infantry ($1 per month retained from privates until end of enlistment), corporals $10, sergeants $13, first sergeants $16. The escort consisted of one corporal and seven privates from B Company, Sixth Infantry, and a corporal and three privates from B Troop, First Dragoons. Of the infantry I remember only the name of the corporal—Barney Dunnigan, a thoroughly good, intelligent, reliable young Irishman; his whole detail was remarkably good. The dragoon detail consisted of Corporal Lowe and Privates Charles McDonald, John Russell, and Edward O'Meara. The personnel of the last three was remarkable among enlisted men of those days. They enlisted about one year ahead of me, hence had greatly the advantage in experience. O'Meara had been wounded in the battle of the Blue in the fall of 1849, losing two front teeth knocked

---

tired in December, 1863, and died September 22, 1882. He was the father of Mrs. Morton, the wife of Major A. G. Morton, Sixth Infantry.

[13] Sackfield Maclin (not Macklin) was born in Tennessee and was commissioned an additional paymaster of Volunteers in 1846 and major paymaster in 1849. He resigned in 1861 and served in the Confederate Army as major commissary of subsistence.

out by an arrow that cut his lip badly. He was the only man I ever saw whose beauty was not marred by the loss of front teeth. The scar on his lip made his smile all the more attractive. He was an Irish lawyer; by birth, education and instinct a gentleman. The troubles of 1848 drove him to America; he secured a position as clerk in a law office in New York and seemed to be well started on the road to prosperity, when some of his young college chums, in this country for the same reason that he was, determined to enlist in the army for want of something better, and he went with them. This man, this private soldier, entering upon his third year of campaigning, possessed one of the most genial, kindly and attractive temperaments I ever knew. His reading and travel had made him a most companionable man. With the opportunities now afforded he would have stood an examination and been commissioned. But there were no such privileges in his time. Russell was a Philadelphian, a printer and jolly joker, had been a sergeant, and volunteered to go on this trip to get away from the troop and temptation. He was the oldest of the party, as I was the youngest. McDonald was a New Yorker, of Irish parentage, and was a genius—a fine draughtsman and caricaturist. Not a man of our party escaped his pencil. If these three men lacked anything to insure a bright future, it was the strong will and sound judgment to act independently—to blaze the way and decide their own destiny.

Our transportation consisted of the Major's four-mule ambulance for himself and clerk (Mr. Reed), one six-mule team for the infantry and their baggage and provisions, one six-mule team for the dragoons' forage, provisions and tent, and the Major's baggage and servant. The Major had a wall tent and fly for himself and clerk, and a small cook tent. The dragoons had one A tent and infantry two. In all, the Major, his clerk and servant, three teamsters, eight infantry, four dragoons, eighteen. Sixteen mules and four horses. Not a very large escort to take so much money 300 miles to Fort Kearney and 350 more to Laramie. As I ranked my friend Dunnigan by a few days in our appointment the Major gave his orders to me. He was a pleasant, even-tempered man, under whom it was a pleasure to serve, and on the whole trip I never heard him complain. Having seen enough of his escort to satisfy himself that all duty would be carefully attended to, he was content.

There was no boisterous rowdyism, but the dragoon camp, with O'Meara in tragedy, "Sallie" Russell in comedy, and McDonald as scenic artist, was the center of attraction. The infantry had several fair singers, every one could tell a story, and the time passed merrily away from dinner, as soon as practicable after coming into camp, until bed time, soon after dark. We were on the road about 7:00 and in camp between 1:00 and 3:00. Our animals had no forage other than grass after the first week. There was much rain during the first part of the journey, roads bad, no bridges over streams and mud holes, sometimes doubling teams and at others hitching lariat ropes on each side of wagon bed and all hands helping to pull, our progress was slow.

After noon of the fifth day we reached Walnut Creek[14] about fifty-five miles northwest of Fort Leavenworth. We had no rain during the day and did not expect to find the creek high, and though it was running bank full and one hundred feet wide, caused by rains higher up the creek, none of us seemed to remember that its bed was very deep. I rode forward to feel the way across, and though very cautious and slow in my movements my horse suddenly began to slide and in a moment nothing but my head was above water. But the noble animal being a well trained swimmer came up as suddenly as he went down and struck out boldly for the opposite shore, which he made safely about one hundred yards lower down. Though I had navigated the quicksands of the Platte and Republican and had been in water so deep that my horse had to swim from one sandbar to another, this was my first experience in swimming a horse in a rapidly

---

14 Big Walnut Creek and Little Walnut Creek are shown on contemporary maps as entering the Missouri River between Atchison and Leavenworth. There is another Walnut Creek that joins the Arkansas River east of Great Bend.

flowing stream, and the venture was so sudden that the good horse sense of the noble brute under me was my only salvation. In that minute of peril to both of us, I thought of all the rules of action in similar emergencies that I had ever heard, the main point being to cling to the mane and the saddle and leave the horse as free as possible, guiding him only to give the right direction. In this case the current took him on to a sloping bank in the bend of the creek, where he landed easily. If I had expected to swim I should have divested myself of saber and belts, pistol, carbine, and every unnecessary thing, even to outer clothing, and strapped all firmly on my saddle. If the west bank had been steep as the east bank was, rider and horse would have been lost, unless some projecting limb gave me a chance to escape. All was so sudden and so quickly over that my comrades had scarcely time to think, as they expressed it, though they instinctively spurred their horses down the east bank in hopes to assist me. Immediately on landing I discharged my pistol and carbine so that the water would not soak in under the percussion cap to the powder. The Major and the dragoons knew why I did it, but it added to the excitement of others who were without experience.

The Major went into camp to wait until the creek ran down. I stripped everything from my horse except the head halter and lariat, and from myself everything except underclothes, and cached them with my arms in some thick brush. Then I looked carefully for a good place to cross. The east bank was such that I must land at the road or my horse could not get out. The current was so swift that if carried below the road I must go down stream. No one could throw a lariat across, and the men took the small ropes from the ends of the wagon covers, knotted them together, tied a stone to one end, carefully coiled the rope close to the bank and stalwart, broad-shouldered Corporal Dunnigan threw it to me. I was afraid to trust the small rope to pull on and told the men to tie several lariats together and to the east end of small rope, which they did, and I hauled them over and tied to the end of my lariat, and they hauled the rope taut on the east side. I then rode to the edge of the stream some distance above where I must land, the men in the meantime keeping the rope taut and ready to quickly haul in all slack. I stuck my toes in behind the horse's elbow joints, and taking a firm hold of the mane with my left hand, urged the horse with my right, and he plunged in and struck the landing nicely; but he could not have stemmed the current, and, slippery and steep as it was, he could not have carried me out without the assistance of the men at the ropes. The Major stood by and watched carefully to see that no mistakes were made, but did not interfere. By this time the Major's and the infantry camp had good fires. The water was cold that April day, and I was thoroughly chilled. After washing in hot water and putting on dry clothes, I drank hot coffee and ate a good dinner with the infantry, and as my comrades had been devoting their time to me, they too were fed. Of course I was congratulated very much, not the least by the Major and Mr. Reed. I deserved little credit, but rather censure, and said so, for not dismounting and trying the crossing of that swift running stream with a pole or stone on a rope—anything to make sure of what I was undertaking.

There is no place on earth where a man gets fuller credit for every reasonable effort, or where exposure to danger is so liberally rewarded as among his comrades in the army. That little adventure became one of the traditions of B Troop, and lost nothing in the telling. McDonald had it down in good shape on paper, and while all three of them would hatch a joke at my expense, it was always in a way that left no sting.

These prairie streams run down as quickly as they rise, and by noon the next day we crossed with little difficulty, more than doubling teams and all hands at ropes, and camped on the west side.

Except continuous rains and bad creek crossings we had no more difficulty until we reached Big Blue River, now Marysville, about 150 miles from Fort Leavenworth. We found it bank full— a wide turbulent torrent, and no prospect of its running down.

The First Two Years

The Major was anxious to get over and seemed to think we could make a raft on which to lash one or two wagon beds and cross over a little at a time, and finally swim the animals. I set about getting some dry logs and lashing them together. My comrades, of greater experience, could see no use in our efforts, though they took hold wherever I asked them to, but I worked with energy all afternoon and fell into the river several times. I went to camp thoroughly exhausted and wet; was going to change my clothes, but lay down in the tent and fell asleep. The next morning when I awoke the sun was high. I heard my comrades talking by the camp-fire wondering how I slept so long. My head seemed perfectly clear, but I could neither speak nor move, though in no physical pain. Russell looked in and seeing my eyes open, spoke. Receiving no answer, he came nearer and spoke again; then he was alarmed, and reported to the Major, who came to the tent, spoke to me, felt my pulse, raised me up, put a flask of brandy to my lips, a little at a time, in the meantime a man at each limb rubbing me thoroughly. I made a spasmodic effort, turned over on my side, circulation seemed restored, and soon I could speak. Having been thoroughly rubbed and properly clothed, I could sit up, and before night could help myself in a feeble way. The Major told me not to worry about anything, he would wait. I doubt if any doctor could have treated me better. In the meantime some large freight trains came along, stretched a rope across the river, lashed two large wagon beds together, and in a few days ferried over fifty wagons and their contents, and our little outfit—all the animals, oxen, mules and horses being compelled to swim.

Major Dougherty, of Clay County, Missouri, en route to Kearney and Laramie, where he was post trader, camped near us, and a young Negro man belonging to him fell into the river and was drowned. The Major had raised the boy, his mother belonging to him and employed in his family, and he felt keenly the distress that the news would bring to his household.

Having crossed the Blue and left the danger of bad roads and high water behind, we made good time. I had recuperated a good deal, but was weak and feverish. The Major, in the goodness of his heart, made me ride in the ambulance more than half of the time the balance of the way, while he rode my horse to Kearney, where we spent several days. Captain Wharton, Sixth Infantry, commanded the post.

From Kearney to Laramie, 350 miles, the journey was pleasant. At the crossing of the South Platte we met several caravans of trappers and traders hauling furs and hides to the Missouri River. These outfits were more remarkable as showing how much a man can make of a little than for their elegance. These men had picked up broken down and abandoned emigrant wagons, crudely repaired and made a large number of carts and wagons, which enabled them to move great quantities of goods to steamboat navigation, their motive power being oxen that they had found broken down and abandoned or had traded for with the emigrants the year before. This was to them luxurious transportation, for until the heavy emigration of 1849 there had been but few cattle in the country. Heretofore traders and trappers had worked their way down the Platte and Missouri in bull boats during high water in May or June, or packed on mules or ponies. We were fortunate in meeting these caravans at the crossing. Here I learned a good lesson in navigating a quicksand river. We reached the crossing on the south side and camped as the traders' trains went into camp on the north side. The river was quite deep for the Platte, caused by melting snow in the mountains, half a mile wide and from one to four feet deep—quicksand bottom. Towards evening several of the traders rode over to our camp to "try the river," as they said. 'Twas here I first met Major Fitzpatrick, "Tim" Goodale, John Smith, and other celebrities with well established reputations as traders, trappers and Indian fighters.[15] I went with them to their camp. "Now," said Major

---

[15] Thomas Fitzpatrick (1799–1854) called Broken Hand and White Hair, was one of the most famous of Mountain Men. One of the original Ashley and Henry men of 1823, Fitzpatrick headed the Rocky Mountain Fur Company, guided the

Fitzpatrick, "if we should hitch up and start to cross with a load without beating down the quicksand, thereby making a firm roadbed, we would get mired in the sand; one side would settle and upset the wagon, or the whole wagon sink; in short, 'twould be impracticable to cross in that way. Now, the way to pack the sand and make a firm roadbed is to travel over it with a lot of animals until it is well beaten down, and then cross your wagons; the more travel over it the better the road gets. Now, in the morning we will have a lot of men mounted and drive all of our cattle over and back, keeping them as near together as possible, and then we will cross as fast as we can, giving the roadbed no rest, and a good way for you to do with your little outfit will be for you to follow us when we drive the cattle back." And this we did, crossing without trouble.

Fifteen miles from the crossing of the South Platte, we entered Ash Hollow and struck the North Platte, up which we traveled to Fort Laramie, passing Court House Rock, Chimney Rock, Scotch Bluffs[16] and other interesting points, all of which have been so well described by Generals Frémont, Cooke and others that I need say no more than that no one can realize how wonderful they are without having seen them.

The Laramie River is a lovely, clear mountain stream, about the volume of the Little Blue or Pawnee Fork of the Arkansas. The post of Fort Laramie is located on its west bank, above and south of where it flows into the North Platte. Our infantry de-

---

first wagon trains to Oregon, guided Frémont, Kearny, and Abert, was an Indian agent, and negotiated the Fort Laramie Treaty of 1851. (See LeRoy R. Hafen and W. J. Ghent, *Broken Hand* [Denver, Old West Publishing Company, 1931]). Tim Goodale was companion of Kit Carson in driving thirty horses and mules to Fort Laramie in May, 1850. M. Morgan Estergreen in *Kit Carson* (Norman, University of Oklahoma Press, 1962) says Goodale went on to California, but apparently he had not started when Lowe caught up with him. John, or Jack, Smith was trader at Bent's Fort and influential among the Cheyennes, with whom he lived for several years. Lewis H. Garrard has much to say about him in *Wah-to-yah and the Taos Trail* (Norman, University of Oklahoma Press, 1955).

[16] Scotts Bluff, now a National Monument. Court House Rock and Chimney Rock were landmarks on the Oregon Trail.

tachment was quartered with Company G, Sixth Infantry; Major Macklin and his clerk were quartered with Captain Ketchum,[17] commanding Company G and the post, and I was sent up the Laramie where the dragoons and teamsters with all the animals were to camp during our stay. Four miles above the post, on the opposite side of the river, which was fordable almost any place, I found a camp, as O'Meara expressed it, "Fit for the gods"—one of the most lovely spots I have ever seen. We owed our good fortune in not being attached to one of the three troops of mounted rifles stationed at the post to the fact that there was no forage except grass, and that was eaten off close to the sandy ground for some miles, and to the fact that most of the rifles were camped out for the purpose of foraging their horses. That was why I went so far from the post and camped on the opposite bank. Here the teamsters had nothing to do but take care of themselves, herd their mules during the day, picket them out at night, and take their turn with the dragoons standing guard. The dragoons had nothing to do except to take care of themselves and horses, and do their share of guard duty. I reported to the Major at the post every day about ten o'clock.

And now followed one of the most happy months of my life. O'Meara described this camp in prose and poetry that would be fine reading to-day, but alas, in youth how little we think of the future! Of all of our trip there is no record, not even a morning report, as with the troop. That report shows Corporal Lowe and Privates Russell, O'Meara and McDonald on detached service escorting paymaster to Fort Laramie, and that is all there is of one of the most interesting trips I ever participated in. But I can see

[17] William Scott Ketchum of Connecticut was graduated from West Point in 1834 and commissioned brevet second lieutenant, serving eighteen months in that rank before being commissioned second lieutenant. He became first lieutenant in 1837, served as regimental adjutant, 1838–39, captain and assistant quartermaster, 1839–46, and was commissioned captain, Sixth Infantry, in 1842. He became major, Fourth Infantry, 1860; lieutenant colonel, Tenth Infantry, 1861, brigadier general of Volunteers, 1863, and ended the Civil War a brevet brigadier general and brevet major general, with assignment as colonel, Eleventh Infantry. He was unassigned after March 15, 1869, retired in 1870, and died in 1871.

the camp now, fifty-five years later, in memory, lovely, green and beautiful as ever—an amphitheater of rugged hills, the pure, clear river with its pebbly bottom running gently by, fringed with willows, orchards of box elders in the bottoms, cedars and pines upon the hills, fragrant flowers on every hand. Any good hunter could bring in a black-tailed deer in a few hours, and the river afforded plenty of fish.

All of our party could cook, but McDonald was excellent, Russell made good bread, and O'Meara, well, he was the epicure of the party; the coffee must be browned just so, a certain quantity of ground coffee to a given amount of water; the venison must be seasoned right, whatever that was, and 'twas always good. Everything was clean, tin cups and plates included. We had new forks at every meal; McDonald insisted on that, and O'Meara whittled them out of tough dry willow—straight sharp sticks. We stretched the Major's tent fly for a dining room, drove down four stakes to lay the endgate of the wagon on, and that was our table; water-buckets and boxes for seats. Russell tore a flour-sack into squares, hemmed them and put one at each man's plate. "Gentlemen," he said, "must use napkins," and he changed them as often as was necessary. Another flour-sack ripped open made a table-cloth. Russell and O'Meara did most of the hunting, and we were seldom without venison. McDonald put out the hooks at night and was almost sure to have nice channel catfish for breakfast. I frequently took down a quarter of venison to the Major. Except reporting to him daily I made it a rule not to be out of sight of camp long at a time. I explored every nook for several miles around and reveled in the pure air, the delicious water and the delightful scenery. We moved a short distance and made a fresh camp every few days for cleanliness and good grass. The Major gave me some papers out of the semi-monthly mail, and we borrowed a few books from G Company. We furnished our three teamsters meat and fish. One of them, "Bill" Anderson, was six feet four inches tall, a comical, good-natured Missourian. One day I sent him down to G Company with one big buck and half of another. When he found the first sergeant he was on parade at guard mounting, standing at "parade rest." Anderson slouched along down to the sergeant and said, "See here, the boss sent me down with some meat and I don't know what to do with it; I'm 'feared my mules 'll git skeered when this here drum beats." The Sergeant said, "Well, you run for your mules and I'll see you later." And Bill ran and got there in time to be escorted off the parade ground by Captain Ketchum's order, with the threat to put him in the guard house if he was caught here again. This man stayed in Government employ, was with me in the Kansas war in 1856 and on the Cheyenne expedition in 1857—served in the volunteers in the war between the States, and died in the Soldiers' Home in 1900, always a faithful, reliable man.

One night there was a heavy storm of rain, thunder and lightning, lasting till morning, when two mules were missing. We had been in the neighborhood two weeks and these mules had not been out of it except when Anderson went with meat or for rations, and no one thought they would leave. O'Meara, Russell and I mounted and circled around awhile without finding their trail. I then told Russell to go down the river and O'Meara up, while I crossed over and struck out toward the post. They were dragging long lariats fastened to picket pins, and the trail ought to be easily found. On an old wood road half-way to the post I found such a trail as they would make, but rain had fallen upon it, and if the trail of my mules, it had been made in the night during the storm. I followed it, passing west of the post to the ferry across the North Platte. The ferryman was just up and had not seen any mules. He was a good-natured fellow who knew everything and didn't "believe no durned mule would do such a fool thing as ter leave camp 'n all his friends 'n pass the post 'n come down ter my ferry ter swim when ther's er boat waitin' fer 'im." However much I might respect the ferryman's knowledge of mules, the fact remained that I had followed this trail more than three miles. I knew a mule's peculiarity for following a trail when once on it, and insisted on crossing and taking a look on the other side. The ferryman crossed me reluctantly, protesting that I would have my trouble for nothing.

Having landed, I pointed out to him the marks of two ropes with pins attached going up the bank. He insisted that it was something else, and I left him, following the trail with ease for several miles along a broad lodge pole trail made by Indians. It was as easily followed as a plain wagon road. Then the trail left the road and the mules had grazed, zig-zagging here and there, but finally came into the Indian road again, and here their trail was fresh—made since the rain; one or two shoes were off as shown by the tracks. I knew that some of our mules were in that condition, and felt sure that, strange as it might appear, I was on the right trail, and urged my horse forward rapidly for some time, hoping every high point I reached to see the mules. The farther I went the more mystified I was, for this trail ran west up the north side of North Platte—straight away from any place these mules had ever been, so far as I knew. Much of the way the trail showed that they were traveling at a trot; and going down some hills there were marks showing that occasionally a picket pin had caught on a tuft of grass and bounded forward several feet, a thing that would not occur at a walk. It was evident they were traveling of their own free will, because there were no other tracks, and if ridden the lariats would have been gathered up and not allowed to drag. As the forenoon dragged along my horse advised me that I was asking too much of him. I had had no breakfast, was feeling keenly the want of it, and while I must do without I must not destroy my horse's usefulness; and so I grazed him awhile, meantime taking off the saddle, smoothing down his back with my hand, adjusting the blanket, washing his legs in a pool of water, and he thanked me, the poor brute, for every kindly touch.

In half an hour I mounted again and started on; and now I settled down to studying my horse's strength and doing all I could within it. The day was lovely, the landscape green and beautiful, the air pure and fresh and not too hot—just right for a long ride. I grazed my horse a little several times, peering anxiously from the top of every rise. Along in the afternoon I found myself on a gradual rise going steadily up, up, for miles, the ridge ahead seeming little nearer for a long time. I knew that when I reached the top of that ridge I would see a long distance unless the country was broken, and so my thoughts and eyes were forward, anticipating the scene that was to open.

Coming up on the level ground my horse stopped, head high, nostrils distended, ears pointing forward, and every muscle strained to the fullest tension—no fear, but eagerness seemed to possess him. In the last ten miles I must have risen three hundred feet, most of which I would go down in one mile farther. Then commenced the river bottom extending as far west as I could see, and one mile wide from river to bluff. On this bottom an Indian camp extending perhaps two miles along the river—a nomadic city of magnificent dimensions. It was a mile to the lower end of this vast camp, and I looked down upon every part of it. Many lodges were just being put up; quite a number were coming in over the hills from the north. Evidently this was a new camp, growing larger all the time, but none of it had passed over the trail that I had followed. Great herds of horses were grazing above and north of the camp. The scene before me was one of great activity, the building of a new city, and under more pleasant circumstances would have been an interesting study, but to me there was nothing pleasant about it. I dismounted and rubbed "Chub's" nose. I felt the need of friendly company, and he was all I had.

My journey seemed to be ended. Here I was upon the trail, my mules probably with one of the Indian herds, but could I get them? And how? I did not believe the Indians would give them to me without a reward, which I could not give, and possibly some mourner who had lost a friend might try to get even by taking my scalp; this was a way they had of doing, and I hesitated. I could not bear the idea of trailing my mules to the very edge of this camp and then giving it up—weakening, as the boys say.

The First Two Years

But what hope had I of accomplishing anything? My judgment said, get back to Laramie and let the mules go; my pride caused me to hesitate, and the longer I hesitated the firmer my pride held me. In this frame of mind I led my horse behind a low bluff and sat down while he grazed.

It was now probably five o'clock. Suddenly my horse threw his head high as under great excitement. Without looking for the cause I sprang into the saddle. All around me were mounted Indians—twenty or more young bucks—bows and arrows in hand. I was completely surrounded, and to run might insure being riddled with arrows, and so I put on an air of indifference, showed the trail of my mules, and tried to beat into their stolid heads the fact that I wanted them. They let me go through the motions for five minutes with perfect indifference. Finally one of them said, "Kig-e-la." Seeing that I did not understand, he said, "Wa-se-che kig-e-la etoncha tepe," pointing to the Indian camp, all of which was Greek to me, but which I afterwards learned meant: "White man go to chief's tipi (lodge)," and I drifted along with them in that direction.

Having arrived at headquarters, the chief saluted me with, "How, how, cola, how!" and shook hands; numerous others did the same. My escort melted away, and in response to his pantomimic invitation, I dismounted and entered his palace, where he invited me to rest on a pile of robes and furs. A squaw took the saddle and bridle from my horse and led him away. After awhile she returned with the picket pin and laid it inside the lodge. Looking where she laid it I saw two others, worn bright from dragging on the ground, and was sure they belonged to the mules. I gave special attention to the dried venison and buffalo laid before me, hardly realizing how hungry I was until I struck that soft couch and food. A squaw brought me some soup, probably dog, but it was good. I had been twenty-four hours and had ridden all day without food. Women and children peeped in to gratify curiosity, and the warriors and braves came and went continually. A circle of apparently distinguished men was formed, the chief opposite me, a pipe was lighted, passed and smoked by all. Whatever nervousness I had felt was gone. I seemed to be taking on the stolidity of an Indian. Seeming to realize that I must be tired, the lodge was soon vacated and in spite of my peculiar surroundings I slept. When I awoke it was dark inside, but bright fires burning outside all over the camp, and from end to end tremendous excitement. This was my first night with the great Sioux Nation, and I knew little of them, but enough to convince me that something exciting had occurred. I sat down outside of the lodge, leaning against it so that I could see a long distance into the camp. The scene before me was one never to be forgotten—in short, it was a war dance. A war party of Sioux had killed six Crows[18] and brought in their scalps; but it was not all a Sioux victory, for there was mourning for some of the Sioux who never returned.

I will not attempt to describe it. Not all the demons of the infernal region, with sulphurous torches, horns and cloven feet, nor anything else the imagination can picture could excel the beastly human nature here displayed. Gradually the clans joined in until the main display was near the chief's headquarters; the victors came near and shook the bloody scalps almost in my face as they danced and paraded up and down, beating tom-toms and emitting unearthly yells, whether to honor or to intimidate I did not know, but afterwards concluded that it was neither. The warriors just wanted to show the wa-se-che (white man) by the war dance what they could do, and the weeping and howling of the squaws and near relatives of the dead represented genuine grief. This din was kept up long past midnight, and gradually died out from sheer exhaustion of the actors.

On that couch of furs I fell asleep toward morning, and was awakened by the sun shining into the lodge. I sat up and took an inventory of my surroundings. The old monarch, one squaw,

---

[18] Crow or Absaroka, a tribe of Siouan linguistic stock living at this time in and near the Rocky Mountains of present Wyoming and Montana. They were traditional foes of the Teton Sioux and Cheyennes.

The First Two Years

with baby at her breast, and a half a dozen youngsters—boys and girls—were asleep. An adjoining lodge held two or three more squaws and several youngsters of his family; outside was a solitary squaw boiling some meat. From end to end the camp was silent—even the thousands of dogs that had lent their aid to the hellish din during the night were all asleep. I came out and sat down; the old squaw brought me some meat from the kettle on a stick and some of the soup in a cup. I enjoyed it so much that she brought more, and I feasted. We seemed to be the only people awake. Indians never get up early without some special incentive; they want the dew off so that their moccasins will not get wet. Between seven and eight o'clock a couple of bucks came in from a herd driving some horses and mules, and as they drew near I saw mine. Here they came at a rattling gait, my two mules and horse looking little worse for the previous day's fatigue. The old squaw who gave me breakfast caught the lariat of my horse, led him to the lodge, reached in and pulled out my saddle, blanket and bridle, while the men helped themselves at the kettle. The squaw was going to saddle my horse, but I did it to suit myself, while she chattered and laughed with the men. The people in the lodge came out and a few from other lodges gathered around. The big e-ton-cha looked as if he had spent a rollicking night at the club; his eyes were bloodshot and he looked drowsy. He and the men talked some together; he evidently asked the squaw if I had eaten plenty; went to a pile of dried meat, selected a lot of nice pieces and put them in my holster. Then he shook hands with me and said, "How cola, kig-e-la wa-se-che tipi." "How" was the common salutation on meeting or parting with white men, and all the English most Indians knew; the other words meant: "Go, friend, the white man's tipi."

I did not stand upon the order of going, but wanted to reward this prince to whom I was under so many obligations. I had on a very large red and yellow silk handkerchief, a luxury I always indulged in on the plains. I often tied it around my hat and brought it around so as to cover my neck and most of my face to keep off the sun and the pestiferous gnats. If not in use any other way it hung loosely around my neck to keep off the sun and wipe away perspiration. Though it cost me $2.50 out of my munificent salary, I could afford it, for it was cheaper than whisky at twenty-five cents a gallon. This handkerchief I wanted to give to the chief, placed it around his neck, pulled out my four-bladed knife and put it in his hand. I was the most thankful of men and anxious to prove it. If any one thing more than another would tempt an Indian to commit murder or any other bad act, it would be to possess himself of such a beautiful handkerchief. If I were in battle against Indians, I would hide such a temptation quickly, for fear that every effort would be centered upon destroying me to possess it. The chief felt of it, looked at the sun through it, rubbed it over his face and handed it back to me. I opened the blades of the knife; he felt of them slowly and said: "Wash-ta" (good), and handed it back. I pressed them on him, but he only said: "Wa-se-che washta" (white man good), and declined to accept. I offered the handkerchief to his squaw with the suckling babe, but she laughed, shook her head and would not touch it. I could not pay this nobleman for his hospitality, trouble and protection; I even feared that he thought less of me, this savage king, than if I had gone away with more dignity and less patronizing display. Well, having said "good bye," I coiled the lariat ropes carefully about the mules' necks, fastened them securely, mounted my horse and started. The two Indians who brought in the mules started with me and drove them over the bluffs where I first saw the camp and then said, "How," and turned back. I persuaded one of them to stay with me, thinking that he might be of service in case I met other Indians. On we came, down the long slope, making what time I thought my horse would stand, grazing a while two or three times, and reached the ferry while the sun was an hour high. I fully expected my Indian friend to go to camp with me, but he refused and said, "How cola." I bought him two loaves of bread from the ferryman, which he tied in the corner of his blanket, and said, "Skaw-papoose"—that is, he would save it for them, his wife and child, I tried in vain to press my handkerchief upon him, but he refused, and took another loaf of bread, all the ferryman had.

This benighted ferryman had seen no one from the post, and supposed I had recrossed at a ford some miles above. "Well, dog me! ef them mules ain't h—l, I'll never ferry another pilgrim, durn my buttons." I wanted to go through the post to report to the Major, but instead of keeping outside of the parade ground the mules set up an unearthly braying and ran directly in front of the commanding officer's quarters. Of course, I must follow them, and as I got there Captain Ketchum ran out and said: "What are you riding over this parade for?" I halted to explain, when he recognized me. I told him how it happened, which was satisfactory, and asked him to please say to the Major that I had returned with the mules and would report in the morning.

I reached camp about dark. Russell washed "Chub's" back and legs, and rubbed him down good. McDonald got hot water, O'Meara rubbed me down in a hot bath, I got on clean clothes, ate a good supper, rolled myself in the blankets, and told them to wake me in time to get to the post by ten o'clock. Russell had reported to the Major the day I left and the day I returned; all were considerably worried and puzzled at my absence. No one had thought of looking in the direction of the ferry. Russell had been down the road east of the post eight or ten miles, talked with some traders, and concluded that they had not gone in that direction.

I rode McDonald's horse, reported to the Major next morning and told my adventures to him and Captain Ketchum. A guide and interpreter was called in to listen to my description of the camp, and he said it was over 50 miles from the ferry across North Platte, and several traders familiar with the country, with whom I talked, did not put any lower estimate upon it. The puzzle was, why did the mules go there? It turned out that a lot of troops had been camped there about a year before, and it was believed that these mules belonged to that command and had been taken to

Fort Leavenworth in the fall, as all stock that could be spared was taken there to winter. This seemed the only solution to such a freak on the part of these two. Estimating that I lost 10 miles in hunting the trail going, would make 65 miles the first day and 55 the next day—120 miles.

All too soon the time came for us to start on the return trip to Fort Leavenworth, and we left "Camp Macklin," named by me in honor of Major Macklin, with many regrets. We had enjoyed a month of positive pleasure and happiness, the like of which we might not hope for soon again.

At Laramie we were joined by Mrs. Rhett, wife of Brevet Captain Rhett,* of the mounted rifles, and her two small children and a servant, her transportation being a light wagon and four-mule team. Having crossed to the east side of Scotts Bluffs, about fifty miles east of Laramie, we turned south and camped near a trading post belonging to Major Dripps, who was or had been an Indian agent.[19] He was to join us the next morning and travel in our company to the Missouri River. Our camp was made about noon on a plateau where grass was very short. A ravine twenty-five feet deep ran by the camp, sixty feet wide at bottom, with steep banks. At the bottom of this ravine was a small spring from which we got water. It also contained fine grass, and in it we picketed our animals.

About two o'clock there was sharp lightning and loud thunder, evidently a heavy storm some distance in the bluffs, which kept gathering force and coming nearer to our camp. But while the sun was still unobscured by clouds where we were, water which had fallen a long way off came down the ravine, increasing rapidly. We hurried to the animals and got about half of them

19 Andrew Dripps, one of the notable mountain men, served at times the Missouri Fur Company; Pratte, Chouteau and Company; and John Jacob Astor's American Fur Company. Dripps was Indian agent on the upper Missouri in the late 1840's.

* Thomas Grimke Rhett was a native of South Carolina and a graduate of the M.A. in 1845. He resigned in April, 1861, to enter the Confederate Army. He was Assistant Adjutant General from 1861 to the close of the war. He died July 27, 1878.

out and tied to the wagons before the water was ten to fifteen feet deep, and the other animals on the other side of it where we could not reach them, and if their frantic exertions had not enabled them to pull their picket pins they must have drowned. Before the storm struck us the water was twenty feet deep, and great logs coming down at the rate of twenty miles an hour. The Major and Mr. Reed got Mrs. Rhett and her children into her wagon, we drove picket pins into the ground and tied ropes to the wagon-wheels and had everything as safe as could be made, when one of the most fearful storms I ever experienced struck us. The wind did not blow very hard, but rain with heavy hail came down in torrents. Standing in our tent I dipped up a hat full of the mixture and after the water ran out through a hole, the hat was two-thirds full of large hail. On the slightly sloping ground the water was half-way to one's knees, from which may be inferred what a deluge was falling. Fortunately the storm passed quickly, and by five o'clock the sun was smiling as sweetly as ever; the creek ran down as quickly as it came up.

We had two horses, mine and O'Meara's, and on them we started to find the lost animals. The storm obliterated the trail, and we had no guide but the direction of the storm. It came from the southwest, and the stock must drift before that pelting hail to the northeast, and in that direction towards a line of high red bluffs we rode. We must find them before dark if possible, as if they had all night the start we might have a long chase. Fortunately we found them about eight miles from camp on the west side of an amphitheatre of perpendicular bluffs, all together, grazing contentedly at sunset. We managed to catch all of them and take off their picket pins. Excepting a few slight wounds, none of the animals were hurt. We fixed the ropes around their necks and started for camp about dark, where we arrived two hours later.

I had asked McDonald and Russell to keep a bright fire of pine knots, of which they had plenty, so that we could see the light, which was a great help. When the stock was all caught and made safe Bill Anderson said: "Well, I'll be gol durned if they hain't got the last one on 'um." This was one of the best lessons I ever learned, never to camp in a ravine or where the camp could possibly overflow by a sudden rise, never to trust stock where by any possibility one can not reach them. I have seen thousands of camps in attractive places like that ravine, for convenience of water and wood, because the people were too lazy to carry water or wood, and I have almost every year read of some of them being drowned and their outfits destroyed. There was no other incident worth mentioning on the trip, no accidents, no losses and no friction.

We met emigrants continually, in great numbers, en route to California, Oregon and Salt Lake.

Before leaving Laramie, Major Macklin had informed me that soon after we left Fort Leavenworth B Troop had been ordered on a forced march to Fort Adkinson,[20] on the Arkansas River, to relieve D Company, Sixth Infantry, quartered in a sod fort (Adkinson), which was surrounded and threatened by the Kiowa and Comanche Indians. Nothing further had been heard from them. He also informed me that there was to be a great assemblage of Indians near Fort Laramie early in the fall, at which all the tribes that could be induced to come were to meet, smoke the pipe of peace, make treaties between tribes and the tribes with the Government, and to wind up with a general distribution of presents from the Great Father. At Kearney we heard the same report and nothing more.

At what is now called "West End," then the dragoon drill-ground, the Major halted and made us a little speech, in which he recounted the uniform good conduct of his escort and the pleasure and freedom from care they had given him during the trip. The dragoons had taken upon themselves to look after Mrs. Rhett's camp, pitch and take down her tent, and soon after our

---

[20] Fort Atkinson, Kansas, (not Adkinson) was a temporary post on the Arkansas River, not far from the sites of Fort Mann and Fort Dodge and Dodge City, Ford County.

arrival at Fort Leavenworth Mrs. Rhett sent for me, and through me sent her thanks and a nice present to each of the dragoons for special kindness and attention to her and her children during the trip.

And now we heard that B Troop, having relieved Adkinson without serious trouble, had been ordered back, and would, after its return, proceed to Fort Laramie.

The infantry part of the escort was at home with its company. I reported to the commanding officer of the post, Colonel T. T. Fauntleroy,[21] and he excused us four dragoons from all duty except the care of ourselves and horses until the arrival of the troops. We took possession of our quarters and stables, and when the troop arrived ten days later we had everything in good order. Sergeant Hooper was now first sergeant. This was a change extremely gratifying to me. He was serving in his tenth year—a level headed, sober, honest, active man, of good judgment and even temper. I looked forward hopefully.

Private Wiggins was drowned in Grasshopper Creek (now Delaware River) on the way out. After everything else was over, the horses and mules had to swim. They were driven into the river, Sergeant Cook and Private Wiggins bringing up the rear, mounted. Both were washed from their horses. Wiggins struck out to swim to shore, which he would have done, but his horse struck him with his feet, knocked him under and he was never seen again. Cook caught his horse's tail and was pulled ashore. Wiggins was an excellent soldier, a man of good habits, and well liked. No other casualties or serious accidents. The forced march out had pulled the horses down some, but they were in fair condition. At stable call the Major inspected the horses of my detachment critically and found them almost as fleshy as when we started out—not a sore spot on them. As the Major expressed it,

21 Thomas Turner Fauntleroy of Virginia was appointed major of the Second Dragoons when that regiment was organized in 1836. He was promoted lieutenant colonel in 1846 and colonel of the First Dragoons on July 25, 1850. He resigned in 1861 and became a brigadier general of Virginia Volunteers in the Confederate army. He died in 1883.

"No one would think they had been on a long march." We had traveled over 1,300 miles; my horse had traveled eight miles a day for thirty days from the camp at Laramie to the fort and back, 240 miles, besides my trip to the Sioux camp after the mules, 120 miles, making in all more than 1,660 miles. The troop under Major Chilton had traveled 800 miles and the horses looked well, with few sore backs. Two or three horses were changed by the quartermaster, some shoeing done, a little replenishing of clothing, and in a week we were ready for the field again. For my twenty animals six sacks (384 quarts) of corn were taken. One quart each night and morning (forty quarts per day) fed until all was gone, and from that time to the end of the trip grass only. Being used to corn, this two quarts per day kept them up until they became used to the grass and until the early grass gained substance. Major Chilton's command took extra transportation to haul half rations—five pounds of corn for each animal per day to Council Grove; one-fourth rations from there to Adkinson and back.

We were to escort the Superintendent of Indian Affairs, Colonel D. D. Mitchell,[22] who arrived at Fort Leavenworth by steamboat with Colonel George Knapp,[23] of the *Missouri Repub-*

[22] David Dawson Mitchell (1806–1861) was superintendent of Indian Affairs during most of the period from 1841 to 1853. Born in Louisa County, Virginia, he became a clerk for the American Fur Company in St. Louis in 1828 and built Fort Mackenzie in 1832; another fur trading post, Fort Mitchell, was named for him in 1833. In the Mexican War he was lieutenant colonel of the Second Missouri Volunteers, commanded by Colonel Sterling Price. When Price and Colonel Alexander W. Doniphan became involved in Indian troubles, Mitchell was ordered to lead the advance toward Chihuahua. The troops lacked supplies or funds to purchase them. Mitchell then gallantly escorted Señora Tules, the gambling queen of Santa Fe, to a fandango, and so flattered her with his attention that she consented to lend cash to move the troops. In 1855 he promoted the Missouri and California Overland Mail and Transportation Company and became its president. He supplied mules for the army in the Mormon War of 1858.

[23] George Knapp, 1814–83, was lieutenant colonel in the St. Louis Legion during the Mexican War. For forty-six years he was proprietor of the *Missouri Republican,* the oldest English-language newspaper west of the Mississippi River. He became an apprentice in its business office when twelve years of age. By 1837 he was one of the owners.

The First Two Years

lican, and Mr. B. Gratz Brown,[24] correspondent of the *Republican*, and late Governor of Missouri, who was to and who did write up the campaign, the treaty, etc.; in short, a full and well written account from start to finish, and if published to-day would be read with great interest throughout the world. Colonel Cooper,[25] Adjutant General of the Army, was a guest of Major Chilton during the whole campaign to Laramie and back. The Major had my four horses brought up for Colonel Cooper's inspection, and explained to him the service they had performed, and the Colonel seemed surprised at their freedom from sore backs, and their fine condition.

I was questioned, and made this statement: "When near Fort Kearney, on the way out, a Californian en route to 'the States' camped near us and he showed me how he kept a sound back on his horse. In the first place, he had the California saddle-tree, old Spanish style, high and wide at the withers, and otherwise fitting the back. He used a gunnysack—the coarse kind, made of loose soft fiber—the old-fashioned corn sack, clean and put on next to the back, and a common blanket between it and the saddle. The

[24] Benjamin Gratz Brown, 1826–85, was one of the founders of the Republican Party and was Liberal Republican candidate for Vice-President on the ticket with Horace Greeley in 1872. He was born in Lexington, Kentucky. He was graduated from Yale, practiced law in Louisville in 1847, and moved to St. Louis in 1849, where he became a supporter of Thomas Hart Benton. Brown served in the legislature, 1852–59. He was a frequent contributor to Knapp's *Missouri Republican*, especially 1854–59. In 1856 he was shot in the knee and partially crippled in a duel with Thomas C. Reynolds; Col. Mitchell was Brown's second. Brown was a delegate to the 1860 Republican Convention that nominated Lincoln. In the Civil War Brown was a colonel of the Fourth Missouri Volunteers, but resigned when elected to the Senate in 1863. He was governor of Missouri, 1871–73. After his unsuccessful candidacy for Vice-President in 1872, he joined the Democratic Party in 1876.

[25] Samuel Cooper, 1798–1876, became the highest ranking general (four-star) in the Confederate States Army. He was born in Hackensack, New Jersey, and was graduated from West Point in 1815. In 1821 he became first lieutenant in the First Artillery, and in 1831 brevet captain for ten years' faithful service in one grade. In 1836 he prepared and arranged, under the supervision of Major General Alexander Macomb, *A Concise System of Instructions and Regulations for the Militia and Volunteers*, which was long in use. Cooper was promoted to captain in regular grade that year, and brevet colonel in 1848 for his services in the Mexican War in which

claim was that the gunnysack absorbed the moisture without scalding, as would the blanket if worn next to the back. We tried this with great success, always taking care to have a clean sack, that is, wash the sack occasionally and keep the grit or sand out of it." After that the gunnysack was worn by every horse in the troop. Although our "Grimsley" saddle could not compare with the California tree, the sack was a wonderful help.

As I cannot have access to the records which would enable me to give dates, I am compelled to state the events as they occurred throughout the season, one event following another, regardless of dates. It was July when we returned from Laramie, and the troop from Adkinson and July when we left Fort Leavenworth, and August when we arrived at Fort Laramie. I had been consulted a good deal about camping places because of my recent trip over the road, and now when asked by the Major I recommended "Camp Macklin," and there we camped. The Indians were gathering in great numbers. The plain between our camp and Laramie was filled with Indian lodges, mostly Sioux, but there was a large camp of Cheyennes and Arapahos. Here and there were interpreters, squaw men (men married to squaws and living with or near the tribe for the purpose of trading). Now, this was an effort on the part of the Government to get all the tribes together and have them to make peace with each other, swear fealty to the Great Father, and generally to fix up matters so that there should be no friction between tribes, nor between the various tribes and the Government. Runners had for months been circulating throughout the Indian country, from the Missouri River to Fort Bridger[26] and from Canada to the Arkansas. This was in

---

he had served as assistant adjutant general with the rank of brevet major. At the time Lowe met him, Cooper was assistant adjutant general with the rank of lieutenant colonel, his permanent rank still being captain, Fourth Artillery. In 1852 he became Adjutant General of the Army with the rank of colonel. He resigned March 7, 1861, and served the Confederacy throughout the Civil War as Adjutant General and Inspector with the rank of General.

[26] Fort Bridger, on Black's Fork of the Green River (now southwestern Wyoming) was established by James Bridger and Louis Vásquez in 1843 for trade with the Snake, or Shoshone, Indians.

The First Two Years

the heart of the Sioux, Cheyenne and Arapaho country. Thousands came, even from the far northwest, from the upper Mississippi, from headwaters of the Missouri and the Yellowstone.[27]

The grand old Sioux Nation with its numerous branches and bands furnished the greatest number; then the handsome, the dignified, the wiry, agile, intelligent and brave Cheyennes in large numbers, and rich in equipment. The Arapahos were interesting but less numerous. These three tribes were friends and allies, and ruled the country from Minnesota to the Arkansas River and from the Rocky Mountains to a line drawn north and south some forty miles west of Fort Kearney at their own sweet will. They did not want peace with other tribes. Why should they? Their pastures were well stocked with game, the supply of buffalo was unlimited, the way they hunted inexhaustible. They were rich in everything that people of nomadic habits needed, and as to peace, why, what would life be to them without war? Nature supplied all their needs. They did not hunt for the sake of wantonly destroying the lives of animals as did the white man, and how could they amuse themselves? Of what use to live? And how could they hope to raise young men without war? And of what use were men if not warriors? But the Indian Department had become a great branch of the political machine, large amounts of money were appropriated, growing larger annually, and it must be spent. There were many beneficiaries interested—manufacturers of Indian goods, merchants, freighters, officials and hangers-on in large numbers. Whether it led to tragedy or ended in a farce, here was a well laid plan for the largest assemblage of Indians ever gathered at one council or on one treaty ground. The Pawnees and some others were invited but none of them came, presumably because they were afraid to risk it. But the Snakes came. Their headquarters was about Fort

[27] The Fort Laramie Peace Council, lasting twenty-three days, resulted in a treaty signed on September 17, 1851, which provided for peace among the tribes named by Lowe, and defined their boundaries. Because grass around the fort was soon exhausted by the ponies of ten thousand Indians, the council was moved thirty-five miles down the Platte to Horse Creek, as Lowe narrates.

Bridger. The Sioux and Cheyennes had promised to make peace with them, and to take no advantage of them while the treaty was going on.

About noon one bright day, a long line of dust was seen from our camp, looking west, towards Laramie Peak. Soon a long line of Indians came moving slowly down in battle array, arms ready for use and every man apparently expectant, the women and children and baggage bringing up the rear well guarded. It turned out that Major Bridger,[28] the interpreter, had reported to headquarters the approach of the Snakes, and he had been directed to lead them down near to our camp. All the head men of the Sioux and Cheyennes had given assurance that they should not be molested, so down they came, moving very slowly and cautiously, the chief alone a short distance in advance. They were dressed in their best, riding fine war horses, and made a grandly savage appearance. In the absence of Major Chilton down at the post, seeing all this caution on the part of the Snakes, Lieutenant Hastings had "boots and saddles" sounded so as to be ready whatever happened. Just below us was a large Sioux camp, and the people were showing great interest and some excitement at the approach of their hereditary enemies, and a few squaws howled in anguish for lost friends who had died in battle with these same cautiously moving warriors. When the Snakes reached the brow of the hill overlooking the beautiful Laramie, less than a mile away, and the chief commenced the descent, a Sioux sprang upon his horse, bow and arrows in hand, and rushed towards him. A Frenchman, an interpreter, had been watching this Sioux, ex-

---

[28] James Bridger, 1804–81, mountain man, fur trader, guide, scout, and Indian agent, is referred to as "Captain Bridger, as he was then called." These titles of rank probably derive from the militia system, which allowed considerable latitude in election and appointment of officers. J. Cecil Alter, *Jim Bridger* (Norman, University of Oklahoma Press, 1962), 243, says Bridger received an appointment as major from Colonel Albert Sidney Johnston during the Utah Expedition of 1857. In later years it became a custom to call Indian agents "major," probably after several army or militia majors had served in that capacity. Lowe's account of Bridger in the pages immediately following is a much quoted source on the mountain man's career at this point.

Courtesy Kansas State Historical Society

Percival G. Lowe

U.S. Army photograph

Parade ground at Fort Leavenworth, 1865

Courtesy Library of Congress

Fort Kearny, 1858

Courtesy Library of Congress

Fort Laramie, 1855

Courtesy Yale University Library

Soldiers in uniform, from Plate XVII, "Artillery, Infantry, Dragoon (Full Dress), 1835–1850," a lithograph by H. A. Ogden, in the *Army of the United States* (Washington, 1888)

Courtesy Kansas State Historical Society

Colonel Samuel Cooper, adjutant general, U.S. Army

Courtesy Kansas State Historical Society

Major General Philip St. George Cooke, U.S. Army

Courtesy Kansas State Historical Society

Brevet Brigadier General Albert Sidney Johnston, U.S. Army

pecting trouble, and he, too, mounted his horse and was instantly in pursuit. The Snake column stopped and sent up a wild shout of defiance, the chief moved a few steps farther and raised his gun ready to fire just as the intrepid Frenchman reached the reckless Sioux, pulled him from his horse, disarmed and stood over him. Then ensued a harangue between interpreters and chiefs. The wild Sioux, who sought to revenge himself on the Snake chief who had killed his father some time before, was led back to camp while the Snakes held their ground. Their position was a good one; every man had a good gun, plenty of ammunition, besides bows and arrows. Not one out of a hundred Sioux had guns, and the Snakes, though not one to five of the Sioux, would have defended themselves successfully, and the battle would have been the most bloody ever known amongst the wild tribes. They had come prepared for treachery, and with their splendid equipments felt full confidence in their ability to cope with any band upon the plains. Having quickly mounted the troop, Hastings took a position where he could overlook the actions of the tribe.

Here I met Bridger the first time. He spoke on behalf of the Snakes, and told Lieutenant Hastings what he already knew, that the Snakes had been assigned a position near his troop and asked where they could camp without interfering with the dragoons. Hastings told him that I knew the ground all about there, and turning to me said: "Corporal Lowe show Captain Bridger the limits of our camp and give him all the assistance you can." That order was license for me to stay on Bridger's staff until a camp was made. Then and there Lowe became a Snake, and the other tribes were not in it.

I galloped off with the great mountaineer, whose fort I had seen dotted on my atlas at school a few years before, I showed him the finest camp imaginable, and he was pleased. I asked him if he had any objections to my staying with him until the camp was formed. "No, young man, these are the finest Indians on earth; stay with me and I'll show 'um to you." Soon the column was in motion, and they went into camp in their own peculiar way. Every prominent point was dotted by a sentinel, quietly wrapped in his blanket, gun ready for use. Bridger said: "Well, you seen that fool Sioux make the run, didn't you?" "Yes sir." "Well, ———," referring to the brave interpreter, whom he knew well, "saved that fellow from hell; my chief would 'er killed him quick, and then the fool Sioux would 'er got their backs up, and there wouldn't have been room to camp 'round here for dead Sioux. You dragoons acted nice, but you wouldn't have had no show if the fight had commenced—no making peace then. And I tell you another thing: the Sioux ain't goin' to try it again. They see how the Snakes are armed. I got them guns for 'um, and they are good ones. It'll be a proud day for the Snakes if any of these prairie tribes pitch into 'um, and they are not a bit afraid. Uncle Sam told 'um to come down here and they'd be safe, but they ain't takin' his word for it altogether. They'll never be caught napping, and they're prepared to travel anywhere. Awful brave fellows, these Snakes; got the nerve; honest, too; can take their word for anything; trust 'em anywhere; they live all about me, and I know all of them."

I returned to the dragoon camp, in a couple of hours just as Major Chilton, with the Indian commissioner, Colonel Mitchell, and some others came in, and I was sent back with Colonel Mitchell's compliments to request Captain Bridger, as he was then called, to come over. I delivered the message, and returned with Bridger, who spent some hours with the Commissioner's party. Somehow, I had conceived a great liking for and felt great confidence in Bridger. The acquaintance had been short, but he impressed me as a master in his line, and when I related to Sergeant Hooper and others what he had said to me, all seemed to partake of the same feeling, and whatever anxiety was stirred up by the incidents of the day quieted down. While conceding his courage, no one admired the judgment nor the treachery of the Sioux, who fully expected to arouse his tribe to battle, and but for the brave interpreter he might have done so, though sure death awaited him. The attitude of the Snakes, the cool, deliberate action of the chief, the staunch firmness of his warriors and the quiet demeanor of women and children, who were perfectly self-possessed—not a single outcry from that vast parade save the one cry of defiance that went up spontaneously as the chief raised his gun to take aim at the Sioux. The scene was impressive, as showing the faith that band of warriors had in each other; the entire confidence of their families in them; the self-reliance all through. It was a lesson for soldiers who might never again see such a grand display of soldierly manhood, and the lesson was not lost. Every dragoon felt an interest in that tribe.

Major Chilton told me to report to Captain Rhett, which I did, and he very cordially thanked me, and through me my comrades, for kindness to his family while en route to Fort Leavenworth. He impressed me very much—was a good officer and a perfect gentleman. He could show kindness to an enlisted man without the risk of invoking undue familiarity.

Colonel Mitchell and his party left for the fort before sunset. As our camp was rearranged, we were between the Snakes and the other tribes, and half of the troop on guard. Every half hour was called thus: "Number one, ——— o'clock! All's well!" Morning dawned on peace and quiet. There had been some anxiety for fear the Sioux would make a general break. Bridger told me some time afterward that if they had they would have found every Snake ready. In about a week after the incidents above related we moved thirty-four miles east of Laramie to where Horse Creek flows into the North Platte. It was a better camping ground for this great mass of Indians because of more room, grass and water. Horse Creek came in from the southwest, and on the north side of the Platte was another creek coming in from the northwest, so that the camps could spread out.

Being in command, the Major placed his own troop and Captain Ketchum's company below the mouth of Horse Creek. This remained headquarters. Two troops of mounted rifles, now Third Cavalry, were a short distance above. One troop remained to garrison Fort Laramie. The Snakes followed us on the march down, and camped near us. One thing was plain: if there was any trouble between troops and Indians, it would not be between troops and Snakes, and the Snakes in numbers and efficiency were largely in excess of all the troops, so that in case of trouble they were our best dependence. Strategically the arrangement was excellent. The mounted rifles averaged about 60 men to each troop, B Troop about 75 and G Company, Sixth Infantry, about 75—270 soldiers. Considering that there were within fifteen miles of our headquarters more than 60,000 Indians, of whom probably 10,000 were fighting men, ours seemed a slim array of troops. In fact, if there was any disposition on the part of the Sioux, Cheyennes and Arapahos to destroy us they could have done so in an hour if given a chance to camp around us. But this was not done. Our camp was formed with great care. The Sioux, Cheyennes and Arapahos were allowed to camp anywhere on the south side of the Platte not occupied by troops above the mouth of Horse Creek and anywhere on the north side of the Platte or on streams coming in from the north. Horse Creek and the south side of the Platte below it was reserved for troops, transportation, parade and treaty grounds, Snake Indians and such other visiting tribes as might come in. Lines of sentinels were placed, inside of which no one might come without permission.

Major Chilton was a man well fitted for a command of this kind. He was bold, unyielding, self-reliant, quick to comprehend an emergency, and so vigilant that he could not be surprised. No people on earth will discover a commander's weakness quicker than Indians; to hesitate or to show fear of results in their presence is fatal. On the other hand a bold front, to keep them at a distance, treating them well as long as they behave themselves, and drawing the line at the slightest encroachment—to locate them and say: "Thus far shalt thou come, and no farther," is the only policy practicable. It will apply in many places in dealing with men other than Indians. Of course Major Chilton had experienced advisors in abundance if he chose to ask advice. Colonel Mitchell, the Commissioner of Indian Affairs, had spent many years with the Sioux of the Upper Missouri. Then there was Bridger and Fitzpatrick with their great experience, and always reliable and any number of long-haired mountaineers—a large percentage of them worthless characters—but many traders, trappers and guides of good, well earned reputations. Captain Ketchum, commanding Company G, Sixth Infantry, had been stationed several years at Laramie, and few men knew the Indians and the country better than he.

This camp, and incidents connected with the treaty was well written up at the time by Mr. B. Gratz Brown, heretofore referred to, and published in the *Missouri Republican*. So far as I know, no other paper had a correspondent on the ground. Today such an event would draw reporters from most all of the leading papers in the country, including the illustrated papers; the whole camp, including daily incidents, war dances, squaw dances, sham battles, etc., portraits of the principal chiefs and the officials would be seen in these great periodicals, and all the reading public would be familiar with it.

We remained a month in this camp, awaiting the arrival of the ox train that brought the presents from the Missouri, they having been first brought from St. Louis by steamboat to Fort Leavenworth. During the time we were waiting the Commissioner was having made a list of all the head men and the number of each band, and ranking them according to their power and influence, judging by the number of followers; then taking an invoice of the goods to be distributed parceling them off to each band, turning them over to the chief or sub-chief for distribution.

This listing of the bands was an immense job, and the distribution must be made with as little partiality as possible. The chiefs having been given rank according to influence and following, they all sat in an immense circle, smoking with great dignity and passing the pipe, meanwhile some orator entertaining them with a bombastic account of some of his or his tribe's adventures. This part of the entertainment was equal to a political convention waiting for the committee on resolutions to report. Amidst the grunts of approval as the oratory went on a chief was called in to headquarters and soon returned decked off in full major-general's uniform from head to foot. There the line was drawn by the Indian; he still wears his moccasins—he could not walk in boots—wearing a saber, medal with the head of the President on one side and clasped hands on the other, he carries a document with an immense seal and ribbon thereon—enclosed in a large envelope, that he may show all comers what the Great Father thinks of him—what rank and power he wields among his fellow-men. This and his medal he values more than all else. They give him the entree to the camp of the emigrant, who must, perforce, have confidence in and feed him since he comes with these proofs of the love the aforesaid Great Father has for him. Then follows another major-general with decorations substantially the same. Having exhausted the list of major generals, then followed the brigadiers, then numerous colonels, lieutenant colonels, majors, captains and lieutenants—as Bill Anderson said—"Till yer can't rest," all with medals of some kind and all with a paper—"Certificate of Character," Corporal Ferguson called it. These papers had been prepared, probably, in the Indian office in Washington, with a blank space left to fill in the name. Then there were great numbers of braves—a multitude who were entitled to and received some distinguishing mark in the way of medal or other decorations or paper.

Several days were given to this "dignity business," as McDonald called it, and then followed the distribution of goods. In this the roll was called as before, and the pile turned over to the head man, who shouted out his instructions and parceled out the goods, and strange to say there seemed to be little wrangling or dissatisfaction. In each case the goods were packed on ponies and taken to the camp where they belonged. The provisions were given out last and in great quantities, and the feasting and good humor was general. The daily scenes and incidents of our stay there were of the greatest interest, often very exciting; sham battles were a feature daily, and they showed their prowess to the white men, and one tribe to another, with all the savage energy of their bombastic natures. No human being can out-brag an Indian, and they spend hours in oratory over the most trifling occurrences, and often tell monstrous lies in their illustrations.

The presents having all been distributed, the feasts being over, the long talks ended, the great orators having ventilated themselves, while the white dignitaries listened and grunted their approval with the dignity becoming the representatives of the Great Father in Washington, the great camp began to disintegrate, band after band began to move out, until all but a straggling few, camp scavengers who hang around to pick up anything left behind, were gone. The Sioux moved in many directions, some for the far north and northwest, others for various points for winter quarters. The Cheyennes seemed to keep well together and moved off up Horse Creek, the Arapahos soon following. The Snakes were amongst the first to move, and though the head chief and a few others had talked a little in their turn to the Indian Commissioner, their story was soon told. Few complaints, as Bridger told me, were made, and they had no bombastic threats nor false promises to make. All they wanted was to be left alone, but would endeavor to care for themselves; they had never injured the white people and had no desire to do so. Every Sunday the Snakes had church service. They had a minister who had been with them twenty years; preached to them in their own language; several times I heard him. Bridger interpreted to me, and I could readily understand why every one of those people listened to him with close attention. He taught them true Christianity, kindness, brotherly love, honesty, and all the precepts calculated to make men better. No orthodox mysteries, no unnatural or miraculous plan of salvation, nothing that they could not understand. "Now," says Bridger, "I don't know nothing about religion as I used to hear it in the States; but me and the Snakes don't have no trouble in believing what he says, and I tell you he just leads the Snakes about right."

Bridger pointed out to me one day a quiet listener, a man thirty-five years old, six feet, about 175 pounds, gentle face and manner, and told me that this was the most modest and unassuming man he had ever met. A few years before, some Sioux had run off a lot of Snake horses and taken one scalp. This man with others started on the trail. In about a week they all returned except he, they having separated. Another week and he was given up for dead, and there was loud lamentation amongst his friends, lasting for days. One night in the midst of the weeping and wailing this man rode into camp driving all the lost Snake horses and six more and with six Sioux scalps dangling from his bridle and belt. The story was quickly told. Having struck a "hot trail," he followed it down into the foot hills on the east side of the mountains, until one evening he saw a band of horses and one lodge. He watched; he knew the Snake horses, and found that there were six Sioux. Evidently these six had left the lodge standing while they made the raid two hundred miles into the Snake country. Here they thought themselves safe. They feasted around a fire in front of the lodge, and howled and danced around the Snake scalp until midnight, when all went into the lodge and slept. Towards morning the Snake crept to the lodge, ripped it open with his scalping knife and in the darkness killed all, scalped them, and alone managed the herd of horses, averaging seventy-five miles a day until he reached home.

"Now," says Bridger, "how many fellows can you pick out of your troop that could do what that Indian did and make no fuss about it?" I did not know, had not seen them tried, and gave it up. I thought it an inspiration to meet one who possessed such reckless nerve. I parted with Bridger with regret, and when he shook my hand he said, looking at me keenly, "Young man, don't you stay in the army no longer than your time's out, but come right up to Bridger. Thar's more money in the mountains than in all the rest of the world—gold till you can't rest, and I know where some of it is. Now be sure to come to me. Good bye." I certainly thought I would, and told him so. His life suited my notion; he was a genuine article with no alloy.

Colonel Mitchell and his party stayed behind and came down with the mounted rifles, while Colonel Cooper came down with B Troop. No incident worth mentioning occurred until coming along the Little Blue one afternoon, Major Chilton wearing hunting clothes and Colonel Cooper in citizen's dress, riding in a little one-horse spring wagon, belonging to the Major, the Major's servant driving. About a mile ahead of the troop four Pawnee Indians stopped them, highwayman style, one seizing the horse's head, the others demanding that the occupants get out and give up everything. The Major seized his shotgun and would have killed two of them but Colonel Cooper stopped him. The Indians did not seem inclined to kill, but to rob. At the critical moment one Indian saw the troop, and they all ran.

When we returned to Fort Leavenworth we occupied our old quarters and stables of previous winter. There was one company of Sixth Infantry and Light Battery G, Fourth Artillery, at the Post.

A few days later a detail of twenty men of B Troop was ordered to go to Uniontown, a Pottawatomie village, a few miles south of the Kansas River and west of where Topeka now stands. We crossed at a rocky ford near Silver Lake and went a few miles south, distant from Fort Leavenworth about seventy miles. Lieutenant Cuvier Grover,[29] of the Fourth Artillery, commanded the

---

[29] Cuvier Grover, born in Maine, was graduated from West Point in 1850 as brevet second lieutenant, and in September was assigned to the Fourth Artillery as second lieutenant. In 1855 he became first lieutenant, Tenth Infantry, and in 1858, captain. He was commissioned brigadier general of Volunteers on April 14, 1862, and during the Civil War was brevetted lieutenant colonel for Williamsburg, colonel for Fair Oaks, brigadier general for Cedar Creek, major general of Volunteers for Winchester and Fishers Hill, and major general for gallant and meritorious service during the war. At the close of the war he was major, Third Infantry, and was promoted to lieutenant colonel, Thirty-eighth Infantry in 1866, assigned to Third Cavalry in 1870, and promoted to colonel, First Cavalry, in 1875. He died June 6, 1885.

detail. At Uniontown we were to guard the paymaster or agent and his money while distributing cash annuities to the Pottawatomies—so much per capita to be paid to heads of families or to individuals of age having no families. We were there ten days in glorious Indian summer. The lists of persons to whom money was to be paid were so complete that the work went on from day to day, with the aid of interpreters, as smoothly as if it were the paymaster paying off troops. I liked these Pottawatomies; all well behaved men, women and children. All had good horses, seemed to be well clothed and fed, lived in comfortable cabins, did considerable farming in a small way, especially in corn and pumpkins. Every cabin had great quantities of yellow strips of pumpkin hung up to dry. We had seen no vegetables during the last six months, and would steal them if given half a chance. I had charge of the quartermaster and commissary department of our little command, and schemed in every way possible to supply our wants. An influential Frenchman whose acquaintance I made on the way over, who had two Pottawatomie wives and a large family of children—the more children the more money—introduced me to Joseph LeFramboy, fourth chief of the Nation, who lived near Silver Lake, was wealthy and had great influence. He had two wives, one a Pottawatomie and one a Frenchwoman. My French friend made known to this chief, who talked good English, the fact that we had been on the plains the whole season on soldiers' rations and wild meat, and the fact that we probably had nothing to pay with. I asked LeFramboy if the hogs we saw cracking nuts in the woods were wild. He answered, "Yes, so you not let him squeal too much." He soon brought an Indian who pointed out a lot of half grown pigs and said, "Eat plenty." In short, our camp was soon supplied with fresh pig, pumpkin, cabbage and potatoes in abundance. It was too late in the season for anything else. All temptation to steal was removed, and we lived high.

If the reader has never been similarly situated, has never lived for six months at a time on bread, rice, beans—no other cereals and no vegetables—a little sugar and coffee, not half what soldiers get nowadays, bacon and such game as could be killed, he has not the slightest conception of the excellence of pumpkin sauce, with salt and pepper, flavored with a little bacon grease, boiled cabbage, mashed potatoes, baked potatoes, potatoes baked in the ashes by the campfire, eaten with salt or a thin slice of bacon broiled on a stick. Of all the army of to-day probably not one ever had our experience and never will have. I sent Lieutenant Grover his dinner every day in our best style. He sent back his thanks and asked no questions, but I told him how nicely we were being treated. Our rest at Uniontown was a great relief from the everlasting march, march, day after day, until horses and men were weary, oh, so weary. In going to Uniontown, our stay there, and return, we had enjoyed two weeks of absolute peace, and were sorry when we had to return.

And now the winter was before us, and we hoped for rest—rest that every man and every horse needed. To sum up the summer's campaign: I had ridden one horse twice to Laramie and back—2,600 miles; eight miles a day for thirty days at Laramie, 240 miles; to and from Sioux camp, 120 miles; to and from the Pottawatomie payment, 140 miles; total, 3,100 miles, besides considerable riding about from our camp to the Snakes, etc., that the others did not do. McDonald, Russell and O'Meara had ridden 360 miles less, making them 2,740 miles. All the balance of the troop had been to Adkinson and back, 800 miles, and to Laramie and back, 1,300 miles—2,100; and sixteen of them had been to the Pottawatomie payment, 140 miles, making for them 2,240 miles. The horses that went first to Laramie were exceedingly leg weary, but looked well and were sound. All the horses, with the exception of a few slightly sore backs, were sound. All they needed was rest, feed and good care, and they got it. The grooming, leg washing and rubbing down with strips of gunnysack that they got was something that any lover of horse flesh might be proud of. The dirt stalls that they stood in were kept level, each man held accountable for the condition of his own stall.

An officer said to me when talking of this campaign, "Well, you did not have any mounted drill for some time after that!" In a week we drilled an hour mounted in the forenoon and on foot in the afternoon, but we drilled carefully; went through the evolutions, saber exercises and pistol practice at a walk; in a few weeks a part of the time at a trot, and in a couple of months all of the gaits, never missing mounted drill every forenoon when weather and ground was suitable on week days, and, except Saturday, afternoons on foot, with inspection mounted on Sunday morning. One hour drill each time. In case of rain or snow we drilled on foot in quarters. Our horses were ridden to the river for water morning and evening before corn was fed to them which, with the hour's drill, gave them good exercise. They always went to and from water at a walk. I saw other mounted troops go yelping down the hill in outrageous disorder, running races up the hill after watering. B Troop was as orderly and well behaved going to and from water as if on parade; talk was free but no noise. I can say the same for Captain Hunt's Light Battery G, Fourth Artillery.[30] We used the watering bridle bit (snaffle), surcingle and blanket, but no saddle, going to and from water.

And now we were settled down in comfortable quarters for those times. A bed sack, refilled with prairie hay (Arnold called it prairie feathers) once a month, and a pair of soldier blankets, with overcoat, or anything else one could utilize for a pillow. If the Government allowance of wood was not sufficient, we took a company team, made a detail, and hauled more from above the post. Indefatigable commissary and quartermaster Sergeant Cook managed our rations and forage so that men and horses fared well. We got vegetables and apples from Missouri. Nothing of

---

30 Franklin Eyre Hunt of New Jersey was graduated from West Point in 1829 as brevet second lieutenant and assigned to the Fourth Artillery as second lieutenant on the same day. He became first lieutenant in 1836 and captain in 1846. In 1855 he became major paymaster and in 1865 he was brevetted lieutenant colonel for faithful and meritorious service during the Civil War. In 1878 he was made deputy paymaster general with the rank of lieutenant colonel. He retired in 1879 and died in 1881.

The First Two Years

the kind was then furnished by the commissary. Cook got some barrels and had them sawed in two for bath tubs, which we could use in the dining room between supper and tattoo. The troop moved about so much that there was little company fund, and from our small pay we "chipped in" for nearly all the extras.

A Thespian Society was formed, and our troop furnished the lion's share of actors, among them Jim Glennon, Warren Kimball, Forrest, etc. Officers and their families had as much fun out of it as did the men, and the performances did a great deal of good. Our troop raised money for a ball, and I was treasurer. We wanted things that must be gotten from Weston, and I made the purchases. Mr. Ben Bishop, who was first sergeant of B Troop before I joined, was now in the cattle business, doing well and living in Weston, gave me much assistance and took me to the "Weston Club" for dinner, where I was introduced to a lot of gentlemen who would be a credit to any town of ten thousand people, whose friendship I retained. Most of them are now dead—Dick Murphy, Joe Murphy, Perry Wallingford, Merrit L. Young, George Belt, Charles A. Perry, etc. Weston was a wonderful business place—fine stores and heavy stocks of goods. It was at that time the best business town between St. Joseph and St. Louis except Lexington.

Our ball came off, and was a great success from the soldier's standpoint, and did a great deal of good. The men were on their good behavior—their pride was appealed to, and even the roughest seemed to rise a little higher and to think better of themselves.

Part III
Campaigns of 1852–53

† † † † † † † † † † †

In the winter of 1852 Major Chilton went on a six months' leave, which left Lieutenant Hastings in command of the troop. Sergeant Hooper went on a two months' furlough, to the end of his time. Every good man in the troop felt his absence a personal loss. It wound up his ten years' honorable service, and he would never return. It was time for him to make a home for himself and family, which, with land warrants and some money that he and his industrious wife had saved, he did in Iowa, and became a prosperous and prominent man. Sergeant John Cuddy was made acting first sergeant until Hooper's time should be out, and three-fourths of the troop hoped he would keep the place. He was born in Ireland, was well educated, bright, clear headed, and a good judge of men, six feet tall, handsome, and a perfect picture of manhood, witty, cheerful and self-reliant. I never saw a better specimen for a first sergeant. He was just what our troop needed. I knew that good order would reign under Cuddy; but there was an element that did not want such a man, and a few of them would do anything to destroy him. After he had been acting first sergeant a couple of weeks, he was visiting a friend across the parade ground, out of quarters in the night without permission. Some miscreants managed to get fire into his orderly room, and the garrison was aroused at midnight by the alarm of fire. When Sergeant Cook and I reached the door and broke it down, the room was in flames. The fire was soon quenched, but Cuddy's enemies had gotten their work in; this was sure to prevent his promotion. He was placed in arrest and Sergeant Drummond took his place. Cuddy was released in a couple of weeks and returned to duty, but Colonel Fauntleroy would not consent to promote him.

In April, 1852, Major Macklin, the paymaster for Kearney and Laramie, called for an escort and Sergeant Cuddy and ten privates were detailed. Cuddy was glad to get away with his little command, and did not object to some of the toughest cases detailed to go with him, to get them away from the troop. The man who was the instigator of the fire in the orderly room deserted, and with his wife located in Weston. More of him hereafter.

There was a custom at Fort Leavenworth to detail a noncommissioned officer each month who was called "provost sergeant," and whose duty it was to work the prisoners in policing the garrison, cleaning up generally, and to do anything that there were no hired employees to do. If there was a death the provost sergeant had the grave dug. My turn came and I served during April. It was an odd coincidence, to say the least, that three men died of delirium tremens during that month, two of Light Battery G, Fourth Artillery and one of the band. I remember the names of these men and can see how they looked as well as if it happened yesterday. These were the only men I ever saw after death from delirium tremens, and the only deaths at the post during the month. I had two prisoners digging a grave in the soldiers' cemetery where now stands the commanding officer's quarters. They had gotten down half deep enough when one of them, an infantryman, leaned on his spade, turned to me with a sorrowful expression, and in a sad tone said: "Arah, Corpler, aren't it lucky I am?" I could not see his good luck, it was not apparent on the surface, and so I said, "How is that, Mike, have you struck a gold mine?" My question brought no smile. Poor Mike shook his head; leaned harder on his spade, and said: "If I hadn't got in the geard house I might 'ev shared the fate of poor Tom, and yez w'u'd 'ev had somebody digging me grave as I am his." I said I hoped that such a misfortune would never befall any of us. Straightening himself to his full height, looking at me earnestly, he said: "No danger of yez, Corpler, but look at poor Mike." I suggested that this was a good time to swear off. He sighed and went on with his work. I pitied him with all my heart. The only enemy he had was whisky, and he needed a guardianship that would keep him from it, or keep it from him.

Several men deserted the first pay day after coming in from the summer's campaign of 1851. In March, four of the best men in the troop deserted, and as they had been my friends from first to last, I felt the loss keenly. They made a big gap in the efficiency of the troop. A batch of recruits from Carlisle joined about this time, and special attention was given to drilling them preparatory to the summer's campaign sure to follow. They had spent the winter at Carlisle and were pretty well drilled. They came up on a steamboat.

On the twentieth of June I was made sergeant; on the twenty-third, first sergeant. After the order making me first sergeant was read and the troops dismissed, as I was passing a group of men on the way to the steps leading up to the squad room I heard one man say: "Well, we may as well desert now." The man was slightly under the influence of liquor and evidently intended that I should hear the remark. I walked over to where they were standing, and said: "See here; I don't care what anyone says of me so that I do not know that the words are intended for me to hear. In this case you said what you did purposely for me to hear. Now, it lies entirely with you whether or not you may as well desert. If you intend to be a decent, respectable soldier, there is no occasion for you to desert. On the other hand, if you want to make things disagreeable generally, and for me in particular, the future for you is not bright. Now take your choice, for I tell you plainly that I will not be harassed, worried and annoyed by men who can see no good in anything but whisky, noise, opposition to good order and discipline, and other things that make the troop and all connected with it miserable. I may not succeed in having everything my own way, but I will come as near to it as I can, and the nearer I come to it the less cause any one will have to talk as you have." The man was about to speak, I do not think disrespectfully, when a man said quietly, "Shut up," and two of them walked him off. Though I spoke in a low tone, probably half the troop heard what I said. The next day this man made an apology and said he would never give me any trouble, and he never did.

I called the roll at "tattoo" without a light, the first time I had seen it done, and without a mistake—called two absentees the second time and reported them absent. I never used a light, nor read from a list at roll call. A general good feeling seemed to develop from day to day, and many men said they were glad it was settled. The most experienced said they would know about what to expect for the next two years, and there was a great deal in that. Lieutenant Hastings had the confidence and respect of all the men whose opinions were worth anything, and that was a tower of strength to me.

The day of departure soon came and we found our way to the Arkansas via Pappan's Ferry across the Kaw and thence through Council Grove.

Arrived in the vicinity of Cow Creek, now in Rice County, Kansas, it became evident that the Kiowas and Comanches were as energetic as usual, annoying trains, surprising small parties, and driving off stock. Several trains were compelled to corral and stand them off until relieved by the Dragoons. Generally the Indians did not stand much upon the order of going when the "long knives" came in sight. Some inexperienced people have charged Indians with possessing less real courage than white men. There never was a greater mistake. The Indians knew that bows and arrows, good at forty yards, could not compete with musketoons and pistols at one hundred or two hundred yards, so they skirmished for the advantage, and took it whenever they could, as became the sensible robbers and bandits that they were.

Arrived on the Arkansas, from the mouth of Walnut Creek west the danger to trains was great. Nothing short of constant, intelligent, determined effort on the part of the commanding officer, Lieutenant Hastings, served to protect the trains from destruction until he compelled their owners or managers to concentrate in large caravans and proceed with the greatest caution in double column.

One morning near Pawnee Rock, now near the corner of Barton, Stafford and Pawnee Counties, a Mexican train of ten mule teams pulled out of camp. The rear team was made up of seven little mules and three burros. The load was heavy and the team lagged. Suddenly a small band of Indians was seen charging toward this train. The train master did the usual thing, hurried into corral as fast as possible, and succeeded very well except as to this last team, which all expected to see captured and the man and his ten-year-old son scalped. Seeing his desperate situation, the father hid the boy in the wagon under some blankets, in hopes that relief might come to his son, though he must die. The Dragoons had camped west of Walnut Creek, near where Great Bend, the county seat of Barton County, now is, and had made an early start in order to halt this train until others should come up. A few skirmishers on the high ground saw the situation, gave the alarm and charged in time to drive off the robbers, though a shower of arrows had already hit the wagon and slightly wounded the man. One pony was killed, and it was believed that some Indians were wounded, though all got away.

This team was owned by the driver and traveled with the big train for company and protection, and the team being weak for the load it had to haul, was compelled to travel behind, so as not to retard the progress of the train, and frequently lagged. Numerous small freighters were in the habit of traveling in this way.

Probably no better officer than Lieutenant Hastings ever commanded a troop. This was his second campaign with this troop. And now he was approaching ground sacred to the memory of brave men, and there was still with the troop a remnant of those who fought desperately at the mouth of Coon Creek, now in Pawnee County, when in 1846 twelve men out of a detachment of twenty under Sergeant "Ben" Bishop were wounded, some of them fatally, in recovering cattle that had been driven off by Indians. Bishop was shot through the body with an arrow, but survived and was discharged first sergeant of the troop in 1849. Sergeant Peel and Bugler Brydon kept alive the fires that burned in memory of their fallen comrades, and the spirit that pervaded the little command boded no good to the reckless robbers that infested the Santa Fé Trail from the Little Arkansas River to Mexico. The Indians knew the troop, the sorrel horses, the blue shirts worn in the field in place of the regulation uniform, the drab hats—the horses and men seen when they by forced marches relieved Fort Adkinson. In fact they had not forgotten the sorrel troop since 1846.

Having concentrated the trains and escorted them via the so-called Cimarron Crossing on the Arkansas, about where Cimarron station on the Santa Fé Railway now is, to about sixty miles southwest of that point, the troop returned and went into camp about where Dodge City now is, and about four miles below Fort Adkinson. Here the whole Kiowa and Comanche tribes seemed to have concentrated in one vast camp on the south side of the river, opposite the Dragoon camp.

Sergeant Cuddy and his party joined from detached service a day or two later. I quote from what he and others told me: When he returned from Laramie to Fort Leavenworth in July, he was, after a few days' rest, ordered to join his troop. In the meantime the "toughs" of his party got drunk and Colonel Fauntleroy ordered four of them to confinement in the guard house until ready to start—actually had four horses led to the guard house for the prisoners to mount and ride away. Their arms were boxed up in the wagon. The men were mad; they had been kept from liquor, could not get any now, and were going across the plains with no rest except what they got in the guard house. A few miles on the road the mutinous disposition was at fever heat. Four good men rode behind and two in front of them, while Cuddy rode ahead. They cursed the men in the rear because they were not allowed to fall out of ranks, and finally got so bold that they addressed themselves to Cuddy. Then he ordered a halt, wheeled his horse so as to face them, loaded two pistols, placed one—army size—in his holster with flap thrown back ready for use, the other—navy size (his private property)—in his belt, and addressing them reviewed all of their misdeeds during the time he had known them, especially the trouble they had given him during the trip and since returning, and wound up by telling them that now they were sober and had not the excuse of drunken men for being insolent, showing that, drunk or sober, they were utterly bad and unfit to live, and then and there assured them that the first man who did or said anything to him or in his hearing in the least disrespectful he would *kill him—he should die like a dog;* he knew they intended to desert and would do so if permitted, but that he would return them to the troop or give their *worthless carcasses to the wolves.* A desperate man, fearless, outraged and thoroughly aroused, is dangerous, and these villains saw that their race was run. He brought them four hundred miles into camp and they were placed in the guard house at Adkinson. He told me that these desperadoes had caused him the loss of many nights' sleep on the trip to and from Laramie and from Fort Leavenworth to the troop. Cuddy and six good men were a valuable addition to the troop at this time. Cuddy knew that these scoundrels should not have been let out of the guard house to go with him, but fearing that Colonel Fauntleroy would place a wrong interpretation on it if he asked him not to send them, his pride kept him silent; he would not do anything that would reflect upon his *nerve*; if nothing else would do he would kill them. He would have been amply justified in doing so. The Colonel meant well, but he had not been in Cuddy's place, and could not see into his fine character, nor could he imagine the character of the villains he had to deal with.

Company D, Sixth U. S. Infantry, was at Adkinson, Brevet Captain S. B. Buckner commanding (late governor of Kentucky and candidate for Vice-President on the Sound Money Democratic ticket with General John M. Palmer).[1]

---

[1] Simon Bolivar Buckner, 1823–1914, was born in Kentucky. He was graduated from West Point in 1844 as a brevet second lieutenant, First Infantry, and it was

Guard duty was extremely arduous, nearly half the men being under arms among the horses or on post day and night. This constant strain told on the disposition of the men more in camp than on active march. They became tired and morose, and with the cause of their trouble constantly before them, somewhat reckless, and would have welcomed almost anything for a change.

There was no active war. Every day some of the head men of the tribes came into camp to talk with the "white chief," always expressing regret that they could not "control their young men." One day while this kind of farce was being enacted a young buck rushed across the river and reported to the chief, who was talking with Lieutenant Hastings, that a few miles away some of the "bad young men" were attacking a train. Hastings' information led him to believe that there were no trains within 150 miles of him. That a Government train and escort was on the way, with which a caravan of freighters had joined at Council Grove, he knew, and he also knew it to be too strong to tempt the Indians to attack. The actions of the Indians and the commotion in their camp made him believe there was something wrong. When "boots and saddles" sounded the interviewers broke for the other side of the river, and their whole camp seemed to be under arms. Their horse herds were rounded up and hundreds of the horses saddled. Hastings concluded that all of their fine talk for some days had been to gain his confidence, and this report was to induce him

not until 1846 that he was promoted to second lieutenant, Sixth Infantry. He was regimental quartermaster in 1847 and was brevetted first lieutenant for the Mexican War battles of Contreras and Churubusco, and captain for Molino del Rey. He became a first lieutenant in 1851 and captain commissary of subsistence in 1852. He resigned in 1855 to practice law. As brigadier general of Kentucky militia he commanded Confederate forces in Kentucky and surrendered Fort Donelson to General Grant in 1862. As prisoner of war he was taken to Fort Warren, but was exchanged in August, 1862, and as major general commanded a division and then a corps under General Bragg. After Chickamauga, Buckner was made lieutenant general and commanded districts in the Trans-Mississippi Department. In 1887 he was elected governor of Kentucky, and in 1896 he was Gold Democrat candidate for Vice-President. His son, Simon Bolivar Buckner, Jr., 1886–1945, rose to the rank of lieutenant general in the United States Army and was killed while commanding the Tenth Army on Okinawa in World War II.

to send a detail to the relief of the train said to be besieged, thereby dividing his command, so that a sudden rush could destroy the Dragoon camp and probably wipe out the detail afterwards. But instead of dividing his command, Hastings made it more secure by tying all horses to the picket line, all mules to the wagons, and doubling the line of sentinels along the river, thereby plainly indicating that he understood their little ruse.

And now all grass for the animals was cut with butcher knives, Fortunately the grass was abundant, and by moving a little up or down the river it could be had within convenient distance. This episode somewhat dampened diplomatic relations between the wily warriors and the "long knife chief," and the effect on the soldiers mowing grass with butcher-knives was anything but pleasant. Such strained relations could not last very long. We soon got a scythe from Adkinson and relieved the butcher-knives.

Guard mounting while on campaign was always in the evening. When the old guard was relieved it was marched to the river below the camp, and the musketoons discharged down stream. One fine evening, a few days after the incident above referred to, Sergeant Cuddy marched the old guard off, and having given the command "fire" some of the men deliberately turned their pieces and fired across the river into the Indian camp, not at the people, but hitting the tops of some lodges. Having dismissed the guard, Cuddy reported to Lieutenant Hastings and explained the occurrence. The men were called to account and claimed an accident—a falsehood, of course, but might as well go at that. Every precaution was taken, and with the river on one side and a big ditch running from it, there was perfect confidence in the ability of that camp to defend itself.

About nine or ten o'clock, as the gentle south breeze blew across the river, the rattling of lodge poles was heard—not loud rattling, as if being carelessly handled, but an occasional click, as if great care was being exercised to avoid making a noise. The Indians were surely taking down their lodges. The sound of "tom-toms," that made barbarous music for the monotonous chant and dance—the war dance, the scalp dance, the squaw dance, and every other dance that had hitherto made their camp hideous till the wee small hours—was not heard on this lovely night. Nothing but the slight rattle of lodge poles; even the dogs were silent. A mounted messenger left camp with a letter to the commanding officer at Adkinson informing him of what seemed to be taking place. Hour after hour passed, and silence reigned supreme—silence that was oppressive. It was like a dead calm when storm laden clouds hang thick and threatening. The hours from midnight to dawn seemed long and tedious. When the sun sent its glimmering rays up the beautiful valley, not a lodge, not a soul or an animal was in sight. Where a few hours before had stood a large city in all of its savage grandeur, with great herds of horses and mules grazing in the vicinity, not a living thing remained save the prowling coyotes—all had silently stolen away. The Dragoons were puzzled.

Mounted vedettes went to their posts upon the bluffs north of camp; from there and from the tops of wagons the Indian camp ground was carefully examined. Peel, Cuddy and I crossed over at some distance apart, for fear of an ambush, while a line of men on the river bank stood ready to support us. For half a mile from the river bank towards the hills and two miles along the river lodge poles and every kind of Indian equipage lay scattered upon the ground. Where each lodge had stood more or less of the family property was left. The poles were all there. In their haste they had taken their best lodges and whatever they could pack that was of greatest necessity to them. In a few hours they had packed hundreds of horses, and mounted on others had scattered in all directions, to meet at some appointed rendezvous, probably hundreds of miles away. Not a lodge pole trail led from the camp.

The men were in high spirits, notwithstanding the probability that after their families were at a safe distance the warriors under the great war chief Satanta (Sawtanta)[2] might make it

[2] Satanta, Set'tainte, or White Bear, of the Kiowas, born about 1830, first came to notice about this time (1853) and Mildred P. Mayhall (*The Kiowas*, Norman,

warm for them. In two days everything desirable for comfort or pleasure had been moved to the Dragoon camp and the rest burned. Not a vestige of the great Kiowa and Comanche camp remained. The soldiers had killikinnick[3] by the bushel and Indian pipes to smoke it in, and buckskin in every style. Buffalo chips were no longer gathered in sacks for fuel, lodge poles having taken their place.

But these Dragoons were not without sentiment and sympathy. Emblems of motherly love and helpless infancy were found in abundance. Papoose cribs, buckskin clothing for infancy, maidenhood and old age, robes, moccasins, and trinkets of all kinds, told of the terrible sacrifice the women and children had made, and there was general regret that the helpless ones had left so much of home and comfort behind.

The Indian movement could only be explained by supposing that they considered firing into their camp a declaration of war. But the Dragoons could not understand why so many warriors should be so easily bluffed. They had heretofore been very independent and saucy. While very diplomatic and deceitful, the chiefs who visited camp acted in a patronizing sort of way, leaving

---

University of Oklahoma Press, 1962, 186), believes Lowe confused Satanta with Satank, an older chief. Satank, Set-anaya, or Sitting Bear, was born in 1810, and is credited with negotiating peace between the Kiowa and Cheyenne in 1840. Both signed the Medicine Lodge Treaty of 1867. Satanta and Lone Wolf, or Guipago, were arrested by General Custer for violations of the treaty, but were released. In 1871, Satanta and Satank attacked a wagon train in Texas, killing seven persons, shortly after General Sherman had passed that way. At Fort Sill, Satanta boasted of the deed to General Sherman, and he and Satank were arrested. As they were being taken away, Satank sang his death song, then attacked a guard with a knife, and was killed. Satanta was tried for murder and condemned to death, but the sentence was commuted to life imprisonment. He was released in 1873 and resumed his raiding. He was captured in 1874 and returned to prison. He killed himself on October 11, 1878, by jumping from a second-story balcony of the prison at Huntsville, Texas. In 1963 his remains were removed from the prison cemetery and re-buried at Fort Sill.

3 Usually *kinnikinnick,* an Algonquian word meaning tobacco mixed with bearberry leaves, inner bark of red willow, or other leaves or barks. Few Plains tribes raised tobacco. The Comanches got most of their tobacco from Mexico.

the impression that they held the soldiers in utter contempt. They had learned enough to convince them that the superiority of the soldier was in his arms, not in his horsemanship (for the Kiowas and Comanches were the finest horsemen in the world), nor in his strength and prowess as a warrior. These athletic, sinewy sons of the plains were from an ancestry that had been warriors since the race was created, so far as known, and from their infancy through every stage of their existence their normal condition was that of warriors and champions of the chase. From instinct and education they were alert, cunning, strategic, recklessly brave, and capable of subsisting where white men would utterly perish. To say that such men given equal arms and supplies, are not the equals, as rank and file soldiers, of any race known to history is bald nonsense.

Two days after the Indian movement the train and escort heretofore referred to, including some artillery, came up en route to New Mexico. Lieutenant Hastings was not expecting them so soon. It seems that Indian runners brought the news of their approach, and their conclusion was that the troops were coming to help clear them out, and firing into their camp confirmed this belief, hence their sudden departure. It was an odd coincidence.

Major Chilton joined from a six months' leave.

Two weeks had passed, no Indians had been seen, and the two great tribes that harassed the travel and were a standing menace to the commerce of the plains were believed to have gone to Texas, and would probably extend their raid into Old Mexico, as was their habit. This had been a bad season for them. They had captured no trains, no fresh scalps dangled at their bridle bits, and they had met with heavy loss in the destruction of their camp. Peace seemed assured for the balance of the freighting season.

Owing to the great amount of travel, the buffalo kept away from the road, and to procure fresh meat (which we needed very much) it was necessary to go a few miles from it. One bright morning Sergeant Peel and a comrade got permission to go on a hunt as far as what Sergeant Ferguson called "Angel Spring," the head of what is now known as South Fork of Pawnee Fork of the Arkansas, six miles north of camp, it being understood that Sergeant Cook would be out there with a six-mule team about noon to haul in whatever the hunters killed.

At seventeen years of age Langford M. Peel enlisted at Carlisle Barracks as a bugler. His father was a soldier, and Peel was practically raised in the army. He was assigned to B Troop, commanded by Captain E. V. Sumner. In the spring of 1846, in a battle at the mouth of Coon Creek, heretofore referred to, Brevet Captain Lovel commanding the troop, Bugler Peel, then not twenty years of age, was credited with having killed three Indians. Three years and a half later, in a battle with Pawnees near Fort Kearney, he killed two, and a month later, one. He was the best specimen of 160 pounds, five feet, nine inches, naturally bright, clear headed, cheerful and helpful always; as keen as an Indian on the trail, well up in every branch of prairie craft, a perfect horseman, possessing unlimited courage and endurance, he was a man to be relied on and trusted in every emergency. A full set of such noncommissioned officers under a good commander would make a troop invincible against any reasonable odds.

Peel and his companion arrived early, drank from the lovely spring, watered their horses, and hobbled and picketed them for safety. Buffalo were plentiful, and seemed perfectly at ease on the grazing ground, indicating that they had not been disturbed, and giving assurance to the hunters that no Indians were in the vicinity. Waiting patiently for the buffalo to go to water, in a couple of hours they had two fine ones within a short distance of the spring, cut up ready for transportation. Then they built a fire of buffalo chips, broiled meat, and feasted as only an Indian or a plainsman can; smoked and recounted their adventures. Noon, and Cook and the wagon not in sight. The creek from Angel Spring runs a little east of north; on the east, bluffy; in some places, vertical, rocky bluffs from ten to thirty feet above the level of the creek; to the west, some bottom, gradually sloping to high ground. Along the creek, which hugged the bluffs pretty closely, were scattered trees, choke cherry and wild plum bushes, with numerous wild grape vines, forming patches of dense thicket in some places. Little more than a mile north of the spring a herd of buffalo lay in the open bottom. The land lay so that it was easy to approach them, and the wind favorable, the temptation was great.

The campaign had been one of monotonous care and drudgery, and no mounted hunting had been allowed on account of the necessity of keeping the horses in the best possible condition, and this was the first good opportunity to have some real sport. They agreed to make a ten minutes' run to see which could kill the most in that time, the pending bet being a good dinner when they reached "America." Such was civilization called among plainsmen. They approached the herd at a walk, and were within easy pistol shot before the buffalo saw them. Then each went his way, Peel to the west, his companion to the east. The latter dropped his first buffalo in the bottom, the second ran east to the top of the bluff where he fell. The man was down cutting out the tongue, always the sportsman's trophy, when the voice of Peel rang out, as he came up the hill, "Get on your horse!" No time was lost, and looking east he pointed to fifty or more Indians in a half circle half a mile away, their left wing so far advanced that retreat towards camp was cut off. Consultation was brief. Peel led the way down the hill, circling around a thicket, carefully selecting the firm buffalo grass sod so as to leave no trail, and drew into cover not twenty yards from where some of the Indians were sure to come down. Here they sat on their horses, pistol in hand. They had no future plans; they might have to fight to death under that bluff; they would do whatever circumstances seemed to dictate.

They had not long to wait. The Indians came rattling down the rocky trails leading into the bottom, sending out their blood-curdling war-whoop at every jump. They seemed to think the fleeing men would try to escape towards camp, and be enveloped in the circle; did not think they would stop to hide, or that they would do anything but run for their lives, which would be sure death. Their greatest success had been against demoralized men who had given up hope and lost their heads, which soon made their scalps an easy prey. One brawny brave drew rein at the foot of the trail where the men had come down, raised himself in his stirrups and looked sharply towards them. Peel's companion, believing they were discovered, and that a signal would bring the whole pack of howling demons, raised his pistol to shoot; but Peel quietly reached over, and placing his hand on his comrade's arm gently pressed it down. In less time than it takes to tell it the Indian was off to the west, showing by his actions that he had not seen them. Hearing no more noise from the east, the way seemed clear in that direction. Peel led the way out, and they quietly walked their horses up where they had gone down a few minutes before, turned south, and gently trotted towards camp, saving their horses' wind for the critical moment which they knew must soon come.

By this time the Indians seemed confused. The hunters could see most of them riding helter skelter and peering from the highest points to the west of the creek, never dreaming that they had passed the game. More than half a mile had been covered, not away from the enemy, but directly south, slipping by, when suddenly they were discovered, and every Indian charged toward them furiously. But the hunters' horses were comparatively fresh; they were on the high ground, and as far south towards camp as the most southern Indian, with four or five miles of nearly level stretch ahead of them, while the Indians had to oblique to the east and rise considerably to gain their level, and they felt that while the race would be interesting, barring an accident they were pretty safe. The greatest danger was that a horse might step in a prairie dog or badger hole and fall, hence they rode with great care.

When fairly under way and all on a level the soldiers were a quarter of a mile ahead. Soon the wagon was seen, Cook's horse tied behind, while he rode with Matthews on the "lazy board," as they smoked and chatted. Then, to attract Cook's attention, and not lose a shot, the two hunters turned in their saddles and fired at the Indians. Quickly Cook was seen to mount his horse, Matthews turned his team, and Cook "interested" the mules with a "blacksnake" whip. About two miles further, and the hunters were close to the wagon. A vedette on the high point north of camp saw something wrong in the distance and discharged his musketoon; then the other vedette on another high point discharged his. In the meantime the Indians had not been gaining on the men until within the last mile, and then only because the team impeded their progress a little. Not half of them had kept to the front; some were a mile behind. Arrived near the vedettes, Matthews was allowed to go down the hill alone to camp not half a mile away. Cook joined the hunters and shooting began in earnest, including the two vedettes, who had been using their musketoons at long range for all they were worth. Seeing the hopelessness of capturing their game, and knowing that a strong force from the troop would soon be up the hill, having lost two ponies and had some of their number wounded the Indians retreated. At the risk of their lives they always carry off the dead and wounded if possible. When Lieutenant Hastings with half of the troop came up the steep hill the Indians were well on the retreat, and he followed them only a short distance beyond the crippled ponies. Horse flesh was too precious to be wasted in a pursuit that could accomplish nothing.

No fresh meat cheered the camp that night, but it was a jolly camp. All answered to their names at retreat roll call. There was something new to talk about, as the men sat around lodge pole fires and related the traditions of the grand old troop.

The next day Major Chilton with a part of the troop, including those in the excitement of the previous day, went to the spring, killed more buffalo and returned with a wagon load. No Indians were seen, and the wolves were feasting on the buffalo killed the day before. Of course, Major Chilton examined the ground that Peel and his companion had gone over, including the hiding place and the race course.

Now, when Peel discovered the Indians he was half a mile west of his comrade and nearly one and a half from the Indians. He could have easily escaped by going south towards camp. He had scarcely one chance in ten to save his friend, but he took that chance, such as it was, in the face of almost sure death. He saw the thicket and the steep shelving bluff as he went up the hill. To hide there seemed the extreme of recklessness, but he builded better than he knew. Until that moment he had no idea how to act unless they got on a high point and with their pistols stood off the Indians until help should come. The latter was all he hoped for, and he knew that if Cook saw the situation, that hero in every emergency would join the two or die. One iota of weakness would have induced Peel to abandon his friend and save himself, and how easily Cook could have left the teamster and rode to camp for the troop, as many a coward has done, and been counted a hero for the noise he made. But no such weakness troubled his manly soul. Like Peel, he was a born hero. The vedettes on the bluffs could have pulled their picket pins, mounted their horses and ridden into camp after discharging their guns—such were their general instructions; but they saw their comrades in trouble, and Charles McDonald and Edward O'Meara confirmed the faith that they had in them.

And what became of the Indians who pursued the hunters? A freight train returning from New Mexico saw a band of Indians—supposed to be the same—some distance south of the Cimarron Crossing a day or two later, and corralled to stand them off, but the Indians seemed in a hurry and did not trouble the train. These were the last Indians seen on the trail that season.

To put in a little more time and make sure that there was no further danger to trains, Major Chilton went up the river about ten days, traveling about five miles per day—going through the skirmish drill all the way—the principal object being to get fresh grass and exercise for the horses and practice for the men. We returned leisurely along the trail, met F. X. Aubry, the champion rider of the plains,[4] Colonel William Bent, of Bent's Fort,[5] and Maxwell, of Riado, New Mexico.[6] All were of the opinion that the Indians would not return to the trail that season. From Pawnee Fork we made time for home—Fort Leavenworth.

At Council Grove we got corn—the first in two months—and fed a quart to each horse and mule night and morning from there in. Our horses were thin in flesh but otherwise in good condition. We had but the two company wagons for transportation of rations, tents and other camp equipage. Of course, we drew rations at Adkinson when necessary.

All the way in the grass was dead. Plenty of buffalo from Pawnee Fork to the east line of what is now McPherson County, and turkey on every stream. They had never been hunted, hence not easily scared, and were big and fat.

On arriving at the fort the Major found an order waiting for him to escort and act with Major Ogden, quartermaster, to locate a new military post near the junction of the Republican and Smoky Hill branches of the Kaw River. In three days fifty men had clothing replenished, rations and forage drawn, some horses

[4] Francis Xavier Aubrey, Santa Fe trader, freighter, and explorer, rode from Santa Fe to Independence in 5 days, 16 hours, in September, 1848, a record transit of the Santa Fe Trail. In 1851–52 he pioneered a cut-off called the Aubrey Trail, which left the Santa Fe Trail at Cold Spring (Cimarron County, Oklahoma) and took a northeast course to Bear River, and then to the Arkansas east of present Syracuse, Kansas. Aubrey was killed in 1853 in a dispute with Richard Hanson Weightman, captain of Missouri artillery and paymaster in the Mexican War, who became New Mexico's delegate to Congress, and was killed at the Battle of Wilson's Creek as a Confederate colonel.

[5] William Wells Bent, 1809–69, with his brother Charles (1799–1846) and Ceran St. Vrain (1802–70) built Bent's Fort on the Arkansas River near the mouth of the Purgatoire in 1833. It was one of the largest fur trading posts in the West.

[6] This was Lucian Bonaparte Maxwell, 1818–75, whose home at this time was on the Rayado River (Lowe's "Riado" is probably phonetic). Lucian Maxwell trapped with Kit Carson and was hunter on Frémont's 1842 expedition. In 1858, Lucian Maxwell bought a tract of land from his father-in-law, Charles Beaubien, which he enlarged until he became the largest individual land owner in the history of the United States—the Maxwell Land Grant totaled 1,700,000 acres.

shod, and were on the road. Sufficient transportation was taken to haul corn for the animals. The most unserviceable men and horses were left behind, Lieutenant Hastings in charge of them. The Santa Fé Trail was followed to the crossing of Soldier Creek, four miles north of Pappan's Ferry, thence to Silver Lake—up the Kaw through St. Mary's Mission, where Father Deurinck had a flourishing school for Pottawatomie children,[7] thence fifty-two miles to the junction of the rivers above mentioned. A week was spent in that vicinity, resulting in the location of the new post, afterwards named Fort Riley,[8] about 130 miles from Fort Leavenworth. A band of Delaware Indians returning from a buffalo hunt said there were plenty of buffalo twenty-five miles west of the new post. We were never without turkey after reaching the Big Blue River until our return. It was a little late in the season, nights cold, but no rain or snow, and with big fires and plenty to eat, the trip was rather pleasant.

Having arrived in Salt Creek Valley, three miles from Fort Leavenworth, Major Chilton made a speech to the troop, in which he gave them excellent advice concerning their conduct in garrison. (Major Ogden was a strictly temperate, religious man, and I always thought that he inspired this speech.) They had

[7] St. Mary's Mission among the Pottawatomies was established on Sugar Creek in 1841 by Father Christian Hoeken and was moved to the site that became the city of Saint Marys, Pottawatomie County, in 1848. The Rev. Baptist Duerinck (not Deurinck) arrived there in 1849. The mission became St. Mary's College in 1869.

[8] Fort Riley, located in 1852 as described by Lowe, became one of the most famous of army posts. Construction began in 1853 and the post was established in 1854. It was named for Brevet Major General Bennett Riley, colonel of the First Infantry, who died that year. The Seventh Cavalry was organized there in 1866. In 1869 a school for light artillery was established there and was succeeded in 1887 by the School of Application for Cavalry and Light Artillery, which eventually became the Cavalry School. During World War I, Fort Riley was a training school for reserve officers, and at Camp Funston, on the reservation, the Eighty-ninth and Tenth Divisions were organized. Fort Riley continued as the principal cavalry post until World War II, when the Second Cavalry Division was inactivated in 1942. In 1946 the cavalry school became a ground general school. The Tenth Infantry Division was reactivated there in 1948.

made a good campaign, a campaign that should be a credit to any troop. Unfortunately there were men who would become intoxicated, get in trouble and cause trouble for every one having anything to do with them. He advised them that whisky was their worst enemy, and if they drank at all not to get drunk, and assured them that leniency for those who did need not be expected, for he would not have his troop destroyed in that way. I think that speech did much good; moderate drinkers watched the fellows who had little control of themselves, and curtailed the excesses.

Heretofore during winter about 10 per cent of the troop were undergoing punishment in the guard house, much of the time by sentence of garrison court-martial—forfeiture of pay and time in the guard house—nearly all of the offenses growing out of drinking whisky. I talked with the noncommissioned officers about it, and cautioned each one in charge of a squad to give personal attention to their men and stop any man who seemed to be verging on the danger point in drinking, and if he could not control him bring him to me. Sometimes a man was brought to me and I shut him in a store room to sober off and then put him on extra duty for punishment. During the winter we had several company courts-martial, three noncommissioned officers sitting in judgment, and the proceedings reviewed and acted upon by the first sergeant.[9] Of course, the written proceedings were not very voluminous. The result was, no man was tried by general or garrison court-martial; summary courts were unknown. Another result, some men were doing extra guard and fatigue duty instead of loafing in the guard house and letting better men do their duty.

[9] The "company courts-martial" described by Lowe were of course entirely extralegal. Army Regulations of this period were silent on company punishment, but the custom is an old one. Company punishment is not inflicted without the consent of the man accused, but appeals are few, as punishment by a court-martial is apt to be more severe. At this period the only courts-martial authorized were general, garrison, and regimental. As Lowe notes, the summary court, a one-officer court for trial of minor offenses, had not yet been established.

When a man could not be managed without violence he went to the guard house, but much of the time B Troop was not represented there.

If punishment was not immediately meted out to an offender, his record was fairly kept and he was sure to be called on for the next fatigue party (details for fatigue to do some kind of dirty work), and during the whole winter scarcely a decently clean soldier was called upon—always the troublesome fellows got the job. Twice the findings of a court and the approval of the first sergeant were appealed from and the parties sent with a noncommissioned officer to the Major, who heard their complaint, and sent back word to me that if I had any more trouble with them to put them in the guard house. No officer ever saw the proceedings of the company courts; they did not want to. I gave all the dissatisfied ones to understand that if they had any grievance I would send them to the Major to make their own statement.

Of course we did not always have peace and happiness, nor freedom from drunkenness, but we came nearer having *home rule—self government*—government within the troop and by the members of it than any of the oldest members had before seen. It was a little binding on 10 per cent of them who were taught many good lessons in respectful demeanor and language towards noncommissioned officers; they could not hide insolence and abuse under the cloak of drunk, and hence not accountable. There was much whisky drunk and no effort made to conceal it. "Budgen-ken," a sort of company club, in a place fixed up between the two stables, was always supplied, each drinker "chipping in" to buy whisky, and the men were given to understand that any abuse of the privilege would insure its destruction. No whisky was allowed in the quarters, a rule which was closely lived up to.

Soon after returning to quarters, the Major came to the orderly room and broached the subject of a company library. He had learned the cost of "Harper's Classical and Family Libraries"; a pair of book cases, with hinges closing the edges on one side, and two locks the edges on the other side, held the library of uniform size and binding. When open the title of each book could be read, and when closed no book could move or get out of place; the books were all the same length and breadth, and an excellent collection. The Major led off with a subscription of $25.00. I followed with the same, Peel the same, then followed a calculation of what percentage would be due from each man in proportion to his pay to make up enough to pay for the whole. I took the list with each man's name. The Major spoke to the troop on the subject at the retreat roll call, explaining to them the advantages of so much good reading matter, and before dismissing the troop I requested each man who wanted to subscribe to come to the orderly room and sign the list pledging himself to pay the amount opposite his name on pay day. Most of the men off duty and *at liberty* signed immediately and the others soon after, and the library was assured with scarcely an effort. The Major collected the money at the pay table, and the books in their cases came on the first steamboat in February. Of course the library was sure to give me some trouble, but it was so popular and had such a good effect that with Bugler Brydon's help I got used to it and ceased to look upon it as a burden. Compared to present usage there was little writing to be done in transacting troop business, and I never had a regular clerk. Lieutenant Hastings always assisted with the muster rolls and anything else that I asked him to; he liked to do it; and by calling in a man for two or three days in a month I was never much crowded with writing.

Our troop ball came off—a decided improvement over that of the previous winter.

A few recruits from Carlisle came up on a steamboat soon after we came in. The lance sergeant in charge, a cultivated gentleman, said little about himself except that he had experienced ups and downs in business; had lived some time in Cuba, and knew considerable of the business world. He seemed to have no bad habits, and was soon made a corporal. He made the next summer's campaign and spent the following winter with us, and was discharged in the spring of 1854 by order of the Secretary of War. He was the son of United States Senator Clark, of Rhode Island. He was commissioned first lieutenant First—now Fourth—Cavalry when it was authorized in 1855, served a couple of years and resigned to take a position in a business house in Leavenworth. Drifting along with varying fortune, he became hospital steward of the Military Prison when it was established, and died there several years ago. I have mentioned this case to show the ups and downs in some good men's lives.*

Another man in this same squad of recruits was a tall, fine looking, rather polished man, with a fine set of dental instruments, and proved to be a fine workman; a genial, cheerful fellow, he made friends easily (Worrell by name), became a corporal, then a sergeant. But I skip his history until I left the troop, of which he hoped to be first sergeant at the expiration of my time, but through my influence failed, and was the only man that I did not shake by the hand and say "good bye" to when I left the troop.

* Hartford T. Clark was born in 1827, and is a descendant of Revolutionary stock of prominence. His maternal great grandfather was none other than Stephen Hopkins, one of the two delegates from Rhode Island who signed the Declaration of Independence. After learning the trade of a pharmacist he enlisted in the army in New York, and was sent to Carlisle Barracks, Pennsylvania, from which he in due time reached the First Dragoons. Upon his discharge from the service he was appointed a first lieutenant in the First Cavalry, the date in the records being given as March 3, 1855, an appointment which expired by limitation May 1, 1856. He again enlisted in the army, and his knowledge as pharmacist being valuable, was appointed a hospital steward in January, 1860. He served as such much of the time at Jefferson Barracks, having been transferred there from Fort Leavenworth, and was discharged July 30, 1863. He is again found in the army in 1875, for early in that year he was appointed hospital steward again and assigned to duty at the U. S. Military Prison at Fort Leavenworth, where he served until the date of his death, June 7, 1881. Prior to his death he made a request of the military authorities that upon the death of his wife her burial at his side be permitted. A lot was so left vacant, and upon her demise, in 1897, her body was deposited in the spot she had hoped some day to be placed to be near her husband. She was the granddaughter of Count DeSanno, who came to the United States with Lafayette and later located in Pennsylvania. Mr. John Clark, the eldest of two sons and the second of five children of Hartford T., is at present employed as assistant engineer in the Quartermaster's Department at Fort Leavenworth.—EDITOR. [From Lowe's original book.]

Campaigns of 1852–53

To be brief, he got discharged, and when the First, now the Fourth Cavalry, was raised, enlisted and was made first sergeant of one of the troops, served about a year and then with some company funds and the farrier of his troop deserted, taking with them horses and equipments and pistols. Down towards Jefferson City, Missouri, they stopped at a plantation for the night and there met a Mr. Gordon, chief engineer of the Missouri Pacific Railroad, then being built between St. Louis and Jefferson City. In the morning all three left the plantation on horseback traveling the same road. A few miles on the road Worrell shot Gordon from behind, robbed him of considerable money and hid his body in some brush. But the history of this case, the capture of the murderer and his execution after several trials, in which his good father and mother spent much money, is recorded in the proceedings of the courts, and I refer to it here to prove the correctness of my judgment in regard to this man's character.

Spring came, and early in April we were on the way to the Arkansas. The desertions during the winter were not numerous, and they not damaging. A few horses had been turned over to the Quartermaster and new ones received, so that we were again well mounted.

Fort Adkinson was to be abandoned, and in its stead a camp established on Walnut Creek near its confluence with the Arkansas. We took along teams and citizen teamsters to transport the Government property from the Arkansas to the new camp, and utilized them to haul forage for our horses, so that we were able to feed two quarts of corn to each horse every day for some time, and finally came down to one quart. We were supplied so that we had some corn all summer.

This was one of the most trying seasons in my experience.

Having spent the night at Cow Creek, the next camp would be "Big Bend" of the Arkansas, eighteen miles. About midway between these points, now in Rice County, was a line of high sandy hills, called "Sand Buttes," sometimes "Plum Buttes." With his usual prudence and fore-thought in passing through broken country and in crossing streams, a habit which had enabled him to travel with one troop through all the tribes from the North Platte to Mexico, and from the Missouri to the mountains without being surprised, the Major threw out skirmishers, a corporal and four men, riding twenty-five or thirty yards apart. Having reached the highest "Butte" the corporal discharged his pistol, the four men rallied on him, the troop moved forward quickly, part thrown out in line of skirmishers. Ten yards from the corporal was a dead Mexican, and within a hundred yards two more. One was still breathing, and blood was trickling from their scalped heads. Away down towards the Arkansas was a large Mexican train. The dead men belonged to it, and were hunting antelope in the hills when killed. Ponies and arms were gone. They were evidently completely surprised. After following the Indian trail a short distance it was completely obliterated by countless thousands of buffalo tracks. The Mexican train was corralled on the plain below and the Dragoons moved to it, but they had corralled to let the herds of buffalo pass by, and had not seen any Indians.

From Cow Creek to Coon Creek travel was nearly blocked by buffalo. Standing on any high point as far as the eye could reach, a vast moving mass could be seen, making the earth tremble with their trampling and bellowing.

We arrived at camp near Adkinson; D Company Sixth Infantry moved to the new camp on Walnut Creek; Major Chilton and Lieutenant Hastings located in the commanding officer's quarters, which was a pretty comfortable sod building, and the men of the troop occupied the soldiers' quarters.

Sergeant Cook, acting wagonmaster, made regular trips to and from the new camp, moving everything that could be utilized in completing it. On one of his trips, one morning after leaving camp on Pawnee Fork, Cook was asleep in the front wagon; he never got a good night's sleep on these trips. His little escort of two infantrymen to each wagon was also asleep. The teams were moving along up the incline from the Pawnee Fork bottom to the "dry route," by the head of Coon Creek, when suddenly a band of Indians came up, stopped the train and demanded a feast, etc. Cook hurried out and mounted his horse. He was pointed out as the chief, and to their demand for "tobac" he said "No," when the leader hit him a vicious blow with his "quirt" or riding whip and raised his bow and arrow. Cook shot the Indian, who fell from his horse, and shot two more who clung to their horses as they ran off. The escort was out of the wagons by this time, but Cook had done the work and the band was gone, about a dozen. Realizing that probably this was only a small party from a larger force near by, Cook straightened out his teams, left the dead Indian and made the best time he could. This happened about 9 A. M. The next morning before sunrise a vedette called attention to a train down the road some miles traveling unusually fast. I reported to Major Chilton, who told me to mount ten men and go down to meet the train, which I did, and met Cook two miles below camp. He had traveled over fifty miles in twenty hours, watering and feeding a little twice. He knew the Indians to be Osages, supposed to be entirely friendly, but stealing and robbing whenever they could bluff a small party. A detachment of dragoons accompanied the train the next day, which wound up the moving.

News had come that a "pow-wow" was to be held at or near Adkinson during the summer, and large amounts of presents would be distributed; that in addition to the Kiowas and Comanches, the Prairie Apaches would be there, and that Major Fitzpatrick on the part of the Indian Department would superintend the distribution. Of course it meant the three tribes in full force.

Until the final movement of Indians after the distribution of presents one-half of the troop was on guard at night and one-fourth during the day. Sentinels called the number of post, the hour and "All's well!" every half hour during the night. In daytime the horses were herded a short distance below the post. The Indians were not allowed north of the river unless visiting by permission.

This condition of things lasted two months. Major Chilton had a great many talks with leading men of the Kiowa and Comanche tribes. Satanta, the war chief of the Kiowas, always came rather neatly dressed in fine buckskin, and wore a handsome cavalry saber and belt. He was a man about five feet ten, sparely made, muscular, cat-like in his movements—more Spanish than Indian in his appearance—sharp features, thin lips, keen restless eyes, thin mustache and scattering chin whiskers that seemed to have stopped growing when one to three inches long. At the time of which I write he was about thirty-five years old. He invariably came with one servant, a Mexican Indian, to the line of sentinels, dismounted, leaving his handsome horse and Spanish equipments with the servant. Always before allowing an Indian to come inside the line of sentinels the sergeant of the guard was called, who escorted the visitor to the commanding officer, permission having been given for the visitor to come in.

Usually the conversations between the Major and Satanta were apparently pleasant, though sometimes the latter became somewhat emphatic. He complained of the treatment the Indians received from the whites, the manner in which they overran the country, destroyed the game and ignored the Indians' rights, and his eyes flashed as he jammed the end of his saber scabbard into the ground. Sometimes the Major recounted the efforts made by the Government to look after the welfare of the Indians, and the treacherous manner in which such efforts were taken advantage of. Satanta, excited, and his black eyes flashing, was scarcely a match for the Major, whose big black eyes fairly blazed when he chose to be emphatic. The Major always tried to be pacific and just, admitting many wrongs complained of, but never permitting a threat, even by innuendo, to pass without an emphatic rebuke. He felt that Satanta was a superior, intelligent man, and treated him as such. There was a good deal in common with these two men. Both had tempers easily excited, unbounded energy, boldness and courage. Educated and civilized, Satanta would have been a match for the Major anywhere. In cunning, Indian duplicity and shrewdness he was a full match; but the Major was not a man to be trapped, flattered, coaxed, driven or bluffed, and if the combined Kiowa and Comanche tribes had him surrounded he would roll his black eyes with their broad white borders, defy them and threaten to "wipe them off the face of the earth," and no man living could come nearer making them believe it. Every man of his troop capable of imbibing a stern determined spirit of defense knew that his threats, though sometimes extravagant in the face of overwhelming thousands, would be defended to the bitter end. His watchfulness, care, prudence and clear conception of Indian character were his best safeguards. He could never be caught napping; there was no earthly danger of surprise, and no seventy-five men under such discipline, with such a commander, armed as we were, had been overwhelmed by men carrying bows and arrows and lances only; hence staunch, steady confidence, from which there was no swerving, reigned supreme in our camp, and men endured the hardships without complaining. About the most comfortable place during the heat of the day was under a tent fly stretched near my orderly room, and there I had a good opportunity of seeing and hearing what passed between the Major and others.

One day when the conversation had been quite animated, the Major looked steadily at Satanta and made an emphatic assertion of what he would do if certain trains then on the road were interfered with. Satanta always spoke Mexican Spanish in talking with the Major, who could understand fairly well what he said, but when in doubt had the interpreter tell him. The interpreter talked wholly by signs, never speaking a word to Indians. He was a wonder in that way, and understood the sign language of every tribe on the plains. The Major talked entirely through the interpreter. Although a mountaineer and desperado, the Major's threat was so bold that he was afraid to interpret it correctly, hesitated and made few motions, all of which the Major noticed, and Satanta's mild, unconcerned attitude convinced him that he had not been fully interpreted, and he called for a file of the guard, which came quickly, and Pyle (the interpreter) found himself tied to the wheel of a cannon which stood near by, and there he remained until dark, when he was confined in the guard house, to remain, as the Major said, "until he could tell the truth." "A life sentence," said O'Meara. Satanta was made to understand the threat, and why the man was tied to the wheel. He soon took his departure, and did not come again until Major Fitzpatrick came to make the "big talk," as the Indians called it. Strange as it may appear at this time, there was no representative of the Indian Department except Major Fitzpatrick, none of the army except the officers of B Troop, and no correspondent to write up the grand "pow-wow"—thirty thousand Indians, Apaches, Kiowas and Comanches. To-day the principal newspapers of the country, including the illustrated papers, would have special correspondents on the ground. At that time any one except the necessary officials, attachés and military officers would have been an incumbrance.

In a smaller way this was as important a distribution of presents to the Indians as was that in 1851 at the mouth of Horse Creek. If it had any newspaper record I never heard of it. The big ox train came in, the wily Apaches (called Prairie Apaches to distinguish them from those ranging in southern New Mexico and Arizona), the Kiowas and Comanches having assembled in full force, the goods were unloaded, boxes and bales opened, the nabobs of the tribes decorated in brilliant uniforms, medals and certificates issued, goods parceled out, winding up with plenty to eat, feasting, sham battles, etc. The Apaches were off their home ground and anxious to return. Major Fitzpatrick seemed equally anxious to have the job over with and kept his little working force and a couple of clerks pushing things. The long drawn out dignity of the Horse Creek treaty was lacking.

Major Fitzpatrick had the confidence of these as he did of all other Indians on the plains. They claimed that in the twenty years they had known him as agent or trader he had never lied to or tried to deceive them in any way, and that his advice had always been good—a certificate of character that few could get.

The presents having been distributed, the Indians went south, probably not to return during the season; all the available material at Adkinson had been moved and the sods level to the ground. We had not seen a buffalo in more than two months or any fresh meat of any kind except some prairie dogs which Peel and I killed with the only rifle in the troop; no one hunted with it except us. The musketoons did not shoot accurately enough, and no one was permitted to waste ammunition. From time to time we killed enough of the little barkers to make a stew, and found them quite as good as the common gray squirrel. Parboiled and then stewed with a little fat bacon made them taste pretty well to men who had been so long without fresh meat. Owing to the proximity of the Indians there was no other game to be had.

From our surroundings during the last month we were in a critical position. It would take but a spark to inflame the powerful tribes confronting us, and several happenings seemed to have brought the climax. A lot of trains were corralled a little below and not permitted to pass on until the distribution of presents and the Indians had moved off. To detail the incidents would be tedious and unnecessary to this narrative. For a month Lieutenant Hastings and I divided the night between us, half and half, each acting as officer of the guard and often walking from sentinel to sentinel all the way around the line, half the company on guard and half the guard on post at one time. I relieved Lieutenant Hastings at midnight and tried to make up sleep by an afternoon nap. The quarters were full of fleas, the old sod walls full of mice and snakes, and were soon abandoned for the more comfortable tents. Compared to fleas, bedbugs are pets. Spread out a soldier's blanket and see thousands of fleas hopping from an inch to a foot high, enjoying the warm rays of the sun and exercise, after a successful night with a soldier. The two dozen cats that Lieutenant Heath brought from Fort Leavenworth two years before were perfect wrecks; they could not digest mice enough to counteract the ravages of fleas, and moped about utterly discouraged.

The Indians had been gone a week, the Mexican trains straightened out up the river, the troop escorting them to the Cimarron Crossing and two days south of it, returned to the crossing and went up the Arkansas to "Big Timbers" (Bent's new fort), and returned to Adkinson, now only heaps of broken sod leveled to the ground, so that from it the Indians could not ambush mail carriers, express riders or other small parties.

It was the first of October when we left the vicinity of the dismantled fort to return to Fort Leavenworth. One day we camped at the mouth of Coon Creek, on the Arkansas, about noon. This was B Troop's battle ground, where in the spring of 1846 Sergeant Bishop with twenty men recovered a herd of 400 oxen that had been stampeded by Indians heretofore referred to. Peel explained to the Major all the interesting features of the fight.

On the opposite side of the river was a line of high bluffs, craggy and abrupt, with some buffalo trails leading out on to a narrow strip of bottom land between the river and the bluffs. Buffalo on the south side were numerous, and little bands came out of the bluffs across the bottom to the river to drink. I took Company Teamster Matthews with his saddle mule with me and crossed over. When a buffalo had been killed we were to pack Matthews' mule and bring to camp all the meat he could carry. After winding around through the trails in the bluffs for some time I killed a fat cow between the bluffs and the river. We picketed our animals and proceeded to prepare the meat for transportation to camp. We were busy cutting up the buffalo when we heard a splashing in the water; looking up we saw Lieutenant Hastings with half the troop coming at a trot. This trotting crossing the river meant urgency, and we mounted at once. It was all clear to me that nothing less than Indians skulking after Matthews and myself induced the rapid movement towards us. We joined Lieutenant Hastings, who said that some Indians had been seen watching us, and the last seen of them they were creeping towards us through the bluffs. Lieutenant Hastings wanted to get around them or behind them so they could not escape. I showed him a trail that I thought might lead to their rear. He left half the men to watch the trail that the Indians were believed to be on while we moved quickly on the trail that I believed would cut off their retreat. Sure enough we drove them out, found them to be Osages, four in number, and did some loud talking to keep Cuddy, Cook and others from shooting them as they came out. They professed all sorts of friendship, but did not succeed in convincing any one but that Matthews and I owed the safety of our scalps to the fact that they were seen by a vedette near camp, and the prompt action of the troop. We finished the buffalo, loaded the mule with all he could carry and brought the Indians to camp. Major Chilton turned them loose with a threat to "wipe the Osages off the face of the earth" if they did not keep off the traveled road and leave white people entirely alone.

Nothing of special interest occurred until we reached Diamond Springs, now in Morris County. The weather had been frosty at night and days sunny—a continuous Indian summer all the way—grass dry as powder. We had barely a quart of corn per day for each horse, and they were poor. All day we had seen little bands of Indians a mile or two off the road traveling the same direction that we were and apparently watching us. This was the Kaw country and probably no other Indians were there, and we could hardly understand why they kept aloof and watched our progress. Of course the Kaws knew our troop by the horses, and we knew they had no love for it, but were slow to believe they would attempt to do us any harm. We camped on high ground a little east of Diamond Springs, on the south side of the road. We had been very careful of fire all the way in, and here we were especially careful on account of the dense growth of grass and consequent danger of burning the camp. We had finished dinner, about two hours before sunset when, as if by one act, fire broke out in a circle all around us not more than a mile from camp. A stiff gale was blowing from the south, and when we noticed it the fire in the tall grass was roaring furiously and the flames leaping twenty feet high. Quickly we commenced firing outside of our camp, whipping out the fire next to it, thereby burning a circle around it. Every man used a gunnysack or saddle blanket and worked with desperate energy. The utter destruction of our camp was imminent, and we faced the fire like men who had everything at stake. Success was ours, but the battle left its scars on nearly all. I have never seen fifteen minutes of such desperate work followed by such exhaustion—scarcely a man could speak. Blinded by smoke, heat and ashes, intuitively we found our way to the creek, bathed our burned hands and faces, many of us terribly blistered. My hands and face were blistered in several places; my mustache and whiskers, the first I had ever raised, were utterly ruined; even my eyebrows were badly scorched. I could not wash on account of the blisters, and dipped my face and head deep down into the lovely spring water and held my hands under to relieve the pain. My experience was that of most of the troop. We had quite a quantity of antelope tallow, which was warmed and gently applied to our sores. Undoubtedly the Kaws had set the fire to burn us out, and while they did not quite succeed, if they had seen us they should have been fairly well satisfied. I think that Major Chilton and Lieutenant Hastings were better satisfied with the troop than they had ever been before. Men who could stand together in such a fight and win could stand against desperate odds anywhere. I was instructed to notify the troop at retreat roll call that we would start at daylight. The guards were doubled, and we rested as best we could.

Just out of camp we met the sun squarely in the face, but fortunately it soon became cloudy, which was a great relief. At Council Grove we got some corn from Hays & Company and went on to Big John Spring, three miles east, where we camped at noon.

Major Chilton told me to be ready to go back to Council Grove right after dinner. When I asked if I should take any one with me, he said, "No, you will go alone." About half past one I reported myself with horse saddled (an extra one which I took to save mine). He gave me a sealed letter directed to myself, and told me I could read it on the road to save time. Inclosed in my letter I found one directed to Mr. Hoffaker, a young man who was school teacher of the Kaw Indians, requesting him to furnish me an interpreter which he (the Major) had spoken of when he came through the Grove. My instructions were to proceed with the interpreter to the Kaw village, said to be three miles down the Neosho River, and there make a demand of the chief that he have five horses, stolen the spring before from some "mounted rifles" camped at Walnut Creek (now in Barton County), brought to his (Chilton's) camp at Big John Spring.

Mr. Hoffaker had the interpreter ready, one Batteese, a Pottawatomie by birth, but married to a Kaw and living with them. Batteese talked good English and was quite intelligent, but when I told him that I was after stolen horses and would make a demand on the chief he seemed reluctant to go or would rather go without me (he lived with the Kaws and was afraid to make enemies). Of course, I could not send him; my orders were to go myself. When we arrived at the village three miles down, we learned that the chief was at the lower village, two miles farther down, and there we went. We found the chief, whose name I regret to have forgotten, in a round house built of mud and willows at the west end of the village. An Indian woman came out as we went to the door and we found the chief alone, lying on a willow mattress, not feeling very well, as he told the interpreter. However, he was dressed and talked pleasantly in reply to all I said. He believed there were some Government horses among the Kaws that some of the young men claimed to have *found*. While we talked, Indians came in and packed the house full, and a crowd stood outside. Most of them had no arms.

My appearance seemed to be quite a source of amusement for a lot of young bucks, and they nodded and chatted about me in a merry way, and I knew they had reference to my burnt face and hands tied up in rags, and doubtless the scoundrels who set fire to the grass were before me. For some time I had not said anything; I wanted to kill a lot of Kaws; they seemed to know that I was suffering mentally as well as physically, and were amusing themselves at my expense. I could see that the chief was embarrassed. He seemed to be a sensible, good man, and these thieving scoundrels were riding over the country committing depredations and causing him a lot of trouble. Finally I rose to go, and told the interpreter to say to the chief that my captain knew the Kaws had the five horses, and that they stole them from a camp on Walnut Creek last spring, and that unless they were delivered in camp at Big John Spring the troop would come down and take them. I did not want to offend the chief, but to impress the thieves. I spoke in rather an angry tone, and the interpreter hesitated. I turned to him abruptly and said: "Interpret what I say, quickly, every word of it." An Indian about thirty years old, who was known as Clark, had been watching me closely, and at this juncture he spoke in plain English: "Who tole you I stole um horses?" "No matter," said I, "who told me, I know you stole them, and unless they are in my camp by the time I get there I'll make you sorry you did steal them." I shook the chief's hand and said "good bye" and came out through the crowd, the interpreter following. We mounted and galloped off. About four or five miles, mostly up Big John Creek, brought us to camp.

I reported to Major Chilton all that had happened, and wound up by saying that I hoped my threat would be carried out. The interpreter was much agitated, and said that he thought the horses would be brought in by to-morrow. "To-morrow!" said Major Chilton, "they'll bring them to-night, or I'll teach them a lesson they'll never forget, the thieving scoundrels. I don't propose to make another campaign against the Kaws in winter. I am here now, and while I don't want to hurt innocent men, half the Kaws ought to be wiped off the face of the earth, and my men have a mighty good excuse for doing it. Sergeant Lowe, take twenty men and bring the horses or the chief; I'll show them."

My saddle was changed from the extra horse I had been riding to my own, and in a few minutes twenty as good men as ever roamed the plains were in column of twos on the way with me to the Indian camp. We left our sabers in camp, they rattled too much, taking our revolvers only and plenty of ammunition. The interpreter was cautioned by the Major to interpret as I directed him. As I rode away the Major cautioned me to be prudent, and not hurt the chief. A low line of bluffs or hills formed the east bank of Big John Creek to within half a mile of the chief's house, which was at the upper or west end of this village. Before passing this point I halted and told the men to follow the leader in each rank, pistol in hand but not cocked, to keep their ears open for orders, and to do just what they were told and no more. Privately I told Cuddy I would go to the left door, which was on the east side, and he would go to the right and meet me. This part I did not want the interpreter to know, fearing that he would not go with me if he did. Sergeant Peel was in the rear of the line behind Cuddy, and Corporal Ferguson in rear of the line behind me; they would see that my plan was carried out, good or bad. We passed the point at a walk, then "Trot!" "Gallop!" "Charge!" came in quick succession.

I sprang from my horse at the door just as it was opened by the chief, who ran out at the sound of the horses' hoofs. Cuddy dismounted almost at the same instant. I seized the chief by the left arm and Cuddy by his right, and placed him on a horse behind another man, we mounted and were off in less time than it takes to tell it. The chief saw at once that he was a prisoner and went willingly. Instantly there was an uproar all over the village, men, women and children howling in every style. The bucks rushed out with guns and bows and arrows as if to give battle. The chief turned on the horse and rode backward, gesticulating and talking at the top of his voice. I told the interpreter that if a shot was fired at the dragoons I would kill the chief and him too, and impressed upon him the importance of repeating this, which he did vigorously and continually, and the chief kept up his exhortation till we were out of reach.

We moved off at a walk in extended line a pace or two apart, every man with pistol in hand turned in his saddle ready to shoot, Ferguson and Peel giving strict attention to the men. Just as we reached the point of bluff heretofore referred to, a man was seen coming as fast as his horse could bring him riding bareback. It was O'Neil, and he had been sent in haste by the Major to tell me to return, that three of the horses had been brought in and the other two promised. It was too late, and we took the chief to camp. He was one of the Major's prisoners of January, 1851, and they shook hands. The chief was much agitated and distressed. As I made my report, I felt sorry for him.

While the troop's verdict was a justification of the action, the more I thought of it the more I did not feel at all proud. Only for smarting from the outrage of attempting to burn our camp and the wounds from which we were suffering, we would all have condemned it, and I became convinced that I had been guilty of an outrage on a man who had been guilty of no wrong, in order to recover some horses that had been stolen by some thieves of his tribe. And now came the other two horses and some head men and sub-chiefs, but none of the thieving young bucks. A very earnest talk followed, in which the Major recounted the wrongs they had been guilty of, including the attempt to burn his camp the day before, and promised them if he had to come from Fort Leavenworth another cold winter to look after them he would "wipe the young bucks off the face of the earth." And he exhorted the chiefs and head men to control the bad young men in their tribe, if they had to kill them. This story has been told ever since the occurrence in various forms, often greatly exaggerated. The reckless element undoubtedly predominated with all of us at that time. Smarting as we were, we were unfit to be trusted to deal out justice in such a case. Whatever of wrong was committed the blame was all mine, and it took me some time to realize the extent of the outrage upon a harmless man. In camp and quarters men delighted to relate the incident, never for a moment dreaming that a wrong had been done; but fifty-three years later, while few remember it (probably I am the only living member of the party), all false pride has passed, and I see nothing to be proud of save the faithful conduct of those who followed me. While painfully smarting under the cowardly and treacherous outrage of the day before, they kept themselves under perfect discipline and self-control. I do not believe a word was spoken on our side save by myself and the interpreter.

In Salt Creek Valley, before marching into Fort Leavenworth, the Major made quite a little talk to the troop, recounting the hardships of the campaign and the faithful and creditable service rendered, cautioning them to remember that they were men capable of heroic acts and not to brutalize themselves with whisky, but try to keep up the good name they had so well won on the plains, at the same time reminding them that no amount of service rendered would condone future wrong doing; good behavior should be continuous.

Few incidents worthy of note occurred during the winter of 1853 and 1854. The traditional B Troop ball came off, routine of drills, etc. Not a man was tried by court-martial during the eight months we remained at the post, except by company court. One night at "tattoo," as I was calling the roll I heard the click of a pistol as if being cocked in front of me. It was quite dark, but standing close to a man I could recognize him. I stopped in the midst of the roll call, stepped forward to where I thought I heard the noise, reached over to the rear rank, seized a man, jerked him out in front of the troop and caught his right hand in his pocket holding a cocked pistol, which I took from him. All was done so quickly that hardly any one realized what was going on. Several seized the man, and I was obliged to protect him. I sent him to my orderly room with Sergeant Peel, finished the roll call and dismissed the troop after cautioning the men not to allow the incident to create any excitement, but all go to bed as usual. In the orderly room the man claimed that he bought the pistol (Derringer) to shoot rats with and had no definite object in cocking it at that time. He was pretty drunk, or pretended to be—an all around bad man, who had done an unusual share of extra duty for punishment. He had been a good while in the army, and had the reputation of having murdered a comrade during the Mexican War. I let him go and gave him his pistol the next day, at the same time telling him that I believed him to be at heart a cowardly murderer. I had no doubt but that he intended to shoot me as I passed him on the way to my quarters, which I would do as soon as I dismissed the troop. He had braced up with whisky for the act and rather overdid it. I could not prove that he intended to murder me, and if I sent him to the guard house the verdict would have been that I was afraid of him.

I may as well dispose of this man here. He would have deserted, but was anxious to go to New Mexico, where he had served before, and where the troop and regimental headquarters were now under orders to go. And from the happening of the incident above related he was silent, sullen and on his good behavior, having little companionship in the troop. It leaked out that in his drunken moods he had said he would desert when he got to New Mexico, accompanied with many threats. He never again gave me any trouble, but I was keenly on the lookout for him always.

When I left the troop Corporal Ferguson was made first sergeant. He joined the year before I did and re-enlisted a year before my time expired. He was a remarkable fine man, an Irishman by birth, had been clerk at regimental headquarters a good deal and was familiar with all company and regimental papers. Up to within a year he had never cared to serve as a noncommissioned officer. He had been made corporal once before, but resigned. He was a fine horseman, an excellent shot, a superior drill and all-around athlete; a man who would attract attention anywhere. Not much given to words, he held a quiet control of all around him without an effort. The last time he was made corporal was about a year before my discharge, through my influence, and I held up to him the fact that Sergeants Cuddy, Cook, Drummond and others would not re-enlist, Peel would not accept first sergeant, and the timber for that place in the troop was scarce, and

Campaigns of 1852–53

I had no doubt but that he would be appointed if he would take interest enough to accept it. And he did take interest, and showed so plainly his superiority that the appointment came to him almost as a matter of course. The troop and its commander knew that it was my wish, all became educated up to the idea and expected it. And so when I was furloughed I left him acting first sergeant.

One night after "tattoo" roll call the man of the pistol above referred to plunged a knife into Ferguson's heart, killing him instantly. By great effort the murderer was saved from being mobbed by the troop; was tried by civil court and sentenced to hang. I have refrained from mentioning the names of men of whom I had to speak in uncomplimentary terms, for the reason that most men have family relations and friends, and to mention them in a way to leave a stain upon their character might be unjust and is altogether unnecessary, and most men who have come under my observation in the army and on campaigns pulled out in fair shape and led good lives, many of them raising families afterwards. But this murderer had no friends on earth that his comrades ever heard of, and sure I am that he had no family near or remote to weep over his crimes. His name was Jackson, and it is but just to his comrades that no mistakes be made in the name.

Sergeants Cuddy, Cook and Drummond were discharged towards the last of the year 1853, and new noncommissioned officers took their places. All three were employed by the quartermaster, and the following spring Cook and Cuddy went with Colonel Steptoe's[10] command, the former as wagonmaster and

---

[10] Edward Jenner Steptoe of Virginia was graduated from West Point in 1837 as second lieutenant and assigned to the Third Artillery, promoted to first lieutenant in 1838 and captain in 1847. In the Mexican War he was brevetted major for Cerro Gordo and lieutenant colonel for Chapultepec. He became major in the Ninth Infantry in 1855. On May 17, 1858, he commanded four companies in a fight with eight hundred or more Spokane Indians near Spokane Lake, losing two officers and six enlisted men. He resigned in 1861 shortly after being commissioned lieutenant colonel, Tenth Infantry. He died April 1, 1865.

the latter in charge of strings of lead horses to Salt Lake the first year (1854), wintering there and going through to California the following season.

When Walker[11] went on his filibustering expedition to Nicaragua, Cook served as a captain in his command, escaped when Walker was executed, came back to San Francisco and died in poverty. He was a native of Nova Scotia, had been a sailor, and I never knew a stauncher, braver man.

Cuddy was a shrewd man, with money-making tendencies, dropped into the cattle ranch business in California, married a Spanish woman with large Spanish grant, cattle and horses, and the last I heard of him he was raising a good family.

Russell, O'Meara, McDonald, Bostwick and others were also discharged and went their various ways—Russell to setting type on the *Missouri Republican*; Bostwick, the farrier, married a wife and farm in Clinton County, Missouri, and was killed at Vicksburg in 1862, while a major in the Confederate Army. O'Meara declared he had money enough to take him back to the "Old Dart," and he was going there. I will have occasion to mention McDonald later.

Recruits came from Carlisle before the close of navigation on the Missouri.

The Major applied for and was given authority to purchase twenty-five horses for his troop, subject to his own inspection, and made an arrangement with a Mr. Calvert, of Weston, to furnish them. Two or three times at evening stables the Major pointed out to Mr. Calvert the kind of horses he wanted, the models that suited him best, all to be sorrels of solid color—chestnut or red sorrels would do, but no light colored ones, no white noses—

---

11 William Walker, 1824–60, was born in Nashville, Tennessee, and was graduated from the University of Nashville. In 1853 he led a filibustering expedition into the state of Sonora, Mexico, but was driven back across the border. In 1855 he landed in Nicaragua and for a time controlled that country, proclaiming himself president. In 1857 he surrendered to Commander C. H. Davis of the United States Navy. In attempting an invasion of Honduras in 1860, Walker was captured and put to death by firing squad.

white feet not absolutely barred, but unless exceptionally sound would be rejected. Sound feet, flat, sinewy legs, sound hocks and knees, arms and quarters well muscled, short, sinewy back, high withers, rangy neck, bony head, bold eye—no "hog eyes"—fine ear, deep chest, plenty of room to carry his forage, five to seven years old, fifteen to sixteen hands, preferably fifteen and a half, all natural trotters and well broken to saddle—about filled the Major's idea, reserving the right to reject any of them for any reason satisfactory to himself. The quartermaster paid for the horses on the Major's order. They came in fine shape, were put in our stables, and thoroughly tried before being received. They were a fine lot and the deal satisfactory all around. The old and least serviceable of the troop horses were turned over to the quartermaster to make room for the new ones, and mine was one of them. I saw him sold at auction to a Missouri farmer for $50.00 and requested him to see that the horse was well cared for, which he promised to do, told me where he lived, and invited me to see him, which I did two years later, dined with him and told him and his wife the horse's history. His wife was riding him in her visits about the neighborhood, and she declared that he should never do any other kind of work. In those days everybody rode horseback. A few wealthy people had old-fashioned, roomy carriages for use on special occasions, but every man and woman, boy and girl, generally rode horseback.

I had the choice of the new lot of horses, and chose a deep chestnut, without a white spot, sixteen hands, fine from ear to hoof, a little nervous, but had not been spoiled, and soon became a great pet. And now came the task of adjusting this fine lot of horses so as to make the best use of them. It was an ironclad rule that every man must be gentle with his horse. Abusing a horse was the unpardonable sin. Peevishness, kicking, jerking, swearing at, unnecessary spurring or violence of any kind would not be permitted to go unpunished, and noncommissioned officers were sure to report any infraction of the rule. Everything must be done for the comfort of the horse. The noncommissioned officers who wanted to change old horses for new did so, and then came the privates with the least serviceable horses. If, after assignment, a horse was found unsuited to the man or the man to the horse a change was made, whether the man liked it or not, be he non-commissioned officer or private, and from first to last, whatever would add to the efficiency of the troop was done, whether in drilling horses or men. Within five miles of the flagstaff west of the river there was not a nook or corner that we did not drill over, giving strict attention to the skirmish drill.

I have heretofore not mentioned the manner of feeding our horses; they were always watered before feeding. Prairie hay was used—there was no other in the country at that time—and *there was no better "roughness" for horses.* Ear corn was the kind of grain always used in garrison. One can easily see whether corn on the cob is sound or unsound. Shelled corn might be musty or some bad corn mixed with it and none but an expert could tell, while any man would know a sound ear of corn; and more than that, horses do not eat ear corn so fast; they like to bite it from the cob—masticate, relish and digest it better. Of course on the plains one must use shelled corn, but in garrison, in a corn growing country, there is no feed equal to ear corn and prairie hay. I know that now there is a great habit of feeding oats to cavalry horses; farmers, teamsters and livery men did that in the Northern States when I was a boy; it was the best feed they had and oats were nearly always well cured and free from must and dust, and they did not raise corn as they do in the West. Here oats do not do as well as in New England or Canada, are not so easily cured, and are often both musty and dusty, and as a rule chaffy and light, with little nutriment compared to Northern oats. Corn is the cleanest and best feed; there is nothing equal to it for strengthening or fattening man or beast. Barley and wheat are good feed where corn is not raised, but where it grows in abundance there is nothing equal to corn; for man, for horses and mules, for cattle, for hogs, for fowls, it is the king of products to make muscle and fat. The Southern planters fed corn and bacon to the Negroes because it made them strong and healthy; they fed corn to their plantation mules for the same reason. At the salt mines in the Island of Bonair the strongest Negro men and women I ever saw were allowed a bushel of corn a month and no other food except some fish that they could catch occasionally. They could parch the corn, grind it between two rocks, or eat it without cooking—no mills to grind it with; 'twas corn that made them big and strong. Probably this has nothing to do with cavalry horses, but all the same I have never seen better or more enduring ones than were in B Troop, and *prairie hay, corn* and *good care* made them what they were. The nutriment in prairie hay does not equal that in timothy, clover or alfalfa when well cured, but it is much easier cured; the nutriment is in sound ear corn.

As heretofore stated, the man who was the instigator of the fire in Cuddy's orderly room deserted, and with his wife stayed about Weston. His occupation was "recruiting deserters"; that is, he would find men with money after pay day, persuade them to desert if he could, and often robbed them. One Sunday I tried to capture him but he escaped on horseback while I was hunting him. I found the shanty where he lived with an ill-assorted set of vagabonds in a little corn-field, and represented to Major Chilton that a dozen men could surround it and effect his arrest. The next Sunday Lieutenant Hastings and a dozen men, including Sergeant Peel, went over to Weston, surrounded the house, half the men dismounting and hunting through corn shocks. Out of a shock ran the man into the house, with Peel after him. Peel searched thoroughly in vain. A man and half a dozen women, including the deserter's wife, were sitting at a table apparently in the act of commencing to eat dinner. 'Twas when big hoop skirts were worn, and being a small man Peel felt sure that he was under his wife's skirts and a blanket thrown round her lap and feet, told her so, and declared that he would have him if he had to go under her skirts. At this juncture Lieutenant Hastings rode up and called Peel out, told him he had no right to enter and hunt through a man's house without a search warrant, which he did not have, and now that he had laid himself liable to arrest they must mount and get across the river, which they did. It was understood that an indictment was found against Peel, and after that he kept away from Weston. A month later the man gave himself up, a consumptive wreck, and died soon after. He confessed that he was under his wife's skirts when Peel was after him.

In March, 1854, I was made a Mason in the Weston lodge and took the first three degrees. I have seen something of masonic lodges since that time, but have never seen a finer set of men or brighter Masons than that lodge contained. "Old Jimmy" Miller was the secretary and "father" of the lodge, and Perry Wallingford conferred the degrees in a manner that the "novice" could never forget. One night every week, when it was convenient for me to be absent, I spent in Weston and attended the lodge. I asked the captain's permission to ride over to Weston in the evening and back in the morning, and it was cheerfully given.

And now the time was approaching for the annual campaign. Headquarters, staff and band and B and D Troops were ordered to New Mexico and would leave about the first of July. Brydon re-enlisted and was transferred to the band. He was getting old, and settled down to the fact that the best way to provide for old age was to go to the Soldiers' Home in Washington. The Government had just commenced to collect twelve and one-half cents per month from each soldier for its support. While regretting to part with him I encouraged him to take the step, for, old and out of the army, he would be helpless. He was the only man who had shared my tent for the last two years, except on a few emergencies, and had been my constant friend since we joined the troop.

Towards the last of May D Troop, Captain John Adams,[12]

---

[12] John Adams of Tennessee was graduated from West Point in 1846 as brevet second lieutenant of the First Dragoons. He became second lieutenant in December, 1846, brevet first lieutenant in 1848 for the Mexican War battle of Santa Cruz de Rosales; first lieutenant in 1851 and captain in 1856. He resigned in 1861, became

Campaigns of 1852–53

came from Fort Snelling[13] by steamboat and camped on the "blue grass," a little southwest of where is now "Merritt" Lake, and the month of June was a busy one for every one preparing for a move that admitted of no return for probably some years.

a Confederate brigadier general, and was killed in the Battle of Franklin, November 30, 1864.

[13] Fort Snelling was established in 1819 at the mouth of the Minnesota River (between Minneapolis and St. Paul, Minnesota).

Part IV
From Soldier to Civilian

† † † † † † † † † † †

On the second day of July, 1854, headquarters First Dragoons, B and D Troops, with a large number of army officers, some families, a large supply train and six hundred extra horses led on strings of about forty horses each, left Fort Leavenworth for Fort Union, New Mexico,[1] Colonel Thomas T. Fauntleroy commanding.

From start to finish, the two troops alternated daily in front and rear guard. During my experience I had never campaigned with another troop, hence did not know very much about the management of other troops on the plains and I learned to think B nearly as perfect as the conditions permitted. I was as proud of it as I ever have been of anything under my immediate charge. On every hand the troop attracted attention—the manner of marching, care taken of their horses, appearance of horses and men, the short time necessary to put up their tents, and the lightning speed with which they were struck, folded and loaded in the wagons, the neatness and dispatch in everything, and the quietness and lack of confusion on every hand, seemed a wonder to many of the officers of long experience. There was no special effort on this trip more than on others, but somehow we were settled down to one way of doing—a uniformity of thought and action—changes were few and only when circumstances forced

---

[1] Fort Union, New Mexico, on the Santa Fe Trail, was established in 1851 by Lt. Col. Edwin V. Sumner, First Dragoons. It was located on Coyote Creek, about six miles north of the junction of two branches of the trail, the Cimarron Cutoff, and the Mountain Branch via Raton Pass. Fort Union was abandoned in 1891 and became a National Monument in 1955.

them. Officers and noncommissioned officers did not have to reiterate from day to day and from camp to camp, for no man could plead ignorance of a general routine, hence there was little friction; the men had grown into the habit of taking pride in doing everything, having "some style about them," as McDonald used to say, and every man had grown to know that he must do his share cheerfully, all working together for the general good.

D Troop was composed of a fine lot of men and drilled well, but they had been stationed for some years at Fort Snelling, and did not have the long summer campaigns that B had, and for that reason were not up to the daily routine of making themselves comfortable. Most of the men were comparatively new to campaigning, and while fine garrison soldiers, had much to learn and to suffer before they could hope to compete with men who had traveled from fifteen hundred to three thousand miles every summer, always in an Indian country, always on the alert and obliged to move with little transportation, little or no forage save the grass that grew in abundance everywhere, and with short rations, depending largely on game which was also generally abundant. Of course, more or less recruits were received every winter (generally fore part of winter) from Carlisle Barracks to replace those discharged, etc. These recruits had special attention in drill, and imagined they were full fledged soldiers by the time we went on the plains, but soon found that half was not learned.

A good deal can be done to discipline men in garrison; but in the field, on the march, in bivouac under the blue sky, in storms, cold and heat, on the trail, caring for self and horses, with always a helping hand for comrades, bearing cheerfully every hardship,—there was where the thorough dragoon was made, and a man in his first year's service was not worth half as much as in after years. This applies to a troop where three-fourths of the men were "old soldiers," which includes all men after the first year. This being true, how about a troop or company where there is not more than half a dozen who have seen service before? Take the experience of any man who has served in the regulars and volunteers. See the amount of sickness in the latter compared to the former; see the difference between strict discipline and the reverse; see the comfort of one against the suffering of the other under trying circumstances; see the difference between men who accept their instructions as ironclad law, never doubting the correctness thereof, and men who argue the point in their minds, if not aloud, the instructor himself in doubt, lacking confidence in himself and the men he addresses—"the blind leading the blind." To hear the rabble, and politicians in particular, talk of how "our brave volunteers" performed such and such feats in battle, one would think the regular army did not amount to anything, and were only a stumbling block in the way of the "gallant men" of this or that State. Who ever doubted the courage of any respectable American—the peer of any man on earth? Surely, not I. But how can a man know anything until he has learned it? Is there any sense in marching young men, after a few months of camp life, into battle against disciplined troops? It won't do to tell us they are brave. Who doubted that? The fact that he is brave does not make his adversary less brave nor his aim less accurate. To stand up and receive the death blow because too ignorant to avoid it, may be admirable, but it is pitiable, and no credit to the nation that places men in such a position. No country on earth has superior material for soldiers, but it is no credit to the United States to expect this material to be transformed from peaceful pursuits to military experts in a few months to meet the stern necessities of battle.

Some one may point to the performance of the First Volunteer Cavalry ("Rough Riders") at Santiago to prove that the very best work was done by that regiment. Such comparison is no criterion. Nine-tenths of them were men who had lived for years in the field, in the mountains, on the plains, accustomed for years to Indian warfare; the best shots and the best horsemen in the world; accustomed to follow the trail and protect themselves and their property everywhere. Turned loose anywhere, singly or in squads, they were self-supporting. Even that portion of the regiment which came from the colleges and society circles of New York were remarkable for athletic accomplishments of all kinds, including target practice. Probably there is not on record an organization of similar numbers where each individual was so nearly self-made and self-reliant at this. The Colonel had distinguished himself as an Indian follower and fighter in the regular army in Arizona and Mexico as few men ever did, and the Lieutenant Colonel from boyhood up had trained himself in every line of athletics; had ranched with the cowboys of Dakota, Wyoming and Montana, and was the champion hunter of big game in the United States. In his experience in public life he had learned human nature in every grade, and above all, at the age of most complete manhood—not too old for strength and energy nor too young for mature judgment—had learned self-control and the management of men. With their superb courage and patriotism, no wonder Colonel Wood and Lieutenant Colonel Roosevelt led that magnificent band of men, equal to those who died with Crockett at the Alamo, to glorious victory. It will not do to compare this regiment with average volunteers. Every man was a soldier, tried in a school than which there is no better in America. But the officers and men of this regiment will ever stand in respectful acknowledgment of the grand old regulars, who were shoulder to shoulder with them, and without which there would have been few of the "Rough Riders" left to tell the tale. Dogged, stubborn discipline came in time to mingle with desperate gallantry at the crucial moment. Young America, I honor your courage and manhood, but keep your eye on the regulars, and when you want to be a soldier enlist in a good company, in a good regiment, and go to a home where order and decency prevail, and every well behaved man finds peace and comfort.

Of course there was the usual confusion of starting a big caravan on a long journey, but things improved from day to day. Our troop had easy times compared to other organizations. After passing Council Grove, guards were doubled, as they always were on the route west, always expecting depredations of some kind from the Indians if the utmost vigilance was not maintained.

On Coon Creek, now in Edwards County, we met Kiowa Indians in great numbers, mounted on fine horses. They cavorted about us, saucy, insolent and defiant, in fact it looked like trouble was inevitable. B was advance guard, and as we were strung out on the road, D was more than two miles in rear. Our horses on strings were a great temptation to the Indians, and they could have charged in and stampeded the whole lot with little loss to themselves. Colonel Fauntleroy was riding with Major Chilton and other officers ahead of me, as I rode at the head of the troop, and I heard the conversation. I saw that the Colonel and the Major were disagreeing, and finally the Major lost his temper and said with some spirit, "Well, if I were in command I would corral these trains and horses and wipe these Kiowas off the face of the earth; this is no way to deal with Indians." In answer the Colonel ordered the Major in arrest and to the rear. The Major turned, his eyes flashing, his bristling mustache looking unusually fierce, and rode to the rear. He had taken his last ride in front of his troop. Lieutenant Hastings was detached from the troop, acting commissary officer, hence, when the Major was arrested there was no officer left in command of it. The Major had been consulted all along about camps, and had been of great service. Immediately after his arrest, the Colonel called me and said he wanted to go into camp. It was about eleven o'clock. I told him he could not find a better camp than about where he was, where the town of Kinsley now is, and at his order I rode off to assist the quartermaster, Captain Mastin,[2] to arrange the camp. To the troop I gave the order, "Dismount! Graze your horses!" The Colonel looked surprised, but said nothing. I was carrying out a standing rule to rest and graze the horses at every opportunity.

[2] Frederick H. Masten (not Mastin) of New York was appointed second lieutenant, First Infantry, in 1838, and was first lieutenant in the same regiment from 1841 to 1850. In 1847 he became captain and assistant quartermaster. He resigned at the end of 1857 and died September 8, 1874.

I was an hour with the quartermaster, during which time the troop were enjoying the finest grass on the plains.

This camp was made more compact than any we had heretofore, and the guard considerably strengthened. It was but a few miles from the old battle ground.

I reported to the Major after retreat and guard mount for any suggestions he might desire to make. Evidently he felt chagrined at the position he was placed in, and anxious that whatever happened his troop should not be found wanting. While we were talking, Lieutenant Robert Williams[3] called and stated to the Major that he had been detailed to take command of his troop. He had called to pay his respects and to learn from the Major anything he desired to impart concerning it. The Major thanked him and said about as follows: "This is Sergeant Lowe, Lieutenant Williams. He has been first sergeant more than two years, knows all about the troop, and will certainly serve under you as faithfully and cheerfully as he has under me. I congratulate you on being detailed to command my troop. You will not be likely to have any trouble with it." Lieutenant Williams commanded the troop two days, when Lieutenant Hastings took command. Lieutenant Williams was one of the best specimens of manhood I ever met. Nothing ruffled the even tenor of his ways; he always spoke in the same gentle tone, the same perfect English, in the same refined manner. I conceived a friendship for him that a more intimate acquaintance in future years increased to admiration. He was one of the most refined and noble characters I ever knew. His military service ended with his retirement as Adjutant-General of the Army in 1893 on account of age.

---

[3] Robert Williams of Virginia was graduated from West Point in 1851 as brevet second lieutenant, First Dragoons; he became second lieutenant in 1853 and first lieutenant in 1855. In 1861 he became brevet captain as assistant adjutant general, then captain; served briefly as colonel of the First Massachusetts Cavalry, 1861–62; then resumed as assistant adjutant general with the rank of major in 1862. He was brevetted colonel and brigadier general for Civil War service. He became lieutenant colonel in 1869, colonel in 1881, and the Adjutant General with the rank of brigadier general in 1892. He retired in 1893 and died August 24, 1901.

On leaving the Coon Creek camp we moved out in double column, troops traveling by fours, wagons and horse strings two abreast. The rear guard furnished a line of vedettes along the bluffs, and orders were strict to keep everything closed up. A few days later we crossed the Arkansas at Cimarron Crossing, thirty miles above where now stands Dodge City, and camped on the south bank. We seemed to have left the Indians all behind, twenty miles below, and the talk that the Colonel had with them the evening before indicated no trouble.

The camp was west of the road, extending up the river fully a mile. D Troop was at the upper end (west); B was rear guard that day and camped just west of the road, forming the left flank of the camp, the wagon train, except headquarters, company and officers' transportation, was well to the front (south), away from the river, and the horse strings immediately in rear, while headquarters, officers' families, etc., were strung along the bank of the river between the two troops. A bend in the river where B Troop was, threw it north of the east and west line of the other camps. The ground occupied by the supply train, the horse strings and D Troop was sandy and treacherous. Picket pins went down easily and were easily withdrawn. Our camp occupied firmer ground, and with care we made our horses perfectly safe, knowing well the terrors of the stampede, taking in the treacherous nature of the ground occupied by all except us, and the fearful effects of hundreds of animals with lariats and flying picket pins sweeping over our camp. We hugged the bank of the river below the bend closely, occupying as little room with tents and the two company wagons as possible, and arranging horses so that a direct stampede east would pass them. In other words, a stampede would have to come around the bend to strike any part of our camp.

It was noticed by all of our troop that the six hundred led horses were always badly picketed; that is, picket pins driven half way down and in many cases two or three lariats tied to one pin. A stampede had been feared by all of us. The man in charge of the horse strings was very ill most of the time, and each man in charge of a string of horses seemed to have no conception of the crash that was sure to come sooner or later. D Troop did little better than the horse strings and B was spurred up by me and other noncommissioned officers to see that every picket pin was securely driven in the best ground. I have seen men stick their picket pins in an ant hill because it went down easily. Such a thing in our troop, or the fact that a horse got loose in any way, unless proven to be no fault of the rider, would insure his walking and carrying his arms the next day. Carelessness in picketing horses would not be condoned on this or any other trip that we ever made. A stampede was the terror of terrors on the plains, and this location was like camping on a volcano liable to erupt at any moment.

It was a perfectly bright, starlit night, and peace seemed to reign from end to end of the camp. Visiting was general among the officers, and a feeling of safety prevailed, now that we seemed to be clear of trouble with Indians. A little before nine o'clock the earth seemed to tremble as if in the violent throes of an earthquake. Like a whirlwind a stampede commenced with D Troop horses, rushing down through the extra or "led" horses and on through the mules, sweeping everything before it, barely missing officers and B Troop camp. On they went a little south of east down the river, in the mad rush trampling everything under foot, upsetting and breaking a dozen six-mule wagons by catching picket pins in the wheels as the moving mass rushed on; picket pins whizzing in the air struck an object and bounded forward like flying lances. To condense: D Troop lost two-thirds of their horses. All the string horses (600) and six hundred mules, besides some private animals, were in the mad rush of destruction. One B Troop horse, an extra, succeeded in joining the gang. Realizing the full meaning of the terrible calamity, I ordered "boots and saddles," and when Lieutenant Hastings, who was visiting some officers, arrived, the troop was ready to mount. The quartermaster sergeant was left in charge of the camp with a cook and bugler. Lieutenant Hastings rode over to headquarters and reported. Returning immediately, we mounted, and were off in the direction of the stampede. A few young officers en route to join their troop in New Mexico, and who were fortunate enough to have their horses down near the river out of the line of the stampede, mounted and struck out.

The stampede was a mystery at headquarters, one opinion being that it was caused by Indians, another that wolves had frightened some horses and they had started all the others. There was more experience in B Troop than in the balance of the command, and the conclusion was that it would be no trouble to bring about a stampede from either cause. One Indian in a wolf skin might have done it, or one horse frightened at anything running the length of his lariat and scaring a few more might bring about the whole thing. We did not believe that any number of Indians were near us, or were making any hostile demonstrations. In short, the treacherous character of the ground made it unfit to picket a large number of horses and mules, and the stampede was almost a matter of course. We might have escaped such a calamity as inexperienced campaigners sometimes do, but the chances, considering the number of animals and want of care were against us.

It was nine o'clock when the troop started on the trail, feeling its way out through the wilderness of wrecked wagons, crippled and dead horses and mules and their lariats and picket pins, met with in the first two miles, within which nearly a hundred horses and mules were found dead or injured by being pierced with flying picket pins or by being tangled in the ropes and dragged. We did not stop for any of these, but rode on to head off those animals that had escaped in a condition to travel. Within five miles of camp we headed off probably two hundred mules. Most of them had broken their lariats and lost their picket pins by being trampled upon by other animals. We rounded them up and sent half a dozen men with them, following the river bank towards camp. Then we spread out and in a mile or two, rounded up another large band nearly all mules, and sent another squad of men with them. It was my experience then, and always has been in a stampede, that mules tone down after a short run, whereas frightened horses never know when to stop, and run until exhausted. A herd of mules without horses to lead them in a stampede will hardly ever run more than two miles, circle around a little and then either stop to graze or strike a trail at a moderate gait. Within twelve or fifteen miles of camp we had turned back with different squads of men probably four hundred mules and half as many horses; and now Lieutenant Hastings and three or four men started back with quite a band, mostly horses, leaving with me about twenty-five men. Following the same tactics and having driven in whatever we could find within a few miles, a small squad of men was started up the river towards camp. A couple of young officers, Lieutenants Lloyd Beall[4] and ─── Craig,[5] joined me with quite a band of horses about daylight.

At that time I was with a few men in the sand hills, probably a mile from the river. We swung around driving about sixty horses before us towards the river, and suddenly found ourselves close to an Indian camp, a little below it. There was no changing our course so as to avoid the village altogether without abandoning our captured animals. I put spurs to my horse to get between the horses and the Indian camp, followed closely by Hand and the two officers. The horses did not seem to notice the lodges until close on to them, and we rushed through the south edge of the

[4] Lloyd Beall, born in the District of Columbia, was a resident of Missouri when appointed second lieutenant, Second Artillery, in 1848. He became first lieutenant in 1851, transferred to the Second Infantry in 1859, and became captain in 1861. He was dismissed Sept. 12, 1862, and subsequently was a Confederate artillery private (and sergeant, says Lowe).

[5] William Craig of Indiana was graduated from West Point in 1853 as brevet second lieutenant, Third Infantry. He became second lieutenant, Eighth Infantry, in 1855 and first lieutenant in 1858. He was captain and assistant quartermaster in 1861 (as mentioned by Lowe on p. 135). Craig resigned April 5, 1864, and died May 27, 1886. (This was a march of the First Dragoons, but casual officers of other commands would go along for transportation and protection from Indians, in cases of transfer, return from leave, or other official business).

village at a fast gallop. In the meantime the dogs set up a terrible barking, and as we looked back the whole camp seemed to be alive, as men, women and children hustled out of their lodges. Attracted by a large number of Indian horses, two of ours started to join them. Craig made a break to head them off, and pistol in hand chased them through the Indian herd. Beall joined Craig and with the two horses joined my party in little more time than is necessary to tell it. And now the sun was coming up; we had ridden our horses at all sorts of gaits seven hours. In the band we were driving were several good ones. We rounded them up in a bend of the river and made a change and helped Beall and Craig to change. Knowing that the Indians would be soon scouring the country for horses, and with my small party of men I could accomplish nothing, I determined to scatter out two hundred or three hundred yards apart and drive all we could find to camp. I knew that the camp we had passed was composed of Kiowas and Comanches, about thirty miles below our camp. When about twenty-five miles below our camp, I saw horses on the opposite side of the river. They must be a part of ours that had crossed over; they were loose and grazing. Through my glass I could count about a dozen. Leaving the balance of the party to go on, driving everything they could before them, I took three men and crossed the river. Below the horses first seen there were no signs of any having passed down. We drove before us all that we saw and probably all on that side and arrived in camp near sunset with thirty-two. At retreat roll call every man of B Troop answered to his name. Among the big bands brought in by Lieutenant Hastings and others the dismounted portion of D Troop found mounts, and with citizen employees did good service in gathering in and caring for horses and mules.

To the fact that B Troop was able to mount promptly, and work systematically and vigorously, Colonel Fauntleroy owed his ability to move without abandoning many wagons, only those badly wrecked. If pursuit had been delayed until morning the Indians would have had most of the horses. It did not take them long to scour the country and pick up what we left. They brought a good many to the camp, for which the Colonel paid them. Two days after the stampede we recrossed the river and found a fine safe camp on the north side.

Nearly all mules not killed or fatally crippled were saved, so that we were short only about 50. About 150 horses were dead or desperately crippled, and many more not accounted for, probably found by Indians after we left; shortage, 200 or more.

Lieutenant Beall had been in arrest ever since we left Fort Leavenworth, and now he was released. He volunteered to go in pursuit of the stampeded stock, and on Craig's report he was restored to duty. This I understood at the time. Eight years later Captain Craig told me at Fort Union, New Mexico, where he was then quartermaster, that on the way to camp after I left to cross the river, Beall said: "Why the ——— didn't I think to lead off after those two horses? Here I am a first lieutenant and you just from the Academy; I am under a cloud and ought to have done something to recommend myself." "You did," said Craig, "you followed those horses through the Indian herd, pistol in hand (which was true, following the example of Craig), and I shall so report." And that report induced Colonel Fauntleroy to release Beall.

The history of these two men is interesting. Beall was captain of artillery at the commencement of the Civil War, resigned and enlisted in the Confederate Army. Dr. M. S. Thomas resided in Leavenworth previous to the war, joined the Army of Northern Virginia as a surgeon, and after the battle following the capture of General Pope's headquarters, while riding over the battlefield near a Confederate battery he recognized a dog that used to belong to Beall at Fort Leavenworth. He knew that the dog was not far from his master, and proceeded to investigate. He soon found Sergeant Beall. A long conversation followed, in which Beall stated that many times he had been recommended for promotion, but on account of his reputation for drinking his endorsements were overruled before they reached the appointing power. I do not know his end. Colonel Craig married a wealthy lady in Ohio, resigned from the army at the close of the war, prosecuted a claim to a large Spanish grant of land in southern Colorado, won it, and was independently rich, and died before he was fifty.

Colonel Fauntleroy sent for me and said some very nice things to me and of the troop, but there was no mention of the happenings in "orders." I take it for granted that Colonel Fauntleroy included the stampede in his report to the War Department, and that the quartermaster, Captain Mastin, reported the loss of public animals and other property, but no mention of it in newspapers, nor in "orders" anywhere. Men were supposed to do their duty without hope of special commendation. A troop that would do now what B did then would be commended by the colonel, by the department commander, by the division commander and by the general of the army in his annual report.

After recrossing the river I called on Major Chilton as soon as I could. I never saw him better pleased with the troop. "B Troop saved the command," said he. "Mr. Hastings tells me that you had 'boots and saddles' sounded and the troop ready to mount when he reached it after the stampede. I am glad you were so prompt and did not wait."

And now we moved off up the north side of the Arkansas by easy marches for several days, on up the river to Bent's Old Fort, and crossed; thence south to Timpas, Water Holes, Hole in the Rock, Hole in the Prairie, crossing Purgetwa—generally pronounced Picketware—below where Trinidad now is.[6]

It was nearly one hundred miles farther by this than by the Cimarron route to Santa Fé, hence it had been abandoned; had not been traveled since the Cimarron came into general use.

[6] Bent's Old Fort was on Horse Creek near La Junta; U. S. 350 follows roughly this stretch of Santa Fe Trail from La Junta to Trinidad. Timpas still exists on Timpas Creek; Hole in the Rock is near Thatcher; Hole in the Prairie is near Model. From Earl to Trinidad the trail followed the valley of the Purgatoire, sometimes Anglicized to Picketwire and misspelled Purgatory, but Lowe's Purgetwa is a weirdly phonetic version.

Trees had fallen across the trail, mountain torrents had made great gulleys, and it took Lieutenant Craig's pioneer party[7]—details from B and D Troops—several days to make the road passable. In the meantime our animals had the finest grama grass I ever saw, and I never saw animals improve so much as ours did in so short a time.

One day while camped here Sergeant Peel went hunting; he was riding a mule, and when a mile or two from camp a thunder storm overtook him, and he sought shelter under a thick clump of pines. A flock of turkeys ran under a big, low branched pine, not more than ten yards from him. The rain and hail came down in torrents while the wind blew a fearful gale. Peel had tied his gentle mule securely, and deliberately shot seventeen turkeys, every one in the head. They seemed to think the crack of his rifle a peal of thunder, and the fluttering of the dying turkeys did not frighten them. He finally wounded one and it flew away, the balance of the flock—half a dozen—following. Peel came into camp about dark with all that his mule could stagger under.

Just before this storm I had marched my detail for guard to headquarters, and guard mounting was just over when the storm struck us. I put spurs to my horse and rode with all speed for camp. I had crossed a dry ravine going, and returning found a mountain torrent. I very imprudently dashed through it, looked back and saw a tree a foot through going down at railroad speed. A second later and I and my horse were hopelessly lost. As it was, nine horses out of ten would have failed, but my noble "Bruce," with courage that knew no faltering, having full confidence in his master, landed me safely and bounded away as if there was nothing the matter. This horse was my special pet; every soldier's horse ought to be. It may be a little hard for a good soldier of fine feelings to pet a miserable plug, and on the other hand, it

---

[7] "Pioneers or working-parties are attached to convoys to mend roads, remove obstacles, and erect defenses. The convoys should always be provided with spare wheels, poles, axles, etc."—Revised Regulations for the Army of the United States 1861.

may be a little hard for a good horse to think much of his plug master—both combinations that ought not to exist. Good men and horses having faith in each other will follow the right kind of leader to victory or annihilation without a murmur. The horse need not be of any particular strain of blood so that he is of a saddle horse breed, made to gladden the heart of the proud man who rides him; not a thick shouldered, fat headed, short stepping thing, only fit for a huckster, but a horse with flat, muscular legs, short back, well quartered, well cupped sound hoofs, high crest, lean head, bright eyes and brainy. With this latter combination, he may be Spanish broncho, Arabian, Kentucky thoroughbred, or mixed—never ask a man to ride a plug off the farm where he is used to plow. One of the greatest mistakes this Government is making is in not using a part of the Fort Leavenworth and Fort Riley military reservations to breed a sample of saddle horse, if for no other reason than to show the farmers of the surrounding country the kind of horse the Government requires for cavalry and artillery.

Having gotten the road open and the animals well rested, we moved over the Ratton Pass[8] and camped at a pond at the foot of the mountains. We were rear guard this day and had a tedious time; some wagons wrecked, and we came into camp late. The next morning we were in advance at sunrise. Approaching Red River, a big flock of turkeys were plainly to be seen on the trees; they had never been frightened and knew no fear. I asked permission of Lieutenant Hastings to ride ahead and kill one of them, which I did, shooting a big fellow from the tree with my pistol.

The first settlement that we struck in New Mexico was Maxwell's Ranch, on the Cimarron; the next was Rayado, where I Troop was stationed. We here heard the first account of the battle fought six weeks before between I Troop and the Apaches, here-

---

[8] Raton Pass (not Ratton) between Trinidad, Colorado, and Raton, New Mexico, was almost on the border. After the Civil War Uncle Dick Wootten made some improvements and established a toll road across the pass.

From Soldier to Civilian

tofore referred to. I met my old friend Byrnes, whom I had not seen since we parted at Fort Leavenworth the first of April, 1850. Now he was first sergeant as heretofore related. Headquarters, band and D Troop stopped here, while B went on.

Arrived at Fort Union, we went into camp by ourselves about two miles from the post. And now the troop was under orders to proceed to Fort Stanton in a few weeks. Major Chilton found his commission as major and paymaster, was ordered to report at Washington, and was released from arrest. As my time would be out in less than two months I was promised a furlough before the troop would go. Colonel Cook[9] would leave Fort Union for Fort Leavenworth in two weeks with a miscellaneous command, and this was my opportunity to go to the "States."

Pitching two wall tents facing each other and stretching a fly to cover the space between, I had a good orderly room and office, and with Corporal Ferguson for a clerk, assisted by Lieutenant Hastings, we proceeded to straighten up all company accounts, and bring everything up to date before my departure. Nothing in the way of clerical work was left undone on Major Chilton's account as well as Hastings'. I had never had a company clerk and no assistance except what Lieutenant Hastings was always glad to render, and assistance from Ferguson or some other in comparing muster rolls. The records will show that when I left the clerical work was complete and there would be no unsettled matters between the troop commander and any of the departments, and there would be no dispute or confusion about any man's account.

I bought a mule, and Hastings gave me a saddle, bridle and blanket. I got permission to put my provisions, blankets, clothing, etc., into a Government wagon in which I might sleep at night. Transportation was scarce and teams heavily loaded. A man on

---

[9] This is Philip St. George Cooke (not Cook), lieutenant colonel, Second Dragoons (see note 3, Part I) who was recalled from Fort Union in the fall of 1854 to join General Harney in the campaign against the Sioux that resulted in the fight at Ash Hollow the following year. See Young, *The West of Philip St. George Cooke,* 262–69, citing an article by Lowe that gives a little more detail on the Santa Fe Trail journey than does *Five Years a Dragoon.*

furlough had no status and no rights. The wagonmaster, Mr. Rice, very kindly invited me to mess with him, which I was very glad to do. The day of my departure came, my last roll call was made at reveille, and I passed from right to left of the troop and shook hands with every man. I was obliged to nerve myself to the utmost to meet this trial, one of the greatest of my life. My work was done, I had turned my back upon my best friends. I would never make better. I never saw any one else similarly affected. I had met and stood as severe shocks as any man of my age that I had ever known, and inwardly prided myself upon being equal to any emergency, but now I seemed bewildered. I went to my tent and pretty soon Hastings came in and said: " 'Tis not too late to re-enlist; perhaps you had best reconsider your determination to leave the troop." This seemed to bring me to my senses. I straightened up and replied: "Lieutenant Hastings, I appreciate all you say and all of the good will that you have ever shown for me, but I have matured my plans for the future. I am tearing myself away from the best friends I ever had and am doing it as a matter of duty to myself. There is nothing in the army for me from my standpoint. I am nearly twenty-six years old, and in another five years I would be thirty-one. I have learned all that I can hope to learn in the army that would assist me in civil life. Surely my services will be worth more out of the army than in it. At any rate I have nerved myself for the trial, the bridges are burned, and there is no retreat." There was one man, Sergeant Worrel, in the hospital. Hastings mentioned the fact thinking I might have overlooked him. I said that I did not have to say "good bye" to him. I had no use for him; he was a thief, and would be guilty of any crime he dared to commit, and I gave the Lieutenant satisfactory evidence that what I said was true, and told him that sooner or later he would find that I was right. I have heretofore stated the end of this foul murderer, and will now drop him.

There were two married men in the troop, Sergeants Peel and Espy. Mrs. Peel and Mrs. Espy gave me a farewell dinner, learning which Mrs. Hastings sent them some delicacies not to be had otherwise. Peel's only son, Percival Lowe Peel, was two years old. Having said "good bye" to Lieutenant and Mrs. Hastings and their lovely children, and to Mrs. Peel and Mrs. Espy and their boys, I started out for the first camp, ten miles. When half way I saw Colonel Fauntleroy, staff, band and D Troop en route from Riado to Union. The short cut that I was on and the road that they were traveling were a mile apart. I wanted to see Bryden, now of the band; in fact I would have been glad to salute the Colonel for the last time, and the adjutant, Lieutenant Magruder,[10] and to say "good bye" to genial old Bandmaster Hooper, who had been my dancing master several winters. I got under a clump of pinyons, sat on the ground and saw them pass. To go down and shake Bryden's hand would never do; it would be a severe trial to say "good bye" to him, and I did not want to trust myself. And so I watched the column, the dear old fellow near the front, his trumpet over his shoulder, the cheering notes of which I would never hear again. It was my last look at all of them except Sergeant Candy of D Troop, now Colonel Candy of the Hampton Soldiers' Home.[11]

Arrived in camp Major Chilton's servant came to say that the Major wanted to see me. When I reported he wanted to know

---

[10] William Thomas Magruder of Maryland was graduated from West Point in 1850 as brevet second lieutenant, First Dragoons; became second lieutenant 1851; regimental quartermaster, 1854–58; first lieutenant, 1855; regimental adjutant, 1860; and captain, 1861. He resigned on October 1, 1862, became assistant adjutant general in the Confederate Army and was killed July 3, 1863, in the Battle of Gettysburg. (Lowe calls him adjutant at a time when he seems to have been quartermaster).

[11] Charles Candy, born in Kentucky, was a resident of Ohio when he enlisted on May 14, 1850, and was assigned as private to Company D, First Dragoons, in which he served to May 14, 1855. He re-enlisted January 28, 1856, as private general services; later was assigned to the First Infantry, and served to January 1, 1861. He became captain and assistant adjutant general of Volunteers on September 21, 1861, and resigned December 3, 1861, to become December 17, colonel of the Sixty-sixth Ohio Infantry. He was commissioned brevet brigadier general of Volunteers for faithful and meritorious service during the Civil War on March 3, 1865, after his muster out on January 14.

how I was fixed for the trip. I told him I would be all right.

We came in the Cimarron route, leaving the old trail near Diamond Springs, turned north to Fort Riley and thence to Fort Leavenworth. At Riley I left the command, and arrived at Fort Leavenworth two days later, and by invitation of Levi Wilson, who was general superintendent of teams, etc., I took my meals at his house, a room having been furnished me elsewhere.

Major Ogden told Mr. Wilson to employ me, and I was put in charge of a small train, five six-mule teams for Fort Riley and met Colonel Cook's command ten miles out. I was warmly congratulated on being so well employed.

This was the beginning of five years' continuous service in the Quartermaster's Department, the most interesting part of which I will sketch hereafter.

Part V
At Fort Riley

† † † † † † † † † † †

LATE IN THE FALL OF 1852, Major R. H. Chilton, with his Troop B, First Dragoons, of which I was then first sergeant, escorted Major E. A. Ogden from Fort Leavenworth on an expedition to locate a new military post in the vicinity of the forks of the Kansas River—the confluence of the Smoky Hill and Republican. The site selected was afterwards named Fort Riley,† now one of the finest military posts in America. Some buildings were erected in 1853 and 1854, most of them temporary, and the post was garrisoned by infantry. I quote the following from an address* delivered by me before the State Historical Society, January 14, 1890:

> "Of all charming and fascinating portions of our country, probably there is none where Nature has been so lavish as within a radius of 150 miles, taking Fort Riley as the center. In rich soil, building material, in beauty of landscape, wooded streams and bubbling springs, in animal life, in everything to charm the eye, gladden the heart, and yield to the industry of man, here was the climax of the most extravagant dream, perfect in all its wild beauty and productiveness; perfect in all that Nature's God could hand down to man for his improvement and happiness."

The Congress that adjourned March 4, 1855, made an appro-

† The post was named in honor of Brevet Major General Bennet Riley, U. S. Army, who entered the service in 1813, and died in 1853. He distinguished himself in campaigns against Indians in Florida, and was brevetted brigadier and major general for meritorious and gallant conduct in the war with Mexico.—EDITOR. [From Lowe's original book.]

* Address delivered before the Kansas State Historical Society, at its twenty-fifth annual meeting, January 15, 1901.

priation for preparing Fort Riley for a cavalry post by erecting new quarters, stables for five troops of cavalry, storehouses, etc., the plans of which were prepared in Washington; and Maj. E. A. Ogden, quartermaster U. S. A., was ordered to take charge of the work. The buildings were all to be of stone to be taken from quarries in the vicinity of the post. The major made contracts with Sawyer & McIlvain—or McIlwain, of Cincinnati, for the necessary woodwork, doors and frames, window-sash, etc., to be made at the factory in Cincinnati and shipped with the necessary lumber, hardware, glass, etc., by boat to Fort Leavenworth, and thence by wagon to Fort Riley. Mr. Sawyer was employed as architect and superintendent. I was post wagonmaster at Fort Leavenworth when the order came to furnish transportation for the men to Fort Riley, and a request from Maj. Ogden that I be placed in charge of it. With fifty six-mule teams, I met, on the Fort Leavenworth levee, about five hundred men, mechanics, laborers, etc., just landing from steamboats, and camped them in Salt Creek Valley. Excepting a few Mexican War veterans, none of these men had ever been in camp. They were just from their homes in Cincinnati or St. Louis, and, as a large percentage of them were married men, this was a novel experience. Fortunately, the day was fine and we got into camp early.

Without incident of much importance we arrived at Fort Riley in four days, without a storm or other serious discomfort. The men cheerfully walked, turn about, in order to make time and get permanently settled. All were located in quarters or camped under canvas, and work in all branches commenced the first week in July. Excavations for foundations, quarrying rock, burning lime, making brick, cutting wood for burning them, hauling rock, sand, wood, etc., burning charcoal—in short, in a few days all of the gangs of mechanics and laborers were adjusted to their work and everything was moving as smoothly as possible. The messing was the most important and the most difficult feature. Some cooks had been brought, but most of them had much to learn about cooking in camp. The carpenters seemed to get along the best, and were from the first to last a fine lot of men and gave no trouble. It fell to my lot, under Major Ogden's instructions, to look generally after all camps, and from my experience to advise the cooks about preparing the food—the same as allowed to soldiers—and to see that the camps were well located.

By the end of July a kiln of brick, lime, and charcoal had been burned, and one two-story stone building finished, except hanging the doors and putting in the windows, and a number of others well under way. This completed building was taken possession of for offices, and two iron safes containing the funds for paying the men were put in the front room. By contract, the men hired to work until the fifteenth of November, and were to be paid half their wages at the end of each month and the balance at the end of the time for which they were hired. They were then to be returned by wagon to Fort Leavenworth, and thence by boat to St. Louis and Cincinnati, whence they came.

Major Ogden, on horseback or on foot, was conspicuous for his general supervision of everything, ready to call attention to any neglect of work that did not seem to be going on to the best advantage, and in that one month of July I learned more than I ever have during the same length of time. There was very little friction, as the major's experience with men and material was extensive, and his well-directed energy and good judgment made all of the departments move as nearly in harmony as was possible among men suddenly taken into camp from their city homes. More than half of them lived in tents. The teamsters probably lived better than any other class of men on the work, as they were accustomed to camp life; some had served in the Army, and were therefore fairly well disciplined and well versed in cooking Government rations. Towards the end of the month a few men became ill, and one or two men died of what was undoubtedly cholera. All hands received their half-month's pay on the first of August and that evening Major Ogden and I rode from camp to camp inspecting all the messes and the manner of living. He talked freely and cheerfully, notwithstanding the feeling of unrest caused by the few cases of sickness, which had been promptly sent to the hospital. He dwelt carefully upon all the details and expressed the opinion that there would be little danger of cholera if the men lived well. He entered into the matter with his usual gentle earnestness, and restored courage and confidence in many whose homes and friends were far away. But this was his last effort; the last cheering words to the men he had brought to this new territory to build what was then considered a great military post. We also went through all of the quarters occupied by the men, accompanied by Mr. Sawyer, in whom the mechanics had great confidence. When Major Ogden arrived to build the post, all of the troops had left for the summer's campaign on the plains, so that of the military there were left only the Army surgeon, Dr. Simmons,[1] Chaplain Clarkson,[2] Bandmaster Jackson and a few other members of the band of the Sixth Infantry, the hospital steward, whose name I am sorry I do not remember,[3] and a young soldier whose term of service would expire in a few months. He acted as orderly for the major. During the night of

[1] James Simons (not Simmons) of North Carolina was appointed assistant surgeon in 1839 and came to the hospital at Fort Riley in April, 1854. At the height of the cholera epidemic in 1855 he left Fort Riley and went to St. Mary's Mission. He was tried by court-martial for deserting his post and was dismissed on January 15, 1856. Lowe in his "Recollections of Fort Riley" (*Kansas Historical Collections*, Vol. VII, p. 112) tells how he, Sawyer, Hopkins, Clarkson, and Martin gave written statements to Major John Sedgwick investigating the affair. Lowe says, "I believe he was reappointed at the foot of the list some years later." Actually Simons was reinstated on October 24 of the same year, and in 1859 was commissioned major surgeon to date from August 29, 1856, the year of his dismissal. Apparently he produced convincing excuse for his defection. He was brevetted lieutenant colonel and colonel for faithful and meritorious service during the Civil War, and was promoted to lieutenant colonel surgeon in 1876. He retired in 1882 and died in 1885. (See also George E. Omer, Jr., "An Army Hospital: From Dragoons to Rough Riders—Fort Riley, 1853–1903," in *Kansas Historical Quarterly*, Vol. XXIII, No. 4, [Winter, 1957], 341–43).

[2] Daniel Clarkson was chaplain at Fort Scott, Kansas, from 1850 to 1853, and at Fort Riley from 1853 to May 14, 1860.

[3] The acting hospital steward during the cholera epidemic was John A. Charters, private, Sixth Infantry (Omer, *loc. cit.*, 341).

At Fort Riley

the first of August cholera developed rapidly. The morning of the second dawned on a camp in great anxiety and distress. Major Ogden had been taken sick and, although every effort was made to keep this information from spreading, it flew like wildfire and caused a panic. A burial party and a gang of men to dig graves were organized. Several died that day. Work was generally suspended, though Sawyer tried to keep men at work, and a few did work, without stopping. I have no idea how many men were sick, but much of the illness was caused by mental anxiety. The slightest indisposition was attributed to cholera, and often resulted in bringing it on. All sorts of wild reports were afloat, and a stranger coming in would think half the garrison in a dying condition, everything was so exaggerated.

Sawyer and Hopkins, the chief clerk, gave special attention to Major Ogden. Martin, whose business it was to keep the men's time, mingled with them in camp and quarters, including the hospital, and gave much attention to burying the dead and nursing the sick. I never saw a cooler or more intelligently nervy man.

I moved all the teams four miles up the Republican River to a fine, dry camp, partly for the safety of the men and partly to prevent mules being stolen to ride away on, several having been already taken. I instructed the men not to leave camp or allow anyone to approach it; built a corral of the wagons for present use; gave orders to corral the mules every night, and set the men to cutting cottonwood poles and building a large corral, which was needed. I knew that the distress was great enough to justify sending an express to Fort Leavenworth for medical assistance. The doctor was utterly unable to meet the demands upon him, and I told Mr. Orton, a wagonmaster, to report to me, ready to go, and mounted on his best mule, but not to let anyone know that he was going. I called to see Major Ogden in the fore part of the evening. There was no hope for him. Sawyer and Hopkins knew it, and asked me for a reliable man to carry letters to Fort Leavenworth. I told them that Mr. Orton was ready, and that I had selected him, much as I disliked to part with him, because

I knew he would get there as quickly as it was possible to go. He left about 10 P.M., August 2, and delivered his letters at Fort Leavenworth about 2 P.M., August 4, having ridden 130 miles on one mule in forty hours. He fed himself and mule several times, but did not sleep.

After Orton had gone, I went to the hospital with Martin. Sawyer had appointed nurses, with promise of extraordinary pay, and they seemed to be trying to do their best, but all the sick had not been brought there. Many were in the camps. The hospital steward was a good man, and stuck to his post cheerfully, but the doctor seemed to have given up, and had not been seen about the sick since morning. Murmuring and discontent were general, and it was known that many men had gone—struck off down the road on foot. About midnight Martin promised to keep moving about if I would lie down awhile, which I did on a buffalo-robe in the office where the safes were. I had scarcely closed my eyes when I heard groans in the room next to me. I looked in and found Hopkins in great agony, with a bad case of cholera. Two men were doing their best for him. I stayed with him a few minutes and then went to the steward, at the hospital, who gave me some brandy. On my way back I called at the doctor's quarters. He came to the door himself. I told him of Mr. Hopkins' illness, and asked if he could go and see him. I saw that he was nearly a physical and mental wreck. He shook his head sadly and said, while he shoved up his sleeves and rubbed his arms and hands: "Mr. Lowe, I am unstrung—unfit for anything. I want to take my family to St. Mary's Mission. I wish you would send me an ambulance. I want to get off as quickly as possible." I told him I had no ambulance under my immediate charge—in fact, there was not then an ambulance at the post. I returned to Hopkins with the brandy, and then went to Major Ogden's headquarters. Sawyer was about receiving his last message to his wife. "Tell her," he said, "that I appreciated her love to the last."

The distress on August 2 was as nothing compared with the horrors of the third. Brevet Major Wood[4] had gone to Fort

At Fort Riley

Kearney with his company, leaving his wife and two children. All had cholera. Brevet Major Armistead, afterwards Major-General Armistead of the Confederate Army,[5] had gone up the Smoky Hill with his company, leaving his wife and two children. His wife had cholera. Additional cases were noted all over the post. Thus the morning of the third opened. An ambulance had gone after Major Armistead. Reverend Mr. Clarkson, the post chaplain, with his wife and niece, were the only nurses for Mrs. Wood and her two children and Mrs. Armistead. I never saw braver or more devoted nurses and friends than the Clarksons. They took Mrs. Armistead's two children home, and did everything that could be done for the others. But Mrs. Wood and her two children and Mrs. Armistead died during the day. Mr. Sawyer wanted to use the messenger—the young soldier acting orderly for the major—but I found him in the room over the office where I had tried to sleep, dying of cholera. Sawyer procured the lead linings from the tea-caddies in the commissary, and had Major Ogden's coffin made air-tight.

Fifteen in all died on the third of August—Major Ogden, Mrs. Armistead, Mrs. Wood and two children, the major's orderly, and nine workmen. A few men were at work all the time, and Mr. Sawyer encouraged them to continue, but their surroundings were distracting. A delegation waited on Mr. Sawyer and earnestly insisted that the balance due them should be paid and they allowed to go. Sawyer explained to them that, even if they were entitled to more pay, it could not be given to them, as there was no one to pay them, and the money was locked up in the safe, which could not be opened. A little after noon I galloped off to

[4] Not identified. Heitman lists no Wood who was an officer of either Sixth Infantry or First Dragoons in 1855, and none who was a brevet major.

[5] Lewis Addison Armistead, born in North Carolina, was appointed to West Point from Virginia in 1834, and was a cadet until February 15, 1836. He was commissioned second lieutenant, Sixth Infantry, in 1839; first lieutenant in 1844; brevet captain for Contreras and Churubusco, brevet major for Molino del Rey, and captain, Sixth Infantry, on March 3, 1855. He resigned on May 26, 1861, became a Confederate brigadier general, and was killed at Gettysburg while leading his brigade in the charge on July 3, 1863 (Pickett's charge).

my camp on the Republican, found everything all right, and no sickness among the fifty men there. I did not dismount, nor did I allow anyone to come near me. I returned to the post about three o'clock, and saw Mr. Sawyer and Rev. Mr. Clarkson sitting on the latter's front porch looking at a band of men in the middle of the parade ground. Sawyer called to me, and I hitched my horse and joined them on the porch. Mr. Clarkson made the following statement: Mr. Robert Wilson, the post sutler, who had a very large stock of goods in his store, had locked up everything and taken his family away in the morning, accompanied by one of Major Ogden's clerks. Soon after I left, about one o'clock, the store was broken into by a gang of men, some goods scattered about, a barrel of whisky rolled out, a head knocked in, and, with tin cups, the men helped themselves. When well liquored up, led by a big stonemason, some of them broke open the building used for the post ordnance department, and armed themselves with guns, pistols, and ammunition.

And there they were, in a half-drunken condition, on the parade ground, airing their grievances, threatening to break open the safes and pay themselves, etc. But a small portion of the revelers armed themselves (about twenty-five), and they formed a circle, with their leader inside, while all sorts, drunk and sober, looked on. We could hear plainly most that was said, and they meant that we should hear; and, if carried out, it looked serious. A committee headed by this fellow had waited upon Sawyer before they broke into the sutler's store and demanded the pay they claimed was due them. Sawyer was a man of good courage, but of quiet disposition, and not a very strong man. Seeing the apparent determination of the fellow and his following, Sawyer parleyed a little, and said that when I came we would consult about it. The man said that if I did not come d——d quick, they would not wait. And this violent demonstration on the parade ground seemed to be a warning to accede to their demand. Of course, Sawyer's reference to me was a mere ruse to gain time and form some plan of action. I suggested that I go and talk to the men,

At Fort Riley

since my name had been mentioned. I knew the leader pretty well, and thought he would listen to me; at any rate, I might check him up until we had a little more time, and perhaps bridge over until he would sober up. I never was more anxious for a good company of soldiers under a good officer.

Sawyer rather demurred at my trying to pacify these men—it was against his judgment, and might precipitate trouble. I assured him that I would not make matters worse. The day was exceedingly hot and I took Sawyer's umbrella. As I approached, I saw that most of this valiant chief's followers were hopelessly drunk. The leader stood in the center flourishing a pistol, which was apparently cocked. A drunken man noticed me, and cried out, "Hurrah for the mounted chief!" a name given me and by which I was generally referred to, because I was always moving about pretty lively on horseback, while others in charge of work or exercising any authority were on foot. I stepped into the circle and said to the leader, "What is the matter, Mr. ———?" Quick as lightning he sprang back and leveled his pistol, and if it had been at full cock, I would have been shot. Up to this time I had no definite plan of action—had no arms and no fixed notion of what I would do. Whatever I did dawned upon me instantly. The violent threats of the man caused me to act; the impulse was irresistible. Dropping the umbrella, I seized his pistol, gave him a trip and quick jerk, and his huge body fell so heavily that the breath was knocked out of him. I had his pistol and threatened to kill him if he moved. As soon as he could get breath, he begged for his life. The crowd seemed dumb. With my left hand I jerked a gun from the nearest man, who was so drunk that he fell over. Throwing the gun on the ground, I told the others to pile their guns and pistols on it. I never saw an order more promptly obeyed.

The mutiny, or rebellion, so far as these men were concerned, was over. I called to a lot of carpenters and asked them to carry the guns and pistols to the quartermaster's office, which they did, and put them by the two iron safes. Quite a quantity of ammunition was disgorged by the disarmed men, and a ridiculous part of it was that much of it was not suitable for the arms they had. But few of the guns were properly loaded, and some not at all. It was a drunken outfit all around. I said but little to them beyond the plain and emphatic statement that no Government property should be molested; no noise or drunken rioting would be permitted; no misbehavior of any kind; and the man who broke one of these rules would do so at his peril, for henceforth the line was drawn, and this was to be considered a notice to all bad men. While I believed that nine-tenths of all the men employed would do their best in this trying time, I exhorted them to stand by and help each other. The fallen and bruised leader protested his sorrow, laying it all to whisky. The indignation expressed by many good men reached the manhood that was trying to assert itself through the fumes of the whisky he had taken. He was a foreman, a fine workman, came to Mr. Sawyer highly recommended, and had a respectable family in Cincinnati. The terrible condition so demoralized him that with the heat and whisky he became crazed. I learned afterwards that he had no hand in breaking into the store, but drank freely when he found the whisky. There had to be a severe check somewhere, to set the reckless element to thinking, and bring the better element to the front and establish leaders.

This was the turning-point. It happened oddly enough, but was effective. Men of different trades organized themselves into squads to keep good order and to assist each other. Nurses volunteered for the hospital and in the camps. Voluntary help came pouring in, though I found that many men had left the post. There was no way of stopping them, and under the circumstances perhaps it was well that they should go. But where could they go? There was no settlement in the immediate country. There was one family at the bridge across the Big Blue, nineteen miles east, and the Catholic mission and Pottawatomie village of St. Mary's, fifty-two miles east, where good Father Duernick had established a college and was gathering in the young Pottawatomies and teaching them, with admirable success, to become good citizens. Here Mrs. Bertram kept the only hotel worth the name between Fort Riley and Leavenworth. Captain Alley's store at Silver Lake, the Pottawatomie homes and the eating-place at Hickory Point finishes the list of settlements, save here and there at long intervals a squatter's shanty. (I do not say "cabin," because that indicates a home built of logs, with a fireplace, where warmth, comfort and contentment abound in winter and cool restfulness in summer.) Such houses did exist at long intervals along the streams, but seldom on the high prairie. A shanty, boarded up and down, with a stovepipe through the roof, was the rule, and a decent man ought to have died alone rather than intrude himself on one of these poor families, under the circumstances.

A small steamboat had run up the Kaw to Manhattan, twenty miles east of Fort Riley. (At the time I write of I had not seen Manhattan, and do not know what settlements were there.) A lot of the stampeders from Fort Riley took possession of her and ran down the river for a few miles, got aground and had to leave her. Martin told me of a raft of logs down in the river, tied to some trees. He learned that the men who had made the raft were waiting for night, when they would cover it with lumber from a pile of pine flooring near by. I went with him, cut all the ropes, and set the logs floating singly down the river. This saved the lumber. The men probably deserted.

Major Armistead's quarters were the second west of the quartermaster's office. Mrs. Clarkson and her niece had prepared the body of Mrs. Armistead for burial, but it was not to be coffined until the major's arrival. Entering the hall through the door from the south porch, one walked about ten feet north and entered a room through a door on the left. At the left of the door stood a bed, with head to the east. From the mantel at the west end of the room a candle shed a dim light over the room and the bed, on which lay Mrs. Armistead, the white bed-clothes covering her as if asleep. Her face was not covered, and to one standing a little way from the bed she seemed to be sleeping peacefully, and no one not cognizant of the fact would have thought her dead—a lovely picture of a lovely woman. Mr. Clarkson informed me that his wife and niece were worn out, but would attend to Mrs. Wood's quarters, where she and her children were coffined, ready for burial in the morning, and he asked me to take charge of the Armistead quarters, which I promised to do.

Counting the time that the ambulance had been gone, I expected the major sometime before midnight. I knew that the faithful driver, K. B. Cecil, now a wealthy farmer of Platte County, Missouri, would spare no effort to bring him quickly. About ten o'clock I heard an ambulance rattling over the stony road, knew it was the major, and dreaded to meet him. As the ambulance stopped at the porch, I opened the door and the major sprang out, shook my hand and inquired: "How about my family?" I hesitated a little, which he interpreted as a bad omen and continued: "Are they all gone—wife, children and all?" "No, major," said I, "your children are safe at Mr. Clarkson's." He said no more then. Taking hold of his left arm, we walked to and stepped inside the room. Taking off his hat, he cried out: "Oh, my poor wife! Oh, my poor wife!" The agony of that minute during which he gazed on her was terrible. I led him gently away. When on the porch, he said: "I will take my children on the plains with me. I will take them away to-morrow." I assured him that I would have his quarters cared for, and he went to Mr. Clarkson's, where his children, a boy and a girl, were located. Martin came to me about midnight; he said he had gotten quite a nap and would relieve me. I went to the office, put an unhung door on the two iron safes, two robes on that, and tried to sleep. I did not fear an attack on the safes, though I was well prepared for it. For two days and nights I had scarcely closed my eyes. I thought I had seen enough suffering and wickedness in this one day to haunt me a lifetime. In the room overhead was the dead soldier; Hopkins, in a critical condition, was in the adjoining

At Fort Riley

room; Major Ogden, Mrs. Armistead, Mrs. Wood and her two children were dead—all within a short distance of each other. Others were still unburied and an additional one reported dead from time to time. Several new cases were reported to me while at Major Armistead's quarters. At the rate of increase the outlook was alarming.

How good comes of evil was illustrated here. The outrage of breaking into the sutler's store and of taking arms from the ordnance building created great excitement throughout the post. Disarming the rioters and their probable immediate departure soon after relieved the minds of the better element, gave new courage, cemented a brotherhood among those remaining, and created a determination to help—to assist instead of destroy; and I have always believed that if I had met nothing but the continued distress prevailing, I should have collapsed. But this exciting episode cleared my head and stirred my energies to greater action, and many others were similarly affected.

I had not slept long when I was aroused by some loose animals rubbing against the front porch. It was three o'clock by my watch. I was surprised that I had slept at all. I then went over to the Armistead quarters. Martin had fastened the door leading from the hall into Mrs. Armistead's room, and he lay asleep in the hall. I mounted my horse, rode to my own tent, where the cavalry stables now stand, and got breakfast. I then went over to the hospital. The dead were being coffined and carried out, while others took their places. Heroic efforts were being made to keep the hospital and bedding clean. Mr. Sawyer had made the best arrangements possible, under the circumstances, for nursing, washing, cleaning quarters, etc., and it was a surprise to me how well the attendants did. To change bedding and attend to the necessities of a long room full of men in the agonies of the fatal disease required attentive and intelligent work. Burial parties were under way, and I rode over to the cemetery and found the grave-diggers already at work under a foreman. I am writing now of the morning of the fourth of August. The doctor and his family had gone; fifteen had died on the third, and probably fifty were under treatment.

In writing this I would like to refer less frequently to myself, but I only tell what came under my own observation—what I saw or knew of. I went to Mr. Sawyer and reported the status of affairs as I saw them. He and Martin would attend to the burial of the major, Mrs. Armistead, Mrs. Wood and her two children. Leaving Sawyer, I went to the dispensary in the hospital to get from the steward a bottle each of brandy and port wine to carry with me on my rounds among the camps. The steward introduced me to a young man who had just come in on horseback, Doctor Whitehorn.[6] He came from Dyer's Bridge, nineteen miles east, near which he had a claim. For fear of doubts of his being a doctor, he was showing the steward his diploma and other testimonials, including a letter from Mr. Dyer. He was a light-built, wiry, sunburned youth, and carried on his saddle the old-fashioned doctor's saddle-bags. I told him that Mr. Sawyer was now at the head of affairs, but that I would introduce him and then show him around, which I did, and he was warmly welcomed. Cholera was a new disease to the doctor, and he was very young; but he was cool, quiet, self-reliant, intelligent, and possessed good judgment. When he entered the hospital, word passed from one to another, "We have a doctor," and this had a good effect. He soon impressed them very favorably. A spoonful of brandy or port wine by the doctor's order would do more good than from me. I spent the forenoon with him, and showed him the quarters, camps, etc.

I then rode to my teamster camp on the Republican River during the afternoon, and found all well. Towards evening, while riding around, I stopped to talk with a young stone-cutter from St. Louis. I had often talked with him and liked him. Major Armistead had selected a stone to be put up at his wife's grave, and this young man was cutting the letters and figures on it. He

[6] Dr. Samuel Whitehorn, recently of Michigan.

At Fort Riley

seemed well and said that he felt so, but he was not as cheerful as usual and I tried to encourage him. The next morning this handsome young fellow joined those on the side of the hill beyond the deep ravine. I mention this instance to show how suddenly and unexpectedly the strongest and best were taken away. I do not know just how many died this day, but about the same number as on August 3. Miss Fox, step-daughter of Foragemaster Lowe, was among those who died on the fourth. I am sorry that I do not remember the names of the men who worked day and night to help those who could not help themselves.

George W. McLain,[7] a newspaper man of Weston, Mo., was driving through the country in a buggy, and came into Fort Riley from Council Grove. On asking for the commanding officer, he learned that he was dead. He found me, and I advised him to drive on and to hold his breath until miles away. He seemed inclined to do that, but could not resist the temptation of getting items enough to write up the conditions. As we passed a small house on our way to his buggy we heard a female voice in great distress. On going in, we saw a woman, wife of a corporal who was away with his company, apparently in the agonies of death. On a bed, with hands, feet and limbs cramped, and a frenzied expression, she was a terrible picture. She had been ill but a short time. There was no one to help her—a woman could not be found to attend her. McLain took off his coat and hat, laid them on a chair, rolled up his sleeves and went to the stove, where there was a kettle with warm water in it—in short, took an inventory of the surroundings. I went to the hospital for brandy and port wine, and when I returned McLain was rubbing the woman vigorously

[7] George Washington McLane (not McLain) started the Leavenworth *Ledger* in the winter of 1856–57, and continued its publication until the war, when he sold it to the *Conservative,* according to *Kansas Historical Collections,* Vol. I–II, 171, which credited the *Ledger* as the first daily west of the Missouri. Nyle H. Miller, secretary, Kansas State Historical Society, says it was preceded by the Lawrence *Kansas Daily Tribune,* a short-lived Free State organ, reported to have been first issued on July 4, 1855. Harry E. Kelsey, Jr., of The State Historical Society of Colorado, reports a McLain (no initials) was editor of the Vulcan *Enterprise,* 1896–99, but finds no record of him in Leadville, where, says Lowe, he died.

and talking to her in the most cheerful manner; told her he was a doctor and would surely cure her. No woman could have handled her better than he did, and, being a strong man, he was not easily tired. He gave her some brandy, and turning to me, said in a low tone: "Lowe, my heart is in this thing. This woman, without a friend within reach, her husband serving his country in the Army, must not be left here to die. She is going to live; I'll see that she does." Turning to her, he said: "I'll wait on you all night and all day tomorrow, until you are well."

I left him in a few minutes, had his team cared for, sent him something to eat, and called early the next morning. The woman was asleep, and McLain said that her symptoms were good. She got well. If she had not thought him a doctor, the shock would have been fatal. This man afterwards became very prominent. He was known throughout the country as General George Washington McLain, started newspapers, and was always a correspondent. He was generous when plenty smiled, and patient when poverty stalked abroad, and after a life of ups and downs, he balanced his accounts, paid off all his earthly debts and passed to his reward a few years ago in Leadville, Colorado. He had lived much at the national capital, knew the prominent men from every State in the Union, and had friends everywhere. He possessed a brilliant mind, and with an unlimited fund of information, was a most charming companion. I never knew his lineage, but the blood that coursed through his heart and fed his brain was not of the common sort. Whatever his faults, and he had them, he deserved a better fate than that which overtook him. His virtues covered his faults miles deep.

Hopkins improved. I firmly believe that much of the sickness was caused by mental trouble—the horrors of the surroundings. There were not so many deaths on the fifth as on the third or fourth, but a good many. The outlook was better. We had lost 150 or more men by desertion. All discordant elements were now gone, and we were getting used to working together.

We had a good deal of pine tar in barrels, brought to the post

At Fort Riley

to mix with gravel as a covering for the stable roofs. Someone suggested that it was a good disinfectant, and on the evenings of August fourth and fifth, when a gentle south wind favored, we had fires built where the fumes and smoke would float into the open windows, and burned tar at all of them. Whether this did much good or not, it counteracted offensive odors. The doctor thought well of it. The night of the fifth I slept well on the top of the safes. There were not so many new cases reported the morning of the sixth, and every good report gave renewed hope. As the sixth wore on I thought it time to hear something from the message sent by Orton. Down the road I saw a four-mule Government ambulance a mile and a half away. I knew it must contain a doctor and probably an officer, and I galloped down to meet it. Just before I met the ambulance my horse sprang suddenly to one side and came near throwing me. He was frightened by a dead Negro, who had died of cholera and been buried in a shallow grave, and the wolves had dug him up and pulled him into a leaning posture, his body mostly uncovered and one arm raised above his head. He was a horrible-looking sight. This had been the camp of the Government hay contractors, Messrs. Dyer & Co.; the Negro was their cook. All the other members of the party had left for their homes in Clay County, Missouri.

The ambulance contained Lieutenant Carr,[8] now General

[8] Eugene Asa Carr (1830–1910) was born in Erie County, New York, and was graduated from West Point in 1850 as brevet second lieutenant in the Regiment of Mounted Riflemen, becoming second lieutenant a year later. He took part in Indian expeditions from Fort Leavenworth in 1852 and 1853, and was wounded in a fight with Mescalero Apaches at Mount Diavolo, Texas, on October 10, 1854. He was promoted to first lieutenant in the new First Cavalry (later Fourth) on March 3, 1855, his commission while temporarily commanding Fort Riley as described by Lowe. He was in the Sioux expedition of that year and was employed in the Kansas border troubles during 1856 and 1857. He was promoted captain in 1858 and took part in the Utah expedition of that year. He was in an expedition to the Antelope Hlils in 1859 and fought Kiowas and Comanche in 1860. In 1861 he led his company from Fort Washita to Fort Leavenworth. At Wilson's Creek he led off the field the only organized remnant of Franz Sigel's brigade and was brevetted lieutenant colonel. He became colonel of the Third Illinois Volunteer Cavalry in 1861. He commanded a division at Pea Ridge and was awarded the

Eugene Carr, retired, and Dr. Samuel Phillips,* my room-mate at Fort Leavenworth, a young contract doctor. I never was more pleased to see a man in my life. Carr I knew as a young officer en route to New Mexico the year before. I was anxious for a commanding officer with authority. The discretionary power of the military commander is very great, no matter what his rank. If not hampered with instructions, he can often do what a man with less power would hesitate to do. I have always admired a man who would not hesitate to take responsibility. Lieutenant Carr was not sent to replace Major Ogden permanently, but to take charge in the emergency and do whatever a good officer could do under the stress of circumstances. These remarks apply also to Phillips. No better man could have been selected for such an emergency. While Carr received from Sawyer an account of the situation, Phillips proceeded at once to the hospital, met Doctor Whitehorn, and went from place to place to examine the sick. The medical department was now under Phillips' control—it had

---

Medal of Honor for holding his ground while several times wounded there. In 1862 he was promoted brigadier general of Volunteers and major, Fifth Cavalry, in permanent rank. He was brevetted colonel for Vicksburg, brigadier general of Volunteers for the capture of Little Rock, major general of Volunteers for the Mobile campaign, and major general "for gallant and meritorious services" during the war. In 1868 and 1869 he commanded the Fifth Cavalry in campaigns against Cheyennes and Sioux, defeating Tall Bull's Cheyennes at Summit Springs, July 11, 1869. He was promoted lieutenant colonel while commanding the regiment in Arizona in 1873. He was with the Fifth Cavalry during General George Crook's campaign against the Sioux in 1876, and became colonel of the Sixth Cavalry in 1879 and brigadier general in 1892. He retired in 1893. It was said of him that he would rather be colonel of a regiment of cavalry than President of the United States. Few officers of the army saw more Indian fighting. See James T. King, *War Eagle, A Life of General Eugene A. Carr* (Lincoln, University of Nebraska Press, 1963).

* Dr. Phillips volunteered for this duty to General E. V. Sumner, then commanding Fort Leavenworth, every one of the many young physicians practicing in the city at Leavenworth declining this service. For this professional work Dr. Phillips was paid by General Sumner less than forty dollars, though his inclinations to pay him a much larger sum were the best. It was all he had at his disposal. Dr. Phillips continues to practice his profession in the city of Leavenworth, and is a vigorous man for his advanced years.—EDITOR. [From Lowe's original book.]

a head with authority. To show the effects of confidence in a doctor, good nursing and encouragement, each day brought fewer cases, men settled down to work more cheerfully, until there was no more cholera. I do not know how many died—in fact, I think I never did know, but the number was not less than seventy-five nor probably more than one hundred.[9] Of the men who left in the excitement, a few were known to have died. I presume the records show all who left, all who died at the post, and all who remained.

The post, since its establishment, had been supplied with water from the Kaw River, just below the junction of the Smoky Hill and Republican. The Smoky Hill was milky and brackish, the Republican clear. The two mingled where the water was dipped up. On the morning of the second I went with the water-wagon and showed the men where they would get water until further notice. Surely the Republican was clear and pure; but feeling some delicacy about assuming authority in a matter of so much importance as the water supply, I took a jug full from each place, and one from a large spring, to Doctor Simmons, and asked him to examine and see which was best. He seemed in great distress about his family, and said that he could give me no advice. Sawyer, Hopkins, Clarkson and Martin thought it a good move, and often afterwards expressed the opinion that, while the water formerly used did not cause the cholera, the Republican water was much safer and probably had something to do with restoring health. For several nights before the cholera broke out, and continuing to the night of the third, we had violent storms of rain, thunder and lightning, lasting several hours and ending about midnight. One would think that this would purify the air—perhaps it did. I do not suggest that the cholera grew out of it, but merely mention it as a peculiar circumstance. No doubt the germs of the disease were brought originally with the men.

Near a spring west of where Junction City now is, two men were attending a lime-kiln. On August 5 I sent a team over after

---

[9] Omer, *loc. cit.*, 342, uses Lowe's figures on the deaths.

a load of lime. A little German from Herman, Missouri (I cannot remember his full name—Henry, we called him), one of the most faithful men I ever knew, drove the team. As he did not come in as soon as I expected, I rode down to the river about dark and met him coming across. He said that one man was "bad sick" when he got there. He helped the other man care for the sick one until he died. They put the dead man in the wagon and started, and the other one was now sick. The teamster had to stop many times to help the sick man, who "go died" just before the team reached the river. The poor teamster was greatly distressed, and apologized for not bringing the lime. He had volunteered to go because the lime-burners were his friends, and he wanted to see how they were getting along. He lived through and conveyed the dying messages of the two to their friends.

From day to day there was improvement, work went on in all departments, and more men were sent from Fort Leavenworth to take the places of those who died or deserted. Lieutenant Corley,[10] Sixth Infantry, relieved Lieutenant Carr, and by the first of September everything was in full blast and work progressing rapidly. Some building supplies were needed and work would be retarded unless they were brought quickly. I was ordered to take thirty six-mule teams and go after them. I got the order at three o'clock P. M. The wagons were all dismantled, covers and bows stored away, and the beds arranged for hauling stone, sand, lime, wood, brick, or any sort of building material. By sunset I had thirty wagons full rigged, thirty of the best mule teams ready to hitch to them, and rations and forage drawn, all ready to start.

An expressman started about that time with requisition for the supplies that I was to bring, and I told him to say to the shipping clerk at Fort Leavenworth that I would not be long behind him,

---

[10] James Lawrence Corley of South Carolina was graduated from West Point in 1850 as brevet second lieutenant, Sixth Infantry. He became second lieutenant in 1851 and first lieutenant on March 3, 1855. He served as regimental quartermaster from June 17 to November 27, 1855, and then as regimental adjutant until April 29, 1861. He resigned on May 4, 1861, and served as quartermaster colonel in the Confederate Army through the Civil War. He died on March 28, 1883.

At Fort Riley

and would start back as soon as I could load, and to please have the loading so arranged that there would be no delay. I wrote a note to my friend, Levi Wilson, general superintendent, requesting him to look a little after the requisition, because several hundred men might be delayed more or less on the work at Fort Riley, and I wanted to make a trip that would beat any record for moving six-mule teams. The expressman laughed at the idea of my reaching our common destination soon after he did. I started at sunrise the next morning and camped in Salt Creek Valley, three miles from Fort Leavenworth, the third evening—127 miles in three days—about 42 miles per day. I rode to the post that evening, only twenty-four hours behind the expressman; and he had started eleven hours ahead of me on a good saddle-mule. I spent the evening with friends talking over the exciting events at Fort Riley, of which they had heard many exaggerated accounts. I had been reported dead of cholera at one time and killed by a mob at another. I returned to camp at midnight, and at seven o'clock the next morning was loading at the warehouses and steamboat landing, and by four in the afternoon I was back in Salt Creek Valley, heavily loaded. There was much talk that day about the quick trip I had made, and everybody expected to see the mules in bad condition, and was surprised to see a fine lot of mules and active, wide-awake teamsters—no one hanging back in a tired way, but all pushing and trying to help along. I rolled out of Salt Creek Valley the next morning, and before sunset of the fourth day parked my train at Fort Riley having made about thirty-two miles per day. The mules were turned into the herd up the Republican, tired but uninjured. We had been eight days and seven nights traveling 260 miles, including loading. No one expected me for two days more, and the fact that no mules were killed or injured, beyond being tired, which they would make up in a week's rest, was a surprise.

Government teams generally make one drive per day. I have seldom met an Army man who did not insist upon doing his day's work, long or short, and then going into camp. I had learned on the Santa Fé Trail how Aubrey, Bent, Maxwell and all the Mexican freighters worked their teams—two and three drives a day. To drive teams with empty wagons forty-two miles a day, or loaded thirty-two miles a day, would soon ruin them, if the drives were continuous. Having made about one-half of my day's drive, I halted, took off harness, and turned the mules loose with lariats on, but without picket-pins. They rolled, drank freely, and grazed an hour, while the men ate dinner. Arrived in camp for the night, the mules were turned loose again the same way, and before dark were caught up, fed corn, and picketed for the night. The first thing in the morning they were watered, then fed corn, and, breakfast over, were hitched up and started usually by sunrise. No corn was fed at noon, but the grass was fine and much better for them. On the evening of my return I showed the quartermaster and Mr. Sawyer my memorandum of the contents of each wagon—each numbered and its contents put down under the number. From this they knew where each wagon should be unloaded.

From this time there seemed to be no check, deficit, or friction: a sort of steady discipline, rare among large numbers of men of various trades in civil life, prevailed all the way through, and all that could be expected was accomplished. Undoubtedly the retained pay had a steadying influence, but I think that after the exodus, during the prevalence of cholera, there was a remarkably good set of men left. I have always thought that sending the troops away during the building of the post was a mistake. Taking five hundred men there who were governed only by self-interest, with no law to curb the bad element sure to exist in any body of men, seemed to be not a wise move, when Armistead and Wood, with their companies, could just as well have remained in the vicinity, changing camp from time to time, and been within call if needed.

I will now refer briefly to the Ogden monument. The original was designed by Mr. Sawyer, and prepared and erected by quarrymen, stone-cutters, laborers and teamsters, under the direction of

At Fort Riley

Mr. Sawyer and myself, without other cost to the Government than the pay of the men while the work was being done. The stone was of the kind used in the buildings of Fort Riley. In time, neither the Government nor anyone else heeding it, cattle made of it a rubbing-post, vandals chipped pieces from it and scratched their names on it, and it became a wreck. It was not expected to be permanent, the hope of the builders being that it would be replaced with something worthy of the man whose memory it was intended to perpetuate—commensurate with his ability and devotion to duty; a monitor to all entrusted with the care and control of others. Another shaft was afterward erected, much better than the original, but not what it ought to have been. I do not know how nor where the money was raised, nor under whose direction it was put up. This, too, was neglected, left a rubbing-post for cattle after the wooden fence around it rotted down; and vain simpletons, who like to "see their names and faces in all public places," defaced the stone.

In 1887 General James W. Forsyth,[11] then colonel of the Seventh Cavalry, took command of Fort Riley. He had never known Major Ogden, and until I, while on a visit to Fort Riley, told him the story of the death of Ogden and the erection of the

---

[11] James William Forsyth of Ohio was appointed to West Point in 1851; was commissioned second lieutenant, Ninth Infantry in 1856; and during 1861 was promoted to first lieutenant and captain and transferred to the Eighteenth Infantry. He was awarded brevets as major for Chickamauga, lieutenant colonel for Cedar Creek, colonel for Five Forks, brigadier general of Volunteers for Opequan, Fisher's Hill, and Middletown, and brigadier general for gallant and meritorious service during the war. Meanwhile he served as major assistant adjutant general of Volunteers in 1864 and lieutenant colonel assistant inspector general until he became brigadier general of Volunteers on May 19, 1865, serving until January 15, 1866. That year he was promoted to major in the new Tenth Cavalry. From 1869 to 1878 he was lieutenant colonel on General Sheridan's staff, at first as aide and later as military secretary. He became lieutenant colonel of the First Cavalry in 1878 and colonel of the Seventh Cavalry in 1886, leading that regiment in its encounter with the Sioux at Wounded Knee. He was promoted brigadier general in 1894 and major general in 1897. He retired that year. He is often confused with George Alexander Forsyth, also of Sheridan's staff, who commanded scouts in the Beecher Island fight.

shaft, he did not know its history. He then knew that it was in memory of a brother officer who died at his post in the discharge of duty under the most trying circumstances, and he took prompt measures to preserve it. He secured a small allowance from the Quartermaster's Department with which, and some labor within his control, he had it repaired—scratches worked out and a permanent iron fence put around it.[12]

About the first of November, Major Ogden's remains were disinterred and shipped to Unadilla, New York, where they now rest under a beautiful monument erected by his brother officers and friends. *Requiescat in pace.*

A part of the Second Dragoons came up from Texas in October, 1855. Colonel Cooke came in from the Harney expedition against the Sioux, with more of the Second Dragoons, to take command of the post. On the fifteenth of November, all of the workmen who were entitled to be paid off and transported back to St. Louis and Cincinnati loaded their effects into wagons that I had ready for them—fifty six-mule wagons—and in four days I landed them on the levee at Fort Leavenworth, where boats were waiting to take them away.

[12] Lowe's "Recollections of Fort Riley," follows Part V word for word to this point. Here is interpolated the material summarized in note 1 and two further paragraphs and a footnote on the later history of Fort Riley.

Part VI
The Kansas War of 1856

✝ ✝ ✝ ✝ ✝ ✝ ✝ ✝ ✝ ✝ ✝

AND NOW THE KANSAS WAR WAS ON. I was acting post wagonmaster at Fort Leavenworth, when one night in May, about ten o'clock, Lieutenant J. E. B. Stuart,* regimental quartermaster, First Cavalry, rode in with a requisition for forage and rations for Colonel Sumner's command, camped southwest of Westport, Missouri. He had ridden from there, thirty-four miles, since noon. The command would be out of forage and provisions the next day, and the order was to have the supplies there in time for issue the day after. I was instructed to have teams in from the nearest train, camped nine miles south, as early as possible. I sent word to the watchman at the stable to bring my horse and wake me at two o'clock, which he did.

* James E. B. Stuart was born in Virginia and graduated from the Military Academy at West Point in 1854. He was then promoted brevet second lieutenant of United States Mounted Riflemen and reported to his regiment in Texas. In March 1855 he was promoted second lieutenant of the First United States Cavalry (now the Fourth), and served as quartermaster of that regiment from July 1855 until May 1857. He became first lieutenant of the First Cavalry in December 1855. and captain in April 1861.

In May 1861 he resigned and accepted a commission in the Confederate service as lieutenant-colonel of a Virginia regiment. His promotion in the Confederate Army was rapid, and he was a lieutenant-general commanding the cavalry of General Lee's army when he received his mortal wound at Yellow Tavern. He died May 12, 1864.

Stuart saw varied and active service during the time that he was a lieutenant in the First United States Cavalry. He was in several expeditions and combats with various Indian tribes, and was severely wounded in a fight with the Cheyennes in 1857. He took an active part in the Kansas disturbances of the fifties, and was in Colonel Albert Sidney Johnston's Utah Expedition in 1858. He was at home on leave of absence in 1859, and accompanied Colonel Robert E. Lee as a volunteer aide-de-camp in the expedition to suppress John Brown's Raid.

At 3:30 in the morning I was in nine-mile camp, breakfasted and started back at 4:30, and before 7 we were loading at the forage yard and commissary. At nine o'clock the train started down the road. We arrived at nine-mile camp, fed and watered the mules, and lunched and at 1:30 were on the road again. I did not expect to go any further, but Stuart came along just then and said the quartermaster had left it with him, and he wanted me to stay with him all the way through, which I did. The roads were exceedingly bad the last few miles before reaching the ferry, and it was dark when we got the last wagon over the Kaw. The way to Colonel Sumner's camp was over a crooked road little traveled, much of the way through timber and mud holes, with no bridges over creeks and deep gullies. Fortunately, the moon gave a dim light. Several wagons were upset, several trees had to be cut down where the road was too narrow and crooked, and in many places limbs must be cut to give room for wagons to pass. In short, at 1 A.M., after the most incessant toil, we camped near Colonel Sumner's command. I rode with Stuart to headquarters, where he reported his arrival with train and supplies. He loaned me a pair of blankets, and we both lay down in his tent for a nap. I was nearly worn out. Stuart had been a quiet witness of a very hard struggle, and but for his piloting we should not have gotten there that night, for he was the only one of the party who had been over the road.

At sunrise I started for my camp about two miles out and overtook Lieutenant Ransom,[1] late General Ransom of the Confederate Army, and said "Good morning," calling his name. He looked at me very sharply and returned my greeting pleasantly enough, but I thought coolly, as we were on the best of terms. I asked where he was going so early, and he said "To Fort Leavenworth." I replied that I was going there too. Just then we crossed

[1] Robert Ransom of North Carolina was graduated from West Point in 1850 as brevet second lieutenant, First Dragoons, became second lieutenant, 1851; first lieutenant, 1855; regimental adjutant, 1855–57; and captain, 1861. He resigned on May 24, 1861, and became a major general in the Confederate Army. He died January 14, 1892.

The Kansas War of 1856

a clear stream of water, I dismounted, dropped my horse's rein, and remarked that I would bathe a little and overtake him. He looked askance at me and turned off to ride up to a group of officers' tents on the hill near by. In a clump of willows I took a pretty good bath, wiped myself with a towel that I carried in my holster, combed my hair and whiskers with my fingers, and went on to the group of tents where Ransom had stopped. With him were several officers in front of a tent, seemingly paying considerable attention to me. As I rode up they all laughed heartily. The joke seemed to be on Ransom. He said that he had no idea who I was, but that I was the hardest looking man he ever saw. I was haggard and weary from want of sleep, my hands and face were black with dust and mud, my clothes muddy from head to foot, and my horse and equipment no better. Ransom's description of me was weird indeed, and he declared that he was afraid to ride with me. He had started without arms, and called on Lieutenant Johnson[2] to borrow a pistol. Now that I was cleaned up a little they all knew me. At my camp we got some breakfast and rode to Fort Leavenworth, where we arrived about two o'clock. I was as good as new the next day.

Things kept getting worse in Kansas; marching columns and guerrilla bands of both parties (Pro-Slavery and Free State) were moving about all along the border. Outrages were committed by both parties, but the worst feature of the warfare was the raids on homes, ostensibly for political reasons, really very often for robbery and plunder. It seemed necessary to keep United States troops in camps and on the move as protection to good citizens of both parties and to keep the threatening columns apart. United States troops were stationed near Westport, Franklin, Prairie or Baldwin City, Lecompton, etc. These camps were headquarters from which troops could move quickly when neces-

[2] Probably Robert Johnston (not Johnson) of Virginia, who was graduated from West Point in 1850 as brevet second lieutenant, First Dragoons; second lieutenant, 1853; first lieutenant, 1855; resigned in 1861; and became colonel of the Second Virginia Cavalry in the Confederate Army. He died July 8, 1902.

sary, and must be supplied every ten days with forage and provisions. Something like one hundred wagons were required for that purpose, and I was detailed by the quartermaster, Major Sibley,[3] to look after them. Most of the supplies went by Lawrence, crossing the ferry there, when the wagons for Franklin were sent off under an assistant wagonmaster, those for Baldwin City under another, and those for Lecompton, the largest command, under another, etc.

After crossing at Lawrence, I generally went on to Lecompton, ten miles, and after finishing there, rode across country to other camps if necessary, returning to Lawrence about the time the wagons from different points reached there, and then to Fort Leavenworth for another ten days' supply. While the teams were not overworked, I was very much so. I never worked so hard and so continuously from May to October as I did this season; five months of exposure and overwork, which would have ruined any man of weak constitution; and it nearly ruined me.

The last trip I started on was with a train of supplies for some troops opposite Topeka. Having delivered them I was to ride across to Lecompton and then to Lawrence. The train under Mr. Beery started early, but I did not get off until afternoon. I was ill enough to be in bed, but said nothing of it. I rode alone, and was so sick that I could scarcely sit my horse, and afraid to dismount lest I could not mount again. In this condition I arrived at a house on Stranger Creek, east of the crossing near Easton. I did not know the people, but dismounted, staggered into the house, and was unconscious. About eight o'clock the next morning I opened my eyes and recognized the woman standing over me bathing my temples and forehead as the one I had seen when I dismounted. I felt a little light headed, but my mind was clear.

[3] Ebenezer Sprote Sibley was born in Ohio and appointed to West Point from Michigan. He was commissioned second lieutenant, First Artillery, in 1827; first lieutenant, 1834; and captain assistant quartermaster in 1838. He was brevetted major for Buena Vista. He became major quartermaster on December 22, 1856. He became lieutenant colonel deputy quartermaster general in 1861. He resigned April 15, 1864, and died in 1884.

The Kansas War of 1856

I imagined, however, that I had been there three days, from Tuesday to Friday.

The supplies in the train were for two commands some distance apart, and I had the papers, invoices, number of wagons to go to each place, the contents of each wagon, etc. The wagonmaster knew nothing about the distribution of goods, and, if this was Friday, they were a day behind and there would be confusion. However, I soon learned that my idea of the time I had been there was but a delirium, and this was Wednesday morning. I had been there from five o'clock Tuesday to eight o'clock Wednesday. This good woman had watched over me all night. Mr. and Mrs. Martin Hefferlin were the people, and I might have died but for their kindness. My fever lasted nearly all night, during which I was quite violent, requiring close attention; and now I was nearly helpless, but my mind was clear. I inquired what time the stage for Fort Riley would pass, and Mrs. Hefferlin said in about an hour. I bundled up my papers and memorandum book, wrote a short explanation and gave it to the stage driver, whom I happened to know, and who promised to give them to the wagonmaster. I found I could not ride, and returned to the fort with Lieutenant Buford* (afterwards General Buford) who

* John Buford was born March 4, 1826, in Kentucky, and graduated from the Military Academy at West Point in 1848. He was then promoted brevet second lieutenant of the First Dragoons, and the next year second lieutenant of the Second Dragoons. In 1853 he became first lieutenant, and in 1859 captain of the same regiment. In 1861 he was appointed major in the Inspector General's Department, brigadier general of Volunteers in 1862, and major general of Volunteers of the sixteenth December, 1863. He died in Washington a few minutes after his major general's commission was placed in his hand.

There are no names upon its honor roll in which the American cavalry feel a keener and a juster pride than in that of General Buford. He was an example to emulate from the beginning to the end of his brilliant but too short career. He died at the age of thirty-seven.

From the date of his graduation until the outbreak of the Civil War, he was constantly and actively engaged with his regiment on the Western frontier in various Indian wars, the Kansas disturbances, and the Utah expedition. As an inspector he remained on duty about the defenses of Washington during the first years of the war, but was then assigned to the duty his active spirit yearned for—the command of cavalry of Bull Run, but in less than a month was back on duty as chief was en route from Fort Riley in an ambulance. For two weeks I alternately shook with chills and burned with fever, but finally pulled out.

The incidents of this summer's work were numerous, but would be mostly uninteresting now. The history of the Kansas War has been written by many able pens, some truthful and some garbled and exaggerated. My part in it was that of an humble employé of the Government. It was not my right or privilege to carry the news from Lawrence, the Free State headquarters to Leavenworth, the Pro-Slavery headquarters, nor vice versa. Of course a great deal came under my observation that might have been useful to either party, but my life was at stake every day if I became a newsbearer in either direction. Both parties contained zealots and enthusiasts who would hesitate at nothing to crown themselves with glory by killing some one on the other side. Most of the men on either side were merely struggling for a principle—whether Kansas should be a free or a slave State—whether they should build homes, as most of them wanted to, in a free or a slave State; and most of both parties were honest, and willing to abide the result of a fair vote; but neither could shake off the element that joined for adventure, for revenge, for robbery, for murder; and that element was a curse to both parties.

I was present at Lecompton when the compromise was effected, and both parties settled down to peace in the fall of 1856. Pro-Slavery and Free State agreed to keep the peace and frown down every disturbing element. Captain Sam Walker[4] was placed in

---

of cavalry in the Army of the Potomac in the Maryland campaign. A history of this cavalry is a history of Buford from the time he joined it till he was borne away from it to die of a brief illness.

Buford chose the field for the battle of Gettysburg, and with his cavalry division held back Heth's Confederate infantry division until General Reynolds arrived with his corps. The Union owes to him, more than to any other man, its victory at Gettysburg.

[4] Samuel Walker was born October 19, 1822, in Franklin County, Pennsylvania. In 1848 he went to Ohio where he worked as a cabinetmaker. After a visit to Kansas in 1854, he returned in April, 1855, at the head of an emigrant party and settled near Lawrence. When the sheriff of Douglas County warned Walker to leave the

The Kansas War of 1856

command of a company of Free State men, and Captain John Wallace[5] in command of a company composed of the best ele-

country, Walker instead raised a free state company of eighty-six men, called the Bloomington Guards, in which he served as first sergeant. When James H. Lane appeared at the head of an "army" at the Kansas border, Walker was sent to persuade Lane to abandon the idea of entering Kansas with an armed force. Walker escorted Lane personally to Topeka; the "army" drifted in without fanfare, although John Brown was at hand to pilot the main body. Walker was elected to the lower house of the legislature under the unrecognized Topeka constitution; he also served as colonel of the Fourth Cavalry and took part in the sieges of Lawrence and Fort Sanders and commanded at the capture of Fort Titus. In September, Governor John W. Geary invited Walker to come to Lecompton, promising him safe conduct. At the Executive office Walker met Colonel Titus, whose house (Fort Titus) was burned by Walker's orders. Walker's home had been burned in retaliation. Says the "Executive Minutes of Gov. Geary": "These men were, perhaps, the most determined enemies in the Territory. Through the Governor's intervention, a pacific meeting occurred, a better understanding took place, mutual concessions were made, and pledges of friendship were passed; and, late in the afternoon, Colonel Walker left Lecompton in company with, and under the safeguard of, Colonel Titus. Both these men have volunteered to enter the service of the United States as leaders of companies of territorial militia." This is the Lecompton compromise to which Lowe refers.

Walker was four times elected sheriff of Douglas County, the first term beginning in October, 1857. He was also deputy United States marshal, and in this capacity he was ordered by Governor James W. Denver in 1858 to arrest James Montgomery, a Free State leader who was planning a raid on Fort Scott. After hearing Montgomery's side of the story, Walker accompanied him and his following to Fort Scott, where Walker arrested George W. Clarke, a Pro-Slavery leader. Walker then arrested Montgomery. When Clarke was released on a writ of habeas corpus, Walker released Montgomery.

In the Civil War, Walker became captain of Company G, First Kansas Volunteer Infantry on June 1, 1861; major of the Fifth Kansas Cavalry in 1862; and lieutenant colonel of the Sixteenth Kansas Cavalry in 1864. He led that regiment in the Sioux campaign during the summer of 1865, remaining in service until December 6. He was brevetted colonel and brigadier general. He was elected state senator in 1872. He died at Lawrence on February 6, 1896.

(William H. Coffin, "Settlement of the Friends in Kansas," *Kansas Historical Collections*, Vol. VII, 349, note cited from Vol. VI, 249; "Executive Minutes of Governor John W. Geary," *Kansas Historical Collections*, Vol. IV, 559; William E. Connelley, *A Standard History of Kansas and Kansans* [Chicago, New York, Lewis Publishing Co., 1918], Vol. II, 688–90; Jay Monaghan, *Civil War on the Western Border* [Boston, Toronto, Little, Brown & Co., 1955], 72–78, 83–86, 92–94, 101–108, 147, 171, 323.)

5 John Wallis (not Wallace) was a Kansas slaveholder and captain of Company

ment of the Pro-Slavery party—all pledged to act together for the common good and the peace and prosperity of the Territory. Homes became safe, murder and arson were unpopular.

One lovely Sabbath, while encamped near Lecompton, I saw half a dozen houses burning—all belonging to Free State people, who were afraid to remain at home and were at Lawrence. Colonel Cooke entrusted to my care a Free State minister who had been captured by the Pro-Slavery party, and whose home was near Leavenworth, and requested me to see that he got home to his family. He was the Rev. J. H. Byrd. I kept him concealed in a wagon, and he got home safely, was in charge of the Government farm at Fort Leavenworth during the Civil War, and died on his farm near Lawrence in September, 1897.

The ferry at Lawrence was a flat-boat run by pulleys on a rope stretched across the river and fastened to a tree on either side and propelled by the force of the current. The boat was not large enough to hold a wagon and six mules, so the leaders were detached from the team and led around to a shallow ford higher up stream, where one might cross on horseback or with loose animals, but could not cross wagons. A Frenchman, married to a Delaware woman and living with the Delaware Indians on the north side of the river, built a boat and stretched a rope; and when I came along one day he met me two miles north of the ferry and wanted me to cross some of my wagons on his boat. I galloped on and found that he had made a good road and had a good boat that would carry a wagon and six-mule team, with room to spare; so I divided the train, going to the new ferry, about forty rods below the old one, myself with Mr. Lanter, an assistant wagonmaster, while Mr. Beery went to the old ferry. Just as the first wagon got

---

A, Mounted Riflemen, Kansas Militia, from September 15, 1856, to November, 1856. Wallis also lived in Douglas County, just south of Lecompton, according to information from Nyle H. Miller, Secretary, Kansas State Historical Society. Lowe probably meant Wallis, but the "Executive Minutes of Gov. Geary" (see preceding note) make Col. Titus the opposite number of Sam Walker in the Lecompton compromise.

on the ferry, I noticed that the old boat was on the south side and Beery was calling the ferryman. As we were about shoving off, the man who ran the old ferry called to me not to attempt to cross wagons on that (the new) ferry; if I did, he would cut the rope and send me down the river; and suiting the action to the word, he caught up an ax and started at a run for the big cottonwood tree where the rope was fastened. We were now in the stream and rapidly nearing the south bank. Standing on the front of the boat with pistol ready, I warned him to stop, and that if he attempted to cut the rope, I would surely kill him.

The boat landed and he stopped within ten feet of the tree. I ordered him back to his boat, at the same time asking him what he meant. He declared that the Frenchman had no charter to run a boat, hence, no right, while he had a charter from the Territorial Legislature for fifteen years. On the other hand, the Frenchman claimed that the Delawares owned the land on the north side, and had just as much right to land on the south side without any charter as the other fellow had to land on the Delaware reservation, over which he claimed that the Legislature had no jurisdiction. I ended the controversy by telling the Frenchman to cross all the wagons he could, and that I would protect him. I told the old ferryman to get his boat in motion quickly or I would run it with my men, and that the ferry which crossed the most wagons would get the most money. As to their quarrel, they could settle that before the courts or any other place—I knew nothing, nor did I care anything about their rights or the law; here were two ferries, and I was going to use them. I had the teamster of the first wagon drive close to the tree and told him to shoot any one attempting to approach it; and he, that same gentle, quiet, nervy "Bill" Curran, would have done it if necessary. Then I got aboard the old ferry and gave the ferryman one more chance to run his own boat, and just as I was about to let go, he and his man jumped on. He was sulky and threatened to report me to Colonel Cooke at Lecompton. I cut him off short with the answer, that I did not care a ——— what he did, so that he lost no time with the ferry; and I told Beery to push things with the new ferry, while I stayed with the old one. All worked with a will, but the old ferry lost two trips to start with, and in the end the new ferry had six wagons the most. All, more than seventy wagons, were crossed in time to camp south of town before dark, whereas without the new ferry half of them would have camped in the bottom north of the river.

The next day, after finishing my business at the camp at Lecompton, I called at Colonel Cooke's headquarters, as I always did before leaving his camp, and there was the complaining ferryman. Having finished his business with me, the Colonel said that Mr. ——— had made serious charges against me. I asked what they were, and the Colonel told the man to state his case in my presence. He did so with a good deal of feeling, but substantially correct, and I so admitted. "Well, what did you do it for?" asked the Colonel severely. I then stated that being in charge of a trainload of supplies for troops in the field, some of whose rations and forage would be exhausted the next day, I came to a river where I had been in the habit of using the ferry, and found another one complete and ready for use. Knowing nothing of any one's rights, and caring for nothing but to use all the means within my reach to get across with the least delay, I had used both ferries, and in doing so was obliged to treat Mr. ——— very harshly; and if he thought I would permit him to cut the ferry-rope and send me sailing down the Kaw River he was much mistaken; and if he ever attempted it again, he would fare worse. "Well, what have you to say to that?" asked the Colonel, turning to the ferryman. The man bristled a little in a loud voice, when the Colonel said, "Stop, sir, stop! You are a ——— fool, and I will give you this advice: never try such a thing again on a good soldier. Mr. Lowe seems to know how to move trains to supply troops in the field—that is what he is employed for." The man left, and the Colonel remarked that he did not think I would have any more trouble with that fellow; to which I replied that I did not think he would "balk" again. This made the Colonel smile, and "balk" became a by-word among the officers, applied to any one who failed to move freely when told to do anything.

I crossed many times afterwards, and each ferry worked its best for the most money. The Frenchman generally captured the best of it by two or three wagons. The Frenchman kept the approach to his ferry in perfect shape, so that there would be no delays, and the old ferryman kept up the competition—result, a great saving in time and talk.

I saw John Brown but once. He came walking into Lawrence, looking like a shaggy lunatic. The class of people who shouted for "Captain John Brown" were the negative characters, always ready to be mixed up with any kind of notoriety, though not amounting to anything themselves. The substantial, thinking portion of the populace looked on, shook their heads, and, if they expressed themselves at all, it was an expression of contempt for that class of people. Brown was no hero among them, but was looked upon as a disturbing element. I never expected him to gain any respectable notoriety, and he did not in the Kansas War; and if he had not made the Harper's Ferry raid and been executed therefor, he would soon have been forgotten, or remembered only for his crimes. I do not know of one generous, manly, high-minded act that he did in Kansas, nor one for which he deserved honorable remembrance. On the other hand, his ranting lunacy and bad advice caused many murders on both sides. He was so wrapped up in the idea of the freedom of the slaves, that with others of like ilk he did not hesitate to steal Negroes from their masters in Missouri, and this always justified him in stealing provisions for them to subsist upon, and transportation to carry them off. Many poor "darkies" were taken from homes against their better judgment through the persuasion and semi-coercion of the disturbing element who came to Kansas in the name of freedom, and made themselves notorious as border robbers and thieves. This element, with that which came from Missouri to carry the elections and override the will of the genuine settlers, together with the political adventurers, caused all the trouble. No better people ever settled a State than those who came to Kansas to make homes.

A young man, well dressed and well mounted, rode one evening into my camp west of Little Stranger Creek, and told me of a terrible battle that had been fought between Big Stranger and the home of Tonganoxie, a Delaware chief, about half-way between Leavenworth and Lawrence. Though he was not a participant in the battle, he thought his information correct. He said I should find dead men scattered about in considerable numbers; that the Free State and Pro-Slavery forces had met there, etc. A few words about this young man. He took supper with me, fed his horse and slept in my tent, and after breakfast left for Leavenworth, promising to take my advice and leave Kansas, which he did; but after peace was declared he returned, went to Denver and Montana, came back, drifted into the cattle business, became a millionaire, raised a prominent family of worthy people, and died in Kansas City a few years ago. He was always thankful that he had kept away from Captain Miller's band of "peace makers," allied himself with good men and led a good life.

The next morning at a point two miles east of Tonganoxie's house, at a place now called Moore's Summit, after the Hon. Crawford Moore who owned a large tract of land there, I found lying in the road a dead man, about thirty years old, dressed like a respectable mechanic. He lay upon his back, pockets turned out as if he had been robbed, a small bunch of keys near his trousers pocket. He had been shot twice, the last time evidently after he fell, in the top of his head. Evidently a number of horses and men had been there, but after riding in a circle a long distance round, I failed to find another body. Captain Sacket came along and had the body buried. I related the circumstance of finding the dead man, as I went through Lawrence, but no one knew who it was.

On my return a man met me at the ferry on the Lawrence side, G. W. H. Golding by name, and stated that he and three others, Roberts, Zimmerman and Brown (not John) had been driven out of Leavenworth on account of their open confession that they wanted Kansas to be a free State. Golding was a gunsmith, Roberts a carpenter, Brown and Zimmerman other trades. All had worked at their respective trades and had not been mixed up in any difficulties. They had been notified to leave, and had started to walk to Lawrence. When near Tonganoxie's house, a mounted company of fifty or more men made them prisoners. They told their story and were damned as Abolitionists. Everybody who wanted to live in a free State and wanted Kansas to be a free State for that reason, was denounced as an Abolitionist and a dangerous character. The percentage of Abolitionists among the Free State men was very small. The sentiment of nearly all men from Northern States and many from Missouri and other Southern States, was in favor of making Kansas a free State. They did not care to meddle with slavery where it existed, but wanted the new State free, where they hoped to make homes, because they believed it best for themselves and families. I met men from Kentucky, Georgia, Virginia and Maryland who wanted Kansas to be free, and they were among the best settlers.

The captain of the troop of rangers who captured these men did not want to be encumbered with them, and concluded to leave them at Tonganoxie's house under guard, and four men volunteered to guard them. Tonganoxie had gone off, as many others had, to remain away until the troubles were settled. These four guards with their prisoners took possession of the house. About midnight they started under pretence of taking the prisoners back to Leavenworth, but really to find an excuse for murdering and robbing them. The prisoners were required to walk, one on the right side of each of these mounted men, and at a signal all were shot at. Golding was shot near the left ear, the bullet ranging downward. He fell and bled profusely, but lay quiet, nearly choking to death with blood, for fear they would shoot him again. The ruffians felt his pulse and one was about to shoot him again, when another said, "Don't waste your shots; no man ever bled that much and lived." Roberts struggled some and was shot again. Brown lay still; they felt his pulse and pounded him on the head with the butt of a gun. Zimmerman was pronounced dead. All were robbed (they had considerable money), the robbers riding off at a gallop. Golding supposed his companions dead, turned over and relieved himself of the blood in his throat, found that he could walk, and finally made his way through the prairie and timber, keeping off the road, and got to Lawrence. Hearing that I had found Roberts and no others, made him hope that Brown and Zimmerman might have escaped as he did. It turned out that Brown was not hit by the shot, but fell and lay still, even holding his breath a long time, and the only injury was caused by the blows on the back of his head. He, too, thought his comrades dead and crept away; but he found that the blows on his head had so affected his eyes that he could scarcely see. In this condition he made his way to the Kaw River, living on green corn for several days, until he was found below Lawrence. I do not know what became of him. Zimmerman escaped badly wounded, but recovered. Golding was the first Free State sheriff of Leavenworth County, and was a useful citizen and good officer. He settled in Labette County and died there in 1895. The above is all there was of the terrible battle described by my friend.

To show the character of the four men who committed this outrage, I happened to know one of them personally, and I suppose the others were of like makeup. This one had been a trapper up the Yellowstone, committed one or two murders up there, and had to get out of the country to keep from being killed by other trappers. I hired him to go to Fort Riley in 1855 and discharged him on the road. He returned to Leavenworth and opened up a headquarters for toughs, his apparent business being that of a saloon keeper. Many men told me that it was only a question of time when he would kill me, if he got a chance. Everybody went armed, and, of course, I was not behind others in having good arms and being prepared to use them. One thing I was pretty safe on, I did not visit the town or tough places at night, and never feared that any man would assassinate me face to face. He

The Kansas War of 1856

might waylay me, but that was hard to do in broad daylight, with a man who was always sober and accustomed to care for himself. But his threats caused me to keep the run of him. One day I met him at the corner of Main and Shawnee Streets; I was going north, as he came round the corner and turned south with a rifle on his shoulder. I stepped to the edge of the walk, drew my pistol quickly and motioned him to continue on south, which he did. Neither spoke. When he got to Delaware Street, he turned west, and I went on north to where my horse was hitched and rode to the Fort. I never saw him afterwards, but heard the next day that he had joined one of the companies of "peace makers."

In the fall, soon after peace arrangements at Lecompton, which destroyed all the business of irresponsible "peace makers," a promiscuous lot of men were assembled in a saloon in Leavenworth, some drinking, some playing cards, talking over the past, conjecturing the future, etc. My "friend" was of the number—swaggering, swearing and bragging—telling of his prowess, and among other outrages he bragged of killing Roberts. "I did not let my man escape," said he. Some Georgians present had come to Kansas to settle, not to steal or rob, but to settle—preferably to make Kansas a slave State, but to settle any way and make the best of it. In the meantime some of them had become so disgusted with the so-called "Pro-Slavery" gangs, as represented by the "peace makers" above referred to and the crowds that came over from Missouri to carry the elections, that they leaned towards the Free State party as representing the better element, and finally some of them concluded to and did act with that party. One of these Georgians, who had been much disappointed and disgusted, now slightly under the influence of liquor, sprang to his feet, rifle in hand, faced the big ruffian and spoke, as reported to me, about as follows: "You scoundrel! you thief! you characterless murderer! You who had nothing at stake, neither character, home, friends, nor hope for the future, you and others like you have roamed this country to our disgrace and the destruction of all that we hoped to build. By murder, arson and robbery you have made us a stench in the nostrils of all decent men. I am going back to Georgia, but for the sake of my comrades who must stay here and struggle for a living, I am going to kill you, so die, damn you, die!" And he shot the ruffian dead.

During the Georgian's speech the ruffian had braced himself up, fumbled his pistol and acted as if he was going to use it, but the Georgian had the "drop" and would have killed him any instance that he thought it necessary. A friend of mine who was present told me this two hours after in my camp fifteen miles away, and of the scenes and incidents previous to and following the killing. The Georgian's speech caused a sensation, not only among the tough element, who thinned out a good deal afterwards, but among the better element who had looked with suspicion upon all Southerners who came to make Kansas a slave State. Gradually it dawned upon them that there were good men of the Pro-Slavery party who would fall into line and work for Kansas anyway, build homes and be good citizens. But the Georgian who did the killing did not return home, but found Government employment, went with me on the Cheyenne Expedition in 1857, to Utah in 1858, where I left him, and thence to California. Frugal, industrious and honest, he made all good men respect him. Two of the other Georgians who were in the room when the killing was done, worked for me in Government business more than two years, saved their money, and made homes in Kansas. Better men it would be hard to find.

At Lawrence, one of my first acquaintances was Lyman Allen. He was in the stove and hardware business, a genial, companionable man. After crossing the ferries, I always went to his office to write my certificate on which the ferry-men collected their pay from the quartermaster at Fort Leavenworth. So that every time I passed through there, going or coming, I saw him. A few days after peace was patched up at Lecompton, I met Governor Charles Robinson[6] in Allen's office. I had seen him frequently as a pris-

---

[6] Charles Robinson, 1818–94, was the first state governor of Kansas, 1861–63. He was born in Hardwick, Massachusetts, attended Amherst College, and was

The Kansas War of 1856

oner at Colonel Cooke's camp at Lecompton, but now made his acquaintance for the first time. Having some leisure, and the Governor seeming to want to talk with me, I remained in conversation with him and Mr. Allen until two distinguished leaders of the Pro-Slavery party came in and introduced themselves to the Governor, who introduced them to Mr. Allen and me. They talked a little, evidently without any very congenial feeling on either side, and treated each other courteously for a few minutes, when the visitors rose to go. After shaking hands reservedly all around, one of them turned to the Governor and said that he had lost a Negro man, and had reason to believe he was in Lawrence— he had the man in camp during the campaign and some one had stolen him. He asked the Governor if he had heard of such a man, describing him, to which the Governor replied that he had not. The other man said: "Well, if the nigger does come under your notice, I wish you would try to save him for me," to which the Governor replied: "Well, if I see him." And the gentlemen were off. After they went out the Governor turned to me and said, that he had been informed that each of these two men had declared that they would shoot him on sight, "And now," said he, "they come in here to inquire after a runaway negro, and while both are armed and I am not, neither acts as if inclined to shoot." These men, then young, were among the wealthiest in Platte and Buchanan counties, in Missouri; both were Union men during the War of the Rebellion, one was a colonel, several terms a congressman, and died a congressman from the St. Joe district in Missouri—one of the ablest men from that or any other State. And so the change referred to by Governor Robinson was not so great, in the light of what followed. When Robinson became

---

graduated from Berkshire Medical School in 1843. In 1849 he accompanied an emigrant train to California and was a miner, a restaurant keeper, and an editor in Sacramento. He was elected to the legislature in 1850. He returned to Massachusetts, edited the *Fitchburg News* for two years, and went to Kansas in 1854 as agent for the Emigrant Aid Company. He was elected governor under the illegal Topeka constitution and was indicted for usurpation of office, but was acquitted.

governor he made his friend Lyman Allen Adjutant General of the State.

Lieutenant Stuart, acting commissary officer at Fort Leavenworth, found himself with four hundred work oxen on hand in the fall of 1856, turned over to him by the quartermaster to be fed for beef. He employed me to take them to Platte County, locate them, buy feed for them, etc., and I was transferred to the commissary department for that purpose. I placed them on the farm of Mr. Daniel Carey, near which I had been the winter before. In the spring of 1857 the oxen were very fat. I had spent a pleasant winter with nice people, and the last of April I returned the cattle to Salt Creek Valley, transferred back to the quartermaster's department.

Part VII[1]
The Cheyenne Expedition

† † † † † † † † † † †

The first of May, 1857, I was placed in charge of transportation for the Cheyenne expedition, to be commanded by Colonel E. V. Sumner, First Cavalry, with Lieutenant J. E. B. Stuart, quartermaster and commissary of the expedition. It was at Lieutenant Stuart's request that I was detailed for this duty.

After the necessary preparations for the long campaign, Major Sedgwick,[2] with four troops of the First Cavalry (now Fourth), five Delaware Indian scouts and forty six-mule teams, Mr. "Nick" Beery as chief wagonmaster, was to go up the Arkansas by the Santa Fé route to about where now stands Pueblo, then strike across to where is now Denver, and down the South Platte to Fort St. Vrain,[3] where it was expected he would arrive on or about the fourth of July. Colonel Sumner, with two troops of his regiment (First Cavalry) would proceed to Fort Kearney,

[1] Part VII is reprinted in *Relations with the Indians of the Plains, 1857–1861*, edited with introduction and notes by LeRoy R. Hafen and Ann W. Hafen (Glendale, Calif., Arthur H. Clark Company, 1959), 49–96. Their notes have been useful and suggestive.

[2] John Sedgwick, born in Cornwall, Connecticut, September 13, 1813, was graduated from West Point in 1837 and commissioned second lieutenant, Second Artillery. He was promoted to first lieutenant in 1839. In the Mexican War he was brevetted captain for Contreras and Churubusco, and major for Chapultepec. He became captain in 1849; major First Cavalry in 1855; lieutenant colonel, Second Cavalry on March 16, 1861; and colonel, First Cavalry on April 25. (It became Fourth Cavalry on August 3.) On August 31 he became brigadier general of Volunteers, and in 1862 major general of Volunteers. He commanded the Sixth Corps at Chancellorsville and Gettysburg, and was killed by a sharpshooter at Spotsylvania on May 9, 1864.

[3] Fort St. Vrain was on the South Platte River, about thirty-five miles north of the site of Denver.

where he would be joined by two troops of the Second Dragoons (now Second Cavalry), and thence to Fort Laramie, where three companies of the Sixth Infantry would join him. At Laramie he would take provisions for his whole command, including Major Sedgwick's, up to the end of July. Major Sedgwick's column started on the seventeenth of May; on the eighteenth and nineteenth we loaded Colonel Sumner's train, and at 8:00 A.M. on the twentieth the column moved out, cavalry in advance.

The transportation consisted of the Colonel's four-mule ambulance, fifty wagons (six-mule teams) and twenty extra mules. Traveled eighteen miles and camped on Stranger Creek.

Without incident worthy of note, the command camped near Fort Kearney June 4, Captain Wharton,[4] Sixth Infantry, commanding; drew forage and provisions to last to Fort Laramie. Two troops of the Second Dragoons joined here, Lieutenant Smith[5] in command of Troop E and Lieutenant Vilipigne[6] of Troop H. Lieutenant Higgins,[7] Sixth Infantry, also joined with one hundred recruits for Companies B, C, D, and G, Sixth Infantry, at Laramie. Colonel Sumner employed five Pawnee scouts, "Speck-in-the-Eye" chief of the band, and ten wagons were added to the train.

June 6th. Command left Kearney, and without incident of importance camped four miles below Beauvais' Crossing of South Platte[8] June 13.

[4] Henry W. Wharton, see note 4, Part II.

[5] William Duncan Smith of Georgia was graduated from West Point in 1846 and commissioned brevet second lieutenant, Second Dragoons. He became second lieutenant in 1847, first lieutenant in 1851, and captain in 1858. He resigned January 28, 1861, became a Confederate brigadier general, and died October 4, 1862.

[6] John Bordenave Villepigue (not Vilipigne) of South Carolina was graduated from West Point in 1854 as brevet second lieutenant, Second Dragoons. He became second lieutenant in 1855 and first lieutenant on May 27, 1857. He resigned on March 31, 1861, commanded the Confederate Army of Mobile temporarily as colonel in 1862, was promoted brigadier general, and died November 9, 1862.

[7] Silas Parsons Higgins of Alabama was graduated from West Point in 1853 as brevet second lieutenant, Eighth Infantry; became second lieutenant, Sixth Infantry, in 1855, and first lieutenant December 24, 1856. He died July 18, 1860.

The Cheyenne Expedition

June 14th. Command lying by; thankful for this. It gives men a chance to clean up, and men and animals a rest. Threw covers off every wagon and let in the sun to dry out dampness sure to accumulate.

Lieutenant Stuart resigned as Acting Quartermaster and Commissary June 1, and Lieutenant R. H. Riddick[9] succeeded him.

June 15. Leaving trains in charge of one wagonmaster, I took the others and assistants with me at five o'clock and rode to the crossing. The river was very high, banks full, and just half a mile by measurement from bank to bank; current three to four miles an hour; usually half the width was bare sand bars, but now all was covered with water; it is the "June rise." Large numbers of emigrants waiting for river to get lower. On account of the melting snow in the mountains, they may have to wait a long time. I pointed out the landing on the north side; told Eskridge, who had quick perception and a clear head, to remain on the south bank and direct me step by step in case I got to drifting down. The others followed a short distance apart. The bottom was very uneven, sometimes a foot deep, suddenly becoming two, three, and in a few places, four feet deep. The changes were sudden, as often three feet as one, but mostly two or three. On a small island just above the crossing on the north side grew many tall, slim willows; we each cut several, ten or twelve feet long, and trimmed them so as to leave a few leaves on the top. Each took several of these long switches. Standing on the north bank, I directed them straight to Eskridge. In the shallowest water, where the current would have little force, a switch was stuck deep in the quicksand. By a tedious struggle we got a straight line from bank to bank.

Along came the cavalry, and I explained to Colonel Sumner and the Quartermaster that if they would keep close up to the line

---

[8] Beauvais' Crossing was also called the Lower Crossing or Lower California Crossing. It was notorious for quicksand.

[9] Richard H. Riddick of North Carolina was appointed second lieutenant of the new First Cavalry on March 27, 1855, and became first lieutenant in 1860. He resigned in 1861 to join the Confederate Army, became colonel of the Thirty-fourth North Carolina Volunteers and was killed at Gaines Mill June 27, 1862.

of willows, they would beat down and level the quicksand bottom so as to improve the crossing for the wagons. The Colonel knew this very well, as he had been here in 1850, though, he said, the water was not then high. I volunteered to show the way and rode in ahead. The head of the column kept up fairly well but some men a few files back had trouble, drifted, and before the north bank was reached the column was a rainbow—the center three hundred yards below the direct line—many horses floundering in the quicksand and several men nearly drowned. For a wonder all got out, but my road-bed was not benefited. However, experience had shown me that there could be no helter-skelter hurrying, and the chance of losing some mules, wagons, and possibly men was very good. That tumbling, boiling cauldron of sand and water was dangerous for the strongest and most experienced men with teams. Be it remembered that the man, horse or wagon standing still will soon sink in the sand; one must keep moving constantly or sink; a blockade of wagons meant the loss of some. I asked the Colonel and Quartermaster if they had any instructions or directions to give me. The Colonel said, "Be very careful," and left me to work it out my own way. The company teams were looked after well under the instructions of officers and noncommissioned officers interested, and there was no friction, each team following in turn, all cheerfully helping. In addition to the wagonmasters I had a dozen teamsters on their saddle-mules strung along the crossing ready to help. A strap or rope tied to the bridle of the lead mule was held by a mounted man starting in ahead of the team, while one or two more mounted men rode at the lower (off) side to whip up the mules and keep them from drifting down, and the teamster on his saddle-mule did the best he could to keep moving. In this way the first wagon got safely over.

Each wagonmaster and mounted teamster understanding his part of the programme, the wagons were started in about fifty yards apart, care being taken to have no more than half a dozen in the river at the same time. Most of the teams had more or less trouble, causing outriders to get off into the water to help out, so that all clothing was soon wet through. The day was dark and cloudy, the water cold from snow-clad mountains and the north wind cold, and all suffered much. As soon as a team was over, the teamster unhitched his saddle-mule and came back to help. Half the teams were safely over when the oldest wagonmaster started in with a wagon for the first time. It was the lightest loaded, and it seems that he thought it would go over easily, and it would, with good management. It was the hospital wagon, containing all medicines for the command. In the middle of the stream, the team tangled up, the leaders swung round and the saddle-mule sank in the sand and got under the tongue, the lower (off) wheels sank, and the wagon rolled over in the deepest water. The boy who drove the team, eighteen years old, was trying to extricate himself from his saddle-mule and crying for help. The man on the lower side could not reach him and the wagonmaster sat on his horse like a wooden man. I was fifty yards away, but put spurs to my horse and reached the boy in time to keep him from going under the tongue with the saddle-mule, which drowned. The men cut the harness from the other mules, and they found their way out. I took the boy on behind me, rode to the north shore, and he was soon made comfortable by his comrades.

At last all but one of the wagons were over—one mule, wagon and medical stores lost. And now, with plenty of mounted men we crossed the beef herd with little difficulty. I did not hear a complaint then or ever afterwards about the management. No one interfered with me from first to last. For my part, with some others, I had been in the cold river, mounted and dismounted, more than six hours; others had been in three, four or five hours; all at least one or two hours. About two infantry recruits climbed into each wagon and were the only ones who got over dry, except a few of the cavalry. Fortunately none were in the hospital wagon.

As soon as the last wagon was over, the cavalry column moved out. Lieutenant Stuart's servant came with the Lieutenant's compliments and presented me with a fine hat; Stuart had gotten it out of his trunk when he saw me lose mine in saving the boy. My ever present bandana was tied on my head.

Lieutenant Riddick said we were going six miles to some water hole; we found the holes but no water. Water kegs contained enough for cooking purposes and to drink, and there were buffalo chips enough to make coffee and heat water for whisky toddies, but no fire for the benumbed, worn-out men to warm themselves and dry their clothes by that dreary, miserable day. I had a few bottles of fine whisky which had not been touched since I left Fort Leavenworth, and now I gave it all out in small doses to the men. I insisted on every man changing his clothing, and with coffee and plenty to eat, it was surprising how cheerful all were. My drowned boy had been well cared for, laid away in blankets, and was all right.

That boy's name was Hayes, a German of Leavenworth, and when he returned home with one arm, at the close of the Civil War, he came to see me. He became a prosperous farmer in Jefferson County, Kansas—a good soldier and citizen. The Colonel sent for me and seemed well pleased at the manner in which the crossing was effected, and when I expressed impatience at the loss of the wagon and medical stores, he said he thought I should be well satisfied. He made me feel a little more reconciled to the unnecessary loss.

June 22d. We reached Fort Laramie, and camped one and one-half miles above on the south side of Laramie River. Orders were received by Colonel Sumner for E and H Troops, Second Dragoons, to be ready to go with General Harney[10] to Utah, so that they are no longer a part of the Cheyenne expedition.

10 William Selby Harney of Louisiana was commissioned second lieutenant in the First Infantry in 1818, first lieutenant in 1819, captain in 1825, and major paymaster in 1833. He was commissioned lieutenant colonel in the new Second Dragoons in 1836 and was brevetted colonel for gallant and meritorious conduct in several successive engagements with the hostile Indians in Florida. He became colonel of the Second Dragoons in 1846 and brevet brigadier general in 1847 for Cerro Gordo. He led the expedition against the Sioux that resulted in the victory at Ash Hollow, September 3, 1855. Cooke was on his way to join this expedition when accompanied by Lowe from Fort Union to Fort Riley (see note 9, Part IV).

The Cheyenne Expedition

23d. Everybody getting ready for the Cheyenne campaign. This is the last chance for any sort of outfit until it is over. Mr. Seth E. Ward,[11] the sutler here, has a good stock of campaign goods. Fitting out more teams, having mules' shoes fitted, drawing provisions, forage, etc. Laramie probably presents a busier scene than ever before in its history. We left Fort Leavenworth with about 300 fat oxen, had been killing some from day to day for beef, and to-day we drew 150 more from the Commissary. We have not seen a buffalo since leaving Freemont's [sic] Spring. The Colonel employed two guides—one a mountaineer white man, the other a Mexican.

27th. Three companies of the Sixth Infantry, under Captain Ketchum[12]—his G, Lieutenant Carlin's[13] D, and Captain Foote's[14] C, marched from Laramie at eight o'clock, passed our

Harney commanded the Utah expedition until replaced by Albert Sydney Johnston. Harney became brigadier general in 1858 and retired in 1863. He was brevetted major general in 1865 for long and faithful service.

[11] Seth Edward Ward was appointed sutler at Fort Laramie in 1857 and remained as the post trader for fifteen years, most of that time in partnership with Colonel William G. Bullock. The sutler was a civilian licensed to trade with army personnel, predecessor of the canteen, or post exchange, PX. See, "The Sutler's Store at Fort Laramie," by Merrill J. Mattes, reprint from *Annals of Wyoming*, Vol. XVIII, No. 2, (July, 1946).

[12] William Scott Ketchum, see note 17, Part II.

[13] William Passmore Carlin of Illinois was graduated from West Point in 1850 as brevet second lieutenant, Sixth Infantry, and became second lieutenant in 1851, first lieutenant in 1855, and captain in 1861. On August 15, 1861, he accepted a commission as colonel of the Thirty-eighth Illinois Infantry and in 1862 became brigadier general of Volunteers. He was brevetted lieutenant colonel for Chattanooga; colonel for the battle of Jonesboro, Georgia; brigadier general for Bentonville, North Carolina; major general for gallant and meritorious service in the field during the war; and major general of Volunteers for gallant and meritorious service during the war. Meanwhile he had been promoted to major, Sixteenth Infantry in 1864. He was transferred to the Thirty-fourth Infantry in 1866, and back to the Sixteenth in 1869. He became lieutenant colonel, Seventeenth Infantry, in 1872; colonel of the Fourth Infantry in 1882; and brigadier general in 1893, retiring late that year.

[14] Rensselaer W. Foote of New York, who attended West Point 1834–35, was commissioned second lieutenant, Sixth Infantry, in 1838; first lieutenant, 1843; and captain, 1853. He was brevetted major for gallant and meritorious service at the battle of Gaines Mill, Virginia, where he was killed on June 27, 1862.

camp with the guides and Pawnees—trains following. Gradual rise eight miles south to top of steep, rocky hill; an hour going down 500 yards; crossed and camped on Cherry Creek at north side of "Goshen's Hole."[15] This "Goshen's Hole" is a level plain thirty miles across from north to south, and is said to be the hottest place this side of the home of Dives, and, except at the extreme south and north ends, about as dry.

28th. Infantry and Pawnees marched at 6:00; cavalry and train at 7:00, eighteen miles over flat plain, the sun shining on the light sandy ground, creating such intense light and heat that men and animals suffered much—blinding heat without a breath of air. Our camp on Box Elder [sic] looked like an old apple orchard minus the fruit. Scattering box-elders and good grass made as lovely a camp as one could expect without a drop of water. Water kegs were full and cooking went on all right, but the poor horses and mules were great sufferers. The white guide said that the water always sank in the sand during a hot day, but there would be a good running stream at 11:00 P.M. In sympathy with my part of the caravan, by permission of the Colonel and Quartermaster, I told the herders to turn the mules up the creek towards a high point of bluff a mile away. The horses occupied all the shade near camp except that monopolized by the men, and I saw nothing but hours of suffering with stifling heat for the mules before the broiling sun would go down. It was the hottest place I have ever seen without artificial heat. Horses stood at the lariats and chewed the grass they were unable to swallow, and spat it out.

Taking some pieces of "hard tack" to nibble on, I mounted my horse, and with "Billy" Lowe, a Cincinnati youth, who, with his brother, was roughing it for adventure, I leisurely drifted off ahead of the herd. Arrived at the point of bluff I noticed under

---

[15] Goshen's Hole, called the Valley of Goshen by Theodore Talbot, and "Goche's hole on one of the affluents of Horse Creek," by Rufus B. Sage. Cherry Creek and Horse Creek flow into the North Platte near the Wyoming–Nebraska border. See LeRoy R. and Ann W. Hafen, editors, *Rufus B. Sage's Correspondence and Papers ... and His "Scenes in the Rocky Mountains,"* (Glendale, Calif., Arthur H. Clark Co., 1956), Vol. I, 217.

Courtesy Kansas State Historical Society

Monument to Major E. A. Ogden, quartermaster, U.S. Army, Fort Riley

Courtesy Kansas State Historical Society

Cavalry stables, Fort Riley

Courtesy Kansas State Historical Society

Post exchange, Fort Riley

Courtesy Kansas State Historical Society

Post hospital, Fort Riley

Courtesy Kansas State Historical Society

Monument at Fort Riley in memory of the Seventh Cavalry officers and enlisted men who died in the Battle of Wounded Knee

Courtesy Kansas State Historical Society

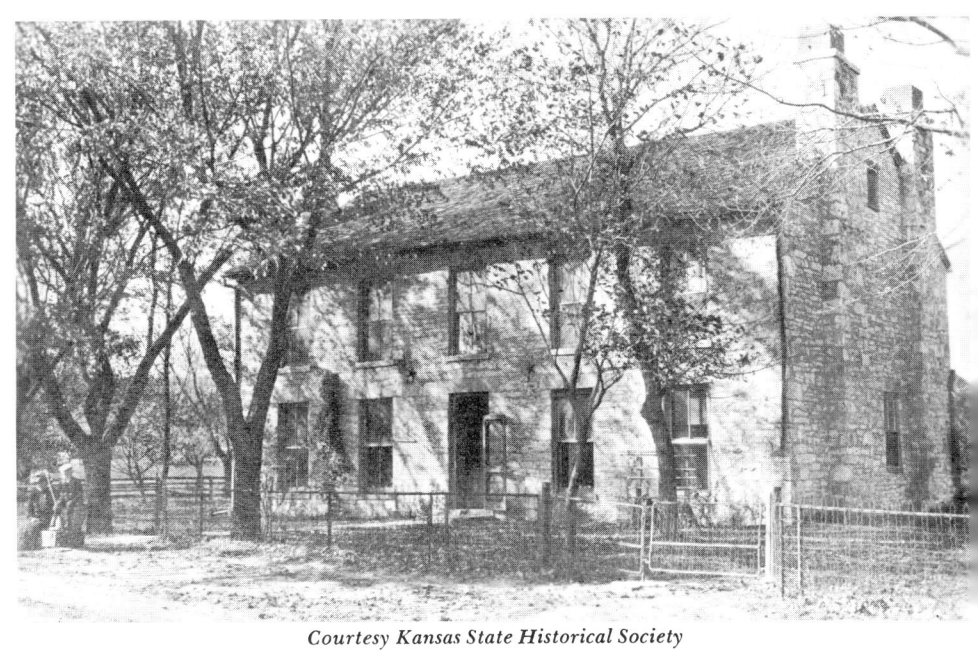

Kaw Methodist mission, Council Grove

Courtesy Kansas State Historical Society

Pioneer store on the trail, Council Grove

Courtesy Library of Congress

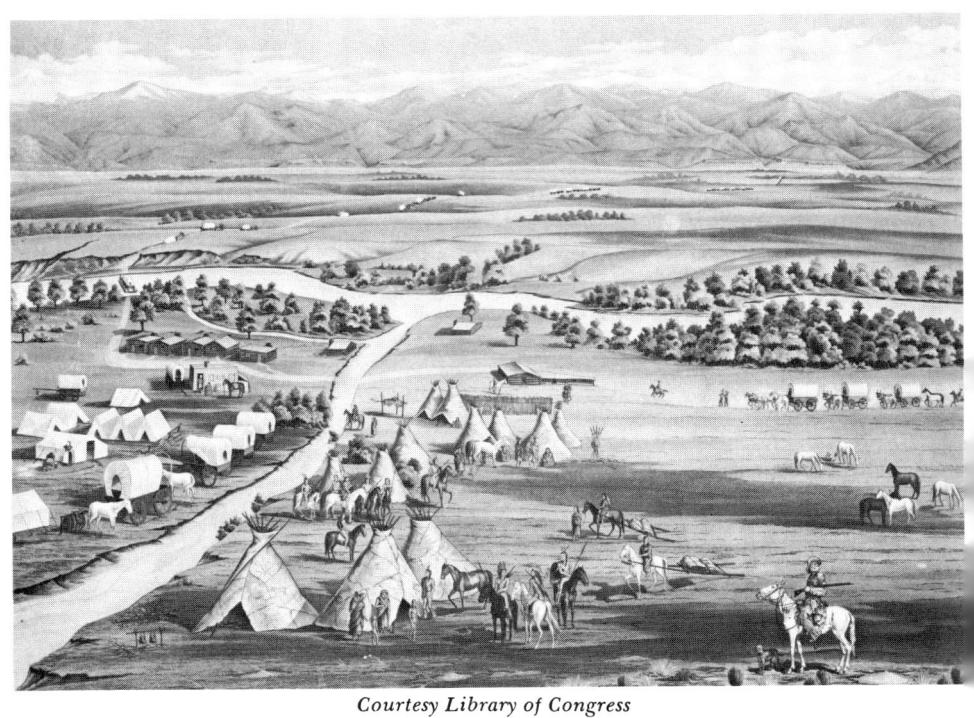

Denver in 1859

The Cheyenne Expedition

the north side, where the sun had not struck since early morning, a trickling stream which ran into the sand twenty feet away. Then I began to hunt up the creek, the water increasing as I went. Two miles from camp the bluffs were high and brush and trees shaded the creek-bed, and our animals drank comfortably. Half a mile further I found a long hole worn in the sand-stone and a good stream running into it, but disappearing in the hot sand within two hundred yards. I wrote on a leaf of my memorandum book to Lieutenant Riddick, telling him that if the Colonel would permit the mules to be driven three miles from camp, they could get plenty of water, and could graze leisurely back before the sun set; also, that there would be plenty of water for the cavalry horses. I told "Billy" to deliver the note to Lieutenant Riddick as quickly as possible. It was now two o'clock. With my glass, from a high point, I could see the camp and the mules. In less than an hour I saw the mules moving towards me, and as they came towards the water and smelt it, they struck a trot and finally a stampede, and such braying from four hundred mules I never heard before or since. The bluffs resounded with their music until their noses were buried in the lovely stream.

And now a column of dust indicated that the cavalry were coming; I showed them some nice holes above the mules. There was great rejoicing over the water, Captain W. N. R. Beall[16] said to me, "Are you the guide of this command?" I replied that I was not, but, that if I were I should know what was in the country or try to find out; I had no use for guides who could only follow a trail and knew nothing of the surroundings; anybody could follow a trail without a guide. When I reported to the Colonel at sunset, he seemed greatly pleased, and questioned me about how

---

[16] William N. R. Beall was born in Kentucky and appointed to West Point from Arkansas. He was graduated in 1848 as brevet second lieutenant, Fourth Infantry; became second lieutenant, Fifth Infantry in 1849; and was named first lieutenant of the new First Cavalry on March 3, 1855, and captain on the twenty-seventh of the same month. He resigned in 1861, became a Confederate brigadier general, and was district commander in Mississippi and Louisiana. He died July 26, 1883.

I thought of looking for water. I thought of it as a matter of course, but admitted that it was an accident.

29th. Infantry off at 6:00, cavalry and trains at 7:00, ten miles and watered at Willow Creek; three more to pass through high bluff, the outlet from "Goshen's Hole"; four hours getting train up the hill and through the pass, half a mile—steep quicksand hill; three more, and camped on Bear Creek at seven o'clock. Fine camp, but everybody and everything too tired to enjoy it.

30th. Off as usual, one mile to a branch of Bear River. This small stream, ten feet across, had by recent rains been made a bog one hundred yards wide. The slough grass was as high as a man's head, and one could cut with a butcher-knife an armful a minute. All soldiers and teamsters had butcher-knives. Cavalry dismounted and all cut grass, and a causeway was soon made. It seemed a huge job to cut with butcher-knives sufficient grass to causeway one hundred yards of bog. All took hold in good shape and we crossed without accident, greatly to the surprise of officers and men, to whom this causewaying with grass was a new thing. Seventeen miles more, crossing five branches of Horse Creek, and camped at 4 P.M. on Mud Creek.

July 1st. Off as usual. Looking from a hill at the course the guides were taking the infantry, I suggested another course for the wagons. I could see with my glass a smooth plain that would save trouble. The Colonel said, "Well, go ahead," and I did, he following with his ambulance. Captain Beall said that we saved two miles. These guides have no idea of a wagon-road; they have been following Indian trails on ponies, and do not know very much about them. Eighteen miles over a hard gravel road and crossed Pole Creek. This is called "Pole Creek" because the Indians get large numbers of lodge-poles near the head of it in the mountains. Four miles more and camped on big "Mud Creek"; heavy rain-storm in the night.

2d. We have a butcher named Smith who has charge of the cattle herd. He never was on the plains before, and imagines that he can handle cattle here as he could on his father's farm in

Rhode Island. I cautioned him to have his Mexican herders on the alert during the storm for fear of a stampede. This morning he came in greatly distressed and swore there "Wa'n't a critter in sight." And sure enough, with the exception of one cow owned by him and one lame beef, there was not a horned "critter in sight." Fortunately for our command, Quartermaster Sergeant Clark, who was commissary clerk, and my mess mate since leaving Leavenworth, overtook us about ten o'clock with all the cattle, having found them ten miles from camp, nearly in the direction of our line of march. Off as usual, ten miles to main branch of Crow Creek; road muddy and bad from last night's rains; ten miles more, and camped on south side of slough, which delayed us three hours in causewaying with grass. Good many mules gave out to-day.

3d. Off as usual, one and one-half miles to slough that occupied two hours in crossing, with assistance of cavalry and plenty of slough-grass. Six miles, and struck spring branch of Crow Creek—four more to crossing. Much time spent in crossing nine wagons, and Captain Beall found a good crossing half a mile below. This shows the worthlessness of the guide. Here the Colonel called me, and said, that by the guide's estimate it was eight miles to where we will camp to-night, twelve more to crossing of South Platte below the mouth of Powder River, and thirteen more to Fort St. Vrain, where he wanted to meet Major Sedgwick the next day; that is twenty-five miles by the usual trail from to-night's camp to St. Vrain, besides crossing the river. The guide also says, that if we could go direct from to-night's camp to St. Vrain, it would be only twenty miles, and crossing at St. Vrain much better than below the mouth of Powder River. Guide thinks the route practicable. So far I had not been impressed by anything the guide had done—if he had given any valuable information it had not come to my notice; so I told the Colonel that the guide's statement could be easily verified—that I would ride that twenty miles to St. Vrain, and back to his camp before starting-time in the morning, and then there would be no uncertainty about it. "All right," said the Colonel, "take both guides and any others that you want with you." I took with me Simeon Routh, a teamster in whom I had confidence, soon overtook the infantry, and got both guides, and struck out west towards the mountains at three o'clock. In referring to the guide, I mean the white man—the Mexican talked little English and kept quiet. The guide pointed out what he called "South Fork Peaks," and said that St. Vrain lay in a direct line between us and them, and we traveled straight as possible towards them.[17]

We first came in sight of the Rocky Mountains at Scott's Bluffs, forty-six miles east of Laramie, Laramie Peak being the only spur then in sight. Since leaving Laramie we have been traveling nearly south and about parallel with the main chain, which now we estimate to be about forty miles distant. Over nearly level plain we went—walk, trot, gallop—pushing along at an average of six miles or more an hour. We have been traveling a little up grade, and at five o'clock, as we reached high ground, we could see the timbers of Powder River in the distance. The afternoon was lovely and the scene before us beautiful beyond description—vivid lightning, clouds, and rain—storms on various peaks along the snow-capped range could be seen far beyond the sound of thunder, the sun shining brightly on tempest, peak and plain, the scenes changing with the rapidity of a kaleidescope. At last we are on the bank of Powder River at seven o'clock, certainly twenty-five miles from where we started, and I do not know how

---

[17] The guides were lost, and so may be the modern reader trying to trace the route on maps that neglect natural features, complicated by probable changes in nomenclature and Lowe's frequent carelessness. Hafen, *op. cit.*, has an outline map. The route was generally south from Fort Laramie, and maps of the Wyoming State Highway Commission and of the Colorado Department of Highways show most of the creeks mentioned by Lowe: Cherry, Boxelder, Willow, Bear Creek (Little Bear Creek), Bear River (Bear Creek), Horse, Crow, Pole (Lodgepole). "Powder River," of course, is the Cache La Poudre. I do not find Mud Creek. Lowe's references to Scott's Bluffs and Laramie Peak in the paragraph following may be confusing, but he is reverting back to a time before the expedition reached Fort Laramie in pointing out that since then the expedition has been moving south, parallel with the mountain chain.

The Cheyenne Expedition

much farther to St. Vrain; and it makes little difference. The river is a raging torrent, overflowing its banks from ten to twenty feet deep, from the effects of rains at its source, which we have been viewing all along. This settles the question about going that way, and, as I concluded then and have since proved, not a mile could have been saved by going that way—another damper on the guide's knowledge of the country. Troops and trains would have traveled over an untrodden plain half covered with cactus—one mile worse than two over a partially beaten track. For half an hour, with my glass I watched the glittering rays of the setting sun upon clouds, storms and white-capped peaks; I might never view such a sight again, and, though I have seen much of the magnificent range since, to me nothing has ever equaled that view.

I do not want to retrace the twenty-five miles to camp, and the guide says it is but twelve miles to the Platte below the mouth of the Cache le Poudre. So that, miserable as the prospect is, we will camp here. Our horses are tormented with mosquitoes that rise from the thick grass and cover them all over, so we fill canteens and betake ourselves to a hill half a mile from the river, but they follow. The animals are hobbled, fuel is brought, and in a few minutes we have a fire, pile on green grass and make a big smoke, to which all animals—biped and quadruped—come for protection. Each man puts his slice of meat on a stick and broils it while seated in the smoke. Armijo, the Mexican guide, has a coffee pot and some coffee—each one has a few pieces of "hard tack," and we feast. Having both guides, I determined to send one back to Colonel Sumner, and wrote the following note:

CAMP ON CACHE LE POUDRE,
July 3, 1857, 10 P.M.

To Colonel E. V. Sumner, Commanding Cheyenne Expedition, Camp on Crow Creek:

Colonel:—On leaving you I traveled due west about twenty-five miles over a fairly level country and arrived here at 7 o'clock. Found the water from ten to twenty feet deep and storms in the mountains indicate that it will continue so, rendering this route impracticable for the train. I will meet you on the South Fork of Platte to-morrow. I send Armijo with instructions to be in your camp by sunrise.

I am, Colonel, very respectfully,
P. G. LOWE.

Armijo saddled his horse and with rifle across the pommel said "Adios, Señor," and was gone. Before he left camp we all agreed upon a star that he should follow, believing that that course would take him close to Colonel Sumner's camp. We kept up the smoke; the night was cool, and by midnight the mosquitoes had settled down into the grass and there was peace for man and beast.

4th. Coffee, small piece of meat and "hard tack" made our breakfast, and at five o'clock we started down stream. Arrived at usual crossing of South Platte below the mouth of Cache le Poudre at 8:00. Unsaddled and let horses graze while we rested an hour. Then I proposed to try the crossing, but the guide said, "No, it is impracticable." Routh was willing to try it, but I would not permit it with his mule. Divesting myself of everything except underclothes, and with nothing on my horse but myself and a bridle, I felt my way into the river cautiously, and was half way over without much trouble. Then my horse had a hard struggle in deep water and quicksand, being hard pressed for some time to keep his head above water, but he took it quietly, rested when he could, and finally landed safely. I took the bit from his mouth and let him graze for half an hour while I fought mosquitoes with switches, and then we recrossed with the same difficulty. Our wagons cannot cross here at this time. The guide said: "You'll take the advice of a guide next time." Feeling nettled at what I conceived to be his utter uselessness, I admonished him that guides and other employees were supposed to furnish information to the commanding officer, and if not, I could see no use for them. The dust of the command is visible four miles away. I selected a camp a mile lower down and rode out to meet the Colonel, who was in his ambulance in advance. He said that Armijo reached him in time. He was anxious to know about the crossing, and I was able to tell him, and he

The Cheyenne Expedition

went into the camp that I had selected. Our battery was manned and salute fired just as we heard Sedgwick's guns up the river on the other side.

Someone cried, "A horseman on the south side of the river!" and all rushed for a sight of him. After long exertion, everyone having given him up for lost half a dozen times, the horseman emerged from the river, and proved to be "Fall Leaf,"[18] one of the Delaware Indian guides, from Major Sedgwick. He brought a letter from the Major to the Colonel, who sent "Fall Leaf" back with an answer, requesting the Major to move down opposite to him to-morrow. Overcome by excitement and fatigue, and the effects of a good dinner, I retired to my tent and was soon fast asleep. But, alas! "there is no rest for the wicked." I was soon aroused by the alarming cry of "Stampede!" oft repeated. Twenty steps from my tent stood my horse (Ben). Always after coming into camp he was saddled and ready to mount. (I always rode a mule during the day.) This time I had left the saddle off to give him a rest and had him picketed so that he could graze. I mounted without saddle or bridle, put the lariat in his mouth to guide him, dropped the picket pin, and was soon three miles back on the road with the horses and mules headed toward camp. Others came promptly, and every animal was safe. A few cavalry horses stampeded and ran among the mules, which were being herded. Two or three horses were hurt by picket pins, but no other damage.

5th. While at breakfast Lieutenant Riddick came and said we were to try to cross the river, therefore three metalic water-tight wagon-beds, tools to work with, etc., were needed at the river. These, with six coils of rope, wheelwright, blacksmith, etc., were soon there. The Colonel and his adjutant, Lieutenant Colburn,[19]

[18] Fall Leaf was a notable Delaware guide. Gold that he found on this trip inspired the Lawrence party of prospectors which entered Colorado the following year.

[19] Albert V. Colburn of Vermont was graduated from West Point in 1855, becoming brevet second lieutenant, Second Cavalry on July 1. Promoted to second lieutenant, First Cavalry, on October 1, he was regimental adjutant February 17,

and Lieutenant Riddick were the only officers who participated in the work. A strong detail of men was made from each troop and company. I was not supposed to work any of my men unless asked to, and I was glad not to be called upon. The first thing was to stretch a rope from the north shore to an island in midriver. The water was over a man's head in some places and current strong. The three metallic wagon-beds were to be lashed together and the raft so made attached by two pulleys to a rope at each end and pulled over by men on the raft. After a long, hard struggle, wading, swimming and pulling, exposed to the hot sun when not under water, they succeeded by noon in getting a rope stretched to the island and two wagon-beds in position to use, but the other one got away and floated down the river.

While three men were working with the rope in mid-river, they lost their hold, and, being exhausted, one of them drowned, while the other two barely escaped. One of them caught overhanging willows at the island with his left hand, and reached back with his right and caught the hand of his comrade, and held on until the men on shore pulled them out. They were cavalrymen of the best type. Fifty men saw this fine young soldier, Daugherty by name, go down to death, with no power to assist him, in that stream of yellow sand and water, and his loss caused deep regret.

Major Sedgwick's command camped opposite to us. At five o'clock the Colonel gave orders to take tools to camp, including ropes, indicating that the effort to cross here was abandoned.

6th. Two commands moved down the river on opposite sides, eighteen miles, and camped on river. Lieutenants Lomax[20] and Bayard[21] crossed over from Major Sedgwick's to Colonel Sum-

---

1857, to May 24, 1861. He became first lieutenant in 1861, then had a succession of staff appointments as brevet captain, captain, lieutenant colonel, and major. He died June 17, 1863.

20 Lunsford Lindsay Lomax of Rhode Island was graduated from West Point in 1856 as brevet second lieutenant, Second Cavalry, and became second lieutenant on September 30 of that year and first lieutenant in 1861. He resigned and became a Confederate major general.

ner's camp. The river is wider and shallower here, and current not so swift. Major Sedgwick having exhausted most of his forage and provisions, his wagons are nearly empty, and he will cross to our camp.

7th. Major Sedgwick's four troops crossed with little difficulty. With my wagonmasters and a number of good teamsters mounted on saddle mules, we helped Beery's trains over without serious accident. Mr. Beery brought my metallic wagon-bed, lost yesterday, which he found on a sand bar. Colonel Sumner calls this "Camp Buchanan," in honor of the President. This evening orders are out, dated "Camp Buchanan, July 7, 1857," in which we are informed that pack and riding mules must be made ready to accompany the six troops of cavalry and three companies of infantry in pursuit of the hostile Cheyennes. Pending the campaign, the train is to return to Fort Laramie, be refitted and loaded with provisions and forage, to meet the command at some time and place not named in the order.

8th. Centrally located is the blacksmith shop, under awnings of wagon covers, supported by poles, with portable anvil, bellows, etc., soon in full blast. Small coal pit burned during the night, and another being made ready; saddler shop near by under similar awnings, trying to make pack-saddles of all sorts of old wagon saddletrees found at Laramie. We found but few real pack-saddles there, and brought none from Leavenworth. Carpenter and helpers are fitting panniers—everybody busy doing the best under the circumstances.

9th. Selected mules, taking care to use those that are broken to ride, including saddle mules belonging to teams, and the teamsters are breaking others. Except a few Mexicans, I have not a man who is a practical packer; among the soldiers there are none.

[21] George Dashiell Bayard of New York was graduated from West Point in 1856 as second lieutenant, First Cavalry. In 1861 he was commissioned first lieutenant and captain in the same regiment (renumbered Fourth Cavalry) and colonel of the First Pennsylvania Cavalry. He became brigadier general of Volunteers on April 28, 1862, and died December 14 of that year of wounds received in the Battle of Fredericksburg.

With the Mexicans I established a sort of school, but they are hardly able to impart to others what they know themselves; however, they are much help to the officers, who want a few men instructed.

10th, 11th and 12th. To sum up: One hundred and eighty pack and riding mules, 170 blind bridles, and all saddles and saddle blankets belonging to train turned over to Lieutenant Wheaton,[22] acting quartermaster and commissary of the expedition.

13th. With best six-mule teams I could rig up, crossed the packs and infantry to south side of river without accident, and returned to camp. Before parting, the Colonel complimented me on the good work done, told me what he expected in future, and as he shook my hand, said that my pay had been increased twenty-five dollars per month from the first of June. I was to return to Laramie, 150 miles, turn in all surplus wagons and harness, refit the train, and make as many six-mule teams as I could, load the wagons with corn and commissaries, and meet him at Beauvais' Crossing of South Platte, where we crossed coming out, by the first of August, 175 miles from Laramie.

And now the "good byes" are said and the command is gone. Lieutenant Riddick is left acting commissary and quartermaster of the train and in command of about fifty men on their first campaign, who, having bunged up their horses or themselves are no longer of any use to the Cheyenne expedition, and are left dismounted with the train. I immediately proceeded to fix up

[22] Frank Wheaton of Rhode Island was appointed first lieutenant of the new First Cavalry in 1855. In 1861 he became captain in his regiment, and also lieutenant colonel and colonel of the Second Rhode Island Infantry. In 1862 he became brigadier general of Volunteers. He was brevetted lieutenant colonel for the Wilderness; colonel for Cedar Creek; brigadier general for Petersburg; major general of Volunteers for Opequan, Fishers Hill, and Middleton; and major general for gallant and meritorious service in the field during the war. When discharged from volunteer service he was major, Second Cavalry, and became lieutenant colonel, Thirty-ninth Infantry, in 1866, transferred to Twenty-first Infantry in 1869; colonel, Second Infantry, in 1874; brigadier general in 1892; and retired a major general in 1897.

The Cheyenne Expedition

teams, and found myself with 109 wagons, 25 six-mule teams, 18 five-mule teams, 66 four-mule teams, equal to 504 mules, Riddick's horse and mine, and a few broken-down cavalry horses, which we will turn in at Laramie. Not a saddle nor saddle-blanket for the teams, 170 bridles short. I had been preparing for this condition of things, and had men breaking in leaders and saddle mules all the time that we had been here; also had to rig out bridles, using ropes and straps for that purpose. By noon we were straightened out, traveled twelve miles and camped above Cottonwood Grove on the Platte. Lieutenant Riddick found the remains of Daugherty on an island a little below camp and had them buried, and called the place "Daugherty's Island."

Mr. Beery went with pack train as chief "muleteer," and took Sim Routh and his pick of other men in the train. The Colonel left the "white guide" with the train, to be discharged on arrival at Laramie. I may as well dispose of him now. He was well-behaved and of rather good disposition—a pleasant man to get along with. The day after our arrival at Laramie he married a young Sioux Squaw—that is, he tied four ponies to the tipi of a warrior, they were accepted by said warrior, and the girl, his daughter, became the bride of the guide. Four years later I saw this same man married in due form to a white woman by a clergyman in Denver, while the squaw bride witnessed the ceremony through a window as she stood upon the porch.

19th. Camped one mile above Fort Laramie. Reported here that General Harney was to have left Fort Leavenworth on the fifteenth en route to Utah.

20th. Turned in twenty-nine wagons, traveling forge and surplus harness, and found myself with eighty six-mule teams complete (including saddles, blankets, bridles and a few inferior surplus mules which we drew from the quartermaster here). Drew commissary, medical and other stores and loaded everything but corn.

21st. Loaded 130,000 pounds of corn, drew fifty rifles and two boxes of ammunition for the same and eight boxes navy pistol cartridges, issued rifles to teamsters and made ready to start in the morning. One wagon was loaded exclusively with supplies for officers when we should meet at crossing of South Platte. Jimmerson was the teamster in charge of this wagon and, strange to say, none of its precious contents were lost, stolen or *evaporated*.

22d. Passed Bordeau's trading place[23] and camped below Major Dripps's trading house,[24] nineteen miles from Laramie.

23d. Fifteen miles and camped at mouth of Horse Creek. We are told by Mr. Reynolds, an Indian trader, that the Cheyennes are but three days' travel south.

If Colonel Sumner meets and whips them, they will likely go north, Reynolds thinks, and may meet us. The management of the train is left to me and I take no chances. The camp is, and will be while traveling along the river, by making the train form three sides of a square, river forming the fourth—say twenty-six wagons fronting west, twenty-six south and twenty-six east— wagons about twenty feet apart—river forming north line of the camp where the dismounted soldiers and their mess wagon and my mess wagon will camp. Mules herded outside of the square until an hour before sunset and then picketed on half lariat inside. Lieutenant Riddick places sentinels pretty well out from the wagons. I make a regular detail of teamsters, with a wagonmaster and assistant in charge, who divide the night between them, and I am to be called at any and all times that the man in charge sees or hears anything suspicious, or that he does not understand. The detail for sentinels is twelve teamsters each night—half being on post the first half of the night and half the last part. This gives two sentinels on the west, two on the south and two on the east— the roster kept so that each man will do his fair share of guard duty. From my experience as a dragoon I send two or three men mounted on mules to highest points in the vicinity of camp, there to dismount and let the mules graze while they keep a look out

---

[23] The trading post of James Bordeau was eight miles below Fort Laramie on the North Platte.

[24] Andrew Dripps, see note 19, Part II.

and keep me informed of everything of interest from the time we camp until sunset.

24th to 27th. Camped each night on Platte.

28th. Soon after leaving camp, saw a party of Indians on the opposite side of river, supposed to be Sioux. Indians seen along bluffs about two miles from camp. We saw some Sioux squaws along the bluff between Indian camp and ours, and Riddick and I rode out to see what they were hunting for, and found they were after rattlesnakes, and they found them plentiful. I dismounted and watched one squaw for half an hour, during which she got three. With a forked stick in left hand and butcher knife in the other, she crept towards the snake until he was ready to "strike," when quickly and skillfully she pinned him down by placing the forked stick close to his head, pressing down firmly and amputating the head. By killing them in this way they had no chance to bite themselves, which they do when hurt or angry. When they do not bite themselves, thereby poisoning the meat, it is good to eat, and that is what the squaws wanted them for. Having severed the head from the body, the squaw caught the latter and thrust it into the folds of her blanket next to her buckskin shirt.

Arrived at Ash Hollow at ten o'clock and camped. Storm subsided and left a bright, sunny day. After lunch mounted my horse, and with "Billy" Daniels for a companion, went in search of a road out of Ash Hollow to avoid the one already in use, which is altogether impracticable for us with our heavy loads—3,500 pounds in each wagon. The teams could no more than pull up the empty wagons, and we should have to double teams and haul up a little at a time, straining mules and breaking chains. We found and staked out a route that can be traveled without much difficulty—five hours' hard riding to find a route three miles through the bluffs.

30th. Off at 5:00, took the new route and at eight o'clock all wagons were at the top of the hill in safety, with no accident except upsetting one wagon by carelessness.

Having fairly straightened out the train at the top of the hill, a band of Indians came in sight from the east at a fast gallop. I started the train into corral, giving the sign by riding my horse in a circle; the movement was quickly commenced, wagonmasters and teamsters moving with a will. Riddick quickly formed his soldiers in line ready for business, while I rode to a high point, with Manuel for an interpreter, and motioned them to stop. They came down to a walk, and when within hailing distance were told to stop and let their chief come up. This they did, "Man-Afraid-of-His-Horse"[25] approached, "Howed," shook hands, and asked for something to eat. I cut the talk short by telling him that we must keep all we had for Colonel Sumner's command, which was after the Cheyennes and would be very hungry when we met. The chief promised not to come any nearer and I shook his hand, galloped to the train and straightened out on the road. The Indians had no hostile intent.

Fourteen miles brought us into camp one mile above crossing of South Platte. Immediately after lunch, about one o'clock, I retired to my tent to sleep off the fatigue of yesterday, and told my cook not to allow any one to disturb me unless for some good reason. At five o'clock he woke me and said that Lieutenant Riddick wanted me to come to the river bank; there were Indians on the other side. I took no arms, contrary to my habit of always being ready. There were four Indians, and I sent a man with a white towel for a flag to a small island to wave it as an invitation to come over, hoping to hear something from Colonel Sumner. As soon as the man beckoned them to come over, one galloped off up the river and the other three took off their saddles and commenced to cross bareback. It was easier and safer to cross without saddles. They were soon in camp, claimed to be Sioux but proved to be Cheyennes. I advised taking them prisoners, which Riddick agreed to, and I explained to him the difficulty

---

25 Man-Afraid-of-His-Horse was generally recognized as head chief of the Oglala Sioux after 1854. He was prominent in the Red Cloud War of 1866–67. His son, often called Young-Man-Afraid-of-His-Horse, succeeded to his influence in the later years of the nineteenth century.

of doing so without injuring them, which we must avoid if possible.

The teamsters were now bringing in the mules and picketing them on half lariat between us and the river. The soldiers had been cleaning their guns for inspection, and stood idly by. Having arrived at my tent, Manuel Vijil, a Mexican who had lived with the Sioux and understood the Cheyenne language, especially the sign language, was called to act as interpreter. The Indians seemed frightened on seeing the soldiers, but were assured that no harm would come to them: that we would feed and take care of them, etc. We all sat upon the ground, Riddick facing one Indian, I another, and Manuel the third. At Riddick's request, I played the part of "White Chief," and did the talking. They were asked why they came into our camp, and replied that, being very hungry and thinking it a freight or emigrant train, they hoped to get something to eat. Asked where their people were, they said that some of them were on the South Platte, near the mouth of Pole Creek, about twenty miles above us. This corroborated my suspicion that the fourth Indian, who rode off up the river, had gone to some camp. Asked if they knew where Colonel Sumner's command was, the big brave said that they did, but did not want to talk about that. They were then informed that this was Colonel Sumner's supply train, and that they were prisoners; that they would be well treated and fed; that we would take care of their arms and ponies until Colonel Sumner's arrival, which would be in a day or two. To this their leader, a large, powerful fellow, six feet four inches high, and strongly pock-marked, appeared to agree, but said something very low to the others, which Manuel afterwards interpreted to be: "You young men can do as you please, but I am no longer a boy to give up my bow." It was a trying moment. I realized that their compliance with my request would come only after a physical struggle. We did not want to do violence to these three Indians in a camp of 150 men; it would seem shameful; yet we must keep them prisoners. We all stood up, 50 men standing around, half of them with loaded rifles. Quick as thought the big fellow sprang on his pony, and was off towards the river. Twenty or more shots were fired after him, but his pony tangled in the mules' lariats and fell, pitching the Indian into a slough separating some small islands from the main land.

All but Manuel and myself rushed after the escaping Indian, while Manuel, a big, broad-shouldered, powerful man, seized one of the others from behind, pinioned his arms tightly, laid him on the ground and there held him; I reached for the bow of the third one, when he eluded me and I struck him a powerful blow in the face, thinking to knock him down; but he only bounded like a ball, drew his scalping knife and came near stabbing me. I seized him by the wrists and held up his hands, realizing that to let go meant death to me, while he sprang into the air like a wild tiger, trying with all his might to break away, and yelling like a maniac. This lasted a minute or two until "Billy" Daniels, a fine young teamster, came to my assistance. I told him to get behind the Indian, pinion his arms and lay him down on the ground, which he did; and with both hands I took his knife, bow, quiver and arrows. His saddle, lariat, bow, quiver, arrows and scalping knife fell to me, and on my return to Fort Leavenworth I gave them to my friend Levi Wilson, who sent them to his father, Dr. Wilson, of Pittsburgh, Pennsylvania.

Small rope was brought and I soon had both tied hand and foot. Then I mounted my horse and searched the small islands near shore for the big brave, thinking he must be wounded or killed; but did not find him. If he was hit, he might have sunk in the muddy stream, and one could not see a foot under water; and if not, he could lie on his back under over-hanging willows with nose far enough out of the water to breathe until dark, and then make his escape. His pony, lariat, blanket, bow, quiver and arrows were left behind. For want of proper irons we used small chains and padlocks from the front boxes of wagons to iron the two prisoners, the right hand of one fastened to the left hand of the other. We had a tent pitched for them, and a soldier sen-

The Cheyenne Expedition

tinel placed in front and one in rear. And now the interpreter, Lieutenant Riddick, and I commenced a pumping process to find out from the young fellows all we could of Colonel Sumner. We learned that he had had a battle the day before, that some Indians were killed and wounded, as well as some soldiers, that the Cheyennes were scattered, most of them going north, crossing the South Platte near the mouth of Pole Creek. We believed these statements to be fairly correct. The Indian that I captured was a son of the head chief, and the other was his cousin, each about twenty-two years old, tall, well built, and very handsome Indians—the best type of Cheyennes.

And now the suspicion arose that there might be a large camp of Cheyennes in the vicinity of the mouth of Pole Creek. We had the chief's son, and there might be an effort made to stampede or capture our train to give the youngsters a chance to escape, and I immediately set to work to corral the wagons so as to make a solid fort, with room for men and animals inside. Setting the first wagon, the next came up and struck its left front wheel against the right hind wheel of the first, with tongue on the outside—each wagon coming up so as to make the circle more complete; when the last wagon but one was in, that one would close the mouth of the corral so that nothing could get in or out. All this we did by hand in two hours, put all of the animals inside and closed the gap with the last wagon. Then I examined all arms in the hands of teamsters, and saw that each had fifty rounds of ammunition. Riddick did the same with the soldiers. A strong guard was posted, and all was quiet.

A candle was kept burning in the prisoners' tent, and lying a few feet from the open front, without being seen, I watched them. They whispered together a good deal and seemed to be listening, wrapped in a state of expectance. There was a dismal sound of wolves howling in every direction. That was nothing new; we heard them howling every night; but one of them sent out a peculiar howl, unlike any of the others; he howled at intervals directly south across the river. To this the young chief and his

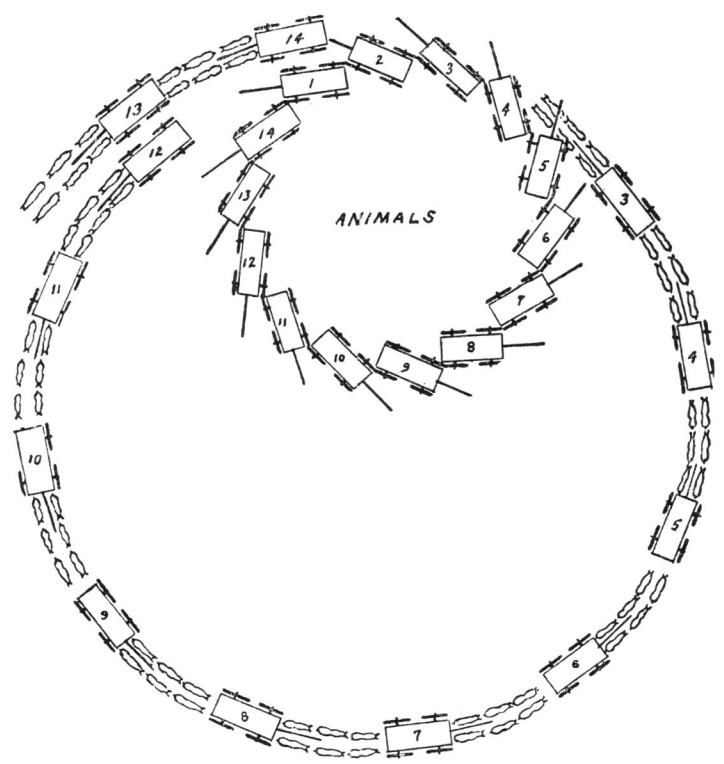

Sketch reproduced from the 1906 edition
WAGON CORRAL

fellow prisoner sat up and listened eagerly. Wolves wading across a shallow river make about the same splashing noise that a horse does, and quite a number crossed during the night. An hour had passed since I had heard the peculiar howl referred to, when it broke out again on our side of the river above the camp. I now felt convinced, as I had before believed, that this particular howl was by an Indian, by which he conveyed information to the prisoners. There was no sleep for me, for I believed that there was a large band of Cheyennes in our neighborhood, but we had no fear of the whole Cheyenne Nation, the way we were corralled. Vigilance was all that we needed.

July 31st. Camp aroused an hour before daylight in anticipa-

The Cheyenne Expedition

tion of an attack, about dawn being a favorite time with Indians to surprise unsuspecting sleepers. Daylight came, but no enemy in sight. After breakfast, with three men mounted on mules, I scoured the country to the highest bluffs north, and then posted them as vedettes on three prominent points half a mile from camp. I then rode a couple of miles up the river, but discovered nothing but the tracks of two ponies which crossed the river during the night. About 4:00 P.M. an Indian approached the river on the opposite side to within half a mile of the bank, reconnoitered a while and then rode away. About five o'clock an express arrived from Laramie with mail for the command, which failed to reach Colonel Sumner by a former express; it was brought by a mountaineer called "Big Phil,"[26] accompanied by a Sioux Indian. No news from Colonel Sumner; mules herded close to corral under strong guard, ready to rush them in quickly if necessary.

August 1st. Vedettes posted and mules herded by strong mounted guard near by corral. I crossed the river and met one of Majors & Company's[27] trains en route to Salt Lake. No news from Colonel Sumner and none from the "States." Rode five miles up the river and found plenty of Indian pony tracks. Some soldiers crossed over and found two saddles belonging to our prisoners. This shows that the Indian who escaped took his saddle for another horse, when he joins his tribe or gets a chance to steal one. No Indians seen to-day. This evening Lieutenant Riddick consented to send out two Mexican spies, Manuel Vijil (pro-

---

[26] LeRoy R. Hafen identifies "Big Phil" as Charles Gardner, so called because he came from Philadelphia. He carried mail between Denver and Fort Laramie, 1858–59. See L. R. Hafen, "Mountain Men—'Big Phil, the Cannibal,'" in *Colorado Magazine*, Vol. XIII (1936), 53–58.

[27] The firm of Majors & Russell—Alexander Majors and William H. Russell—of Leavenworth, Kansas, obtained a two-year contract in 1855 to transport military supplies west of the Mississippi River. The contract was renewed for one year in 1857, the year of the Utah expedition, and losses that year, including three trains burned by the Mormons, threatened the firm with financial disaster. In an attempt to recoup their losses the associated firm of Russell, Majors and Waddell—William B. Waddell was the added partner—established the famous Pony Express in 1860. The eventual result was bankruptcy.

nounced Vi-heel) and Malquis Mestos, for the purpose of ascertaining the location of the Cheyenne camp, supposed to be near the mouth of Pole Creek, perhaps twenty miles above us. Manuel was given a letter from Lieutenant Riddick to Colonel Sumner, in case he should meet him, and he was instructed to find the Cheyenne camp if possible, count the lodges, see which way they faced, take cognizance of every ravine or pass leading to the camp, etc., and to return to our camp by evening of the 3d inst. They were furnished horses, feed and arms, and passed the guard at 12:00 midnight.

2d. The expressman, "Big Phil" and the Sioux Indian left us at sunrise. They had been permitted to talk with the prisoners, it being known that they would tell of it to any Indians they happened to meet, and by that means the safety of the prisoners would be known to their friends; and it was believed that the Cheyennes might be induced to come in and make terms for peace. Moved camp one and one-half miles up river for fresh grass. Improved this time to practice in corralling, so as always to be ready to corral quickly by driving round in a circle without confusion. A hundred men well armed inside of my corral could stand off thousands with bows and arrows.

After the vedettes had been posted on high ground and I or one or two wagonmasters had explored a little, the mules are turned out to graze and kept out until within an hour of sunset, and then shut up in the corral for the night. We feed corn to wagonmasters', Mexicans' and Riddick's and my horses to keep them in condition for long rides or stampedes at any time; no other animals are fed. We save the corn for the command when it reaches us.

August 3d. Mexicans return this evening, and report having found a camp of seven lodges on the south side of South Platte, nearly opposite mouth of Pole Creek, where there had been two other camps. They found a chart in one of the camps marked on a buffalo skull, showing that the Indians had taken the route up Pole Creek to a point opposite Smith's Fork, thence north across

The Cheyenne Expedition

North Platte. The Mexicans saw one Indian today, but could not get near him. No news or sign of Colonel Sumner. Heavy rain and electric storm during the night.

August 4th. I called for volunteers to go to the camp of seven lodges. Twenty teamsters and the two Mexicans above mentioned got ready, armed with rifles and revolvers.

August 5th. Off at sunrise; teamsters on mules, Mexicans and myself on horses; crossed river opposite camp, up south side to the seven lodges. There they stood, but no Indians in sight, and a careful reconnaissance revealed none. Everything indicated that they had gone in a hurry, leaving besides lodges, many useful articles; live coals of a small fire still smouldering, and cooking utensils that would not be abandoned except in case of necessity. Looking across the river, up Pole Creek, we saw a band of Indians in rapid retreat two miles away. Undoubtedly my party had been seen, and the Indians were in too much of a hurry to encumber themselves with lodges. The party seemed quite large and their precipitate retreat indicated that they were greatly demoralized. The Indian trail coming from the south was broad and quite well worn, showing that many had traveled it recently, and quite a number since the rain night before last. Manuel and I were so impressed with the indications of recent Indian travel over this line, that we instinctively looked south for some portion of Colonel Sumner's command in pursuit. We saved one of the lodges, a nice small one, pack-saddle and a bushel or two of kinnikinnick (the inside bark of red willow, dried), enough for all hands to smoke for a month, piled everything else together and burned it. Placing sentinels on several high points, with the Mexicans and "Billy" Daniels, I rode to the camp two miles above; found a chart on a buffalo head and everything to corroborate Manuel's statement; had him bring the head to camp. To me it revealed the fact that the scattering bands were going to concentrate somewhere north of North Platte, and it might be valuable information for Colonel Sumner. Returned to my party and thence to camp without incident, except plentiful signs of

Indians having traveled up and down the river opposite our camp—surely Cheyennes. There were tracks of two American horses, with shoes on, that had passed the camp both ways since the rain, indicating that Colonel Sumner may have lost some horses.

August 7th and 8th. Nothing new. Several false alarms. Each sunny day the wagon covers are thrown off so that the sun may dry out any dampness that may have accumulated. If rain has beaten in, the loading is taken out and repacked. Damp commissaries and corn soon spoil under wagon covers exposed to the hot sun. Many horses and mules die of colic caused by eating corn thus exposed. It gathers dampness, swells, heats, gets musty, moldy and finally rotten, unfit for any animal to eat. There is nothing so demoralizing for men as idleness, and examining loads, unloading and re-loading wagons is a great benefit to men and stores.

The Indian prisoners seem to have outgrown their fears of violence, and to have overcome their aversion to Manuel and myself, who were the prime cause of their captivity; in short, they have become quite communicative. The one who fell into my hands says that after the fight the Cheyennes scattered, agreeing to go north and meet from time to time at some point north of the North Platte. When told of what we found near the mouth of Pole Creek, the buffalo head with chart having been shown them, they said that that camp was a sort of depot of supplies and information to assist those going north. Being closely questioned, the young chief said the wolf that made the peculiar noise the night of their capture was his father, and that two other nights he had heard his father. He thought the Cheyennes too much scattered to attack our train, and thought his father would not do so for fear of what might happen to them; in fact sufficient assurance had been given through the peculiar wolf howl, that they would not disturb the train. And we believed that their captivity would have a strong influence in inducing the Cheyennes to come to terms and sue for peace.

The Cheyenne Expedition

August 9th. This morning one of Childs' ox trains passed en route to the "States." By it we learned that the mail passed west during the night. Sent two men and caught mail at Ash Hollow.

August 10th. Crossed train over river without accident, and camped one mile below where we had so much trouble in June. Water is low; half the river bed a dry sand bar; Lieutenant Riddick took 211 sacks of corn from one of Major Russell's[28] trains en route to Laramie, believing that Colonel Sumner's command would soon be here. Some Indians seen this evening supposed to be Sioux.

August 11th. This morning a band of Sioux, under "Man-Afraid-of-His-Horse," crossed from north to south side of the river. Only the chief allowed to come into camp. He was told to keep away from the mule herd, and not to allow his men to come near. In the meantime the mules were corralled. The Indians soon left, and the mules were again turned out. A wagonmaster or his assistant is with the herd all of the time, and he is instructed to corral on the appearance of Indians, whether there seems to be danger or not. One of the herders leads a horse with a bell on his neck, and when the herd is to be corralled he rattles the bell violently and gallops for the corral. The passageway is always kept clear when mules are out. The mules have now gotten so used to this that they run for the corral when the bell is rattled, and could hardly be kept from it. About noon a train came in sight down the river. Of course we are all expectancy, hoping that every outfit that comes in sight may be ours. I rode out and met Colonel M. F. W. Magraw[29] and his surveying party, en route to Cali-

---

[28] Should be Majors and Russell—see preceding note.

[29] William M. F. Magraw, a friend of President Buchanan and a deserving Democrat claiming influence in Virginia, Maryland, and Pennsylvania, was named by Secretary of the Interior Jacob Thompson as superintendent of construction for the improvement of two sections of a wagon road from Fort Kearny to Independence Rock and City Rocks in 1857. Magraw dawdled at Independence, Missouri, until July; after he got started he was accused of wasting funds and carrying goods for personal profit. He partly redeemed himself by offering his services and those of his party to the Army of Utah, but the Interior Department construed this as resignation of his superintendency, thus ending a prolonged and long-

fornia, with "Tim" Goodale,[30] the celebrated mountaineer, as guide. I had met him here in 1851. Major Johnson,[31] Sixth Infantry, en route to Laramie, is with Magraw. Magraw with his fifty wagons camped near us, and half the night was spent in gathering the news from him, Goodale and Johnson. They left us a few old papers.

August 12th. Magraw's train crossed the river and camped on north bank. He, Goodale, and Major Johnson dined with us. Goodale belonged to the class of mountaineers who ranked with Sublette, Fitzpatrick, Bridger, etc., with Carson as the recognized head—reliable characters, unmixed with false heroism, intelligent and trustworthy. The young Cheyennes knew him, and he learned from them about what they had told us, and he thought the information pretty correct. Of course Goodale knew nothing of Colonel Sumner's fight, but judging from what the prisoners said, it was forty hours afterwards that they came to my camp, and he thought the Cheyennes were sure to retreat north; they would not be likely to go south or west, and surely not east; they

---

distance squabble. See W. Turrentine Jackson, *Wagon Roads West* (Berkeley and Los Angeles, University of California Press, 1952), 175, 191-211.

30 Lowe had met Goodale in 1850—see note 15, Part II. Goodale had spent the winter of 1856-57 on Green River, and came to Kansas City in the spring. There he reported that at Ash Hollow the Sioux chief Long Chin had told him of rejecting Cheyenne proposals that the Sioux join them in warfare against the whites. When Goodale and Magraw reached Fort Laramie, they quarreled over a profit-making scheme and "the guide pulled the superintendent's beard and tromped on his feet to invoke a fight as a means of settling the matter in true mountain style." Officers of the post patched up the quarrel. See Hafen and Hafen, *Relations*, 18-19, 85-86; Jackson, *op. cit.*, 197.

31 Edward Johnson was born in Chesterfield County, Virginia, April 16, 1816. He was appointed to West Point in 1833 (from Kentucky, says Heitman, who also gives that as state of birth) and was graduated in 1838 and commissioned second lieutenant, Sixth Infantry. He became first lieutenant in 1839; brevet captain for Molino del Rey; brevet major for Chapultepec; and captain, Sixth Infantry in 1851. He resigned in 1861 and in 1862 was Confederate brigadier general under Major General T. J. Jackson. In 1863 he became a major general commanding a division of the Second Corps, Army of Northern Virginia; and in 1864 he commanded a division of the Second Corps, Army of Tennessee. He died in Richmond, Virginia, March 2, 1873.

The Cheyenne Expedition

could get north of the North Platte more easily, and soon be in a comparatively safe country, at that time almost unknown to the whites. He wondered why Colonel Sumner was not hot after them, as they passed within twenty miles of his supply train, and some of them much nearer, unless he was himself too much crippled to follow; at any rate, if the Cheyennes were whipped anywhere on the branches of the Kaw River they would retreat north if possible; and we had ample proof that the chief (whose son and nephew were our prisoners) and most of his people did go north. Any one who knew the country north of North Platte would know they would do that, and then old "Tim" expressed the opinion that Colonel Sumner's guides knew nothing about the haunts of the Cheyennes in the northern country.

Mr. R. M. Peck,[32] of Whittier, California, has written an interesting account of the Cheyenne expedition, as he remembers it; and as a soldier in the First Cavalry he participated in the battle and in pursuit of some of the Cheyennes, the command going to the Arkansas afterwards, undoubtedly opposite to the route taken by most of them (see Mr. Peck's letter in Kansas State Historical Society's collections, Volume VIII).

13th. Went with Colonel Magraw to Ash Hollow. He passed his train over my new route without difficulty, and named it "Lowe's Route Avoiding Ash Hollow Hill."

14th. In the evening one mule left the herd and ran down the road, followed by Assistant Wagonmaster Stanley and two teamsters. They soon returned and reported that they saw Indians on the north side of the river. Messrs. Patrick, Cecil and I went in pursuit as far as Nine Mile Tree, where we found Captain Van Vliet,[33] quartermaster of the Utah army, camped. His men had

---

[32] The article by Robert Morris Peck in *Kansas State Historical Society Collections*, Volume VIII, 1903–1904, 486–506, is reprinted in Hafen and Hafen, *Relations*, 97–140. R. M. Peck also wrote a series of "Reminiscences" published in the *National Tribune*, 1901.

[33] Stewart Van Vliet of New York was graduated from West Point in 1840, becoming second lieutenant, Third Artillery. He became first lieutenant in 1843, captain assistant quartermaster in 1847, and major assistant quartermaster in 1861.

caught my mule. Captain Van Vliet is on the way to Salt Lake, to return immmediately. He informed me that while Colonel Sumner's whereabouts are unknown, four of the six troops of cavalry now with him are to go to Utah, while the Colonel with the other two troops returns to Leavenworth. The three companies of infantry now under Colonel Sumner (C, D and G, Sixth), with the company at Laramie (B, Sixth), are also to go to Utah. Colonel Alexander,[34] Tenth Infantry, with advance troops for Salt Lake, expected in a day or two. Returned to camp at midnight.

15th. Captain Van Vliet passed this morning. I led the command over the river, as I did every other military outfit while we were camped near the crossing, and was able to serve many of them to good advantage.

17th. An express from Laramie, "Big Phil" arrived at sunrise. Received several letters from friends. No news from Colonel Sumner. A party of returning Californians camped near by. The party was managed by Mr. D. O. Mills, a banker of San Francisco, and a sea captain whose name I have forgotten. They stopped in

---

He was brigadier general of Volunteers 1861–62 and 1865–66; brevet lieutenant colonel and brevet brigadier general in 1864; and brevet major general of Volunteers and brevet major general in 1865, the last-named rank "for faithful and distinguished service in the Quartermaster Department during the war." In 1866 he became lieutenant colonel and deputy quartermaster general, and in 1872 colonel and assistant quartermaster general. He retired in 1881 and died March 28, 1901. When Lowe met him, Van Vliet was on his way to Salt Lake City under orders "to make necessary arrangements for receiving and provisioning the troops in Utah." His reports did much to avert an armed clash between troops and Mormons. See LeRoy R. and Ann W. Hafen, editors, "Mission of Captain Van Vliet," *The Utah Expedition, 1857–1858* (Glendale, Calif., Arthur H. Clark Company, 1958), 35–55.

[34] Edmund Brooke Alexander was born in Virginia and appointed to West Point from Kentucky in 1818. He was commissioned second lieutenant, Third Infantry in 1823; first lieutenant in 1827; and captain, assistant quartermaster, in 1838. He was brevetted major for Cerro Gordo and lieutenant colonel for Contreras and Churubusco. He became major, Eighth Infantry, in 1851 and colonel, Tenth Infantry, in 1855. In 1865 he was brevetted brigadier general "for meritorious service in the recruitment of the armies of the United States." He retired in 1869 and died January 3, 1888.

The Cheyenne Expedition

Salt Lake several days. Mr. Mills and Captain ———— seemed to be very superior men and not inclined to talk romance. This is the D. O. Mills of New York whose name is honored throughout the financial world. They camped near us two days. They needed rest and took it while they could safely do so near our outfit.

21st. Colonel Alexander crossed over and camped on the north side. I led the train and gave him full information of route to Laramie. Saw Mr. Andrew Gartin and son, beef contractors of Clay County, Missouri, who are driving a large herd of cattle for delivery at Laramie under escort of the Tenth. Lieutenant Bryan's[35] party arrived from Bridger's Pass and camped near us. Dr. Covey[36] joined us from Lieutenant Bryan—quite an acquisition to our mess.

22nd. Colonel Alexander marched early. Lieutenant Bryan's party left en route to the States.

Captain Dixon, quartermaster,[37] and Captain Clark, commis-

---

[35] Francis Theodore Bryan of North Carolina was graduated from West Point in 1846 and was commissioned brevet second lieutenant of the Corps of Topographical Engineers. He became second lieutenant in 1851 after being brevetted first lieutenant in 1847 for gallant and meritorious conduct in the Battle of Buena Vista. He was made first lieutenant in 1855 and captain in 1860. He resigned June 10, 1861. Probably he joined the Confederate Army, but several sources consulted have no further information about his subsequent career. He made a number of surveys for wagon roads and at the time Lowe met him, Lt. Bryan, after mapping a route to Bridger's Pass, was returning to Fort Leavenworth—with no authority to furnish guides to the Utah expedition.

[36] Edward N. Covey of Maryland was appointed assistant surgeon on August 29, 1856. He resigned June 1, 1861, and served as surgeon in the Confederate Army. He died in September, 1867.

[37] John H. Dickerson (not Dixon) was born in Ohio and was appointed to West Point from Indiana in 1843. He was commissioned brevet second lieutenant, Fourth Artillery, on July 1, 1847, and second lieutenant, First Artillery on August 19 of the same year. He was promoted first lieutenant in 1850, and retained that commission until 1861, although, after serving as regimental quartermaster 1852–56, he was named captain, assistant quartermaster in 1856, in which capacity he was quartermaster of the Utah expedition. He was brevetted major in 1865 for efficient and meritorious service in the Department of the Ohio. He resigned on March 31, 1864, and died March 2, 1872.

sary,[38] arrived and crossed the river en route to Utah. They bring news that Colonel Sumner had a fight with the Cheyennes on the 29th of July. Large body of Indians formed in battle array, and the cavalry charged with drawn sabers. Twelve Indians were left on the field and many wounded; cavalry lost two men killed, and Lieutenant Stuart and eight men wounded. Captain Foote with his company of Sixth Infantry bringing the wounded to Fort Kearney. The fight is said to have taken place on Solomon's Fork of the Kaw River. Colonel Sumner followed the Indians, burned their lodges and other property, and then followed their trail, as he supposed, en route to the Arkansas. Colonel Sumner established a camp on Walnut Creek, leaving two companies of infantry there, under Captain Ketchum. Sent Lieutenant Lomax to Fort Riley after supplies. This is the first news of Colonel Sumner's command except what the prisoners gave us. Moved camp five miles up river. We think the chances much against Colonel Sumner ever coming to us. For sanitary reasons one camp should not be long occupied; it becomes filthy and the corrals muddy and unclean.

August 24th. Fifth Infantry camped nine miles below crossing en route to Utah. More than half of the regiment said to have deserted since leaving Florida, two months ago.

[38] Henry Francis Clarke (not Clark) of Pennsylvania was appointed to West Point in 1839 and was graduated in 1843 as brevet second lieutenant, Second Artillery. He became second lieutenant in 1846 and first lieutenant in 1847, serving as regimental adjutant, 1852–55. In 1857 he was named captain, commissary of subsistence, in which capacity he served in the Utah expedition (the Subsistence Department was a separate service until combined with the Quartermaster Department in 1912). Clarke had been brevet captain since 1847, for Chapultepec. He became major, commissary of subsistence, on August 3, 1861, and on September 28, 1861, was named colonel, additional aide-de-camp, retaining that commission until 1866. Meanwhile he was brevetted colonel in 1863 for gallant and meritorious conduct in the Maryland campaign and was commissioned lieutenant colonel, assistant commissary general of subsistence in 1864 as permanent assignment. In 1865 he was brevetted brigadier general for gallant and meritorious service during the Battle of Gettysburg and major general for faithful and meritorious service in the Subsistence Department during the war. He was promoted from lieutenant colonel to colonel, assistant commissary general of subsistence in 1882, retired in 1884, and died on May 10, 1887.

The Cheyenne Expedition

25th. Fifth Infantry crossed river. Animals in good condition, the credit of which is largely due to my friend "Jim" Miller, the head wagonmaster, who always herds mules and never starves them at the lariat. He came to me at Riley in the fall of 1855 with the Second Dragoons from Texas, and is one of the very best in his line.

28th. Express arrived from Kearney bringing letters from Captain Foote and Lieutenant Stuart to Lieutenant Riddick, and orders from Colonel Sumner to Lieutenant Riddick for the train to proceed to Kearney, turn in all stores not necessary for use, and proceed to Fort Leavenworth. Colonel Sumner gone to the Arkansas, and will go from there to Fort Leavenworth, where he will probably arrive as soon as we do. Though there has been no hardship in our stay here, there has been a good deal of anxiety. The long suspense is very monotonous, and all are glad to move.

29th. En route to Kearney. When nine miles below the crossing an express arrived from General Harney at Leavenworth, ordering that the train proceed to Ash Hollow and there remain until the arrival of four troops of the First Cavalry and three companies of Sixth Infantry en route to Utah. The order presupposes the train to be at Kearney, and directs Lieutenant Riddick to take supplies from that post sufficient to subsist the four troops and three companies to Laramie. As he has not sufficient supplies, Lieutenant Riddick determined to proceed to Kearney and procure them, and, unless otherwise ordered, return to Ash Hollow and remain as directed. Camped at Nine Mile Tree.

31st. Camped below O'Fallon's Bluffs at Fremont Spring, the head of big slough that runs parallel with the South Platte, twenty or more miles. When coming into camp, an Indian and two squaws with pack-pony dragging lodge and poles crossed the road from the south going north. The "buck" said that they were Sioux; I thought them Cheyennes. When in mid-river, becoming frightened, they cut away their packs and ran, which confirms my belief that they were Cheyennes. I was sorry to see their effects thus thrown away. The poor squaws were safe enough.

September 7th. Camped at Fort Kearney. And now we must part with our Indian prisoners, of whom I have become quite fond, though glad to be rid of the responsibility of holding them. Lieutenant Riddick turned them over to the commanding officer, and they were confined in the guard house. Thirty-nine days they have been with us, and while we have been obliged to be a little severe in keeping them safely ironed, they have been well fed and safely cared for.

9th. We started to return west and camped seventeen miles above the fort on Platte. Dr. Covey accompanied us. The Doctor and I went after buffalo about sunset and killed one each. Dr. Summers, post surgeon,[39] and John Heath, post sutler, arrived from the fort on a buffalo hunt and spent the night with us.

13th. Camped one mile below O'Fallon's Bluffs on head of Freemont's [sic] Slough. At 6:00 this evening an expressman arrived from Kearney with orders from Colonel Sumner for the train to remain at Kearney until the arrival of Major Sedgwick's four troops of cavalry and two companies of infantry. The order was sent under the belief that the train was then at Kearney.

14th. On the back track en route to Kearney.

16th. Short distance from camp killed a buffalo while crossing road ahead of train, and before going into camp Messrs. Stanley and Eskridge killed another; saved abundance of fine meat. Met George Cater, an expressman, en route to Laramie. Lieutenant Riddick received letters stating that all of the cavalry and infantry that were ordered from the Cheyenne expedition to Utah are now ordered to Leavenworth. Camped on Platte.

17th. Camped on Platte. Killed nine prairie chickens with pistols in camp before train came up. Lieutenant Marmaduke,[40]

---

[39] John Edward Summers was appointed assistant surgeon in 1847. In 1861 he became major surgeon; he was lieutenant colonel, medical inspector from February 27 to October 31, 1863. He became lieutenant colonel in 1880, colonel surgeon in 1885, and retired in 1886.

[40] John Sappington Marmaduke of Missouri was graduated from West Point in 1857 as brevet second lieutenant, First Infantry, and one month later became

The Cheyenne Expedition

with detachment of recruits for Seventh Infantry, en route to Laramie, arrived and camped with us.

18th. Lying by. Rained all forenoon. In the afternoon Marmaduke and I "still hunted" (hunted on foot) buffalo, but did not kill any. His transportation consisted of two dilapidated wagons, each drawn by six broken-down pack-mules that Captain Foote had brought into Kearney with the wounded men from the Cheyenne campaign. We were going in, and could exchange and give him fine teams and wagons, which we did, and turned over to him another team and wagon for which he receipted; and with it I turned over an experienced man capable of looking after all of the teams; knew the camps, and would take him to Laramie all right. I never saw a better pleased man than Marmaduke—a future major general in the Confederate Army, and later Governor of his native State of Missouri. We invited Marmaduke to join our mess while camped near us, which he did. He had some potatoes, something we had not seen in four months. I would only accept enough for one dinner, which, with my prairie chickens, made a fine feast.

19th. Lieutenant Marmaduke and party went on west and we east. Met "Sim" Routh and Sarcoxie, a Delaware guide, with letters, by which we learn that Major Sedgwick's command of four troops of cavalry and two companies of infantry are waiting for us thirty-two miles below Kearney. Arrived and camped at Kearney. Found Lieutenants Wheaton and Bayard at the fort with orders for Lieutenant Riddick to turn over the train and all other property to Lieutenant Wheaton. We left here all commissary stores not necessary for troops going in to Fort Leavenworth.

20th. Finished turning over property and started down the

---

second lieutenant, Seventh Infantry. He resigned in 1861 and became a Confederate major general, commanding cavalry in the trans-Mississippi fighting. He was captured in 1864 during Sterling Price's invasion of Missouri, and was imprisoned at Fort Warren, Massachusetts. He became governor of Missouri in 1885 and died in office on December 28, 1887.

river at noon. Met Beauvais' and Bisonet's[41] traders' trains for their trading posts near Fort Laramie.

21st. Camped with Major Sedgwick's command on Little Blue.

22d. Camped on Little Blue. Turned over four teams to Captain Ketchum's command. Feed half rations of corn to horses and mules.

23d. When leaving camp this morning met Colonel Albert Sidney Johnston,[42] of the Second Cavalry, in command of the Utah Expedition, and his adjutant-general, Major Fitzjohn Porter,[43] with a train of twenty four-mule ambulances, several

[41] James P. Beauvais and Joseph Bisonet or Bissonnette were traders in the Fort Laramie region.

[42] Albert Sidney Johnston was born in Washington, Mason County, Kentucky, February 3, 1803. He was appointed to West Point from Louisiana, graduating in 1826. He was assigned to the Second Infantry as brevet second lieutenant, and was promoted to second lieutenant, Sixth Infantry, April 4, 1827, by a commission predated to his day of graduation. He was regimental adjutant, 1828–32. He served in the Black Hawk War and was named temporarily assistant adjutant general of Illinois Volunteers with the rank of colonel. He resigned in 1834 because of the ill health of his wife, who died in 1835. Johnston arrived in Texas shortly after the Battle of San Jacinto, and was appointed adjutant general with the rank of colonel. His promotion to senior brigadier general of the Texas Army resulted in a duel with Brigadier General Felix Huston, who was superseded. Johnston was wounded. In 1838 he was named secretary of war by President Mirabeau B. Lamar. At the beginning of the Mexican War, Johnston was elected colonel of the First Texas Rifle Volunteers, a three months' regiment. When the regiment was discharged, General Taylor named Johnston an acting inspector general. This appointment was disallowed, and Johnston returned home after he took part in the Battle of Monterrey. When Taylor became President, he named Johnston major paymaster in 1849. In 1855 he was named colonel of the new Second Cavalry. In 1857 he was commissioned brevet brigadier general "for meritorious conduct in the ability, zeal, energy, and prudence displayed by him in command of the army in Utah." He resigned in 1861 and became a Confederate four-star general. As commander of the Army of the Mississippi he was killed in the Battle of Shiloh, April 6, 1862.

[43] Fitz John Porter was born in Portsmouth, New Hampshire, June 13, 1822. He was appointed to West Point from New York and was graduated in 1845 as brevet second lieutenant. He became second lieutenant in 1846, first lieutenant in 1847, brevet captain for Molino del Rey, and brevet major for Chapultepec. In 1856 he became brevet captain as assistant adjutant general. He was named colonel of the new Fifteenth Infantry in 1861 and three days later was commissioned brigadier general of Volunteers. He commanded the Fifth Corps in the Battle of Chicka-

The Cheyenne Expedition

officers and an escort of the Second Dragoons, en route to Utah. I received orders to select twenty-five of my best mule teams to be left with an escort of cavalry to await the arrival of Colonel Cooke,* en route to Utah. Colonel Johnston and Major Porter were waiting by the side of the road, and saw the teams go by. I was sent for, and Colonel Johnston said: "I am told that this is the finest train on the plains." To which I replied that we had exchanged a few good teams for broken-down ones from the Cheyenne campaign; otherwise, the teams and equipments were complete. "Well," said he, "we want the best; we will need them," and he got them. Traveled eighteen miles and camped on Little Blue. Unloaded twenty-five wagons, fitted up the best teams and equipments throughout, got volunteers to drive them, drew rations for the men, and have everything ready to turn over in the morning.

24th. Turned over the twenty-five wagons for Colonel Cooke's command to Lieutenant Perkins,[44] and two wagons for himself

hominy and was brevetted brigadier general (Regular Army) for gallant and meritorious conduct in that fight, and was promoted to major general of Volunteers. His action on an order from Major General John Pope in the second Battle of Bull Run led to a court-martial, and Porter was cashiered on January 21, 1863. After many years of fighting to clear his name, he won reinstatement on August 5, 1886, as colonel of infantry, to date from May 14, 1861 (the date of his permanent appointment as colonel, Fifteenth Infantry). He accepted retirement two days later. He died May 21, 1901.

[44] John N. Perkins was first lieutenant, First Cavalry, commissioned when that regiment was organized in 1855. Born in Tennessee, he entered the army from Alabama as second lieutenant of the Thirteenth Infantry, raised for the Mexican War. He was promoted to first lieutenant late in 1847 and mustered out in 1848. He was cashiered from the First Cavalry in 1859 and served in the Confederate Army as captain of Alabama cavalry. He died February 15, 1896. This identification seems probable, but there was another Lieutenant Perkins in the army at this time—Duane Delavan Perkins, first lieutenant, Fourth Artillery.

* Philip St. George Cooke was born in Virginia, and was graduated from the Military Academy in 1827. Brevet second lieutenant infantry, 1st July, 1827; second lieutenant Sixth Infantry, 1st July, 1827; first lieutenant First Dragoons, 4th March, 1833; captain, 31st of May, 1835; major Second Dragoons, 16th February, 1847; lieutenant colonel, 15th July, 1853; colonel, 14th June, 1858; Second Cavalry, 3d August, 1861; brigadier general Volunteers, 12th to 28th November, 1861; briga-

and escort—a small detachment of cavalry. Mr. Patrick took charge of train as wagonmaster; he was an excellent man and very competent. "Billy" Daniels went as assistant wagonmaster—a well earned promotion. Camped on Little Blue. An expressman left this morning and another this evening en route to Fort Leavenworth.

26th. Camped on Snake Root Creek. Express arrived this evening from Fort Leavenworth. Colonel Cooke's command of six troops of Second Dragoons said to be at Big Blue. The troops of Major Sedgwick's command to be stationed at various points in Kansas for the present.

27th. Met Colonel Cooke's command three miles west of Big Blue. Lieutenant Buford, acting quartermaster for the command, had an order to change all the mules he wanted to, taking our best and leaving his worst, which he did, leaving us nothing but a bad lot of mules to go in with. The last of my beautiful train was gone. We were going where forage was plentiful; they were approaching winter, where forage of all kinds would be scarce. Buford trusted to me, and I gave him the best. Crossed Big Blue and camped on Spring Creek. I heard that there were eighty desertions from dragoons since leaving Fort Leavenworth. Captain Ketchum with his two companies of infantry, remains here (Marysville) until after election—first Monday in October, or until further orders.

28th. Arrived and camped at Ash Point, twenty-five miles.

29th. Camped on Nemaha, Seneca is the town (now county seat of Nemaha County, Kansas). Captain Sturgis[45] and Lieu-

---

dier general, U. S. A., 12th November, 1861; retired 29th October, 1873; brevet lieutenant colonel, 20th February, 1847, for meritorious conduct in California, and major general 13th of March, 1865, for gallant and meritorious service during the war. Died 20th March, 1895.

[45] Samuel Davis Sturgis of Pennsylvania was graduated from West Point in 1846 as brevet second lieutenant, Second Dragoons. He became second lieutenant, First Dragoons, in 1847; was regimental quartermaster, 1851–52; first lieutenant, 1853; captain, First Cavalry, 1855; and major in 1861. Later that year he was made

The Cheyenne Expedition

tenant Stockton[46] arrived from Fort Leavenworth. G Troop First Cavalry to remain here until after election, B Troop to go to Palermo, A Troop to Claytonville, E Troop to Atchison. I go with twenty-nine teams and all the extra animals to Fort Leavenworth. Twenty-nine years old to-day, and gray enough to be fifty.

30th. Off for Fort Leavenworth at the same time that the command starts down the Atchison road. Four days later, with Lieutenants Wheaton and Riddick, I arrived at Fort Leavenworth and turned over the remnant of property in my charge; the Cheyenne campaign had ended, but the troops were still in the field, keeping peace at the polls, a more irksome business for soldiers than fighting Indians.

The day after my arrival Colonel Sumner sent for me and inquired particularly about what I saw of the campaign; said he had heard a good account of my part in it from various sources, and especially from Mr. Riddick; said that my train had the reputation of being the finest ever seen on the plains, and the best managed; in short, he was very profuse in his praises. He was especially interested in knowing my idea of the flight of the Cheyennes north, after his battle with them; I told him how things looked where I burned the camp, and all information gained from the Indian prisoners and by scouting in the neighborhood, but I did not venture an opinion, nor did he ask me to. He had probably made history that would redound to his credit, and

---

brigadier general of Volunteers. He was brevetted lieutenant colonel for Wilson's Creek, colonel for second Bull Run, brigadier general for South Mountain, and major general for Fredericksburg. He was mustered out of volunteer service in 1865; meanwhile, in 1863, he had been promoted to lieutenant colonel, Sixth Cavalry. In 1869 he became colonel of the new Seventh Cavalry. The regiment was actually commanded, until 1876, by its lieutenant colonel, General Custer, while General Sturgis was on duty in his brevet rank. After the Battle of the Little Big Horn, Sturgis took command of the Seventh until his retirement in 1886. He died September 28, 1889.

[46] Philip Stockton of New Jersey was graduated from West Point in 1852 as brevet second lieutenant, Eighth Infantry. He became second lieutenant in 1853; first lieutenant, First Cavalry, in 1855; and resigned in 1861. He was colonel of ordnance in the Confederate Army. He died March 25, 1879.

whether he followed the right or the wrong trail after the battle, he did the best that an earnest persevering commander could do, with the light before him; and I think that the general verdict of his command was that he did well, and that is the highest court by which a man can be tried.

After Colonel Sumner's command was "sifted" where he left us on the South Platte, he went into the field with as fine a set of officers and men as I ever saw. The civilians with his pack train—"Big Nick" Berry at the head—were the best we had. (See Mr. Peck's letter in Historical Society's Collections, heretofore referred to.)

The civilians who were with me four and a half months were from all parts of the continent and some from Europe. Probably one-third of them born in the United States, representing a dozen States and Territories, most of them from Missouri and Kansas. Then there was the hardy, cheerful, untiring "Canuck" (Canadian)—more than twenty of them—always skillful and willing, wet or dry, feasting or fasting; and the Mexican, patient and uncomplaining always—he will squat over a fire no larger than his hand with his serape about him, smoke his cigarette or munch his "hard tack" cheerfully. A few Germans, careful of their teams, always ready and willing—and the never failing Irishman with his unbounded energy and snap. In short, as I look back in memory to the motley crowd I see more than an average set of men.

I am told that Mr. Beery still lives in Montana. Except him I know but two living—Mr. K. B. Cecil, a wealthy farmer of Platte County, Mo., and "Sim" Routh of Easton, in Leavenworth County, Kansas—always a good citizen and prosperous. Of all the officers of that expedition, I do not think there is one living. Of the enlisted men I know of but one, Mr. R. M. Peck of Whittier, California. Probably there may be others.

Part VIII
Mule Trains to Utah

† † † † † † † † † † †

IN OCTOBER OR NOVEMBER OF EACH YEAR, all mules not needed for use during winter were sent to Platte County, Missouri, to be fed, where corn and hay were plentiful and cheap, always returning to Fort Leavenworth fat the following spring.

There were four herds in Platte County for which I purchased forage and over which, with a foreman in charge of each, I had general supervision.

One incident of this winter I will relate: Early one cold morning in January, 1853,[1] I rode from the corrals where I had a herd of mules on the farm of Bradley Cox, to his residence half a mile away, and found him talking to two young cavalrymen, who wanted some breakfast. Their horses were branded on the left shoulder with the letter G and Figure 1, which meant that they belonged to Troop G, 1st Cavalry. The men had hitched their horses by throwing their bridle reins over a fence stake, and without dismounting I reached over, unhitched both horses and started towards my herd house, where the men who attended to the herd lived. At the same time telling the men to follow me and I would give them breakfast. These men knew me as Master-of-Transportation for the Cheyenne Expedition and ran after me begging for their horses. I replied that I would talk to them after they had breakfast, but they could not have the horses. At the mule corrals I called a man, had the horses turned loose with the mules, saddles, bridles, blankets and pistols taken to the house. Of course I knew these young fellows were deserters, knew their troop was stationed at Fort Riley, and that it was commanded by

---

[1] The date should be 1858, not 1853.

my friend, Lieutenant J. E. B. Stuart. I asked the cook to give them breakfast. They admitted that they had deserted from Fort Riley and tried to excuse the act in various ways, whereas they had, in a spirit of discontent, left a good troop, as good a first sergeant as I ever saw (my friend Byrnes) and a troop commander that any man should be proud to serve under, and here they were, deserters! And liable to all the penalties attached to that crime. I talked to them until they shed tears of repentance—they were not ordinary toughs, claimed that they never drank liquor, which I afterwards found was true. They promised that if I would give them their horses, they would go to Fort Leavenworth and give themselves up to the commanding officer. This I refused to do and told them that the temptation might be too great and I would not trust them, that I thought it my duty to save this Government property, that I did not want the reward of $30 each which I would be entitled to for delivering them at the Fort, and if they would promise me to deliver a letter to General Harney I would write one in which I would express belief that they were thoroughly repentant, so much so that I felt justified in trusting them to report to him instead of taking them myself as prisoners. They promised to do this and I wrote the facts to the General and stated that I was trusting them on my belief that they would keep their promise to me and report to him, and that I believed they were so thoroughly humiliated that if given a chance they would yet make good soldiers. I felt that I was venturing too far in expressing an opinion to the General—I was not called upon to do so, but was so fully convinced that these youths would make no more mistakes that I made my letter as impressive as possible. They had a few dollars in money between them; I gave them a lunch and they left me at 10 A.M. to walk the twenty-one miles to Fort Leavenworth, which they did that day. Three days later I went to the Fort and took the horses and equipment along with me. When I called at the Quartermaster's office I was told that General Harney wanted to see me. I reported at his quarters and shown into his sitting room, where he asked me many questions, expressed himself well pleased and went so far as to say I made no mistake in trusting these men, I had certainly done them a great favor, and he liked my way of taking charge of the Government property. Of course the men were in the guard house, but in about a month a party was going to Fort Riley and they and their horses and equipments were returned together and they were soon restored to duty without trial. Lieutenant Stuart wrote me about them, in which he thanked me for my part, etc., and I explained the affair to him.

In August of the same year, when en route to Utah, I called at Major Sedgwick's camp, twenty-two miles west of Fort Kearney to pay my respects. Sergeant Byrnes told me that these two men were bound to see me but were afraid to trust themselves in the presence of their comrades, for fear they might show some feeling, and they had walked a mile up the road to wait until I came along. One of them was a corporal, and there were no better men in the troop. They wanted to show how grateful they were for the manner in which I treated them. I never saw them again, but always felt glad that they fell into my hands.

The commands that started for Salt Lake in 1857, and wintered on Black's and Ham's Forks of Green River lost nearly all of their stock, horses and mules, starved and frozen to death, and Captain Marcy[2] was sent to New Mexico to procure mules and

[2] Randolph Barnes Marcy was born in Greenwich, Massachusetts, in 1812. He was graduated from West Point in 1832 as brevet second lieutenant, Fifth Infantry, becoming second lieutenant in 1835, first lieutenant in 1837, and captain in 1846. He took part in the battles of Palo Alto and Resaca de la Palma in the Mexican War. In 1849 he marked out a road from Fort Smith, Arkansas, to Santa Fe while escorting a train of California emigrants. In 1852 he explored the sources of the Red and Canadian rivers, accompanied by Brevet Captain George B. McClellan, who afterward became his son-in-law. His trip across the Rocky Mountains in midwinter for supplies for the Utah Expedition is an epic of heroism. He became major paymaster in 1859, colonel, inspector general in August, 1861, and brigadier general of Volunteers in September. He was brevetted brigadier general and major general for war services, part of it on General McClellan's staff. In 1878 he became inspector general with the rank of brigadier general. He retired in 1881 and died November 22, 1887. He wrote *The Prairie Traveler* (1859), *Thirty Years of Army Life on the Border* (1866), and *Border Reminiscences* (1872). See also

horses before any of the commands could move out of their temporary winter quarters.

The conditions in Colonel Johnston's army were such that the Government saw the necessity of moving other commands to the front as promptly as possible. Great numbers of horses and mules were purchased at Fort Leavenworth, many of the latter unbroken, and the task of organizing and breaking in trains fit to transport supplies for troops in the field was no small matter.

At Two Mile Creek, below the fort, were located extensive corrals and a "catching-out" crew under experienced "mule tamers," and here all mules were first hitched to wagons and sent to camp some place within a few miles of the post.

Mr. Levi Wilson, general superintendent of transportation at Fort Leavenworth, was the most efficient man I ever saw in the Government transportation line, but his services were required inspecting horses and mules from the middle of March to the last of May, 1858.

I was notified to wind up the feeding business, and bring over mules from Platte the first of April, which I did. Three trains had been organized and camped in Salt Creek Valley. The news that many men would be needed brought them from every direction; some, enterprising young men from the country, ambitious to better their condition or work their way to the Pacific Coast; but there seemed an oversupply of the offscouring of the slums—men leaving their country for their country's good. The variety and makeup of these fellows, many of them fleeing from justice, the arms they carried and their outfits generally, were curious enough.

I was instructed to take charge of the trains. Many complaints had come to Mr. Wilson against a train in the Valley, and he requested me to see to it and do whatever seemed best. I rode out and found a drunken mob—mules scattered, harness in the mud, etc. The wagonmaster was asleep. A mouthy fellow called him

---

Grant Foreman, *Marcy and the Gold Seekers* (Norman, University of Oklahoma Press, 1939) and *Adventure on Red River* (1937).

"Captain," and he finally crawled out. In a few minutes I saw the utter uselessness of wasting time. He had come with a railroad gang from north Missouri, the most blear-eyed, God-forsaken looking set I ever saw. I told him that he and his men were wanted at the quartermaster's office; that they should take all their belongings with them, because they would not return to this train. Inquiries were numerous, but I quietly cut them off, and in half an hour they were strung out, poor wretches, with the "Captain" in the lead. I promised to meet them at the quartermaster's office, and then rode down the creek a mile to another train, and asked the wagonmaster togive me his assistant, a fine young fellow (Green Dorsey), and loan me half of his men. With them I returned to the drunken train, told Dorsey to take charge as wagonmaster, hire any men that came who suited him, and I would send him more, but not to hire one of the old gang, and galloped to the post in time to see them paid off. It was remarked at the office that such an outfit had never before been seen there. I called the "Captain" and his men aside and advised them to seek employment elsewhere; that they had mistaken their calling, and were unfit for the plains, and assured them that not one would ever find employment here. The rain and scarcity of whisky had sobered them some, and they started for the Rialto Ferry and Weston.

This incident spread among the trains and camps on the reservation, and I told every wagonmaster not to hire bad men—we did not want to be bothered with them; and it was soon understood that thieves, thugs and worthless characters generally might as well move on. Many of these found employment in ox trains belonging to Government contractors, and were the cause of strikes, mutinies and loss to their employers. Of course, there was no civil law applicable to the management of men on the plains. In a military command the officer in charge was all-powerful, as he must be everywhere within his jurisdiction. Necessity knows no law, and while all well disposed men would perform their duties without friction, the lawless element, sure to crop out from time to time, stood so much in awe of the military power that they did little harm to their fellows or the Government. Where there was no military command the same restraint did not exist, and discontented spirits, schemers and rebellion breeders often caused trouble. The Government trains had more discipline than the contractor's trains transporting Government supplies. The Government train had a sprinkling of discharged soldiers, and the man in charge had himself been amenable to discipline and could not hope to hold a responsible position without maintaining it. He must be a law unto himself or fail. The great contracting firms that transported Government supplies sent numerous ox trains to various military posts, and while they had a good business system, and often accomplished work much better than the Government would have done, yet the immensity of the business left room for many leaks and much defective management. I recall many instances of mutiny—the teamsters in rebellion against their wagonmasters, in some cases possibly with a grievance, and in others through homesickness or the spirit of rebellion that recognizes no authority, always ready to make trouble, delighting in the opportunity to become leaders for more pay, or to show their power when their services were most needed.

Interesting details would be tedious here, and I pass them by. In short, by the first of June more than six hundred six-mule teams, one-half of the mules never before handled, were organized into trains of about twenty-six wagons each, and about five hundred and fifty of them sent out with columns of troops en route to Utah. The whole months of April and May were exceedingly wet, no bridges in the country, and to move the first one hundred and fifty miles west from Fort Leavenworth was something terrible. Captain Van Vliet, quartermaster, had a bridge built across Salt Creek three miles out. The stone work of that bridge still stands.

The first column to move out was Colonel Andrews,[3] with

[3] George Andrews of Washington, D.C., was graduated from West Point in 1823 as second lieutenant, Sixth Infantry. He became first lieutenant in 1827; captain

Mule Trains to Utah

Sixth Infantry, Lieutenant Sawtelle,[4] R. Q. M., with eighty-two six-mule teams. They were three days going the first ten miles.

Between Government and contractors' trains, the road had been made almost one continuous mudhole. One hundred and fifty contractors' teams were struggling in the mud within twenty miles.

On the 20th of May, Colonel Morrison's[5] column with Fourth Artillery moved out, Captain Page,[6] quartermaster, with 104 teams, 99 horses and a few extra mules.

On the 28th of May, Colonel Monroe's[7] column with Third

in 1836; brevet major in 1837 for gallantry and good conduct in the war against the Florida Indians, major, Seventh Infantry, in 1848; and lieutenant colonel, Sixth Infantry, in 1855. He retired February 15, 1862, and died November 13, 1873.

[4] Charles Greene Sawtelle of Maine was graduated from West Point in 1854 as brevet second lieutenant, Second Infantry. He became second lieutenant, Sixth Infantry, in 1855 and served as regimental quartermaster, 1857-61, becoming first lieutenant in 1860. He was captain, assistant quartermaster, in 1861; lieutenant colonel, quartermaster, assigned, 1862-65. He was brevetted major, lieutenant colonel, and colonel "for faithful and meritorious service during the war" and brigadier general "for faithful and meritorious service in the Quartermaster's Department during the war." He was colonel, quartermaster, assigned, 1865-67; then became permanent quartermaster major. In 1894 he became colonel, deputy quartermaster general; and in 1896 he became quartermaster general with the rank of brigadier general. He retired in 1897.

[5] Pitcairn Morrison of New York was appointed second lieutenant in the Corps of Artillery in 1820; he was lieutenant colonel, Seventh Infantry, in 1853.

[6] Francis Nelson Page of Virginia was graduated from West Point in 1841 as brevet second lieutenant, Seventh Infantry, became second lieutenant within four months and was regimental adjutant, 1845-47. He was brevetted first lieutenant for gallant conduct in the defense of Fort Brown in 1846, was promoted to first lieutenant that year, was appointed brevet captain as assistant adjutant general in 1847, and was brevetted major for gallant and meritorious conduct in the battles of Contreras and Churubusco. He died in 1860.

[7] John Munroe (not Monroe) was lieutenant colonel, Fourth Artillery (not Third) and brevet colonel at this time, and is probably the officer Lowe means. A native of Scotland, Munroe was appointed to West Point from New York in 1812 and was graduated in March, 1814, as third lieutenant, First Artillery, and became second lieutenant in May, 1814. He became first lieutenant, artillery corps, in 1818; and captain, Fourth Artillery, in 1825. He was brevetted major in 1838 "for conduct uniformly meritorious and efficient during the campaign against the Florida Indians," lieutenant colonel for Monterrey, and colonel for Buena Vista. He was promoted to major, Second Artillery, in 1846 and lieutenant colonel,

235

Artillery, Captain Cable,[8] A. Q. M., moved out with ninety-seven horses, ninety-two teams and a few extra mules.

On May 30th, Colonel Sumner, First Cavalry, with Lieutenant Garland,[9] Seventh Infantry, A. A. Q. M., moved out with eighty-eight six-mule teams and fifty-six extra horses.

June 5th, Colonel May,[10] commanding fifth column, with Lieutenant McIntyre,[11] R. Q. M., moved out with fifty-eight teams, seventeen extra mules and sixty horses.

Fourth Artillery in 1856. He died April 28, 1861. (The rank of third lieutenant existed in the army 1813–21 and 1832–33.)

[8] William Lewis Cabell (not Cable) of Virginia was graduated from West Point in 1850 as brevet second lieutenant, Seventh Infantry; became second lieutenant in 1851 and first lieutenant in 1855; was regimental quartermaster 1855–58; and was appointed captain and assistant quartermaster on March 8, 1858. He resigned in 1861 and as Confederate brigadier general commanded a brigade of Arkansas cavalry.

[9] Colonel E. V. Sumner has been mentioned many times in these pages. His quartermaster was Robert R. Garland, born in Virginia, and commissioned second lieutenant, Seventh Infantry, from Missouri late in 1847. He was promoted to first lieutenant in 1855 and was regimental quartermaster from May 1, 1858 to April 1, 1860. He was promoted to captain on March 23, 1861, but was dropped from the rolls on May 23. He was colonel of the Sixth Texas Volunteers in Confederate service.

[10] Charles Augustus May, six feet four inches, with full, flowing beard and dark-brown hair reaching his shoulders, was famous for his charge at the head of eighty dragoons at Resaca de la Palma in which a battery of guns and a Mexican general were captured. A native of Washington, D.C., he was appointed second lieutenant Second Dragoons, when that regiment was organized in 1836. He became first lieutenant in 1837 and captain in 1841. He was brevetted major for "gallant and distinguished service" at Palo Alto; lieutenant colonel for "gallant and highly distinguished conduct" at Resaca de la Palma; and colonel for "gallant and meritorious conduct" at Buena Vista. Promoted major, First Dragoons, in 1855, he finagled a transfer back to the Second the same year. He resigned in 1861 and died December 24, 1864.

[11] James B. McIntyre, born in Tennessee and appointed to West Point from Texas in 1849, was graduated in 1853 as brevet second lieutenant, Seventh Infantry. He became second lieutenant, First Cavalry when that regiment was organized in 1855; first lieutenant in 1857; and served as regimental quartermaster from April 15, 1858, until he was promoted captain in 1861. He was brevetted major for gallant and meritorious service in the cavalry action at Franklin, Tennessee, July 10, 1863, and lieutenant colonel for Chickamauga. He was promoted to major, Third Cavalry, in 1866, and died May 10, 1867.

Mule Trains to Utah

June 12th, Major Emory's[12] column, with Captain P. T. Turnley,[13] A. Q. M., moved out with sixty-nine teams and a few extra mules.

June 12th, General Harney and staff moved out, Captain Hancock,[14] quartermaster, with headquarters of the Utah expedition—forty-two six-mule teams, eight four-mule ambulances, twenty-three extra mules and fourteen extra horses.

[12] William Helmsley Emory, a distinguished soldier, is perhaps most often recalled for his *Notes of a Military Reconnaissance from Fort Leavenworth, in Missouri, to San Diego, in California,* published in 1848. Born in Queen Anne's County, Maryland, September 9, 1811, he entered West Point in 1826 and was graduated in 1831 as brevet second lieutenant, Fourth Artillery. Advanced to second lieutenant, he resigned in 1836 to accept appointment as assistant civil engineer, making him eligible in 1838 for a commission as first lieutenant in the Corps of Topographical Engineers. His reconnaissance was made under Brigadier General Stephen W. Kearny in the Mexican War, and Emory was brevetted captain for the battle of San Pasqual and major for the battles of San Gabriel and Plains of the Mesa. He was promoted to captain in 1851 and major in the new First Cavalry in 1855. In 1857 he was brevetted lieutenant colonel for meritorious and distinguished service as commissioner for running the boundary line between the United States and the Republic of Mexico. Stationed in Indian Territory at the beginning of the Civil War, he eluded Confederate forces and brought his command—seven companies of infantry, five of cavalry, and four guns—to Fort Leavenworth without loss. He became brigadier general of Volunteers in 1861. He was brevetted colonel for Hanover Court House, brigadier general for Fisher's Hill and the Shenandoah Valley campaign, and major general of Volunteers and major general, U.S.A. for Cedar Creek. He served as major general of Volunteers, 1865-66, then as colonel, Fifth Cavalry, to which commission he had been promoted in 1863. As brevet major general he commanded the District of the Republican in the Department of the Platte, 1869-71, and the Department of the Gulf, 1871-75. He was retired as brigadier general in 1876, and died in Washington, December 1, 1887.

[13] Parmenas Taylor Turnley of Tennessee was graduated from West Point in 1846 as brevet second lieutenant, Second Infantry; became second lieutenant, First Infantry, in October of the same year; and first lieutenant in 1850. He was regimental quartermaster in 1852 and in 1855 was appointed captain, assistant quartermaster. He retired September 17, 1863, and resigned December 31, 1865.

[14] Winfield Scott Hancock was, said General Grant, "the most conspicuous figure of all the general officers who did not exercise a separate command. He commanded a corps longer than any other one, and his name was never mentioned as having committed in battle a blunder for which he was responsible." Hancock was born February 14, 1824, in Montgomery Square, Pennsylvania. He was graduated from West Point in 1844 as brevet second lieutenant, Sixth Infantry; became second lieutenant in 1846; brevet first lieutenant, 1847, for Contreras and Churu-

237

The seven columns used 26 wagonmasters, 20 assistants, 641 teamsters, extras and expressmen. In addition to the above, each column was supplied with four blacksmiths, one wheelwright and a traveling forge hauled by eight mules.

The above transportation was to go to the end of the journey, and in addition a train loaded with forage and provisions for each column was sent in advance to Marysville, crossing the Big Blue, to replenish the stores consumed and then return to Fort Leavenworth.

In sending out trains with the different columns, great pains was taken to see that men, mules and wagons were as near the best as it was possible to get, and when the last train was off to Utah, the remnants of trains scattered about within ten miles of the Fort were sifted and reduced to perfect trains ready for service in any direction, surplus mules and wagons turned in and inefficient wagonmasters and men discharged—a general cleaning up.

July found Fort Leavenworth as quiet as if preparation for the Utah campaign had never been. Half of the month had slipped away, when I was summoned to the quartermaster's office and informed by Chief Clerk Card (now Colonel B. C. Card, retired)[15]

busco; regimental quartermaster, 1848–49; and regimental adjutant, 1849–55. Meanwhile he had been promoted to first lieutenant in 1853, retaining that commission in the regiment until 1860, although he was appointed captain, assistant quartermaster, in 1855 (his rank in the Utah Expedition). He became brigadier general of Volunteers in 1861, and major general of Volunteers in 1862, commanding the Second Corps after May, 1863. At Gettysburg he was in charge of the first day's fight, and was wounded on the third day, receiving the thanks of Congress "for his gallant, meritorious, and conspicuous share in that great and decisive victory." In Regular Army rank he was promoted to major quartermaster in November, 1863, and brigadier general in 1864, brevet major general in 1865 for Spotsylvania, and major general, July 26, 1866. Commanding the Department of Missouri, he led an expedition against the Cheyennes and Kiowas in 1867. Hancock, as Democratic candidate for the presidency in 1880, was defeated by James A. Garfield. Hancock died at Governor's Island, New York, February 9, 1886.

[15] Benjamin Cozzens Card, a native of Rhode Island, was commissioned first lieutenant, Twelfth Infantry, and captain assistant quartermaster on the same day, September 27, 1861. He was colonel, quartermaster assigned 1864–67, and was brevetted major and lieutenant colonel for faithful and meritorious service during the war and brigadier general for faithful and meritorious service in the Quarter-

that the clothing and some other winter supplies for the Utah army had not been shipped and now it was too late to ship by contractor's trains and must be sent by mule teams; that the goods in bales and boxes were now en route from the East, and it would take nearly one hundred six-mule teams to haul them. These trains must be made ready and loaded as soon as the goods arrived by boat, and I would be expected to go in charge of them. I had no ambition to go, but the man who has good paying employment cannot afford to mix much sentiment with it.

If I could have retired with money enough to settle down for life, I would have done so; but now I banished everything but the idea of successful delivery of those goods in Utah. There was one consolation, it would be my train, I was assured, independent of interference from any source. If I beat the winter in reaching the troops, fourteen hundred miles away, it would be to my credit; and commanding officers and quartermasters along the route would be instructed to lend me any assistance possible.

When the goods arrived, it was found that three trains of twenty-six wagons each would take them—342 boxes and 910 bales.

John Allen's train with William Daniels, assistant wagonmaster (who helped me capture the Cheyenne the year before), and thirty-one teamsters and extra hands loaded July 31, and with traveling forge, wheelright and blacksmith, moved out with instructions to go as far as last camp on Little Blue, forty miles east of Fort Kearney and await my arrival.

John McGilvra's train with Hamilton assistant wagonmaster and thirty-one teamsters, loaded on the first of August and moved out, with instructions to join Allen.

John Wilson's train with Peter B. Jackson (son of the governor of Missouri,[16] a young man in search of adventure, which he

master Department. He became major quartermaster in 1872, and lieutenant colonel deputy quartermaster general in 1883. He retired in 1889.

[16] Hancock Jackson as lieutenant governor succeeded Trusten Polk, elected to the Senate, as governor in February, 1857, and served until August when Robert

FIVE YEARS A DRAGOON

found) assistant wagonmaster and thirty-one teamsters, loaded on the second of August, and with two young Mexicans with cavayard[17] of fifteen extra mules, moved out fifteen miles and camped at Mount Pleasant, where I overtook it at midnight.

The month of July had been very dry, and the roads, with the exception of numerous mudholes, pretty well dried.

Before leaving Fort Leavenworth I was instructed to look at all contractor's trains overtaken on the road, note the number of wagons, number of train, what loaded with, appearance of train, condition of cattle, how many lost or died, and name of wagonmaster, and inform the quartermaster at Fort Leavenworth every opportunity I had of mailing a letter. To save repeating, I overtook ox trains almost daily from start to finish, most of them contractors' trains, most of them well managed, and cattle in as fine condition as shortage of grass would permit; others in every stage of neglect. Up to Fort Kearney losses by death had been few, but the farther west, the greater the losses.

Traveled with Wilson's train until fifth.

August 6th. With my mess wagon left Wilson. Traveled forty-five miles, making three drives, and camped five miles east of Marysville with Colonel J. S. Johnston's train, en route to Leavenworth.

7th. Found McGilvra's train at Marysville. Allen crossed here the fifth.

8th. Wilson arrived. Took on corn and camped west of Big Blue. All trains took forage here. Left two men, E. L. Quintin and Philip Sawyer, at Marysville sick; a Dr. Miller was to look after them.

M. Stuart was elected. In 1860 Hancock Jackson was defeated for governor by Claiborne F. Jackson.

[17] A corruption of the Spanish *caballada,* meaning a band of horses. In cowboy language it meant the saddle horses held for relief uses on a cattle drive or on a ranch. Ramon F. Adams, *Western Words* (Norman, University of Oklahoma Press, 1944), gives the corruptions cavayer, cav-ayah, cavvieyah, cavoy, and cavvy, but not cavayard. Here is meant obviously the herd of unharnessed mules, available for replacement in the wagon teams. It never means unbroken animals.

9th. Met five government teams en route to Fort Leavenworth from Kearney. Changed twenty-one mules, taking the best.

11th. Overtook McGilvra and camped on branch of Little Blue. Wilson joined later.

12th. Twenty-five hundred Pawnees, men, women and children, passed east, running from the Sioux, with whom they had a battle. Some losses on both sides; Sioux got most of the Pawnee horses.

13th. Twenty-two miles, and found Allen camped on Little Blue. The other trains came up, and all ready to move together to-morrow.

As heretofore stated, the early part of the season was extremely wet, the whole country flooded, but July and so far in August was dry and hot; rank and rotting vegetation created malaria, and there was an immense amount of sickness amongst the men of all the trains en route to Salt Lake. A train belonging to Russell, Majors & Waddell, government contractors, lying by here with half the men sick, and, according to my instructions, I examined the train and found the wagonmaster to be a man whom I had discharged in the spring because he was unfit for assistant wagonmaster. I was told that several of the men died. I reported by letter immediately, and advised a new crew as quickly as possible, and reported the same to the agent at Kearney.

Found a number of men sick in Allen's train and a number of fever and ague cases in McGilvra's. My friend Dr. Samuel Phillips, at Fort Leavenworth, had fixed up a box of medicines with carefully written directions, and I prescribed for the poor fellows as best I could, several of whom needed hospital care.

14th. Twenty miles, and camped on Thirty-two Mile Creek (head of Big Blue). Eight men in Allen's, six in Wilson's and one in McGilvra's trains sick. All wagonmasters and assistants driving teams. The outlook was discouraging.

15th. Twenty-four miles and camped at Eight-Mile Point, below Fort Kearney. After prescribing for the sick men I rode to the fort, presented letters to Colonel May, commanding officer, and Captain Cabell, quartermaster; called on Dr. Summers and explained the sickness in trains. He said that he never saw as much malaria and fever and ague as there was in the trains from the East. I spent the night with Mr. Ben Bishop, forage master, who was first sergeant of B Troop, First Dragoons, before I joined it.

16th. Trains arrived and drew rations to last until 1st of September. Captain Cabell examined trains and seemed much pleased. Changed ten mules. On leaving Fort Leavenworth I took but few guns for guard purposes, and now drew fifty more, with ammunition. Dr. Summers was very kind to sick men, and prescribed for eighteen of them. Five were found unable to travel and left in the hospital; I left their time with Captain Cabell. Dr. Summers overhauled my medicine box, replenished it, and gave careful directions. Drew eighty sacks of corn and oats, and camped ten miles up the Platte. Hired three men to drive teams. Need more, but they are not to be had.

18th. Hereafter the traveling forge will be ahead, so as to be in camp first, ready for work. The wagon that hauls the blacksmith and assistant and the wheelwright, and in which they sleep much during the day, travels next to the forge. Off as usual. Killed a buffalo, the last one seen on the trip. Twenty miles, and camped on Platte. Many men sick. Assistant wagonmasters all driving teams. Issued rifles and ammunition to teamsters. From this time I will make my close corral, as on the Cheyenne expedition.

21st. McGilvra and assistant sick; also three of his men, one in Allen's, two in Wilson's, very sick.

22d. Sick list increasing. Tried to hire men from returning freight train, but they can see nothing but home. They would rather be poor and "dance with the gal with a hole in her stockin',"[18] than to winter in Utah for a fortune. Every train had

---

[18] The line is from the song usually called "Buffalo Girls." The other fiddle tunes mentioned are equally familiar.

Mule Trains to Utah

a cheap fidler sawing away by every campfire on "Money Musk," "Dan Tucker," "The Arkansaw Traveler," "Old Kentucky Home" and "The Girl I Left Behind Me"—no seductive $30 a month for them. These fellows, returning home with $100 to their credit, were the most independent millionaires that I ever saw.

And now the wagons are giving much trouble. Until the Mormon War, nearly all the Government wagons used at Fort Leavenworth were made in Philadelphia—"The Wilson Wagon," so called—and they were absolutely perfect. On the Cheyenne expedition I did not have a tire set nor a box wedged. The wagons in my Utah train were of Pittsburgh make, and now on the sandy and dry roads showed that they were hastily put together with timber not properly seasoned. Boxes and tires came loose, and some must be wedged every evening after coming into camp. From now on to Camp Floyd the road was strewn with broken wagons and dead cattle, and the labor and wear and tear to keep my wagons together was something terrible. During each day pieces of pine from broken wagons were saved for use in wedging boxes and tires, and midnight found me and some others still at work. For awhile we rolled some wheels into the water and let them lay all night to tighten them up, but on the hard road in the hot sun they soon dried out.

One day I found a Mormon train setting tires. The old man in charge had a crippled ox killed, skinned, and the hide cut into suitable strips and stretched around the felloes and tacked on with wooden pins. The tire was heated enough to expand it, but not enough to burn, and then put on over the raw hide. The tire cooled and shrank on tightly; the hide dried and made the fit still tighter. I stayed long enough to see that it was a success, and proceeded to adopt the plan. Every day the Mexicans with the cavayard drove along any abandoned cattle able to travel, and sometimes killed one for the brains and liver, and sometimes made soup of some of the meat. From time to time the hide was used as above described, and while not entirely successful in all cases, it saved much wedging. The boxes in the wheels became loose and must be wedged, and gunnysacks and pine wedges were used. Men in distress learn to do many things, and amongst one hundred men new ideas are evolved by some of them, often of great value.

From my memorandum book I quote as follows:

August 21st. Both wagonmasters in McGilvra's train sick, also three teamsters; one man in Allen's train very sick, also two in Wilson's.

22d. Passed O'Fallon's Bluff mail station and camped twelve miles above on South Platte. Sick list rather increasing. In several cases one man walked and looked after two teams, while his comrade rested in the wagon. Surprising how little complaint there is, and how cheerfully all try to help.

23d. Men continue sick; as one gets better, another takes his place.

24th. Met Colonel Bee[19] at crossing of South Platte with volunteer battalion returning from Utah. One of Colonel Bee's teamsters transferred to Allen's train in exchange for a sick man. Colonel Bee's command has no doctor. My train crossed Platte without accident, camped and greased every wagon ready to start in the morning. In crossing a wide quicksand river the grease is all washed from boxes. The usual amount of sickness.

25th. Fifteen miles to Ash Hollow Hill; nine more and camped on North Platte. Hardest day's work since leaving Fort Leaven-

---

[19] Probably Barnard Elliott Bee of South Carolina. He was graduated from West Point in 1845 as brevet second lieutenant, Third Infantry; became second lieutenant in 1846; brevet first lieutenant, 1847, for Cerro Gordo; and brevet captain for Chapultepec. He was promoted to first lieutenant in 1851, was regimental adjutant, 1848–55, and was commissioned captain in the new Tenth Infantry in 1855. Presumably his rank as colonel was conferred by the state or territory raising the Volunteer battalion mentioned by Lowe. Neither Bee nor his battalion is mentioned in LeRoy R. Hafen and Ann W. Hafen, editors, *The Utah Expedition, 1857–1858* (Glendale, Calif., Arthur H. Clark Company, 1958), which reprints many official reports and orders. Bee resigned in 1861, became a Confederate brigadier general, and is remembered for nicknaming Thomas J. Jackson "Stonewall" at the first battle of Bull Run, where Bee was killed, July 21, 1861.

worth. Some mules gave out; obliged to come here to get grass, as there is none below.

26th. Twelve miles over a very sandy road. Hardest day on mules; several gave out. When a mule can go no farther the team pulls out of the line and stops, the train keeping right on; the cavayard comes up, herder ropes a fresh mule which goes into the team, which takes its place in rear of the train. Twenty times to-day this has been done, and in several instances mules have been used twice. When the worn-out mule is turned loose he rolls, shakes himself and drifts along with the herd, eating grass and drinking, and in a few hours will do duty again. His vitality is wonderful.

27th. Ten miles over a heavy sandy road. Effect on mules similar to yesterday. Met Russell, Majors & Waddell's train en route to Nebraska City with discharged men, but I could not hire one of them. With money enough to buy a suit of jeans, pair of boots with a half moon and some stars on the tops, a wool hat and a blanket for an overcoat, and some silver in their pockets, why should they turn their faces to the mountains, sure to encounter cold weather and the possibility of not coming back until next year? To him it matters not that he could clear money enough to buy a quarter section of fine Missouri land and capture the girl whose "heel kep' 'er rockin',"[20] whom he could see afar off in his mind's eye. There were no charms behind that he cared to turn to, and he looked across the prairie to the "cabin on the creek" away over in Missouri.

28th. Medicine nearly all consumed. Fifteen miles and camped on Platte. Colonel Cooke, Lieutenant Buford and small escort of Second Dragoons camped near me. They give bad account of grass.

29th. In Allen's train, Patrick Laughnahan died this morning at five o'clock. He ought to have stopped at Kearney, but was anxious to go on, and the doctor thought he might pull through. A heavy rain fell during the night, and trains took road next to

[20] More of "Buffalo Girls"—see note 17.

the bluffs instead of river road. I rode ahead of train eleven miles to some springs about three miles east of Chimney Rock, where there were some ponds called "The Lakes." Last night's rains would fill them, and I might get some ducks. I found plenty of them, and with my double-barreled shotgun killed a lot. I waded into the water and was in the act of picking them up when my horse snorted and ran the length of his lariat. I lost no time in getting to the picket pin and put my foot on it. Here came a band of Indians at full charge, 300 yards away, and I motioned them to stop and brought down my gun. (I did not tell them it was empty.) They came down to a walk, but I insisted upon their stopping, which they finally did 150 yards away. Carefully I got to my horse, into the saddle and unsnapped the lariat from the halter. The chief started towards me, bow and arrows in hand. I had learned to not trust Indians, and made him stop 100 yards away; he finally rode back and gave his bow to another, and I let him come up and shake hands. Together we rode to the top of the hill, where we could see the train coming two miles away. There were but ten in the band, and "Little Thunder" was the chief. I had met him several times and called his name. He harangued his followers, and pointing to me said: "Eton-cha, kola," meaning "Chief, friend," whereupon all grunted and moved towards us, but I instantly called a halt, and they all dismounted and waited until the train came up. "Little Thunder" wanted something to eat, and I told my cook to give him "hard tack," and pointing to where I would camp, north of Chimney Rock, invited him and his band to dine with me. They came at dinner time and feasted, behaved well, and shook hands to go at five o'clock. Laughnahan had been prepared for burial by being sewed up in a wagon cover four double in a very neat manner by Mr. Allen. His grave was dug and he lay beside it. When the Indians rode by and stopped to look, one of the men thought he would frighten them by telling them that the man died of smallpox, and he succeeded. I came up just as the Indians were about to ride away; they thought that they had been invited to a camp to be exposed to that dreadful disease, of which they stood most in fear. "Little Thunder" looked sharply at me, and taking my knife I ripped open the cover and removed the white handkerchief, revealing the pale, smooth face, and succeeded in inducing all of them to come close and look carefully. I explained to them as best I could the cause of the man's death. They stayed until the burial was finished. The man who had lied to them kept hid in a wagon; he was scared more than were the Indians. At Laughnahan's grave was placed a board marked: "Patrick Laughnahan. Died August 29, 1858." I sent Laughnahan's memorandum book and some letters found on him to Captain Van Vliet, quartermaster at Fort Leavenworth. Mr. Hamilton very sick; others more or less so.

30th. Met Colonel Alexander and Lieutenant Menadier[21] and Captain Marcy and Lieutenant Grover en route to the States. They doubted my ability to get through on account of scarcity of grass.

September 2d. Arrived at Fort Laramie and delivered letters

---

21 "Menadier" is probably Henry Eveleth Maynadier, at this time first lieutenant and regimental adjutant of the Tenth Infantry. A native of Virginia, he was graduated from West Point in 1851 as brevet second lieutenant, First Artillery. He became second lieutenant in 1852 and first lieutenant in 1855. In 1859–60 he was assistant to Captain W. F. Raynolds in exploration of the Yellowstone River. He was promoted captain in 1861 and major, Twelfth Infantry, in 1863. As of March 13, 1865, he was brevetted lieutenant colonel for "faithful and meritorious service during the war"; brigadier general of Volunteers for the same service "and particularly while commanding a mortar flotilla under Admiral Foote, U.S. Navy, during operations upon Island No. 10 and other rebel forts on the Mississippi River"; and major general of Volunteers "for distinguished service on the frontier while operating against hostile Indians and accomplishing much toward bringing about peace with hostile tribes." On March 27, 1865, he was commissioned colonel of the Fifth U.S. Volunteer Infantry, serving until August 30, 1866. Regiments of U.S. Volunteers usually were made up of "galvanized Yankees," that is Confederate prisoners who agreed to serve against Indians. The record seems to indicate that Maynadier was brevetted for this Indian war before he served in it. It is quite probable that the three brevets were recommended at different times, and all confirmed by the Senate in a blanket act predated to March 13, 1865, the last one through oversight. Maynadier died December 3, 1868.

to Colonel Munroe commanding, and Major Babbitt,[22] quartermaster. Drew 284 sacks of corn, 185 sacks of oats, and camped above the Fort. Dr. Johns[23] prescribed for twelve sick men.

3d. Exchanged twenty-eight mules, all I could find here better than mine. Drew rations for 101 men forty days. Changed two wagons. Left two sick men, Nelson Story[24] and Mike Flood, in hospital. Nelson Story, a friendless youth of twenty, got well, found his way to the Pacific Coast, drifted to Montana, mined, and finally got into the cattle business, prospered in cattle, mines and banks, and was a millionaire a few years ago. I have never seen him since we parted at Laramie, but hope he still lives to enjoy his success. I do not know Flood's history beyond the fact that he got well. He was a fine Irish lad, and probably met with success.* Dr. Swift,[25] of the army, was very kind to my men while

[22] Edwin Burr Babbitt, born in Connecticut, was appointed to West Point from Indiana in 1822, ranked twenty-eighth in his class and received commissions both as brevet second lieutenant and second lieutenant on July 1, 1826 in the Third Infantry. He became first lieutenant in 1834. He was assistant quartermaster 1836–38 and then became captain quartermaster, a temporary appointment as he held a commission as captain in his regiment, 1839–46. He was brevetted major May 30, 1848, "for meritorious conduct while serving in the enemy's country." He became major quartermaster May 10, 1861; lieutenant colonel deputy quartermaster general August 3, 1861; and served as colonel quartermaster assigned from 1864 to July 29, 1866, when he was retired as colonel assistant quartermaster general. He was brevetted colonel for faithful and meritorious service during the war and brigadier general for faithful and meritorious service in the Quartermaster Department during the war, both commissions dating from March 13, 1865. He died December 10, 1881.

[23] Edward W. Johns of Maryland was appointed assistant surgeon in 1849. He resigned in 1861 and served as surgeon in the Confederate Army. He died June 13, 1892.

[24] Nelson Story was an early-day horse operator. He started in the upper Yellowstone country in 1876 with two hundred California mares, and soon had a herd of thirteen hundred horses. General James S. Brisbin in *The Beef Bonanza* cited Story's success in selling great numbers every year at $50 and $75, or buyer's choice of the herd at $100. (Philadelphia, J. B. Lippincott Co., 1881, 130–45; Norman, University of Oklahoma Press, 1959, 133–34; cited by Harold E. Briggs, *Frontiers of the Northwest*, New York, London, D. Appleton-Century Co., 1940, 339).

* I am informed by Hon. James A. McGonigle, who was an officer in the First Kansas, that Mike Flood was among the first killed at the battle of Wilson's Creek, in 1861. He was a member of the First Kansas.—*P. G. Lowe.*

Mule Trains to Utah

here; overhauled my medicine box, replenished it, and gave careful directions.

One man asked for his "time," which I refused to give. Every man had signed a contract to go through to Camp Floyd for thirty dollars per month, whereas, the usual wage was twenty dollars, and if I gave one man his time, more than half the train would want to go, and men were not to be had to take their places. Gold had been discovered near Pike's Peak, 250 miles south, and some soldiers had deserted to go there, and if the men could get a month's pay, many would desert me, and I was obliged to be severe and draw the line. This man complained to Major Babbitt and to the commanding officer. When spoken to about it, I requested that he and any others who wanted to be discharged be placed in the guard house. In an hour this man was arrested and in the guard house when I left. This prompt action ended all complaints.

I was sitting on a box in front of my tent writing, when my attention was attracted by some one in front of me. There stood a man with an army size revolver on his belt and leaning on a long rifle. He was thirty-five years old, big, broad-shouldered, long hair and whiskers, unkempt and dirty, vicious and desperate looking. I never saw a more repulsive looking creature. I inquired what he wanted, to which he replied that he wanted employment; was a mountaineer by profession, and wanted to go through to Camp Floyd. Ordinarily I would have said "No," but I needed healthy men so badly that I called to Mr. Wilson and said that if he could use this man to hire him, which he did. I shall have occasion to mention him again.

Left Fort Laramie September 4th. Traveled ten miles. Trains

[25] Ebenezer Swift, a native of Massachusetts, was a resident of Ohio when he was appointed assistant surgeon August 30, 1847. He became major surgeon in 1861 and was brevetted lieutenant colonel and colonel in 1865 for faithful and meritorious service during the war. He was brevetted brigadier general July 20, 1867, for meritorious service voluntarily rendered during the prevalence of cholera at Fort Harker, Kansas. He was promoted to lieutenant colonel assistant medical purveyor in 1876 and retired in 1883. He died December 24, 1885.

alternate in traveling—the front train to-day will be the rear train to-morrow, the middle train having moved to the front.

This divides the hardships in the way of dust and rough roads. The wagonmaster of the front train has charge of the herd until midnight, and the assistant from midnight until time to corral the mules at daylight. Each train furnishes two teamsters to herd during the first half and two the last half of the night, so that there is a wagonmaster and six teamsters on herd at the same time. Mr. Hamilton being sick, I relieved McGilvra at midnight and found the mules very little trouble. And now we have very little sickness among teamsters.

6th. Rained during the night, turned to sleet and then snow, and by ten o'clock we had six inches. Pulled out facing the storm. Ten miles to camp on North Platte. Cleared off cold. Killed ten sage hens. All well in trains except Mr. Hamilton. Found an abandoned Government wagon and took from it three wheels and both axles to take the place of some of mine not so good.

8th. Camped on Box Alder.[26] When the trains rolled in one man had four mules and a big ox with rope on its horns for leader. We drove along with the herd any oxen able to travel, and used some of the gentle ones in harness, always in the lead.

12th. Arrived at Fort Payne[27] where there is a bridge across the Platte River. Two companies of Fourth Artillery here, Captain Roberts[28] (called by his intimates "Jo Bobs") commanding—a

[26] Boxelder Creek enters the North Platte between present-day Orpha and Glenrock, Wyoming.

[27] Camp Payne, described by Heitman as "near Fort Laramie on the North Platte," was temporary, and was not officially designated a fort.

[28] Joseph Roberts ("Jo Bobs") of Delaware was graduated from West Point in 1835 as brevet second lieutenant, Fourth Artillery. He became second lieutenant in 1836, first lieutenant in 1838, captain in 1848, and major in 1861. He served as colonel of the Third Pennsylvania Artillery from March 19, 1863, to November 13, 1865, meanwhile being promoted lieutenant colonel of his regiment in 1863. He was brevetted colonel, brigadier general U.S.A., and brigadier general of Volunteers at the close of the war. On January 10, 1877, he became colonel of the Fourth Artillery, having passed through every grade in that regiment, to which

fine officer. I had taken fifty sacks of corn from a contractor's train the day before against the protest of the wagonmaster, who felt he had no right to let me have it. The country was almost destitute of grass and I could not hope to get through without feeding. "Well," said Captain Roberts, "I have no authority to advise you, but if you do not use forage and lots of it, you will find yourself snowed in and stock frozen to death before you reach Bridger, just as the commands were last winter. I would advise you to run no risk that might prevent this clothing train getting through." This sounded like the right kind of talk. I wanted to feel that officers along the route would be ready to justify me. Six miles above Fort Payne crossed North Platte.

And now we are in the "poison springs" country. We have water kegs for drinking and cooking purposes, and animals are not allowed to touch water other than the North Platte. Passed several more ox trains; one train had lost seven to eight cattle per day. I pronounced it alkali poisoning, and advised driving two miles to North Platte as I did and herd them away from every suspicious looking pool. One man, George Chrisman, had done that and his cattle looked well and his losses few.

14th. Camped near Red Buttes[29] and traded my tired horse with a Frenchman who keeps a trading post here, for an excellent saddle horse. Have mules herded two and three miles from camp outside of where cattle have grazed. A train coralled here drove cattle five miles to Platte for water and grass. Wagonmaster said he was losing a day, but was filling his cattle and losing few. Hot days; mules suffering for want of water, which they must not have until they can be driven to the river at night.

15th. Camped within two miles of Sweet Water. No grass, but fine water, and mules browse among the grease wood and sage brush. Our mule shoeing increases as we move over the hard

---

he had been permanently assigned for forty-two years. He retired July 2 of the same year and died October 18, 1898.

[29] Red Buttes is near the present Mills, Wyoming.

roads, and every man who can nail on a shoe is in demand. Killed two sage hens.

16th. Crossed Sweet Water on bridge at Independence Rock. Mail station here. Camped above.

17th. Eighteen miles and camped on Sweet Water, opposite Split Rock. Contractor's Train No. 62 camped just below me. Examined train, asked the usual questions, and finally asked why he was lying by, and how long he had been there. Three days, and because he and "the boys" had a dispute about guard duty, the hour of starting in the morning, and a few other little matters—the old story of a train without a head. I told him that I would try to send some one with a crew to drive this one out, and let them "hoof" it back without pay. (Bluff, of course.) Two hours later here came the train and went five miles beyond me to camp. The next day they traveled so well that I did not overtake them, and the next day we camped near together. The wagonmaster said that three of the men knew me. They were of the "Captain's" drunken train, whom I discharged in the valley.

The desperado hired at Laramie proved to be such an incorrigible scoundrel that Wagonmaster Wilson told me he would have to give up control or kill him. He boasted of having killed two men, and was an overbearing bully. I told Wilson to let him herd the mules; he would not care for a team, and cursed and abused mules and men. When the mules were turned loose I told him to drive them north and save the grass near camp for night. Some time had passed—mules all loose and grazing around camp. I called to the man and asked if he did not understand what I told him. He yelled back: "Well, ——— ——— 'em, ain't they goin'?" I then told him to come to me. I was in the act of washing in a bucket, clothes all off to the waist, and my cook standing near ready to hand me a towel. As he came sauntering up the slope towards me swearing viciously, I noticed him slip his pistol to the front. When close to me I asked what he meant, when he drew his pistol. Quick as lightning I caught his hand with both of mine, jerked the pistol from him, and with it struck with all my might on the top of his head. He fell as if shot through the brain, and quivered as if in a death struggle, while blood flowed freely. A dozen men came with knives or pistols, and begged me to step aside and let them "finish him." I waved them back and had him carried to my tent, got out my medicine box, gave him a swallow of whisky (here a man said, "What a shame to waste the whuskey!"), and with scissors cut the hair along the edges of the worst scalp wound I ever saw. A thin sliver of bone came off. While two men held his hands I took seven stitches, and with strips of court-plaster drew the edges together the best that I could. In the meantime the man revived, and in an hour was semi-conscious. I let him lay in my tent until my cook made him some tea, and he was able to walk to the wagon, where he slept on sacks of oats. How he rallied from such a wound was a mystery. The next day we passed a trading post, where a vicious looking lot of fellows were loafing, and when the wagon in which my man was riding got opposite to it he asked the teamster to stop, got out his few effects, and said "good bye." After coming into camp the mule that I rode during the day was turned into the herd, and my horse saddled and bridled and hitched to my mess wagon ready for use. He ran in the cavayard during the day. As this desperate scoundrel approached, he determined to kill me, mount my horse and escape, with all the glory that would be showered upon him by his class for murdering the chief of that big outfit. That was the way I interpreted his conduct. When I seized the pistol it was cocked, and nothing but my quick action saved me.

20th. Camped on Sweet Water. A dragoon sergeant came riding into camp and said that he was part of an escort en route to the States with some officers who had learned that I had a forge, and they wanted to get a few shoes set on an ambulance team. He said the officers were Major Sibley,[30] and Lieutenants Norris[31]

[30] See note 1, Part 1.

[31] Charles E. Norris of Indiana was graduated from West Point in 1851 as brevet second lieutenant, Second Dragoons. He became second lieutenant in 1853 and first lieutenant in 1855, served as regimental quartermaster in 1860, and became captain in 1861. He became lieutenant colonel of the Second Indiana Cavalry

and Bell[32] of the Second Dragoons. I asked him to say to the Major that I would be glad to do anything for him that I could, and showed him a good place to camp near my Sibley tent. In half an hour they came in. I knew Norris and Bell very well, and was introduced to Sibley; I invited them to share my tent, which they did. I had instructed my cook to get up as good a dinner as he could, and they dined with me. Of course we talked of both ends of the route, but during a lull the Major remarked that he did not remember having met me before, and was pleased with the cordial manner in which I had told the sergeant I would be glad to do anything I could for him. I told him that there was a reason behind all of it, and went on to state that "once upon a time, etc.," a young man came to his recruiting office in Boston to enlist. That he, the Major, had advised the youth against such a step, told him the consequences, the position in which he would place himself, the probable estrangement from family and friends, and finally, after putting him off some days, enlisted the youth against his, the Major's protest. "That was nearly nine years ago, and this my first opportunity of showing my gratitude for good advice and the kindly manner in which you treated me; and I never sleep in a Sibley tent without thinking of you." "Are you the young sailor with good clothes and hands so soft that I would not believe him?" "Yes sir." "Well, now, will you please tell me how you got through with your enlistment, and how you happen to be here?" Of course I sketched a little of my life, which has been told in former articles.

These officers advised me to "rob" every train that I found with forage; that my train was of great importance; that no effort or

---

on September 27, 1861, but resigned his Volunteer commission February 11, 1862, returning to his regiment, now called Second Cavalry, as captain. He was brevetted major for Gettysburg, and was promoted to major, First Cavalry, in 1866. He was dismissed in 1870. He died October 31, 1875.

32 David Bell, born in Ohio, was appointed to West Point from Iowa in 1847 and was graduated in 1851 as brevet second lieutenant, Second Dragoons. He became second lieutenant in 1852 and first lieutenant in the new First Cavalry in 1855. He died December 2, 1860.

expense should be spared to get it through. I lost four mules in a week. In grazing the short grass the mules eat too much saline matter, which causes them to drink too much water.

21st. Twelve miles to where road forks, right hand over "Rocky Ridge Road," left hand over "Semino's Cutoff"; took the latter up Warm Spring branch three miles, and camped at Springs. Took three hundred sacks of oats from Contractor's Train No. 23, and shipped seven bales of store tents and tent poles by same train.

22d. Camped at Cold Springs. Camped here was Contractor's Train No. 23. It left Fort Leavenworth the 17th of June; had much trouble with wagons; some wheels broken down—iron axle wagons. Contractors and nearly all big freighters crossing the plains used wooden axle wagons made by Murphy or Espenscheidt of St. Louis, or Young and others of Independence, Missouri, and were able to carry their 6,000-pound loads anywhere. I gave the wagonmaster all the information that I could about repairing his wagons, but he seemed much discouraged, and there was a want of confidence look about the men—a sort of awkward helplessness, that made an excuse for them to lie by a day at a time. The appearance of this train caused me to appreciate the cheerful helpfulness of my own men. No matter how hard the day, how warm or how cold, there was a cheerful taking hold, early or late, that kept everything up to date and moving; no sulking, no growling—all that had been left more than six hundred miles east. The men were as anxious to get through as was I, and all had worked into the habit of helping wherever their services were needed. One wagonmaster, Mr. Allen and two assistants, Mr. Jackson and Mr. Hamilton, were new to the severities of such a trip, but they acquitted themselves excellently, and soon became equal to veterans. Many of the men had much to learn, but they came to time under discouraging circumstances and often severe illness. The vim, push, and energy in one of my trains, under either of my wagonmasters, would have landed the contractor's train in Camp Floyd before this time.

While commenting on the contractors' trains, I will say the firm of Russell, Majors & Waddell was a wonderful organization, and while a small percentage of their wagonmasters were by inexperience and want of character unfit for positions of authority or responsibility, a large majority of them were in their line of business the "salt of the earth," possessing unusual courage, perseverance, good judgment and business ability, and remarkable in the management of men.

23d. Crossed South Pass and camped five miles beyond on Pacific Springs Creek. Contractors' Trains Nos. 21 and 22 camped here; Nos. 24 and 15 passed on.

24th. Eight miles to Big Sandy. Twelve more and camped on Little Sandy. Passed trains Nos. 48, 51, 54, 20, 24 and 25. Took from Train No. 20, John W. Hall, wagonmaster, 170 sacks of oats.

25th. Crossed Green River at Bateese trading post.

26th. Eighteen miles to and along Black's and Ham's Forks of Green River, and camped on the latter. This day has been along the route where hundreds of mules and horses were starved and frozen to death last winter. At one place several trains of six-mule teams stood tied to the wagons. The latter had been hauled away, but the mules lay just as they died, their dry skins stretched over their bones, some lying on one side, some with their feet under them, and some standing in a bracing position, generally two on each side of where the wagon stood and two behind—dead horses and mules for miles. This was Camp Scott.[33] There is a bridge here guarded by fifteen soldiers.

27th. Crossed Ham's Fork twice and then Black's Fork, and camped. Left train and crossed Smith's Fork at Jack Robinson's trading post and came on to Bridger. Called on the commanding officer, Colonel Canby,[34] stopped all night and took dinner and

---

[33] Camp Scott (Utah) was on Black's Fork of Green River.

[34] Edward Richard Sprigg Canby, one of the army's most distinguished officers, was born in Kentucky in 1819. Appointed to West Point from Indiana in 1835, he was graduated, thirtieth in his class, in 1839 as second lieutenant, Second Infantry. He became first lieutenant in 1846; was regimental adjutant, 1846-47; brevet captain assistant adjutant general, 1847; brevet major for Contreras and Churubusco;

Mule Trains to Utah

breakfast with Captain P. T. Turnley, quartermaster, and his chief clerk, Mr. John R. Brooke[35] (now Lieutenant General Brooke, retired).

Captain Turnley opened my papers, addressed to the senior officer of the quartermaster's department in Utah, and Colonel Canby directed me to turn over to Captain Turnley 120 bales and two boxes and six sets tent poles. Train came up and camped at noon of 28th. Got hay from Captain Turnley. The whole train unloaded, turned over packages ordered and reloaded. One man left here sick. One discharged on 14th for misconduct, but allowed to travel with the train without pay, was left here—a wiser if not a better man.

29th. Thirty years old to-day. Colonel Canby and Captain Turnley say there is no grass from Bridger to Salt Lake, 120 miles, and not much from Salt Lake to Camp Floyd, 45 more. Captain

---

and brevet colonel for gallant conduct at Belen Gate of the City of Mexico. (Lowe's "Colonel Canby" means this brevet rank). Canby became major of the new Tenth Infantry in 1855, and colonel of the new Nineteenth Infantry in 1861. As brigadier general of Volunteers, he repulsed the Confederate invasion of New Mexico and was brevetted brigadier general, U.S.A. for the battle of Valverde. As major general of Volunteers, he commanded at the capture of Fort Blakely and Mobile, Alabama, and was brevetted major general, U.S.A. for gallant and meritorious service in that campaign. He was promoted to brigadier general in 1866 before being mustered out of the volunteer service. He commanded the Department of the Columbia when he went on a peace mission to the Modoc Indians and was killed by them April 11, 1873. He was the highest ranking officer killed in Indian wars.

[35] John Rutter Brooke of Pennsylvania, quartermaster's chief clerk when Lowe met him, entered the army in 1861 as captain of the Fourth Pennsylvania Infantry, a three months' regiment, and in November became colonel of the Fifty-third Pennsylvania. In 1864 he became brigadier general of Volunteers and brevet major general of Volunteers for Totopotomoy and Cold Harbor. In 1867 he received belated brevets as colonel for Gettysburg and brigadier general for Spotsylvania. He resigned in 1866 but was commissioned lieutenant colonel of the new Thirty-seventh Infantry that year. In 1869 that regiment was discontinued and Brooke was transferred to the Third Infantry, in which he served for ten years. He was promoted to colonel of the Thirteenth Infantry in 1879, but was almost immediately transferred back to the Third. He became brigadier general in 1888 and major general in 1897. He took part in the Sioux War of 1890–91, and in the Puerto Rico campaign of the Spanish-American War. He retired in 1902.

Simpson[36] of the Engineers had laid out a road from Camp Floyd to Bridger, following the Mormon road through Timpanogas Cañon, from the head of which he threw up mounds on high points a short distance apart, so that starting from Bridger one could follow the line of mounds nearly 100 miles to the head of Timpanogas or Provo Cañon, and then through the cañon to its mouth, near which Timpanogas or Provo River flows into the lake of the same name, and thence through the towns of Battle Creek, American Fork and Lehi to Camp Floyd. Neither Government nor contractors' trains had gone that way, and bunch grass was fine. Neither Colonel Canby nor Captain Turnley would advise me, but I thought they leaned toward the new route, and I reasoned that if snow-bound where there was plenty of grass I could winter, and the goods could be hauled in from time to time, when the weather permitted. So that it was a perfectly smooth road by Salt Lake 165 miles to Floyd, with no grass and half rations of corn or oats, or about the same distance on an entirely unbroken road, through sage brush nearly one hundred miles, with the same corn and oats, and fine grass, about thirty miles through a crooked cañon, and the balance an ordinarily good road.

Launched out on the new road. Traveled eight miles over sage brush and camped on branch of Black's Fork of Green River; mules exhausted; plenty of grass and fine water. After dinner started out to explore some distance ahead. Soon struck a trail and followed it about four miles and very unexpectedly came into the old road from Bridger to Salt Lake. Riding along by

36 James Hervey Simpson of New Jersey was graduated from West Point in 1832 as brevet second lieutenant, Third Artillery; became second lieutenant in 1833 and first lieutenant in 1837; transferred to the Corps of Topographical Engineers in 1838, and became captain in 1853 and major in 1861. He was colonel of the Fourth New Jersey Infantry from August 12, 1861 to August 24, 1862, then resigned and returned to his regular rank. In 1863 he became lieutenant colonel of engineers. He was made brevet colonel and brevet brigadier general in 1865 for "faithful and meritorious service during the war." He became colonel in 1867, retired in 1880, and died March 2, 1883.

Sulphur Springs, I met Major Prince,[37] paymaster, who was just from Camp Floyd. He came through Timpanogas Cañon, over the divide to Weber River, down river to mouth of Echo Cañon, thence through the cañon to where I met him. He wrote in my memorandum book a minute account of the route, distances, water, grass, etc., and advised me by all means to go through Echo Cañon and take the route he came. From his account I felt very much encouraged. About forty miles would take me to and through the cañon, and from that on I would have fine grass.

30th. Took the trail down to the old road, crossed Bear River and camped ten miles beyond. In a cañon a mile from camp I found fine grass. Narrow way to enter, and no one seemed to have discovered it. In the night found a herder asleep, turned his mule loose and brought in his saddle and bridle.

October 1st. Ten miles to head of Echo Cañon; ten more and camped in middle of cañon at "Ten Mile Rock." Rained in afternoon, turned to sleet and then to snow; no grass; fed oats.

2d. Six inches of snow. Ten miles to mouth of cañon; mail station. Turned to left and crossed Cañon Creek. Took new road up Weber River two miles, and camped on it. A party of men cutting hay here for mail station. Finer grass never grew, and the mules are making up for shortage last night. Left two mules here unable to travel—effects of storm and freeze. Snow all gone.

3d. Ten miles and camped where road leaves to cross the divide between Weber River and Silver Creek. A signboard here says seventy-three and a half miles to Camp Floyd. Ox Train No. 60 following me camped below; twenty wagons; six have been abandoned for various reasons.

[37] Henry Prince of Maine was graduated from West Point as brevet second lieutenant, Fourth Infantry, in 1835; became second lieutenant in 1836; first lieutenant in 1838; and was regimental adjutant, 1846–47. He became brevet captain for Contreras and Churubusco, brevet major for Molino del Rey, and was promoted to captain in 1847. He became major paymaster in 1855. He served as brigadier general of Volunteers from 1862 to 1866, receiving brevets as lieutenant colonel for Cedar Mountain and colonel and brigadier general for war service. In 1877 he became lieutenant colonel deputy paymaster general, retired in 1879, and died August 19, 1892.

It was estimated that between Kearney and Camp Floyd there were abandoned chains enough, if straightened out, to reach the whole distance, but this is doubtless an exaggeration. Hundreds of wagons, Government and contractors', were strewn the whole distance. The carcasses of cattle, horses and mules were scattered by hundreds. Ranchmen got rich by picking up abandoned stock, driving it away from the main traveled road, and waiting until the next season to trade their recuperated stock for a new crop of broken-down ones and a good price to boot.

4th. Divide between Weber River and Silver Creek is a small mountain, hard, firm road about eight miles. The first and second trains passed over without doubling teams; rain began to fall, and the last train had to double, and were until two o'clock coming into camp on Silver Creek. Mules turned loose in fine grass, and soon filled themselves. Rain turned to sleet, and before dark we corralled the mules in a heavy snow storm, which continued until towards morning.

5th. At daylight opened corral and the mules came out (always the strongest first) quietly and scattered among the willows along the creek. Snow covered the level creek bottom fifteen inches. All but about thirty came out without much urging; they were down in the mud or had lost hope and the energy to move. Men got ropes, and all but two, which died, were gotten onto their feet. A few hundred yards away was a side hill where the snow was blown off the grass, and the mules were driven to it. Men built good fires, took their time and got a good breakfast. The sun came out and snow melted rapidly. With willow brush men knocked snow and ice from harness and wagons, and at noon the mules were brought in and fed oats. After dinner the teams were hitched up, and slowly the wagons rolled out of the muddy camp. About two miles away I had selected a camp on high, sandy ground, where the snow was mostly blown off and the little left was rapidly sinking into the sand. To this point the trains were moved, the round corral was built and the mules turned loose. The sun had done good work, mules had exercise enough to get warmed up, and on a neighboring side hill facing south they found fine grass. The whole outfit was pretty well tired out, but everybody, even the poor mules, quite comfortable.

6th. Two miles to top of hill and one mile down, steep and rocky, to branch of Provo River, down two miles to main river. We were four hours making the next two miles; crossed the river or its branches five times; five miles farther, and camped on river; fine camp and plenty of grass. Snow nearly all gone.

7th. One mule died; down river six miles, crossing it twice. Broke wagon so badly that I abandoned it, having put the load into other wagons. Three miles to head of Timpanogas or Provo Cañon; down cañon one mile and camped. Plenty of grass. From one o'clock until sunset getting the last two miles. The road has been made along the side of the mountain by digging down the bank, sometimes through solid rock and building stone, or wooden embankments on the lower side, thereby making an excellent road for the short teams of the settlers, two horses or two oxen to a wagon, but the curves are so short that a six-mule team could not make the turn. In some places we took off the lead and swing mules and carefully worked around the short curves with the wheel mules and the help of men. It was very tedious, but if a wagon went over it would fall from fifty to one hundred and fifty feet to the rocky river bed and carry with it team and driver.

8th. Down cañon ten miles and crossed bridge. Two more and camped at its mouth. No grass. Rode to Provo City, five miles, and bought eighty-six bushels of wheat and oats, to be delivered at my camp at $2.00 per bushel—wheat and oats same price.

9th. We have left mountains and come into summer weather. Six miles to Battle Creek settlement, three to American Fork, three more to Lehi; beautiful place, surrounded by an adobe wall, with wide gate at east and west sides. It was a lovely Sunday, and the whole town, men, women and children, in their Sunday clothes, crowded to the east side, covering the wall and crowding the gate to look at the long train as it wound its way along the road. I stopped to water my horse at the beautiful asaquia [acequia] which seemed to encircle the town just inside the wall. A very intelligent man, who gave the name of Clark, entered into conversation with me, and when I inquired for a good place to camp, told me that just outside of the west gate was a good place, and the only grass I would find east of Camp Floyd. Leaving Mr. Daniels, who was riding with me, to conduct the train through the town, I galloped on and selected my camp, and by two o'clock we were comfortably settled. I told the man Clark that I would buy one hundred bushels of oats at my camp and pay the customary price in the country, $2.00 per bushel. I paid cash, and in buying a little more than one hundred bushels I dealt with twenty people. Some families brought only two or three bushels on their backs, which probably represented their own hand labor. I took a few bushels more than I wanted rather than see the poor people carry it back.

10th. Train started early. My bridle was missing. Some one had stolen it while I was buying oats. Two mules lost during the night.

Having crossed Jordan on bridge, the mules were watered, trains straightened out, and I rode on with Mr. Jackson to Camp Floyd, where we arrived at 10 A.M., and I reported to Colonel Crossman,[38] chief quartermaster, who was glad to see me. He and every one supposed that my losses would be heavy in the big snowstorm, and probably I could only move a part of the train at a time. At headquarters he introduced me to Colonel Johns-

[38] George Hampton Crosman (not Crossman) of Massachusetts had been lieutenant colonel and deputy quartermaster general since December 22, 1856. He was graduated from West Point in 1823 as brevet second lieutenant, Third Infantry, and as of same date second lieutenant, Sixth Infantry. He became first lieutenant, Sixth Infantry, in 1828; assistant quartermaster in 1830; captain, Sixth Infantry in 1837; and captain, assistant quartermaster, in 1838. In 1846 he vacated his regimental commission and was brevetted major for Palo Alto. In 1847 he became major, quartermaster. In 1863 he was promoted to colonel and assistant quartermaster general and in 1865 received brevets as brigadier general and major general for faithful and meritorious service during the war. He retired in 1866 and died May 28, 1882.

Mule Trains to Utah

ton* and Adjutant-General Porter, who remembered me from the year before. Expressmen had been sent out to look for me, but had not been heard from. Colonel Johnston asked if I had all that I started with, and I told him I had, except what I left at Bridger by Colonel Canby's order. Train arrived and camped near springs out side of garrison.

11th to 15th, inclusive. Unloading trains and turning over wagons, mules, harness and other equipments, and getting clean receipts for all property in my charge. Thirty-four mules dead or otherwise lost, which were covered by affidavits. Colonel Crossman wanted all of my men who would stay to work at Camp Floyd, and I turned over to him a list including all except the wagonmasters and assistants, wheelwright, blacksmith and eight teamsters—including myself, seventeen—who wanted to return.

Selected two six-mule teams, wagons and covers, some extra wagon covers, my Sibley tent, four common tents, and complete equipments, for return trip; also four riding mules, one for myself and one for each of the wagonmasters. I was offered my choice of any mules at the camp, but I found none equal to my best, and my friend Jim Miller, who had charge of the herds in Rush Valley, told me that out of five hundred mules he had none so good.

I was given the use of a desk in Captain Page's office while at the post, and while writing to-day I heard a man tell Captain Page that he had brought in a stray mule. A voucher was made and the man paid. As he was mounting his pony at the door I looked up and recognized Clark, and my lost bridle on his pony. I stepped out quickly, unbuckled the throat latch, jerked the reins from the man's hand and bridle from the pony's head, and struck a blow on his rump with the bridle. He bounded off at a fearful rate, away across the parade ground, out into the country

---

* When Albert Sidney Johnston was graduated, in June 1826, he was entitled, by virtue of his rank in his class, to select which arm of the service he preferred. Had a cavalry corps then existed his taste would have led him to enter it."—*From William Preston Johnston's "Life of Albert Sidney Johnston."*

and out of sight. He was a fine rider and held to the saddle admirably. I never saw him again.

16th. Drew rations for seventeen men and forage for twenty-two mules ten days, supposed to last to Bridger. Two artillery officers, Lieutenants Howard[39] and Talmadge,[40] were ordered to Platte bridge, Fort Payne, and to accompany my party. They were allowed a six-mule team and spring wagon for transportation, which I selected for them. Having no mess or servants, I invited them to join me, which they were glad to do. My cook was among those left at Floyd, but of the teamsters returning one Robinson was an excellent cook, and so far as food made of Government rations was concerned, we fared well. Three inches of snow to-day.

17th. Lieutenant Tallmadge has a white pony which he will use instead of riding in the wagon. The little train left at nine o'clock. I got my papers, said "Good bye," and with Tallmadge left at one o'clock, coming into camp on east side of Jordan River at 4, eighteen miles. Bought hay for mules; snowed all afternoon. This is one of my anniversaries; I enlisted in the army nine years ago to-day.

18th. Out of camp at sunrise. Twenty-seven miles to Salt Lake City, where we arrived at two o'clock. Arranged for corral room and as much hay as mules can eat for fifty cents each. Leaving

[39] Either James Howard of Maryland, appointed second lieutenant, Third Artillery in 1857, who resigned in 1861 and served as captain in Confederate service; or Robert V. W. Howard, an old army man, born in Ireland, who enlisted as a private in the Fourth Artillery in 1839, rose to the rank of sergeant major and in 1848 was commissioned brevet second lieutenant and second lieutenant in his regiment. He became first lieutenant in 1850, captain in 1861, and lieutenant colonel of the Third Pennsylvania Artillery in 1863. He was brevetted major in 1863 for gallant and meritorious service in action at Blackwater Bridge, near Suffolk, Virginia, and lieutenant colonel at the end of the war. He returned to his regiment as captain in November, 1865, and was promoted to major, Third Artillery, in 1869. He died February 1, 1875.

[40] Grier Tallmadge (not Talmadge) of New York was graduated from West Point in 1848 as brevet second lieutenant, First Artillery; became second lieutenant, Fourth Artillery, in 1849; first lieutenant in 1853; and captain, assistant quartermaster, in 1861. He died October 11, 1862.

Mule Trains to Utah

our animals at the corral, Tallmadge and I started out to see the city. Called on Gilbert & Gerrish, C. A. Perry, Livingston & Kincaid, Bradford & Cabbott, Miller, Russell & Cole. Dodson, agent for Hockaday's[41] Salt Lake mail, etc.—all that we knew to be from "God's Country," as we·called the vicinity of the Missouri River. Wagons arrived at 5. Howard, Tallmadge and I out about town. We were extremely anxious to see Brigham Young, but Governor Cummings[42] had given stringent orders against any one seeing him. Dined at the Globe Hotel, kept by Mormons exclusively for Gentile boarders. Went to Mr. Gerrish's room and wrote until midnight, when the room was filled by Gerrish, Brannan, Bradford, Miller, Tallmadge, Stewart and several others. I like to write the names of these bright young business men, so that they may be remembered by old friends.

19th. Breakfast at daylight. Teams and party off at 8. Went to Gerrish's store and bought buffalo overshoes, and went around with him to say "Good bye," and finally at nine o'clock got out of the city.

When four miles out on the "table" took a farewell look at the city, Great Salt Lake, etc. It seemed a pity to have come such a tedious journey to see so little of this interesting country. Five miles from the city entered Emigration Cañon[43] through the Golden Gate. Rough road. Seven miles to foot of Little Mountain, one mile to top of mountain. Snow two feet deep. Ten mules to each wagon; every one pushing; three trips must be made to

[41] John M. Hockaday of Missouri obtained a contract to carry mail weekly from St. Joseph, Missouri, to Salt Lake City in 1858. George Chorpenning took the mail from Salt Lake City to Placerville, California. In 1859 the route was taken over by Russell, Majors & Waddell.

[42] Alfred Cumming (not Cummings) was appointed governor of Utah Territory on July 11, 1857, by President Buchanan, and accompanied the Army of Utah to his post. An executive of great common sense, he was largely responsible for the peaceful solution of the "Mormon War." Cumming was born in Augusta, Georgia, September 4, 1802. He had been mayor of Augusta, sutler with Scott's army in the war with Mexico, and superintendent of Indian Affairs at St. Louis.

[43] It was by way of Emigration Canon that the Mormons first entered the valley of Great Salt Lake.

get the wagons and things up. At the foot of the mountain a man was drunk. From the wagon I had him and all things taken, and found one two-gallon and two one-gallon jugs of whisky. I broke each of them on a wagon wheel, and that ended the whisky part of the campaign. However much a few may have grieved, there were no tears nor protests.

No grass, but some hay brought from corrals. Mules very tired. And now the prospect is that we will have a severe time during the 1,340 miles ahead of us, and no pains must be spared to keep up the strength of the mules. I brought from Floyd some extra wagon covers, and now have a half dozen of them brought out and each torn into four equal pieces, each one covering a mule all over. The mules, not being accustomed to this, offered some gentle protests, but we soon got them used to it. We had no twine, and used wooden pegs to hold on the strings, and used ropes partly untwisted to make soft surcingles of. Of course, the covers were only put on when mules were tied up, which would be nearly all the time during the night.

20th. Night very cold. Off at sunrise. Two miles to foot of "Big Mountain," and one mile to top. Ten mules and full crew to each wagon; snow from one to two feet deep. Seven eight-mule teams belonging to Russell, Majors & Waddell came up from the other side with the help of ox teams; mules looking badly—scarcely able to walk. One mile down met Hobbs & Street's train—cattle dying rapidly. Two miles to East Cañon, and three miles down and camped. Little grass.

21st. Hereafter, for want of space I shall not mention any outfits, unless for special reasons. Nineteen miles and camped in corrals at Weber River mail station, mouth of Echo Cañon. Bought plenty of hay for mules, and some to carry along, of one Briggs, the station keeper (a seceded Mormon) who entertained us with many stories of why his wife would not leave the Mormons when he did.

22d. Off early. Met Branning's train in middle of Echo Cañon. Gilbert, wagonmaster, has lost 150 cattle since leaving the States;

has been reinforced by 40, and 80 now await him above the mouth of cañon. Snowing some. Made two drives, traveled thirty-two miles, and camped at sunset.

23d. Off at sunrise. Six miles and crossed Bear River. Twenty-six more and camped at sunset on Mud Creek, having left the old road and crossed over to the new. Fine grass. Divided the day into two drives.

24th. Off at sunrise. Fourteen miles to Bridger, and although Sunday I had some mules shod. Drew forage and rations for fifteen days.

25th. Finished shoeing mules and started train at noon. Salt Lake mail arrived with United States Senator Broderick of California[44] a passenger. Fourteen miles and camped on Black's Fork.

26th. Thirty-eight miles to camp on Black's Fork, where road leaves for Green River—three drives.

27th. Thirty-one miles to Sandy, and camped—two drives.

28th. Off before daylight. Met fifteen six-mule teams hauling Salt Lake mail, coaches and ambulances. Ten miles and crossed Big Sandy, and lunched. Twelve more and again turned loose. Twelve more and camped on Pacific Creek. I must make short drives, and two or three of them every day. When mules are turned loose they roll, and pick whatever grass they can find. Having water always in kegs for cooking, I stop whenever I find a patch of grass—water or no water—taking care that the mules are watered often en route. We have so many men and so few mules to care for that it makes light work. Mules thoroughly rubbed every night and morning, especially their legs.

29th. Off at sunrise. One mile from camp found Mr. Wilson, Attorney-General for Utah, in camp. All of his transportation for himself and wife consisted of one six-mule ambulance. Mrs. Wil-

[44] David Colbreth Broderick (1820–59) was born in Washington, D.C., and grew up in New York City, where he became a Tammany politician. In 1849 he went to California, was a member of its Constitutional Convention, served in the state senate, and was elected to the United States Senate in 1856 where he became prominent in the anti-slavery movement. He was fatally wounded September 13, 1859, in a duel with Judge David S. Terry.

son cooking breakfast for her husband, herself and the teamster. Fifteen miles farther, and turned loose an hour. Three miles to Pacific Springs, five more to South Pass. Eight more, and camped at dark on Sweet Water, one mile above mail station. Very cold and threatens snow.

30th. Off at daylight over Semino's Cutoff. Made three drives and camped on Sage Creek at 4. Very cold, snow falling and indications of big storm. Arranged my three wagons in half circle on north side; cleared sage brush to give room for good camp, and so brush could not take fire and burn wagons; tied mules inside the semi-circle and fed them well on oats; stretched the outside wagon cover of each wagon to keep off most of the snow; built fires of big sage brush on the south and kept them burning all night; guard instructed to knock snow off wagon cover shelter occasionally. North wind blows fire away from camp, so that there is no danger.

31st. Stopped snowing at daylight. Off at sunrise; snow drifted about the wagons and shoveling necessary to get out. Five miles to Warm Springs, five more to junction of Rocky Ridge road and Semino's Cutoff, twelve more to the fifth crossing of Sweet Water. Turned loose an hour. Three miles farther and met Train No. 34. Took from it twelve sacks of oats. This train left Nebraska City on the seventh of September; beats any traveling that has been done on this road by ox trains. While down on one knee writing receipt for oats, I looked up and saw my victim of the scalp wound leaning on his rifle, as I had first seen him, and looking at me. At one side I noticed all the wagonmasters watching him. I asked the man what he wanted, to which he replied that he wanted me to certify to the time he worked, so that he could get paid when he got over into the valley. I told him that I never paid men for deserting me. The wagonmaster said that he joined back at the trading house where he left me, and asked about him. I advised not to trust him, that he was thoroughly bad. The poor fellow looked sick and moved off languidly. I felt sorry for him, and though convinced that I was sparing the life of a viper, could not find it in my heart to kill the poor wretch. "He will meet you some day, and you will be sorry for sparing him," was the general opinion.

November 1st. Off at sunrise. Half a mile and found two mail carriers camped by the road and three mules near by. These men lay asleep side by side, and fine snow had drifted over them. I told Tallmadge they must be dead, and dismounting, raised the blanket from the face of each before they awoke; each sat upright at the same time, pistol in hand, "dazed but dangerous," Tallmadge said. Self-preservation, active and prompt defense, was the first thing thought of. And they acted in concert, as one man, even before their eyes were open. With their mail sacks for pillows, these men had lain down at midnight. Their poor mules were hunting subsistence in a small willow thicket in a nearby cañon. The men say they had to leave the mail conveyance at Devil's Gate station on account of deep snow. Made two drives and camped at four o'clock. Snow ten inches deep on the level and more in drifts. Day fine but very cold. Under a steep bluff fifteen feet high, which broke off the keen, cold wind, snow more than a foot deep was shoveled away, the tents pitched and snow banked around them. Good fires, from parts of wagons picked up during the day, and a warm supper made all very comfortable. The wagons placed in a half circle, the snow shoveled back from them, and mules standing in the circle, well fed with oats and small handful of hay each, with outside wagon covers stretched, as described at Sage Brush Creek, and the effect of fires, gave very good protection. There was no real suffering for men or animals. A good deal of labor making this camp, and some time consumed, but a good night's sleep for all hands paid well for the trouble.

2d. Off at 8. Bright sun, and sun dogs indicate cold, and though we have no thermometer, I am sure I never felt a colder morning. Mail station seven miles off. After riding four or five miles, Tallmadge and I dismounted to walk. There had been nothing over the road since the snow fell except the two mail carriers and their three mules. Even their tracks were drifted over and we found it, as Tallmadge said, "beastly exercise" trying walk, and stopped to rest. We were clothed from bear-skin cap to buffalo shoes and buffalo mittens, from underclothes to overcoats and leggings, with the best to be had, and did not suffer except about the nose and face, which we were constantly protecting with one hand. Looking back at the wagons and mounted wagonmasters, I knew that none were clothed as I was, and I saw that Mr. Daniels was riding as he had started, ahead of the first team; did not see how he could stand it. When he came up I asked if he was not cold, and why he did not change with some one for a while. He replied that he could not get off his saddle, and had been hoping to reach the station, which was in sight. I told him the station must be two miles away, and to get down. He tried to, but had lost the use of his limbs, and I took him down against his protest that I was hurting him. In short, I caused all the mounted men to get inside of the wagons and give their mules to others. Having hurriedly made arrangements, we started and made the best time possible to the mail station. It was a stockade of two rooms, one with a good fire and the other without a fire; adjoining was a small stable for mules. Leaving the teams standing on the south side of the buildings, all hands came into the house and examinations commenced. Nine men were more or less frost-bitten, but none seriously except Mr. Daniels. I split his boots from top to toe; both heels and all of his toes were more or less frozen. During the next hour his suffering was intense. Others had frosted toes, fingers or ears—some slight, others quite severe. The men were kept from the fire, and snow and cold water used at first, and then turpentine. I had a little, but the station keeper gave me the use of his big bottle so that I could save mine for future use. The station keeper stayed here alone, ready to feed the mail carriers and care for the mules between changes. He was a young man, intelligent and resourceful—a manly man—and I am sorry that I cannot recall his name. He gave all of us a good cup of coffee, and having made the unfortunates as comfortable as possible, we pulled out after a delay of more than two hours, during which our mules had been covered. We could not stay there on the bleak plain, and must hunt a sheltered camp. Every day we heard of men being frozen; nearly every station had one or more sufferers. I was in the habit of condemning men in charge of others for permitting them to freeze instead of compelling them to take care of themselves. I was nearly caught this time. Crossed Devil's Gate bridge; very little snow below it. Fourteen miles and camped on Grease Wood. Mules turned loose amongst grease wood until dark, and then tied up and fed. Same arrangements as last night for comfort. Camp well sheltered and fuel piled up for night. Broken-down wagon timbers plentiful. All the invalids in my tent before a fine fire. All were able to do something for themselves. Even Daniels did not complain; he had the use of most of his fingers, and with his superb courage and nerve made the most of it. All seemed thankful that I happened to stop and think of them, and they never seemed to forget it. Tallmadge, with his cheerful intelligence, was a great help; his companionship was charming. He was as brainy as he was kind—the son of the first governor of Wisconsin, and always my warm friend after this trip. He died at Old Point Comfort, a captain, in 1862.

3d. Somewhat warmer. Off early; snowing a little. Forty-four miles in three drives, and camped on North Platte at sunset. Got supper and carefully examined all the frost-bitten victims. They had been made as comfortable as possible in the wagons, had stood the ride very well, and were pleased that they would so soon reach a doctor. Tallmadge and I left camp at nine o'clock and rode to Fort Payne, six miles, where we arrived at ten, and stopped at Mr. Clark's sutler's store. It was the coldest ride I ever made. Our animals were cared for, and the usual reviver, hot whisky toddies, applied to us. I had not then learned that hot water was far better. Captain Getty,[45] Captain Roberts and other

---

[45] George Washington Getty, born in Washington, D.C., was graduated from West Point in 1840 as second lieutenant, Fourth Artillery, became first lieutenant

officers came to the sutler's store. We listened to the news from the East and they from the West until midnight, and slept at the sutler's, who was prepared to accommodate us. Tallmadge is at home, this being the end of his journey, and he will find quarters to-morrow.

4th. Breakfast with Mr. Clark. No doctor here. Got some medicine from acting hospital steward. Train came in at 10. Lieutenant Howard stopped here; unloaded his and Tallmadge's goods. Fed all hay mules wanted, and made hospital wagon of the spring wagon in which Howard has ridden all the way. Drew forage to last to Laramie, said "Good bye," and started at 2. Eight miles and camped on North Platte. Fine day, but cold. My tent a hospital; took in all invalids who needed doctoring from that time to end of journey.

5th. Twenty-seven miles in two drives, and camped on Box Elder. Invalids improving and being well waited upon by comrades.

6th. Twenty-eight miles to La Bonte, and camped. In this vicinity hundreds of mules froze to death a year ago.

7th. Thirty miles in two drives. Killed two mountain hens. Camped on Cottonwood.

8th. Off before daylight and arrived at Laramie at 11. Got mail from Mr. Fitzhugh.[46] Train arrived at 3. Took on rations and forage for twelve days. I am receiving congratulations from

---

in 1845, brevet captain for Contreras and Churubusco in 1847, captain in 1853, and lieutenant colonel, additional aide-de-camp in 1861. He became brigadier general of Volunteers in 1862 and during the war was commissioned major, Fifth Artillery and brevet lieutenant colonel for the siege of Suffolk, Virginia, in 1863; brevet colonel for the Wilderness and brevet major general of Volunteers for Winchester and Fisher's Hill in 1864; and brevet brigadier general for Petersburg and brevet major general for gallant and meritorious service in the field during the war in 1865. In 1866 he was made colonel of the Thirty-seventh Infantry, and was transferred to the Third Infantry in 1869, Third Artillery in 1870, and Fourth Artillery in 1882. He retired in 1883 and died October 1, 1901.

46 Norman Fitzhugh was partner of Seth Edward Ward in the sutler's store at Fort Laramie, 1857–58.

Mule Trains to Utah

Major Babbitt and other officers for my (as they call it) "wonderful trip." Crossed Laramie and camped—plenty of hay. Dr. Swift[47] examined frost-bitten men. I advised Daniels to go in the hospital and stop here, but he strenuously objected, and the doctor said that inasmuch as he has no duties to perform and had good care, he would be as well off traveling, perhaps better.

9th. Changed four mules, said "Good bye," and started at 2. Fourteen miles and camped on North Platte.

12th. Camped at junction of Lawrence Fork and North Platte.

13th. Off at four o'clock. Of course the mules must be tied to wagons at night, and towards morning they get chilled badly and suffer. I am traveling to make time and keep up the strength of teams as much as possible. Men can find plenty of time to rest; there are so many of us that it is no trouble to hitch and unhitch often. Thirty miles in two drives, and camped on North Platte.

14th. Off at 4. Twenty-eight miles, and crossed South Platte; river low but good deal of ice. Three miles more and camped.

15th. Off at sunrise. Thirty miles in two drives and camped. Killed prairie chicken.

16th. Off at 4. Thirty-five miles in three drives and camped on Platte. Killed one pheasant.

17th. Off at 4. Two drives and camped on Platte.

18th. Off at 6. Thirty-five miles and camped nine miles below mouth of Plum Creek.

19th. Twenty-two miles and camped at Fort Kearney. Drew rations for my party to last to Leavenworth. Drew forage for seven days and took an order for more at Big Blue. Changed three mules, and got three shod, and made ready to move in the morning. Daniels and two others had their sores dressed at hospital. Dr. Summers kind as usual. He informed me that all the men I left sick recovered and returned to Leavenworth.

20th. Off at 4. Three drives and camped on Thirty-two Mile Creek.

21st. Made two drives and camped on Little Blue.

---

[47] Ebenezer Swift, see note 25, this part.

273

22d. Twenty-eight miles in two drives and camped on Little Blue.

23d. Off at 5. Thirty-two miles in two drives to camp on Oak Creek.

24th. Off at 4. Thirty-four miles to Marysville and camped on east side. A party of artillery officers from Laramie, Captain Brown,[48] Lieutenants Mendenhall,[49] Lee,[50] Soloman[51] and Abert,[52] en route to Leavenworth, camped here. Left Laramie

[48] John A. Brown of Maryland was graduated from West Point in 1846 as brevet second lieutenant, Fourth Artillery. He became second lieutenant in 1847, first lieutenant in 1848, and captain in 1856. He resigned in 1861 and served in the Confederate Army as colonel of artillery. He died October 8, 1877.

[49] John Mendenhall of Indiana was graduated from West Point in 1851 as brevet second lieutenant, First Dragoons. He transferred to the Fourth Artillery in 1852, became second lieutenant in 1853, and first lieutenant in 1856. He was promoted to captain in 1861, became brevet major for Shiloh in 1862; major judge advocate of Volunteers in 1863; brevet lieutenant colonel for Chickamauga; and was lieutenant colonel, assistant inspector general from February 27 to September 26, 1864. He then reverted to major of Volunteers until the end of the war, when he received a brevet as colonel and returned to duty as captain, Fourth Artillery. He became major, First Artillery in 1877; lieutenant colonel, Fourth Artillery in 1883; and colonel, Second Artillery, in 1888. He died July 1, 1892.

[50] Probably Stephen Dill Lee of South Carolina, who was the only Lieutenant Lee in artillery at this time. (Charles Cochrane Lee was lieutenant of ordnance). Stephen D. Lee was graduated from West Point in 1854 as second lieutenant, Fourth Artillery. He became first lieutenant in 1856, serving as regimental quartermaster from 1857 to 1861, when he resigned to enter Confederate service. He was one of three men who called on Major Anderson to surrender Fort Sumter in the first action of the war. Lee commanded a battalion of the Washington Artillery at Bull Run and Antietam, and a division at Chickasaw Bayou. He surrendered at Vicksburg, but was exchanged and in 1864 was commissioned lieutenant general commanding a corps in the Army of Tennessee under General John B. Hood. Lee was wounded in the retreat from Nashville. After the war he was a planter in Mississippi, member of the state legislature, and commander in chief of the United Confederate Veterans. In 1880 he became president of Mississippi Agricultural and Mechanical College. He died at Vicksburg, May 28, 1908.

[51] Owen Fort Solomon of Georgia was graduated from West Point in 1853 as brevet second lieutenant, Second Artillery, becoming second lieutenant, Fourth Artillery, on November 25 of the same year and first lieutenant in 1856. He died September 27, 1859.

[52] William Stretch Abert of Washington, D.C., was appointed second lieutenant, Fourth Artillery, in 1855 and became first lieutenant in 1857. In 1861 he was com-

Mule Trains to Utah

two days ahead of me. Philip Sawyer and E. L. Quintin, left sick here last August in care of Dr. Miller, died. Promised to loan Lieutenant Mendenhall one of the wagonmaster's mules to ride with me, and we will try to ride to Fort Leavenworth in two days, 150 miles.

25th. At 4 o'clock sent riding mule to Mendenhall, who breakfasted with me, and we were off at 5. Wagonmasters and teamsters will follow and be at the fort in five or six days. Gave Wagonmaster Wilson money to buy hay, and with plenty of corn, they do not have to hurry. We have passed all danger of freezing up for want of forage. Roads freezing and thawing and will be bad. Mendenhall and I made seventy-five miles the first day, but it was terrible on him; not being used to riding, he became blistered and sore. A tub of hot water helped him some. I offered to wait until my wagons came up, and let him ride in the spring wagon, but he declared he could ride and would keep up with me.

26th. Rain and sleet fell all day, and it was dark when we reached Mount Pleasant, fifteen miles from the fort. And we stopped at the little hotel. Mendenhall's principal stock in trade was sores and pluck—plenty of both. We made arrangements to have our mules ready by 5 in the morning, so we could ride to the fort for breakfast, which we did, arriving at eight o'clock. Mendenhall stopped with Foragemaster Mix,[53] and I with my friend Levi Wilson. Mendenhall married Miss Sophie Mix that

missioned captain in the new Sixth Cavalry and was named brevet major for Hanover Court House and brevet lieutenant colonel for Antietam. He was lieutenant colonel, assistant inspector general assigned, 1862–64, and colonel of the Third Massachusetts Artillery, 1864–65, and was named brevet brigadier general at the close of the war. He resumed service as captain, Sixth Cavalry, until June 8, 1867, when he was named major in the new Seventh Cavalry. He died August 25 of that year.

[53] Possibly John Mix of New York, who enlisted in the Second Dragoons in 1852 and was first sergeant of Company F in 1861 when he was appointed second lieutenant in the same regiment, now designated Second Cavalry. He served as major and lieutenant colonel of the Third New York Cavalry, but resigned his volunteer commission at the end of 1862, returning to duty in the Second Cavalry as first lieutenant. He became captain in 1865 and major, Ninth Cavalry, in 1881. He died October 26, 1881.

evening, in the privacy of the family, and I received announcement card the next day. My reception with all the quartermaster's department, from old Colonel Tompkins,[54] deputy quartermaster general down, was extremely pleasant; but relieved from care I began to realize what a strain I had been under for four months. I had made the round trip of 2,800 miles in 117 days. Fourteen hundred miles going out in seventy days, equal to twenty miles per day with loaded teams; six days at Camp Floyd, and returned 1,400 miles in forty-two days, equal to thirty-three and one-third miles per day—all the way from Camp Floyd through winter weather.

My egotism prompts me to make the claim that for distance traveled, loads hauled, scarcity of feed, inclemency of weather, time consumed in traveling, number of wagons and mules employed, smallness of losses, to say nothing of suffering and sickness among men, this trip has no parallel in the history of the plains. That was conceded at the time by my friends; and old Mr. Majors at one time, and William H. Russell at another, declared to me that "'twas a most wonderful trip;" and two years later when I was freighting for myself, Mr. Waddell said to me: "If you manage for yourself as well as you did for Uncle Sam, you will be a great success." And I want to say that in all of my experience, with the exceptions mentioned, I never saw as little friction among men as there was in those constantly hard worked, overworked trains. I doubt if such men could be mustered and held together to-day.

[54] Daniel D. Tompkins of New York entered West Point in 1814 and was graduated in 1820 as third lieutenant of ordnance. A year later he was commissioned second lieutenant, First Artillery, to rank as such from his original appointment. He became first lieutenant in 1825 and held the rank of captain in his regiment, 1835–46, meanwhile being named captain, assistant quartermaster, in 1838, and major quartermaster in 1842, as well as brevet major in 1836 for the Florida war and brevet lieutenant colonel in 1848 for the war with Mexico. In 1851 he became lieutenant colonel, deputy quartermaster general, and in 1856, colonel, assistant quartermaster general. He died February 20, 1863.

Part IX
Private Business and Government Service

† † † † † † † † † † †

HAVING PASSED THE WINTER AS USUAL, looking after the Government herds in Platte County, Missouri, I took my place under Mr. Wilson in charge of transportation at Fort Leavenworth, but there was little to do—no Indian excitement, no movement of troops, and compared to previous years, there was much leisure. I became restless and conceived an ambition to do something for myself, and the sooner I severed my connection with the Army and ceased to depend upon it, the better.

I was past thirty years old and the last nine and a half years of my life had been wholly devoted to the Army in some capacity, and I realized how hard it would be for me to form business habits necessary to success in civil life.

I made the acquaintance in Leavenworth of George W. Clayton, a young Philadelphian, who was in the mercantile line, and he proposed to form a co-partnership with me and "Jerry" Kershow, another young Philadelphian, who was doing a brokerage business, to make the firm Clayton, Lowe & Company, with a capital of ten thousand dollars, each one furnishing one-third of the capital. I to put my third in transportation, Clayton his third in goods, suitable to the mining trade in Denver, and Kershow his third in money. This co-partnership we entered into. I fitted out a nice train of six four-mule teams, loaded the goods that Clayton furnished with his and Kershow's money, and on the second of July, 1859, left Leavenworth for Denver. Clayton went out on the Overland (Pike's Peak) Coach and when I arrived there the first of August, found him in a rented store room built of logs and adobe, by Morton Fisher, on Blake Street, east of 15th—then called "F."

All the way out I had met swarms of "pilgrims" returning to the Missouri River in every stage of want and wretchedness, firm in the belief that there was no gold in the mountains—that it was all a myth.

During the spring these people rushed out on to the plains, with no assurance of the future, some with good teams and outfits, some with patched-up concerns, of little value, some with pack mules, ponies or horses, some with hand carts, some with wheelbarrows, and hundreds with all their possessions on their backs, to travel seven hundred miles to the mountains. Most of the latter class, who did not die of starvation and exposure, returned and were the first that we met. A few wheelbarrows and hand-carts did get through—twenty years later, a friend up in Central Park pointed with pride to his wheelbarrow, but I may safely say that nine-tenths of all who started to the Pike's Peak Eldorado returned empty-handed, and in more or less distress.

In Denver we found several adobe stores full of miners' goods and tools, and one train load was hesitating whether or not to return the goods from whence they came. Clayton had been advised not to unload—it was no use—there was no money to buy them, they said. I dumped the goods into the store, sent the train to camp, mounted a mule and rode to the "diggins"—Gregory, Nevada Gulch, Central City, etc. I spent two days informing myself. The prospect was not good but there was more or less gold, and some men much encouraged. On the morning of my third day at the mines great excitement was caused by the report that rich diggings had been discovered at "Tarry All" and "California Gulch." The report was undoubtedly true, for men who brought the news had returned to Gregory for tools and partners. I put my mule through forty miles to Denver by dark and found Clayton and a friend, Dan Smith, and a hired man opening goods which were in demand; all night we worked, and for a month worked early and late selling goods. Denver, with its periodical

Private Business and Government Service

ups and downs, continued to prosper. In the meantime I set the train crew to putting up hay, which paid very well. Clayton took the coach for the East to buy goods; I sent the train to Leavenworth to haul them out, attended to the Denver business and built the first frame store in Denver at the corner of Fifteenth and Larimer streets. I bought the two lots from General Wm. H. H. Larimer,[1] his homestead and cabin, for four hundred dollars.

After seeing the train started from Leavenworth, Clayton returned on the coach and was much pleased with the new store which I had moved into. Our goods arrived in good shape and sold well.

I sold the train to J. W. Iliff,[2] and in January, Clayton and I went east by stage, leaving the store with Mr. Kershow. Clayton bought goods and I fitted out five ox teams and six mule teams; both trains leaving Atchison the middle of March. William M. Clayton, brother of George W., accompanied me with the mule train, with which we went through in twenty-four days, while the ox train was forty-eight days en route. The goods were in

[1] William H. H. Larimer, one of the founders of Denver, had been major general in the Pennsylvania militia. He freighted wholesale groceries by Conestoga wagon in that state and prospered in railroad and coal mine investments until the panic of 1854. He attempted to found a town in Nebraska, but failed, and then became a banker in Leavenworth. With his son William, he went to Pikes Peak, heading a party more interested in speculation than in mining. He succeeded in merging two rival settlements on Cherry Creek as the city of Denver. Larimer Street there was named for him.

[2] John Wesley Iliff has been called "the largest and most successful cattle merchant that the West ever produced." Born in McLuney, Ohio, December 18, 1831, he attended Ohio Wesleyan University and in 1837 went West with five hundred dollars. He was one of the incorporators of Ohio City, later Princeton, Kansas, but in 1859 he drove an ox team to the Pikes Peak area and opened a store on Cherry Creek. His biographer says his trade with Lowe may have marked the end of his mercantile business. (See Agnes Wright Spring, "A 'Genius for Handling Cattle:' John W. Iliff," in *When Grass Was King*, by Maurice Frink, W. Turrentine Jackson, and Mrs. Spring, [Boulder, 1956, University of Colorado Press], 345–451). Iliff went into the business of buying up ox teams from emigrants, started a ranch near Fort Lupton, and expanded over the open range lands of Colorado and Wyoming. After his death in 1878 his executors cleared more than one million dollars from his assets.

demand and sold rapidly. We had them on the market ahead of any others for that spring.

I sold the trains and "Wash" and I left the remnant of goods with William M. Clayton and went east—he to buy more goods, and I to fit out transportation.

Clayton bought a large stock of goods, which I loaded as they arrived at Leavenworth and started them out in three small trains—thirty-six ox teams in all, five yoke to each team, following myself with a young lawyer from Atchison named E. P. Lewis, with a pair of mules to my Concord buggy, our blankets strapped on behind and well armed; we carried a lunch and coffee pot, but took meals with a train whenever convenient, as we overtook them. Twenty-two days from Leavenworth to Denver and slept in the open on our blankets behind the buggy every night—rain the day before we left Leavenworth and day after we arrived in Denver, but no rain between.

I became very much attached to Lewis—he was bright, genial, companionable and kind. After a year or two in Denver he went to Montana, and after a brief struggle with adversity, committed suicide by shooting. That such a lovable man could have come to such an end was shocking.

An incident of this trip should be related as proof that man's humanity to man will sometimes return to bother him. One night Lewis and I drove late, expecting to overtake one of the trains, but failing, camped by the roadside, picketed the mules and slept until sunrise, when we found ourselves a few miles west of Cottonwood Springs and half a mile north of "Jack" Morrow's ranch. Changing the picket pins to give the mules fresh grass, taking a good look up and down the road and seeing no one in sight, we walked up to the ranch to get breakfast. Morrow, the whole-souled, good fellow, greeted us cheerfully and ordered breakfast. Furnishing meals was a part of his business and he had a good "prairie" cook. I stood talking with him about his new stockade corral across the road, when the gate opened and a man came towards us. I quickly slipped my pistol to the front, cocked and kept my hand on it. The man stopped, stared at me, and then passed on through a door and out of sight. Morrow noticed the movements of both, reached under the counter for his pistol and asked me for an explanation. I told the man's name, why I knocked him in the head, etc. He was wearing the same pistol, but with a clean hickory shirt, looked much better than when with me. He was traveling under a different name. This was my third chance to have justified myself in killing him, but he made no move towards his pistol—wouldn't have had any show if he did—and I could not commit murder. Morrow said that he had a terrible scalp wound that did not seem to be entirely well, though it was made nearly two years before. He wanted to work and was hired the day before. I never saw him again. He was supposed to have gone with a team for timber in the cedar buffs near by. The reader will recognize this as the man who attacked me on Sweet Water in 1858.[3] Having finished our breakfast, Lewis and I returned to the buggy and drove on.

In December, 1860, Clayton & Lowe dissolved partnership, Lowe selling his interest to the Claytons, taking in part payment a ranch and company cattle on Box Elder, twenty-eight miles east of Denver. We parted as we had always lived, the best of friends—a friendship that was never broken.

My object in leaving the firm was to go into freighting on my own account, and so I severed my business connection with clearheaded, generous George W. and Wm. M. Clayton, both of whom accumulated great wealth, left an untarnished name, and died all too soon, universally respected in business and social circles.

Returning to Leavenworth by coach in January, 1861, six passengers were eight days and nights en route on account of deep snow from Fort Kearney east. Thirty miles east of Kearney, we were most of one night lost in snowdrifts. I got out and hunted the road for hours, and finally found the stage station at

[3] See pages 252–53.

Thirty-two-mile Creek. It was the hardest night I ever experienced. "Jo" Chaffe,[4] afterwards United States senator, was a passenger. I found a herd of mules in the hands of the trustees of the bankrupt firm of Russell, Majors & Waddell, the great Government transporters, and bought them—ten thousand dollars worth on six months' time without interest. I bought wagons, harness and other outfit, let it be known that I would start the middle of March with fast freight, and merchants furnished all the loading that I wanted, at from twelve to fifteen cents a pound to Denver. I may truthfully say that my reputation as a successful freighter brought me the business. I left Leavenworth on St. Patrick's day, 1861, and went through to Denver in twenty-four days, with thirteen eight-mule teams, and cleared five thousand dollars in gold.

I found that the Arapahoe Indians had raided the ranches along Box Elder, mine amongst them, burned my house, and killed a family on the adjoining ranch. The man in charge of my cattle, Wm. Riecke, heard of their coming and ran the cattle to Denver, and when I came in I found them near Golden City, safe. The Indians had left the country and the cattle were driven back and the house rebuilt.

Mr. Hugh Kirkendall was my wagonmaster and a good one, and I sent him to Leavenworth with the train loaded with dry hides, which occupied him thirty days, while I returned on the coach in six days.

And now the great Civil War was on and all along the border the animosities that had slumbered since '56 were again in full force—the line was sharply drawn between Union and Confederate. In Kansas it was all Union; in Missouri, very much mixed, and the peace and friendship of neighborhoods threatened. My "best girl" lived on the line of Platte and Clay counties, and I persuaded myself and the girl, and her parents too, that it was

---

4 Presumably Jerome Napoleon Chaffee, who was Colorado's delegate to Congress, 1871–75, and United States senator, 1876–79. He was long prominent in politics, as well as in finance, including the Maxwell Land Grant.

best to get her away from such surroundings, and I urged the consummation of what we hoped might be brought about in the near future, so that on the fourth of June, 1861, I married Miss Margaret E. Gartin, a daughter of Andrew Gartin, Esq., of Clay County, one of the leading men of upper Missouri, and one of the best families in the State. I fitted up a Dougherty ambulance, got a good campaign cook, and every convenience for the trip. The train came in and I had plenty of loading at ten cents a pound, which, when grass alone was required for forage, was equal to twelve cents in March, when corn must be fed. The trip to Denver was uneventful. I had prepared a nice home in Denver and we moved into our own house. Besides extraordinary expenses, this trip cleared me three thousand dollars.

On the Box Elder Ranch I intended to winter the mules after making another trip, and my brother, P. C. S. Lowe, in charge of it, put up plenty of hay for that purpose. The train was standing on "F" Street, ready to pull out for the States, when Governor Gilpin[5] offered me, through my friend G. W. Clayton, the lieutenant-colonelcy of the Second Colorado. Thanking him, I explained that I had just started in a money-making business and could not afford to abandon it for the sake of showing myself in glittering uniform for a few days—that I did not think the war would last long, etc. He disagreed with me, and his words then spoken were prophetic, showing an amount of forethought and wisdom that has ever since commanded my admiration. I never met a clearer-headed man. The train returned to Leavenworth under Kirkendall, and I returned by coach in time to meet it. For safety I camped on the military reservation for a couple of weeks. Organized gangs of horse and mule thieves overran the country—nine fine horses were taken from stables in Leavenworth one morning. Under the name of scouts they committed all manner of crimes. My friends advised me that things would

---

[5] William Gilpin of Missouri was appointed by President Lincoln as first governor of Colorado Territory in 1861. He was removed April 19, 1862, because of excessive unauthorized expenditures for troops and supplies.

settle down and become safer soon, but the season was getting late and merchants did not like to trust goods with mule teams liable to be run off at any time—ox teams were safer. A friend of mine, "Cliff" Barnes, of Independence, Missouri, had twelve six-mule teams run off. With the United States Marshal he overtook them below Lawrence, but it cost him half their value to get them back.

I had married into a slave-holding family, and that alone was an excuse for so-called "scouts" and "red legs"[6] to raid my train if they dared. For a week I stayed all night with my train, with the wagonmaster and others, expecting a raid, which did not come. Every morning I returned to the Planters' House and slept and in the evening rode back to the train. One morning I met on the Planters' House steps a man who came to me in 1855 at Fort Riley. He was then a mere youth. He had traveled with me from Utah in 1858. I had heard that he belonged to an organized gang of marauders, and determined to sound him I invited him to breakfast, and after breakfast to my room, where we spent two hours. He was a smart young fellow, capable of much good or bad and gave to me a list of thirty-two of the gang he was associating with, claiming that they were honest patriotic scouts and assured me that none of them would bother my train. This man did no more work with his party after our meeting, but most of the party turned out to be the most consummate robbers on the border. My friend soon went east and occupied a lucrative position in and about Washington in transportation during the war.

One day a gentleman whom I had never before met called on me. He was a militia officer, and after introducing himself stated that he had been instructed by the "Committee of Safety" to inform me that I must not move my train over into Missouri. Of course I was surprised and demanded by what course of reasoning

---

[6] "Red legs" or "Red Legged Scouts," were so called because they wore leggings made of red sheepskin used by shoemakers. They were a Union militia or home guard sponsored by Brigadier Generals Thomas Ewing and James G. Blunt, but under such leaders as William S. Tough were little better than guerrillas.

Private Business and Government Service

he or the committee supposed I would do so. He was a thorough gentleman and much embarrassed at the position in which he found himself. I assured him that I did not blame him for delivering the message, but wished him to tell the meddlesome committee of safety that I would move my train when and where I pleased, and that if I ever saw either of those I happened to know about my train I would have them shot like common horse thieves, and wound up by saying that if he could think of anything else mean enough he might add it to what I had said. This gentleman and I became very warm friends, a friendship that lasted until he died thirty-seven years later.

Major Easton,[7] Quartermaster at Fort Leavenworth, advised me to sell my mules to the Government and return to Government employment again, until it was safer to do business, and I sold to him, paid all my debts, and returned by coach to Denver, sold my ranch and hay on Box Elder to the late John K. Faulkner, sold the cattle and mules left there, disposed of household effects, rented my house and with my wife and brother, returned to Leavenworth. I owned a good house there, into which we moved and had a happy home.

Again the transportation business at Fort Leavenworth was immense, and General Easton asked me to take hold and help, which I did, fitting out trains, etc. I left fifteen thousand dollars in gold in quartermaster's vaults at Fort Leavenworth for a year

---

[7] Langdon Cheves Easton of Missouri entered West Point in 1833, and was graduated in 1838 as second lieutenant, Sixth Infantry. He was first lieutenant in his regiment, 1839–51, meanwhile being appointed captain, assistant quartermaster in 1847. He became major quartermaster August 3, 1861; lieutenant colonel, quartermaster, assigned in 1863; and colonel, quartermaster, assigned in 1864. In 1864 also he was brevetted lieutenant, colonel, and brigadier general "for distinguished and important service in the Quartermaster Department in the campaign terminating in the capture of Atlanta, Georgia," and major general in 1865 for meritorious service during the war. His commission as colonel terminated in 1867, but meanwhile he had been appointed lieutenant colonel, deputy quartermaster general, and in 1872 he became colonel assistant quartermaster general. He retired in 1881 and died April 29, 1884.

and a half, for safety, until I could see my way clear to use it in business again.

In July, 1862, came an order for 600 horses and 120 six-mule wagons to be sent to Fort Union, New Mexico, and as I could leave my wife with a part of her family for company, I took charge of this big outfit.

As soon as a train of teams was ready it moved to Fort Riley, 130 miles, with orders for the wagonmaster to report his train to Captain Scott,[8] acting quartermaster, for assignment to camp in that vicinity. As soon as a string of horses was ready it moved to Riley, the man in charge also to report to Captain Scott for assignment to camp. Five trains of wagons—104 four-mule and 16 six-mule—120 teams, and a traveling forge hauled by eight mules, and eighteen strings of horses (614), including some riding horses, comprised the outfit. When all were gone, I drove in my four-mule government ambulance to Fort Riley in two days. Pat Devine, who had been my driver to Denver the previous year, drove for me now, and fed me as well as circumstances would permit. If I lacked anything, it was not his fault. I slept in the ambulance every night from start to finish of the trip, except two nights that Captain Scott cared for me at Riley, one night that Colonel Leavenworth[9] cared for me at Fort Lyon[10] and six nights that my friend Captain William Van Vliet[11] cared for me at Fort Union.

[8] Captain Scott, acting quartermaster, presumably an officer of Volunteers, probably could be further identified by reference to *Post Returns,* Fort Riley.

[9] Jesse Henry Leavenworth of Vermont was graduated from West Point in 1830 as brevet second lieutenant and second lieutenant, Fourth Infantry. He transferred to the Second Infantry in 1831 and resigned in 1836. He served as colonel, Second Colorado Infantry, from February 17, 1862 to September 26, 1863. He negotiated treaties with the Kiowa-Apaches, Kiowas, and Comanches in 1865 and was agent to the Kiowas and Comanches, 1867–68. He died March 12, 1885. He was the son of Brevet Brigadier General Henry Leavenworth, for whom Fort Leavenworth was named.

[10] Old Fort Lyon was established in 1859 and named Fort Wise. The name was changed in 1861 to honor Nathaniel P. Lyon, killed in the Battle of Wilson's Creek. After floods destroyed the fort on the Arkansas River, near Bent's Fort, a new Fort Lyon was built three miles below the Purgatoire River.

Private Business and Government Service

At Riley Captain Scott furnished me all the corn I cared to take.

The object in sending four-mule teams was to get as many wagons to New Mexico as possible with fewest mules; mules could be bought there but wagons could not. A big six-mule wagon is hard on four mules—jerks the leaders painfully and

Sketch reproduced from the 1906 edition

SIX-MULE TEAM

gives them sore shoulders. Six mules can haul 2,500 pounds with less injury to them than four mules can haul the empty wagon, hence as a supply train for the horses the four-mule teams did not amount to much. This I did not realize for some days, as I had never before tried four mules on a big wagon. We loaded about 2,500 to each six-mule team, 1,200 to each four-mule team, and two sacks of 112 pounds each to each horse-string, and the rule was to keep two whole sacks of corn in each horse-string wagon in case of any accident that might separate it for a night from the supply train.

There was in my instructions no limit to the time I should take to reach Union or to make the round trip, but the general understanding was that as the season was getting late, the sooner the horses could be delivered, without too much strain, the better for them. They were not expected to gain flesh on the trip, and were always liable to accidents. Horses naturally travel more freely than mules, and hence the day's travel must, as a rule, be

[11] William A. Van Vliet of New York was appointed captain assistant quartermaster of Volunteers on August 15, 1861, and was mustered out July 28, 1865. He died February 12, 1871.

measured by the distance that the mules were able to make without injury to them.

I may here describe a horse-string and manner of managing it. A three-inch thimble skein wagon was what we used, with double covers and wheel harness for pair of horses. An inch and one-half or two-inch rope is put through the iron at the end of the tongue and spliced. At the other end the rope is put through an iron ring and spliced. About eight feet apart from tongue to iron ring, strong rings were seized onto the rope. In motion a pair of horses are hitched to the wagon, with which and the brake the driver manages it. At the end of the rope, another pair of horses are hitched to keep it straight. A man rides the near horse to manage the pair. Another pair of horses in the middle of the string, each wearing a collar, hames and back-strap with a chain hitched to the inside ring of each hame crossing under the rope to hold it up. A man rides the near horse of this pair to keep them steady. On either side of the rope a horse is tied to lead. Complete, the string may be made of any number of horses, according to its length; in my case there were about thirty-two on a string, including wheelers and leaders. The foreman and another rode horses, one on each side of the string, to be ready to dismount and assist in case of trouble. Horses were liable to get badly hurt by getting a leg over the rope, and often the string must stop to shorten up if the horses were tied too long; so that a string crew consisted of foreman, cook, driver, lead-rider, swing-rider, and outrider—six men in all. The cook slept in the wagon during the day and must see that the other men's attention was not diverted from the horses to get something to eat. Each string crew had its tent, mess-kit and rations, five water-buckets and ten-gallon water-keg which must be kept full, a big maul, and wooden picket-pins with iron rings around the top. Having arrived in camp, the first thing to do was to picket the wagon-wheels, so that they could not be moved, then the cross-jacks, about thirty feet apart, made of one and one-half by three-inch hardwood seven feet long, crossed and bolted together about one foot from the end. These were opened and set

Private Business and Government Service

under the rope, as shown in the cut, raising it about four feet from the ground. In these the rope rests from the end of the tongue to the end of the rope, which is kept straight by another rope which extends from the end about ten feet farther, and is fastened by an iron-bound wooden picket-pin driven deep into the ground. To the picket line the horses stand tied as they traveled, the halter straps being tied long enough to reach the ground to eat hay or corn comfortably.

Always in camp the horses must be untied and led to water, unless the watering place is bad, in which case they must be watered from buckets. During the day they must be watered from buckets, if convenient; but if one trusts to men to water from buckets always some horses will suffer many times—partly the man's fault and partly because the horse never drinks as well from the bucket as when free to plunge his nose into the stream in his own way.

Each horse-string wagon carried two scythes, a scythe handle and stone, and we had a grindstone in one of the trains. Grass in abundance was cut and put along under the picket rope so that every horse could have plenty. Great industry would be necessary to take these horses 752 miles across the plains in good shape, and we started with this understanding and kept it constantly in view.

The mule trains left Riley the tenth of September, 1862, each traveling independently, with instruction to camp on the Smoky Hill River at Salina, then a mere stage station, until I came up. There was a plain road, but little traveled, and this the first Government train of any importance to pass over it. The Kansas Stage Company ran their stages over it to Fort Larned, under the superintendence of my old friend L. G. Terry. The next day the horse-strings crossed Chapman's Creek, where I left them the morning of the twelfth and overtook the trains at Salina that evening—thirty-nine miles in three drives. During the afternoon of that day I was asleep in the ambulance when Pat woke me and said there were two horsemen ahead going the same way that we were. I looked out, and as we drew near found them to be in soldier's uniform. A horse had been stolen from my back yard two days before I left Leavenworth, and one of these horses looked like mine. I told Pat to keep straight on by them until I told him to stop. When three hundred yards ahead I got out and stood in the road with double-barrelled shotgun. When within a few steps I told them to halt and asked if they had any arms, to which they replied in the negative, and seemed extremely surprised at my action. They were mere boys and this their first taste of war, as they told me later. I asked where they were from and where going. They were from Leavenworth and were going to Larned to join their regiment, the Ninth Kansas Cavalry. In short, they enlisted under a rule to furnish their own horses, for which they were to be paid. I told one of them he was riding my horse, to which he replied that he had bought him in Leavenworth. I told him to raise the mane from the right side of his neck and if he did not find the letter "L" branded thereon, he could keep the horse and I would give him his value in money. He immediately said the brand was there, but he did not steal the horse, and I believed him, and invited both to camp with me at Salina and we would talk it over, which they did, and agreed to see me when I came into Larned if I would allow him to keep the horse until that time; to take him now would leave him afoot and he would be over the time allowed to report to his commanding officer. I was sure that the youth was honest and that he had bought the horse of one of the numerous horse thieves, or "red-legs" who shouted liberty and union while they robbed the people right and left.

I found the train all right at Salina. The next day we would lie by until the horse-strings came up and from that time on traveled together.

About midnight a fearful storm of thunder, lightning, rain and hail came up suddenly. I never saw a worse storm. All the wagonmasters knew that in any extreme case of that kind my rule was for every man to get out, pull the picket-pins and tie mules to wagons. I found everyone doing his best except in one train, and the assistant wagonmaster and half of the men were out, and all of the mules made safe. At Riley this train had lost four mules, undoubtedly by neglect, and I made up my mind to dispense with the services of this wagonmaster. Morning came, and men were hurrying fires to dry themselves, the mules were all safe and being picketed out, when I saw the derelict wagonmaster crawling out of a wagon dry and comfortable. I had some whisky of my own, got it out, and with a little gill cup gave to every man who wanted it a "nip." All of the old timers took it. The dry wagonmaster came to explain to me how he got all of his mules tied up before the heaviest hail came, etc. I cut him off with the assurance that I knew that he was lying, and he could not have any whisky; he might take his mule and go back to Leavenworth and lie to the man who hired him, but if he took the mule he must take his "time" from me, in which I would state that he was discharged for gross neglect of duty and general worthlessness. He took it, and I wrote to Major Easton,* quartermaster at Fort Leavenworth, a copy of his discharge. Henry Farmer came to me in 1855, and had been with me most of the time since. He was now in charge of a horse string at $45 per month, and I made him wagonmaster at $65. I did not have to lose any sleep for fear he would not do his duty. My wagonmasters were now John Wilson, who was with me in 1858 in Utah, Reed, Underwood, Farmer and Shehan.

The horse strings came up all right; they escaped most of the heavy storm and had no hail.

There was a family in Salina, and the nice woman had a few days before received a dozen chickens, brought on behind the stage-coach from near Silver Lake. Early she was out looking for

---

* Major Easton graduated at the Military Academy in 1838. He served in the Sixth Infantry until 1847, when he was made a captain in the Quartermaster's Department. He remained in the department until retired, Jan. 24, 1881. He was brevetted lieutenant colonel, colonel, and brigadier general for distinguished and important service in the Atlanta campaign, and major general for meritorious service during the war. Died April 29, 1884.

them; the rooster failed to crow, and there were no hens hunting crumbs at her door. Of course she was sad. I sent Pat to her house for milk and eggs and he found her crying. She told him of her loss, sent me two eggs, all she had, and a quart of milk. I was *mad*. For a family out here in the wilderness to be robbed of precious hens was too much, but I said nothing. Strolling about from train to train, I was looking for evidence of chicken thieves. In Reed's train they had tried to burn the feathers, but failed; there they were, half consumed in the ashes. I lifted the lid from a big bake oven containing three chickens. Reed was with me and much embarrassed. I told him that I would not look any further, he could do the hunting; and the first thing to hunt was a dollar apiece for twelve chickens, and not a cent less, which must be given to that woman, and if a cent's worth of anything was stolen from any one I would break up the whole outfit but that it should be righted. We had come from the border where thieves were stealing and robbing in the name of patriotism and liberty, but such things should not follow my trail. I would not have it said, as was often said of commands passing through the country, that they stole everything they could carry away. Reed was a fine man, did not know of the stealing until it was done, and like many other good men at the head of a troop or company, did not realize that he should teach "the boys" to protect people's property and not to steal it. The woman got her money and every man of my party a lesson.

The fourteenth was lovely and we moved ten miles to "Spring Creek." This was the first camp where we had all been together, and I made it as I intended making it when camping on a stream where there was room. Spring Creek runs from west to east. The first horse string crossed the creek, turned east and stopped; the next string passed beyond and turned the same way, placing wagon and horse string about twenty-four feet beyond the first; third, fourth and fifth go the same distance beyond and face the same way—that is, five wagons in line facing the same way, the same distance apart. The sixth string goes past the rear end of the

Private Business and Government Service

first five far enough to be out of the way of the last one and stops, fronting north; the next string obliques enough to place the wagon twenty-four feet beyond, west of the last one, and so on until eight wagons and horse strings front north. Then the fourteenth string passes west far enough advanced to be out of the way of the thirteenth, the other following in like order until the camp stands thus: Five wagons fronting east, eight north and five west, all horse strings fronting out, rear end of wagons forming three sides of a square and river the fourth side. Inside of this square my ambulance and traveling forge, and room to hobble or picket a few horses that had met with some accident or need extra care, or horses or mules waiting their turn to be shod. Always more or less horses were under special treatment, and this inside space was referred to as "the hospital." And now I made my big round corral two hundred yards in front of the long side of the horse camp. The camp is shown by the accompanying cut. The horse string tents are shown behind the wagons. The wagonmaster's tents were near the corral. And now the mules are turned out with lariats on without picket-pins. All wagonmasters and twenty men besides myself mounted—the mules driven away from the horse strings, for they were sure to stampede the first time they were turned loose. After circling around for a while, all settled down to grazing and there was no more trouble. A man led a gentle white horse with bag bell on his neck, and the mules learned to follow him to the corral. After two or three days the lariats were stored away in the wagons and not used any more. In the middle of the afternoon a large herd of buffalo came in sight, evidently going for water to Spring Creek, moving straight for our camp. They were moving toward the sun which blinded them so that they could not see the wagons until near to them. The mules were corralled quickly and the gap closed, guns were gotten out and a long skirmish line thrown out between the buffalo and the camp. After a good deal of shooting the buffalo sheered off and crossed the creek a mile west of the horses and continued their course until out of sight. Sev-

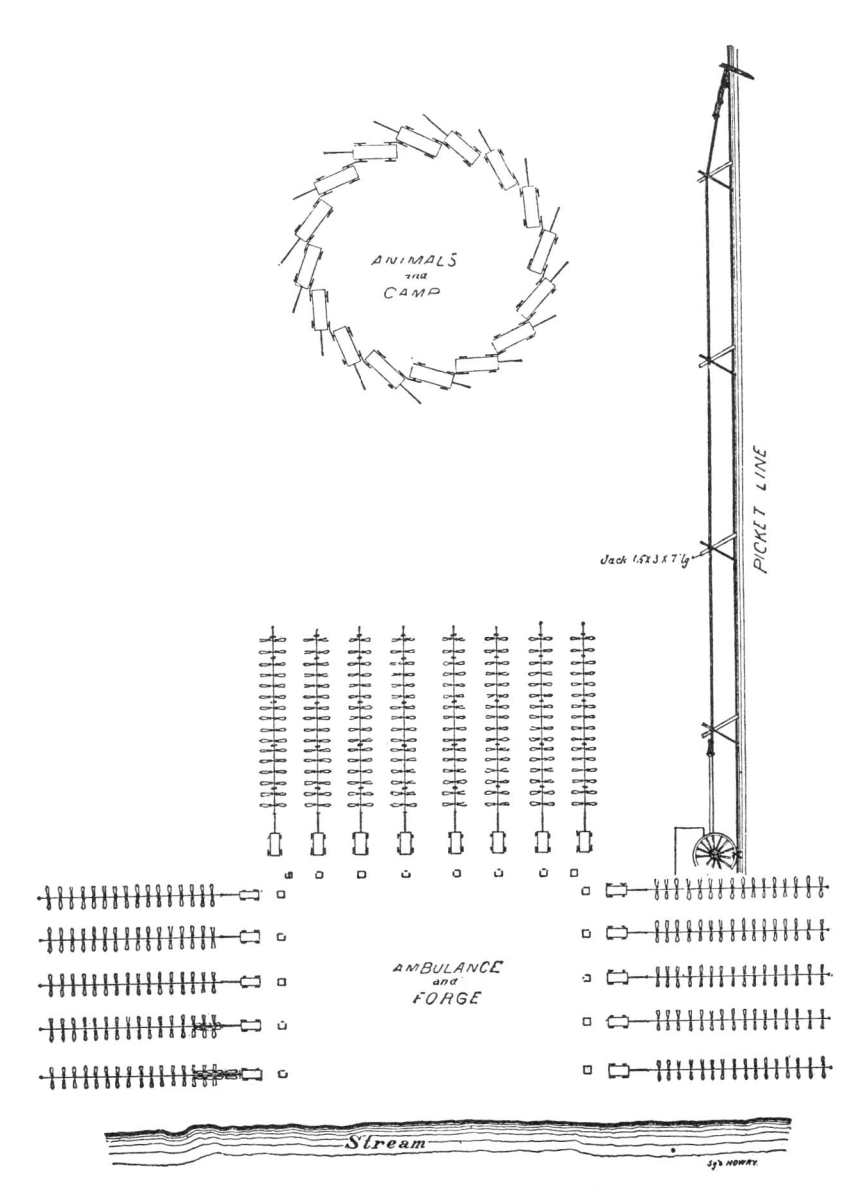

Sketch reproduced from the 1906 edition

THE CAMP; DETAIL SHOWING PICKET LINE

eral buffalo were killed and many wounded. It was quite an exciting battle, but if not turned they would have been in our horse camp before they knew it, and the ruin would have been great.

And here the rules for the future were laid down: The mules would be herded, a wagonmaster or his assistant always on herd with ten teamsters, who stayed on until midnight and were then relieved and the mules corralled at early dawn, and any time in the night that there seemed to be danger; we must not be caught out in a bad storm; in fact, with the gray horse and the bell, they were very little trouble. All hands were roused at early dawn and the mules fed two quarts of corn each—no corn for the mules at night—the grass was good enough. The horses were fed two quarts of corn at night and green grass piled up under their picket lines; in the morning they were fed two quarts of corn each and groomed. Breakfast over they were watered, preparation was made for starting, and at seven o'clock we rolled out, the horse strings in front, the first string to-day the rear string tomorrow, and so on to the end; the trains moved in the same order following the horses. The horse strings naturally traveled a little faster than the mule teams, but where there was no danger of Indians it made little difference if the trains were a little behind. If anything caused a horse string to stop, the others passed on and the delayed one fell in behind; the same way if a team would stop for any purpose. All found their proper place in camp and there was no confusion. And here I made a rule that about two miles out of camp horse strings would pull out of the hard road on to the grass and stop ten minutes, while the men readjusted anything out of place or attended to their own necessities. While waiting this ten minutes, three horses out of four would urinate. The mule teams must do the same way, with like results. The amount of suffering for men and animals thereby avoided cannot be estimated.

On the fifteenth we moved twelve miles and again camped on Spring Creek, the same as yesterday. Only two or three buffaloes seen to-day. As soon as camp is established horses are led to water, and again after feeding corn and grooming.

I am determined that these horses shall go through to Union in the best condition possible. We are a comfortably provided for party, and men need not give way to carelessness and neglect because they are away from home. They fare as well as men do on farms and are much better paid, and must not permit things to go at loose ends because it is "Uncle Sam's" property. And here I will say that the men with me this trip were the best civilians that I ever traveled with. More than half of them had never been on the plains before; had been raised in good homes in Missouri, but on account of troubles growing out of the war, when the news went through the country that this big caravan would go to New Mexico the best young men in the border counties came. There was a singular reticence about them—apparent desire not to talk of themselves from the fear of being condemned for rebels if they hailed from Missouri, and all the way to New Mexico and back there was a quietness unusual on the plains. The men were young and willing to do right, and among the nearly three hundred with me there were no quarrels, no jarrings. Two youths in adjoining horse strings fell out and drew pistols. I rode in between them and made each bring his pistol to me, and each tell his grievance, which amounted to nothing, and I lectured them; told them of home, family and friends. I stated to them that it was no unusual thing in civilian outfits going long journeys for men to fall out and some one be killed, and assured them that no one would be hurt with me. I would allow no man to ill-treat another, especially such men as they were. I was going to send them home to Missouri wiser and better men, and here and now they must shake hands, which they did. I did not tell them so, but imagined each one felt his honor vindicated by showing pluck enough to draw his pistol, and his vanity was satisfied.

I pass my daily journal because too voluminous. Crossed the Smoky Hill at the stage station called Ellsworth, where Fort

Harker was afterwards built. I never rode in my ambulance during the day from Salina to Union, with two exceptions. I rode one horse during the day and had another one saddled to use after coming into camp. Each horse string had a man on guard the fore part and another the last half of the night, whose duties were to walk up and down the horse string and be ready to attend to a horse that got his foot over the rope or in any other trouble, so that the string crew, including foreman and cooks, were on guard half of every night. I had a man to ride all night from one horse string to another around the corral out to the herd and every point about the whole camp, with instructions to report to me if there was anything wrong, if a watchman was asleep, or any one neglecting his duty. He slept in a wagon nicely fitted up during the day. His name was John Gartin, and I never saw his equal for faithful endurance.

I was instructed to go this route because it was supposed to be much nearer than by the old Santa Fé Trail. I arrived on the high ground overlooking Cheyenne Bottom and was surprised at its extent—an expanse of about ten miles of bottom with a mere trail but little traveled and apparently wet. I could not plunge into that without examining it. I had an inkling that there was such a bottom, and had ridden some miles ahead of the horse strings, and now wrote a few lines to the man in charge of the first string telling him and all to halt here until my return, put it on a stick and stuck it in the ground. I kept an assistant wagon-master with me, and we rode across the bottom to a good camp on the west side and back in about three hours. I determined to take the horse strings across, but if I got the loaded wagons into that bottom and it should rain, which was threatening, I might wallow in the mud indefinitely, and so I instructed the trains to corral. If it rained I would have to go south to the old Santa Fé Trail. The horse-string wagons were so light that I could risk them. The horse strings crossed all right, and were in a good camp on the west side before dark. I was off in the morning early, reached the trains by starting time and led them over the bottom, and on across Walnut Creek, the horse strings coming in a little later. The next day we passed Pawnee Rock, and crossed Pawnee Fork at its mouth (where now stands the town of Larned) and camped on the west side. I was told when I left Leavenworth that a strong escort would be ready at Fort Larned to accompany me all the way through to Union, and I sent a man from my Walnut Creek camp with a letter to the commanding officer at Fort Larned, apprising him of my approach and requested that the escort join me en route and save delay. I knew that every mail carried, from Fort Leavenworth to Fort Larned, something upon that subject and had reason to suppose that the escort would be ready. It was eight miles out of my way to go by Larned and I wanted to avoid it. Captain Reed[12] of the Ninth Kansas, commanding Fort Larned, with my messenger met me at camp, where I learned that there were few troops at Larned and they hardly initiated as soldiers, and all that he could possibly spare would be Lieutenant Dodge,[13] of a Wisconsin battery, and twenty-five men of the Ninth; he would select the very best that he had and they would be well disciplined with a good officer. After lunch we drove in my ambulance to the Fort and saw the escort which would move to join me early in the morning. I knew, and so did Captain Reed, that I would have to pass through the whole Kiowa and Comanche Nations, camped along the Arkansas in the vicinity of where now stands Dodge City, and the sight of six hundred fine horses passing close would be a great temptation to possess themselves of some. I ought to have an escort of five hundred men, but they were not to be had. Be it remembered that an Indian's weak point (or strong point) is horse; horses, scalps, and squaws are what contribute to his happiness and make life worth living. Captain Reed said that the young man with

[12] Captain Horatio N. F. Read (not Reed) was mustered out on expiration of three years' service on March 22, 1865.
[13] Lieutenant James H. Dodge was captain commanding the Ninth Independent Battery of Wisconsin Light Artillery when he was mustered out at the expiration of his term of service January 26, 1865. The Ninth Battery is credited with the Battle of Big Blue, Missouri, October 23, 1864.

my horse had reported to him and was in trouble. He was sent for; I believed him honest, and wrote and gave him a bill of sale (or rather "a bill of gift"), reading:

> I have this day presented to Private ———, of ——— Troop, Ninth Kansas Cavalry, one small bay horse seven years old, branded L on right side of neck, said horse having been previously stolen from me at Leavenworth and sold to said ———, who was an innocent purchaser.
>
> P. G. Lowe.

To say that the young man was greatly relieved would be putting it mildly. I liked Captain Reed immensely and am sorry I do not know his career.

The next day we moved up to near where is now Kinsley, and Lieutenant Dodge and command joined us. His party were well mounted, and from first to last Dodge and his men were to me all that that number could be. Having no mess or servant, I invited Dodge to join me, which he was glad to do. He placed his men wherever I asked him to and relieved me of much care all the way through. My horse-string men were armed with revolvers and teamsters with muskets, and I inspected them carefully and saw that they had plenty of ammunition. The next morning, a short distance from camp, we met Company F, Second Colorado—about seventy-five men under Lieutenant Weis, of Denver. They were on the way from Fort Lyon to Larned to report to Captain Reed. "Billie" Weis was a fine saddler and worked in the shop at Fort Leavenworth a number of years. On the Cheyene expedition he went with me as saddler, and was of much service fixing up the packtrains, and went with them. On the Utah expedition he was my cook to Camp Floyd. When I went into business with Mr. Clayton he went as cook to Denver and cooked for our mess until we set him up in the saddlery business, and now he was a good officer, commanding as fine a company of men as I ever saw, every man a pioneer, experienced in everything that makes a man on the plains or in the mountains self-supporting—all recruited in Denver. I knew several of them, and was introduced and shook hands with the whole company. I wrote a note to Captain Reed requesting him to order Lieutenant Weis to join me and go all the way through, and told the Lieutenant where I would camp and wait for him to join me, for I did not want to reach the Indian camp until he did join. He had wagon transportation, could make good time, and he was as anxious to go as I was to have him. At early dawn the next morning John Gartin called me and said that Lieutenant Weis wanted to report. Here he was with his company twenty hours after he left me. The distance traveled to Larned and back to where he joined was sixty-five miles. I told him to let his men sleep as long as he wanted to; I would only move ten miles and camp two miles east of the Indian camp. I had ridden up and selected my camp the night before and would not move early. We moved out about nine o'clock and camped on high ground near the junction of the Dry or Coon Creek route and the river road. For miles along both sides of the Arkansas, commencing two miles above my camp, were Indian tepees with numerous inhabitants. My camp was carefully made, as it always was, and abundance of grass collected. Dodge's men picketed the high points. Weis came up and was assigned a position just west of the horse strings. A line was designated for the sentinels, and all of his men put on guard, and no Indian allowed to cross the line without my permission. Hundreds came, but only two, Satanta and Lone Wolf, were permitted to cross the line, and they stayed and dined with me and Lieutenants Dodge and Weis. "Joe" Armijo, who had been with me nearly five years, was my interpreter; all of the Indians understood Mexican. I left the impression upon the minds of these chiefs that the soldiers were asleep in wagons and that those on post were only a few of what we had. Each teamster placed his musket so that it stuck out from under the wagon covers. I impressed upon them that while we did not believe the Indians would purposely annoy us, the curiosity of young men, women and children might cause them to come too near, frighten the horses and give us trouble, which could be avoided, and they could see the big train pass by just as well at a little distance—a few hundred yards away. They promised that all of their people would observe my wishes and I need feel no uneasiness about it.

I had traveled two horse strings and two wagons abreast during the last two days to keep them more compact, as was always cutomary on the Santa Fé Trail from Walnut Creek to Bent's Fort. There were two, three and sometimes four well broken roads for many miles through the Indian country along the Arkansas River, from the west line of what is now McPherson County to Bent's Old Fort, and now I rolled out three abreast, six horse strings long and three wide; forty mule teams long and three wide. Muskets protruded from under the wagon covers, soldiers were wide awake and plain to be seen. Dodge rode ahead with me with a skirmish line of a dozen of his men spread out wide, indicating that none must come inside of this width, while the balance of his men picketed the hills. For one who knew the curiosity of Indians under such circumstances it was remarkable how by thousands, men, women and children observed the promise the chiefs had made the day before. For more than ten miles these people trudged on foot, or cavorted about on ponies on either side of the train, never approaching nearer than two hundred yards. When we had traveled more than twenty miles and started up over the Seven-mile Journada, most of them were out of sight; but the two chiefs referred to and a few others came to shake hands and say good-bye. Armijo conveyed to them my thanks, and I had a barrel of hard bread and small sack of sugar gotten out for them.

Seven-mile Journada was a rugged bluff running down to the river, very broken—a good place for an ambush. I explained to Dodge, who rode ahead with his skirmish line and examined every break. There could be no traveling abreast, there being but one hard gravelly road only wide enough for one wagon. All horse strings and wagons returned to single file and we reached the Arkansas River and Cimarron Crossing in safety, went into a fine camp at the end of the thirty-five mile drive, without stopping to water. Fortunately the day was cloudy and cool. It is hardly necessary to tell how eager the horses were for water and how, when turned loose, the mules rushed into the river to drink and roll on the sand bars. Possibly I could have made half of the distance and camped without trouble but I should have revealed the weakness of my escort, and the temptation to crowd in would make it almost impossible to restrain a thousand or two young bucks. I never heard the wisdom of my action questioned by any of my party. Dodge and Weis freely expressed themselves as pleased; it was a great relief to have passed safely by that great camp and to feel that they were left behind; but we did not relax our vigilance; the Indians might think we had grown confident and careless, and the guards were doubly cautious.

From the Cimarron Crossing to Fort Union was the best natural road probably in the world, and shorter than by the Raton route by about one hundred miles, but the impression prevailed at Fort Leavenworth that it was very dangerous for my outfit on account of the Confederate guerrillas and Apache Indians, hence my orders were to go the Raton route.

Next morning we rolled out at the usual hour and traveled about twelve miles. There was nothing worthy of note until we reached Fort Lyon, commanded by Colonel Leavenworth* of the "Rocky Mountain Rangers," a son of the founder of Fort Leavenworth. We were two days here; got all the hay we wanted and

* General Henry Leavenworth, the founder of Fort Leavenworth, Kansas, left an only son, Colonel Jesse H. Leavenworth. Colonel Leavenworth graduated at West Point in 1830 and served in the Fourth and Second Infantry until 1836, when he resigned to engage in civil engineering. In 1862 Secretary Stanton commissioned him to organize a regiment of cavalry in Colorado, and this organization became known as the "Rocky Mountain Rangers." It did valiant service in protecting a thousand miles of Western frontier from the encroachment of hostile tribes of Indians. He died in 1885, and his remains rest at Milwaukee. His four daughters reside in Chicago and Tacoma.

turned over 100 horses. Up to this time I had abandoned two horses, hopelessly crippled, so that I left Lyon with 510.

From Lyon west and southwest, there had been a drought and the grass was too short to mow. We filled all the wagons at Lyon and fed sparingly. Crossed the river at Bent's Old Fort and camped ten miles above. Here was a species of canebrake, flat-leaved, and relished by animals in the absence of other long forage. I had all cut, and piled into the wagons all that was not eaten. The next day it was thirty miles to Timpas without water between camps; grass good for mules running loose, but none could be cut with a scythe. On this route from the Arkansas to the Picketwire River (Purgatoire) was always a hard problem for forage and water. My little supply of hay and cane would be all consumed to-night, and I did not expect to use a scythe again this side of the Raton Mountains. The mules could be herded where grass could not be mowed, but it was too late to break the horses to herd, and I would not be justified in trying it, if I met with an accident; but I will here express the opinion that divided into herds of two hundred or three hundred the horses would have gone to Mexico better on grass than they would on strings with plenty of hay and corn. From Timpas to water holes was fifteen miles, and as I knew, no place to camp. Six miles farther was Hole in the Rock, and nothing but volcanic rock and stunted pine and cedar. Twelve miles more to Hole in the Prairie, there ought to be grass and water.

In all these places watering must be done with buckets, and so it looked as if we would travel thirty-three miles and camp at Hole in the Prairie. The horse strings reached the water holes and were well watered. While they were watering the trains came and were told to pass on to Hole in the Rock to save time. The horse strings came up and passed the trains while watering at Hole in the Rock. With an assistant wagonmaster I rode on to Hole in the Prairie, where the ground showed no signs of rain for a long time, and was covered with a white scum of alkali and water strongly impregnated with it. Surely I could not camp anything here and let the animals drink. When the strings got here they would have traveled eighteen miles since watering and the trains twelve, in all thirty-three miles from Timpas. Fortunately the weather was cool.

When the strings came up I sent them right on, not allowing men or beasts to use the water. I showed where the trains should camp on high ground above the alkali bottom; told the wagonmaster in charge to have the mules herded without allowing them in the bottoms or near the water; to corral the mules at dark and start early in the morning. Then I got into my ambulance with an assistant wagonmaster and drove for the Picketwire; arrived there, I found the road had been changed since 1854 and ran up the north side. Following it about three miles, I saw a cabin and some stacks of oats. A young man living here alone had come from St. Louis in the spring, raised a crop of oats and a good garden. It was like an oasis in the desert. In short, I bought his three stacks of oats, as fine as I ever saw, and sent my assistant back to the turn of the road to bring up the horse strings. Two dollars a bushel the man wanted for his oats. That was the Government price at Maxwell's ranch on the Cimarron. I did not dispute the price, and he left it to me to say how many bundles should make a bushel. They were large and I allowed a dozen, which was satisfactory.

Near sunset the horse strings came up at the end of their forty-seven mile drive, and the horses all led into the beautiful clear stream up to their knees. Had we found no feed but the corn we had, they were fortunate to be here instead of at the Hole in the Prairie. All of the foremen of strings and myself stood by to see that the horses were led out before drinking too much. They were watered all they wanted an hour later. Three bundles were given each horse and no corn. A gorge of water with corn might cause some sickness; they ate every straw. After watering next morning they were given two bundles each and ate it clean before noon, and the balance was put into the wagons and taken along. Three hundred dozen bundles of oats the man sold me, and reserved a few dozen for his horse. It was cheap feed under the circumstances for my horses, and none too much for him to get. We bought some nice vegetables from him also.

Half a mile above lived Mr. ———, whose wife was a sister to Kit Carson, and she had a nice five-year-old boy. She brought him with her when she came with some milk and eggs to my camp to sell—a bright little fellow, and I had quite a romp with him. A week later he died from the effects of a rattlesnake bite. I was shocked to hear it on my return.

The next morning I rode up to where now stands Trinidad and selected a camp. A man named Hall, formerly sergeant in the Second Dragoons, lived there with a Mexican wife—the only inhabitants. He had raised a crop of corn and had a stack of fodder cut off above the ears and nicely cured. I bought it. The trains came up and watered where I bought the oats, and camped near Hall's. They found fairly good grass on hills. The horse strings came up in the afternoon.

Since leaving Lyon we had been feeding mules the same amount of corn that we did the horses on account of short grass. The next day we moved about twelve miles up the cañon towards the Raton summit. The mules did well herded on grama grass and the horses had fodder. The next day we had before us three miles to the summit and then down ten miles of steep, rocky, mountain road and three more to water holes. We had passed all the alkali country without losing an animal, but here a horse died.

Colonel Leavenworth assured me that great efforts would be made by guerrillas, rebel sympathizers, etc., of which he claimed to have positive knowledge, to capture my outfit; that said guerrillas were in strong bands ranging through the country; this would be a rich haul for them, and once captured they could easily run to Texas or Indian Territory, and there were no troops in the country to pursue or make them afraid. And the Colonel declared that these same guerrillas were presuming that the civilians of my party would have little incentive to fight, and my hundred soldiers, suddenly surprised by two or three hundred

Texans, might not stand up very long either. To myself I must admit that with a well organized party of such men as I had known I could surprise and stampede a herd of mules and demoralize a lot of horse strings without great loss.

There was nothing strange in the Colonel's story, and why an enterprising enemy should permit such a valuable caravan with so little protection to escape seemed a mystery. Armed as my men were they would seem a strong defensive party, and so they were in corral and could protect it, but a party of rough riders dashing into a herd or a train en route could cause much demoralization, and all the teamsters could do would be to care for their teams, and the horse string men would be too busy to fight, so that as a fighting force my men amounted to nothing en route. On the open plains with my little squad of cavalry on the lookout, we were tolerably safe, but in the mountains or broken country it was more dangerous. I had talked with Lieutenants Dodge and Weis a good deal, and they fully appreciated the danger and were extremely vigilant. Surely if I was to have trouble it would be in getting down the south side of the mountain.

Dodge was off early and covered a wide range without seeing a man or anything to arouse suspicion. As the horse strings worked their way slowly down with great difficulty Weis's men faithfully picketed the way. It was a hard road for horse-strings, but we finally reached camp at the water holes, when some wagons came in sight and kept coming until sunset, when all were in camp and no animals hurt, F Company bringing up the rear. It was a faithful day's work for all concerned and no sign of an enemy.

Early the next morning I sent Mr. Sharp, a man in charge of a horse-string, with a letter to Mr. Maxwell, of Maxwell's ranch, requesting him to deliver at my camp on Vermijo, fifteen miles northeast of his ranch, two thousand bundles of sheaf oats, or an equivalent in hay or other long fodder—whatever he had. It was twenty-eight miles, and I found Sharp and the oats ready for me. Sharp's ride was fifty-eight miles, and if he had not stayed with the Mexican ox drivers, they would not have reached my camp.

Private Business and Government Service

The next day twenty-five miles to Sweet Water. I found men putting up hay, claiming they had the right, and I bought from them enough for one night and to haul along for to-morrow night, for I knew we would find none at Ocate, where we arrived the next day—fourteen miles.

At the Sweet Water camp, a young Mexican complained that two men had come to his sheep herd and taken two young sheep, shot them, took out their entrails and packed the sheep off on their backs. His employer would take $2 apiece out of his wages for losing them, and he wanted that much money. I went around with him, found fresh mutton, and he pointed out the men who took the sheep. I told the men to hustle the $4 and I would make no fuss about it; otherwise, I would find a way to get it. It was soon paid, and notice given that no robbery would be permitted; "the damn greaser," as they pleased to call him, had rights that must be respected. No more sheep were stolen.

Ocate to Fort Union, twenty miles, where I was well received by Captain Craig,[14] the quartermaster (whom I had not seen since 1854), Captain Van Vliet, military storekeeper, old Captain Shoemaker,[15] ordnance officer (whom I had met here in 1854), and Colonel Moore, the post trader. This was the tenth of October, and we had traveled 622 miles from Fort Riley in thirty days, including two days lay-by at Fort Lyon. Our losses had been three horses and four mules.

I turned over all wagons, except the eighteen light ones used by horse strings and my ambulance, all mules except nineteen four-mule teams and five riding mules, and all horses except two. A few men wanted to remain in New Mexico and found employment, but 250 returned with me.

I disliked parting with Lieutenant Weis and Company F and

[14] William Craig, see note 5, Part IV.

[15] William Rawle Shoemaker was born in Pennsylvania and was a resident of Illinois when he was appointed military storekeeper, Ordnance Department, in 1841. He became captain, Ordnance Storekeeper, in 1866, and retired in 1882. He died September 16, 1886. (See Robert M. Utley, *Fort Union National Monument, New Mexico* [Washington, 1962], 36).

Lieutenant Dodge and his Ninth Kansans, but I no longer needed them and they did not need me. I would travel much faster than they, and so we parted, on my part regretfully. I do not know Dodge's career, but fear that he joined the great majority during the terrible war. Major William Weis, after many adventures—ups and downs, can be found at his saddlery shop industriously making an honorable living at 2630 Champa Street, Denver, Colorado.

But about half of the men could ride at one time in the eighteen wagons. I put a wagonmaster or foreman of horse strings in charge of each wagon, and the men were divided off so that each man knew the wagon and mess that he belonged to, and the man in charge must see that they rode turn about. Some men never rode; one, "Dick" Anderson of Platte County, Missouri, left camp as soon as he got breakfast and was in camp in the evening among the first. He came from Utah with me in 1858, and never rode a step except when snow was deep. Weather on the return trip was good until towards the last—just cold enough to make men relish walking.

I measured the road from Union to Leavenworth, 752 miles, with an odometer on my ambulance wheel. The second night from Union we camped at Sweet Water. A high promontory juts out into the plain south of our camp; wagons came around it following the road with half of the men strung along on foot; and bringing up the extreme rear was a cavalcade of about twenty men mounted on ponies, horses, mules or burros. They had improvised bridles of lariat ropes. I inquired where they got their mounts, and they claimed to have found them loose and picked them up as strays and thought they had a right to them. I told them that ranchmen had stock all over this country; all of them were branded; this was a public pasture, and to take an animal from it without consulting the owner, was stealing just as much as was stealing a horse from a farm, and they must turn them loose. One tough fellow said that the people in this country were "nothing but a damn set of rebels anyhow"; to which I replied

Private Business and Government Service

that he was not commissioned to judge of the loyalty of any man, and if he did not go back to the other side of that bluff and turn loose the horse that he was riding and the pony that he was leading I would turn him loose without a scratch to show the amount due him and he should not be permitted to travel with my party. Turning to the other men I told them that my remarks applied to them also. All but two said they had no idea they were stealing, and laughingly rode back and turned loose. I told the two sulky ones not to come near my camp until they got ready to live up to my rule. Two or three men went out and talked to them, and they finally rode around the bluff and returned on foot. This incident stopped all lawlessness. If it had been permitted, all of the unscrupulous fellows would have come into Leavenworth mounted, and flattered themselves that they were brave.

We made two drives, herding the mules night and day, fed two quarts of corn to each animal to Fort Lyon; Lyon to Riley one quart, and then four quarts the balance of the way. I did not want to take much corn from Union or Lyon; nor did I want to haul so much as to keep men from riding. From Riley east grass was dead and I bought hay.

Where the Indian camp stood on the Arkansas when we went west were camped two companies of the Second Colorado, under command of Captain Scott J. Anthony,[16] of Denver. The Indians had gone south for the winter.

Approaching the Saline River to select camp, traveling along the west bank was an immense flock of wild turkeys. I got out with my shotgun and killed two, and the others did not fly; did not seem to know what it was all about, and I killed one with

[16] Scott J. Anthony, born in New York, was a cousin of Susan B. Anthony, woman's rights leader, and of Daniel R. Anthony, editor and newspaper publisher. Scott Anthony came to Leavenworth, Kansas, in 1854 where he became a merchant and was active in the Free State cause, and a member of the Leavenworth Rangers. In 1860 he went to California Gulch (later Leadville), Colorado, and opened a general store. On August 26, 1861, he was appointed captain of Company E, First Colorado Volunteer Infantry, and took part in the New Mexico campaign, including the fight at Apache Canyon. He was promoted to major when the regiment was reorganized as cavalry in 1863.

my pistol. They ran and fluttered along into the thick timber where they roosted. After we were camped, men got after them and one German, who had a double-barreled shotgun, killed a dozen. The weather was cold and I kept my largest one until I got home, November 17.

In the 1,500-mile round trip with more than 250 men, representing all classes, with no doctor, dependent upon the box of medicines that my friend Dr. Samuel Phillips put up for me, without the loss of a man by desertion or illness, with no serious illness or other inability to perform hard duty, we made the return trip from Union to Leavenworth in thirty-one days—more than twenty-four miles per day—half of the way on foot. The cold weather was upon us; we were all anxious to get home, and there was no complaint. I came in two days ahead of my party.

Again my vanity prompts me to challenge comparison with anyone who has ever traversed the Great Plains with horses or mules. Five or ten per cent of loss was not unusual, but here we sent 614 horses 550 miles and 510 horses more than 200 miles farther, and 534 mules 752 miles, and return two horses and eighty-one mules with a loss of but three horses and four mules, and 250 men return in perfect health, after more than two months of out-door exposure and hard work, and no sickness.

But the merit of my trip, if any be due, lies in the safe delivery of so many animals at the end of so long a journey with so little loss, and a bill of health unparalleled for that length of time with that number of men. With few exceptions, wherever I have met one of these men I have felt no hesitancy in recommending him. Men who could work so hard and faithfully without any previous discipline can be trusted anywhere. Most of the men entered trains and continued in Government employ without losing time, and I had the pleasure of placing many of them in good positions. Three men of this party served with me in the First Dragoons— Mr. William P. Drummond, who was a sergeant in my (B) troop, was this trip in charge of a horse-string. Warren Kimball (since dead), who joined me as a recruit, and Mr. James H. Beddow, whom I knew in K Troop, and who is now and has been ever since he returned with me from New Mexico, an employee of the quartermaster's department, now and for many years, having police supervision of the Fort Leavenworth military reservation and wearing the star of deputy United States marshal—universally respected for his long and faithful service. He is now eighty years old.

Probably thirty men of my party had been with me on other trips, and to them I was indebted for much of the good order and discipline.

Part X
Freighter and Contractor

† † † † † † † † † † †

I CONTINUED IN GOVERNMENT TRANSPORTATION BUSINESS until the spring of 1863, when I went east and while in Washington, by permission of Mr. Stanton, the Secretary of War, visited my brother, Prof. T. S. C. Lowe,[1] who was in charge of the Balloon Corps[2] of the Army of the Potomac. I joined him at Falmouth just before the battle of Chancellorsville and remained until it was over. A friend loaned me a good horse and I renewed my acquaintance with several officers who had risen from minor rank when I knew them on the Plains, to be general officers. I was at Gen. Sedgwick's headquarters the evening before he with his Sixth Corps captured the heights of Fredericksburg—called the second battle of Fredericksburg—and saw all the movements of his Corps to the end of the retreat of Gen. Hooker's Army. Returning home I was sent by Gen. Easton on transportation business to Fort Scott and returned to Fort Leavenworth with six

---

1 Thaddeus Sobieski Constantine Lowe was born at Jefferson, New Hampshire, August 20, 1832. After making a first balloon ascension at Ottawa, Canada, in 1858, he took up aeronautics seriously and in 1859 built a mammoth airship—200 feet high with a diameter of 104 feet—which he proposed to control with an aerial propellor mounted on a steam-powered lifeboat. When New York City was unable to supply gas fast enough to fill it, he moved to Philadelphia. There the bag burst. In a smaller balloon he left Cincinnati on April 19, 1861, landing in South Carolina where he was seized as a Union spy. He was freed, gave up plans for a trans-Atlantic flight, and offered his services to the government.

2 Although many writers have called it "the Balloon Corps," it was not a corps, or branch of army service, but was irregularly organized at various times under the Corps of Engineers, Corps of Topographical Engineers, and Quartermaster's, Department. T. S. C. Lowe, although ostensibly in command, was never commissioned, and because of continuous disputes, resigned in 1863. In 1862 the "corps" had seven balloons and a number of trained civilian aeronauts.

hundred head of "contraband" cattle. It was a notorious fact that of thousands of head gathered at or near Fort Scott, this lot was the first to be saved to the Government, all others having been "lost or strayed" or appropriated by *patriots*. It wouldn't do to say that a man who loved his country would steal anything captured from the enemy, or that the sole object in capturing was to open the way to steal it.

En route back to Fort Leavenworth I stopped in the south edge of Lawrence over night where I hired a corral of a milkman named Palmer, who was killed the following night in the Quantrill Raid. I crossed the stock over the Kaw in the morning and rode home. A man by my name was killed in the Raid and my friends thought I was the victim—'twas a narrow escape.

The horse and mule trade at Fort Leavenworth was immense and in the fall of 1863 I left Government employment to become a contractor. My records of business transacted in horses and mules forage and freighting in 1863–66 were in a warehouse vault belonging to me and were all consumed in a fire in 1880 and I must refer to business from memory. The late L. T. Smith was my partner in many contracts for horses, mules, hay and corn on which we made much money. Mr. J. S. Rice was my partner in a large ox train freighting to Fort Halleck. In 1866 Mr. Alonzo Huckins became my partner in the mule trade. We built large corrals and handled many mules. Nearly all the mules used by Shoemaker, Miller & Co. in constructing the Eastern Division of the U. P. Road[3] were furnished by us. We furnished hundreds of mules for Mexican freighters until the railroad got too far west for the freighters to come to the Missouri River.

In 1868 I was the successful bidder for the contract to move all government freight from the end of the U. P. Railroad to New Mexico and intermediate points—from April, 1868, to

[3] The Union Pacific Railroad, Eastern Division was a competing line that hoped to qualify for the transcontinental contract and had no corporate connection with the Union Pacific that made connection with the Central Pacific. The Eastern Division was soon renamed Kansas Pacific. Much later the Kansas Pacific was absorbed by the Union Pacific.

April, 1869. The railroad reached Harker for the spring movement of freight and reached Hays before fall. The contract was in my name, but the firm name of the transporters was Lowe, Newman & Co. I retained one-fourth interest, Newman & Powers one-fourth, J. C. Erwin & Co. one-fourth, and Morehead & Allen one-fourth, and the contract was very profitable. I gave a bond of two hundred thousand dollars, and my partners were the bondsmen.

The following year April, 1869, to April, 1870, the contract was in the name of Powers and the firm was Powers, Otero, Lowe & Co. We freighted from Harker to Sill, Hays to Dodge and Camp Supply and from Kit Carson to Fort Union. Texas fever destroyed fifteen hundred cattle belonging to our sub-contractors, thereby making transportation scarce and high and there was no money made on the contract.

In 1870 I was awarded the contract to move all Government freight from Baxter Springs and Fort Gibson to Forts Arbuckle and Sill. Mr. Alonzo Huckins was my partner in this contract.

The railroads moving west had made such advancement that the Government needed fewer mules, the Mexican and other trade no longer came to the Missouri River and we sold our mule-corrals and quit that branch of the business. There was nothing of much interest in the 1870 contract to move freight except that there was little freight and it barely paid expenses.

Lowe & Huckins handled cattle in 1871. In 1872 the contracts were awarded to me to furnish beef from the block at Forts Leavenworth, Larned, Dodge and Camp Supply. Mr. "Joe" Kirmayer was my partner at Fort Leavenworth and filled the contract. I sublet the contracts at Larned and Dodge and they gave me no trouble and some profit. I gave Mr. Huckins an equal interest in my Camp Supply contract—he to devote his time to it, and we, with a colored man named "Elic" Fields, who was with me many years, with an ambulance and pair of horses, guns and pointer dog, drove from Harker to Larned and Dodge where on account of hostile Indians we were obliged to leave the ambulance, driver,

Freighter and Contractor

team and dog, and travel with the mail escort to Supply, which we did and returned safely. Then we drove from Dodge east to Great Bend, now the county seat of Barton County, Kansas, where I bought cattle, saw Huckins, started with herders enough to handle them, leaving Elic, team, ambulance, dog and guns with him, and returned to Harker by stage and from there by rail home. I was much broken in health and ought not to have made the trip to Supply.

And now follows Mr. Huckins' adventures with the cattle: He camped on the Arkansas River, near where Kinsley now is, had been on guard the last half of the night and came in at four o'clock to rouse the camp. Just as he dismounted from his pony many shots were fired into his camp, the attacking party charging through it driving everything before them except the pony from which he had just dismounted. Some shots struck the ambulance close to him. He believed the attacking party to be Indians and told his men that he was going to Fort Dodge for help and advised them to care for themselves as best they could. The rush through camp was made from northeast to southwest—up the river, and Huckins concluded to look a little in that direction. The night was very dark. About half a mile from camp he saw in the dim dawn two men changing their saddles to the ambulance team, a black and a grey. The two men saw Huckins at the same time, mounted and charged after him, shooting rapidly. Huckins urged his pony in retreat as fast as possible but they were close to him and sending the bullets close, but missing. Thinking they must surely get him soon he stopped, faced them and took a hand in the shooting. At his first shot a man fell from the black horse, the next shot hit the grey horse or the rider—he did not know which, but it stopped the pursuit and he got away. How many were in the attacking party he did not know, but from the number of shots fired into camp he knew there were more than these two. The Santa Fé Railway track was being graded and Huckins rode to Foreman Jackson's camp some miles away, told Jackson of his trouble and rode on to Fort Dodge. A troop of cavalry under Capt. ——— went with him and in the forenoon the cattle were all found with a man driving them. He was confined in the guard house a few days, claimed that he found them and was going to take them to Dodge. As nothing could be proven against him, he was released. Foreman Jackson, with a team and party of men went to Huckins' camp, found the dead man that he shot, who proved to be one of the white outlaws who infested that part of the country at that time, left him lying where he fell and brought the ambulance, harness, dog, gun and other equipments to Dodge. "Elic" went to Boyd's Ranch near Larned where he worked several months before returning to Leavenworth. The other men found their way to Dodge. Huckins, with an escort, got the cattle safely to Supply. In August we bought cattle enough to finish the contract which Huckins stayed with to the end with good success, for which he deserved much credit. Between hostile Indians and outlaws 'twas a hard struggle and a less nervy man would have failed. He married—bought a farm and prospered, raised a good family and is now one of Leavenworth's most wealthy and respected citizens.

And now I was out of business, broken in health and obliged to rest. My chances for the future were not good. I bought property that I thought would make my family comfortable and for the next three years traveled in search of the health I had sacrificed in my efforts to make money. I traveled in Colorado, through Florida and other southern states and gained strength and usefulness.

One incident of my travels is worth mentioning: Mr. Wm. Farrell was my traveling companion. I knew that my captain, under whom I served four and a half years was superintendent of a cotton factory in Columbus, Ga. He resigned as paymaster in the Army, joined the Confederate Army, was a general officer with Gen. Lee, surrendered when he did, and like an honest man had gone to work to make an honest living. We would pass through Columbus and this, in all probability would be my only chance to see him again. I told Mr. Farrell and he said "stop off

Freighter and Contractor

and make the call by all means." Our train arrived in Columbus in the night, we went to the hotel and after breakfast called at General Chilton's office in town. He had not yet arrived from home three miles up the river where his factory was and where he lived. The office boy looked at the clock and said the General would be in the office in five minutes. He might come sooner but not later. It dawned on me that he was living up to his old habits. Sure enough he came in on the minute, said "Good morning, gentlemen," and moved towards us pulling off his gloves. I immediately stood "at attention" and returned his salutation by saying "Good morning, Gen. Chilton." He looked sharply at me, shook my hand and said: "You have the advantage of me, sir." "Yes, General," said I; "I expected that I would have, twenty years is a long time." "Yes," said he, "twenty years of hard work." He sat down and covered his face with his hands. Then noticing that I still stood "to attention," he said "Please be seated," and looked searchingly at me, when I said, "Well, General, you don't know me?" He stood up, took both of my hands in his and said: "Yes, I do know all about you. You are my old first sergeant." I introduced Mr. Farrell who had been much interested in our meeting,—in short I explained why we stopped off and that we would continue our journey that night. The General gave Mr. Farrell a note to the superintendent of a factory who would pass him along to the next and so on, and took me in his buggy, telling Mr. Farrell that we would not be much company for him as we would talk of things in which he would feel no interest. Up the river three miles we drove and he explained that when the War closed he had nothing and no employment with which to support his family. The cotton mills had been burned and there was nothing left but the water power and burned and warped machinery. The company owning the water power offered him, to take charge of the property, a home to live in, small salary and an interest in any business that he could build from the wreck. He found a circular saw, fixed up the water power to run it, sawed lumber, soon started spindles to make thread, which he

317

peddled about town to get money to go on with. In short from these ruins he had built a first class factory of 152 looms and was continually adding to it. He had a mill for grinding wheat and corn, bought wheat and corn by the car load when he needed it, had a complete commissary department, tenements for his employees, employed the poor white people who were in great distress throughout the country, furnished them provisions at the retail price in Columbus, and paid cash for everything. At his home he was very comfortable.

I had been looking at a picture of Gen. Lee when turning to Gen. C., I said that it was reported and generally believed in the North that when Gen. Stuart captured Gen. Pope's[4] headquarters and his famous order "Headquarters in the Saddle" he brought the order to Gen. Lee who remarked: "That is the first time I ever heard of a man's headquarters being where his hind quarters ought to be." Gen. C. replied: "No, Gen. Lee never said that. He could not have said it—there was no levity about him—he was at all times dignified. I was adjutant-general and Stuart brought the order to me and said: "By the way, Chilton, that is the first time I ever heard of a man's headquarters being where his hind quarters ought to be." It sounded like Stuart who saw the ridiculous side of everything. This version of the "Head-

[4] John Pope was born in Louisville, Kentucky, March 16, 1822. He was appointed to West Point from Illinois and was graduated in 1842 as brevet second lieutenant of Topographical Engineers, becoming second lieutenant May 9, 1846. He was brevetted first lieutenant for Monterrey and captain for Buena Vista, becoming first lieutenant in the corps in 1853 and captain in 1856. He was appointed brigadier general of Volunteers in 1861 and major general of Volunteers in 1862. After his capture of Island No. 10 (for which he was brevetted major general at the close of the war), he was called to command the Army of Virginia. His order issued from "headquarters in the saddle" in which he also stated that he had come from the west "where we have always seen the backs of our enemies" was regarded as bombastic, and his only campaign led to the disaster of second Bull Run. He asked to be relieved and was transferred to command of the Department of the Northwest, where he successfully directed the warfare against the Sioux. In 1866 he reverted to his regular rank of brigadier general, to which he had been promoted in 1862, and in 1882 he became major general in permanent rank. He retired in 1886 and died at Sandusky, Ohio, September 23, 1892.

quarters in the Saddle" incident may be accepted as true history. No one who ever knew Gen. Chilton will doubt it for a moment. The General returned me to Columbus and we parted never to meet again, after one of the most interesting days of my life. He was exceedingly interested in what I could tell him about the members of the troop and at that time I knew of but four living, more than half of them had been killed by Indians or overtaken by violent death in other ways.

In the spring of 1876 the quartermaster at Fort Leavenworth employed me to act as guide in chaining the Santa Fé Trail from Fort Leavenworth to Fort Union, New Mexico. I was out of business, my family and property in good shape, and it would be a pleasure trip for which I would be well paid and I ought to be much improved in health by it. We chained by Council Grove, and the old Santa Fé Trail via Raton route, 752 miles to Union. Returning we chained from Fort Riley to Fort Leavenworth. Lieutenant Borden,[5] Fifth Infantry, was in charge of the party and the trip was pleasant and uneventful—no hostile Indians or other trouble. I made my report and was discharged the first of October.

Some friends of mine had taken the contract to furnish beef for the Sioux, Cheyenne and Arapaho Indians at Red Cloud and Spotted Tail agencies in northwest Nebraska, for the year ending June 30, 1877. I do not need to go into details about the trouble in the firm that led up to my employment. I was chosen to go upon the ranges, take an account of cattle and other property and report, which I agreed to do on condition that I should not be more than a month about it. I arrived at Sidney, Nebraska, where I was to meet the manager on the sixteenth of October, who was

[5] George Pennington Borden of Indiana served as private in Company C, One hundred twenty-first New York Infantry from July 23, 1862, to October 12, 1863. He was then appointed to West Point and was commissioned second lieutenant, Fifth Infantry, in 1866. He became first lieutenant in 1878 and captain in 1891. He was promoted to major, Third Infantry in 1899, but succeeded in transferring back to the Fifth; similarly when promoted to lieutenant colonel, Second Infantry, he again effected transfer back to the Fifth.

to show me everything. But he did not meet me. I took stage to Red Cloud agency—120 miles—went with Indian Commissioners Daniels & Howard,[6] with Spotted Tail[7] chief and two scouts—Gruard[8] and Battese[9]—to Spotted Tail agency and returned to Red Cloud, met one of the company's foremen from whom I learned much, went to his camp fifteen miles, to another camp fifteen more and to a third camp ten miles, three gangs of men. I appointed a day to round up the cattle and found about 6,000, whereas the foreman referred to said there should have been 10,000 and that at least 4,000 were on a ranch owned by the said manager. About 500 head were required every ten days, so that by the end of June 12,000 would be needed if none were winter killed and probably many would be. I learned everything

[6] E. A. Howard was agent at Spotted Tail Agency in 1876; in April, 1877, he took charge of the removal of Poncas from Dakota Territory to Indian Territory. (Daniels not identified).

[7] Spotted Tail, 1823-81, chief of the Brule Sioux, as a young man took part in the killing of a detachment from the Sixth Infantry under Brevet Second Lieutenant James Lawrence Grattan, August 19, 1854, and in an attack on a mail wagon in September. After defeat of the Sioux at Ash Hollow by Brevet Brigadier General William S. Harney, Spotted Tail surrendered and was condemned to be hanged. While prisoner at Fort Leavenworth he was given opportunity to realize the power of the United States and after his pardon by President Pierce, Spotted Tail never again went to war against troops, although he resisted all efforts to civilize his people.

[8] Frank Grouard was born in 1850 on the Island of Anaa in the Tuamotu group of South Sea Islands, the son of Benjamin F. Grouard, a Mormon missionary, and Nahina, a native of that island. In 1852 Frank was brought to San Bernardino, California, spending his boyhood in the home of Addison Pratt, notable Mormon elder, where Frank took the name of Ephraim Pratt. When sixteen years old he ran away to Montana and became a teamster. According to his own story, he was captured by the Sioux in 1871 and, being mistaken for an Indian by them, became friendly with both Sitting Bull and Crazy Horse. In 1876 he was employed as scout by General Crook, who regarded Grouard highly, although many officers were suspicious of his relations with the Sioux and reported escape from them. In 1877 Grouard was accused of incorrectly translating a talk by Crazy Horse, leading to the events that resulted in the killing of that chief. Grouard died in St. Joseph, Missouri, August 15, 1905.

[9] By Battese he may mean Baptiste, who could be Baptiste Garnier, called Little Bat, or Baptiste Pourriere, known as Big Bat, both leading scouts of this period and area.

Freighter and Contractor

that I could, reported by letter and asked the firm to send a suitable manager at once to relieve me. They promised but no one came, and it was the middle of the next July, after eight months of struggle including a bitter cold winter, during which I furnished more than 12,000 cattle for the Sioux, Cheyenne and Arapaho Indians, more than 6,000 of which I bought along the North Platte and about Fort Laramie. I was warmly thanked and fairly well paid by my friends and roundly cursed by the other parties.

The incidents of interest in the eight months of my stay in that country would fill a volume if handled by a good writer, but most of my data was destroyed by fire and I don't care to write about it.

I employed Mr. Fielder Philips to buy cattle for me in the vicinity of Fort Laramie where he had a ranch. He bought 2,140 head and I was daily expecting a message from him informing me that the cattle were ready, and had sent a party of men to take charge of them. I needed the cattle and sent "Elic" Adam, my Indian servant and traveling companion, with a letter to Mr. Philips. I gave him two ponies to ride, turn about. He left me at 8 A.M., with instructions to deliver the letter that night. It was 81½ miles from where he left me at Red Cloud Agency to Laramie. My letter to Mr. Philips requested him to exchange ponies with "Elic," giving him fresh ones to return on, and expected him to sleep at Laramie and return the next day. The next morning at eight o'clock—twenty-four hours after leaving me—here came "Elic" with a letter from Mr. Philips. He had delivered my letter at 7 P.M., eleven hours after leaving me. Mr. Philips gave him supper and lunch and two fresh ponies with instructions to deliver letter to me by 8 A.M. the next day, which he did. This faithful, untiring, full-blood Sioux had traveled on four ponies 163 miles in twenty-four hours without sleep. No one can dispute the distance—it has been measured by army officers and is 80 miles between Camp Robinson and Laramie and it is 1½ miles from Robinson to the agency. The road was quite straight and he could not save distance by short cuts—twenty miles of it was deep sand. Now let the long riders with their fine horses come in and claim something better. In half an hour after he had returned he was in my buggy with me on the way back to Laramie, where we arrived the next day at noon. He did good sleeping in the buggy. When I sent this man with the letter I knew he would deliver it before he slept. When Philips started him back he knew that I would get the letter in twelve hours. He could not speak English but could understand a little and I could squeeze out a little Dakota. For seven months he was to me all that an honest, faithful servant could be. When I left that country I parted with him with deep regret. He was one of the most interesting men I ever met, this poor benighted Sioux.

I returned home determined that this should be my last taste of wild life—I would henceforth devote myself to my family. I left a good home and my good wife had managed the two sons and two daughters as few mothers could. Somehow I seemed to be always plunging into some hard task and I determined to resist every temptation and live quietly.

I served in the city council from 1868 to 1870 as its president—1876 was again made president and resigned without serving because of absence from home—and now at the fall election of 1877 I was elected sheriff of Leavenworth County and re-elected two years later, serving four years, the limit allowed by law. In 1885 was elected State Senator and served during three sessions of the Legislature. I served on the Leavenworth school board by appointment, declining election; was appointed police commissioner by Governor Humphrey,[10] serving as secretary of the board one and a half years.

My sons graduated at Pennsylvania Military College, my daughters at Brook Hall, Media, Pennsylvania. My eldest son is

10 Lyman Underwood Humphrey, governor of Kansas for two terms, 1889–93, was born at New Baltimore, Stark County, Ohio, July 25, 1844. He enlisted in 1861 in the Seventy-eighth Ohio Volunteer Infantry and was first lieutenant when mustered out in 1865. He died at Independence, Kansas, September 12, 1915.

Freighter and Contractor

commandant of cadets at the Western Military Academy, Upper Alton, Illinois. He is also a graduate of the law department of Washington University, St. Louis.[11] The other son is retired as a captain in the regular army.[12] My eldest daughter is the wife of Major L. S. McCormack of the Seventh United States Cavalry,[13] and the other[14] the wife of Mr. Samuel H. Wilson, of the Great Western Manufacturing Company, of Leavenworth.

My dear wife died March 5, 1905, and is buried in the National Cemetery at Fort Leavenworth, where I will join her in the near future. A more lovable woman, a purer or more gentle wife, a more sweet and kindly mother I never knew. She made my family and home all that I could hope for, and brightened my pathway for nearly forty-four years.

She was educated at the Liberty, Missouri, Female Academy, under the tutelage of Prof. and Mrs. James Love. She possessed a remarkably good mind and was blessed with superior intelligence and refined tastes.

"I thank my God upon every remembrance of you."

---

[11] Wilson G. S. Lowe was born in Leavenworth, May 7, 1862. He had also been instructor at the Michigan Military Academy, Orchard Lake.

[12] Percival G. Lowe (Jr.) enlisted in Company B, Eighteenth U.S. Infantry, September 29, 1885, and during his first enlistment was promoted to corporal and sergeant. On February 11, 1889, he was appointed second lieutenant in his regiment. He was promoted first lieutenant, Fourth Infantry, in 1896 and transferred back to the Eighteenth the following year. He became captain, Twenty-fifth Infantry, in 1899.

[13] Jane E. Lowe became the wife of Loyd Stone McCormick of Ohio, who was graduated from West Point as second lieutenant, Tenth Cavalry, 1876. As of June 26, the day after the Battle of the Little Big Horn, he was transferred to the Seventh Cavalry. He became first lieutenant in 1878, served as regimental adjutant, 1887-91, became captain in 1895, and was assigned to the Subsistence Department in 1902. He was promoted to major, Seventh Cavalry, in 1903. (His name appears as McCormick, not McCormack as Lowe has it, both in Heitman, *op. cit.*, and in *Of Garry Owen in Glory, The History of the Seventh United States Cavalry Regiment*, by Lt. Col. Melbourne C. Chandler, n.p., 1960, in which, however, his first name appears as Lloyd, not Loyd.)

[14] Ellen.

Index

Abert, William Stretch: 274–75
Adam, Elie: 321–22
Adams, John: 122–23
Adkinson, Fort: *see* Fort Atkinson
Alexander, Edmund Brooke: 218, 219, 247
Alkali poisoning: 323
Allen, John, wagonmaster: 239, 241–42, 244–46, 255
Allen, Lyman: 182–84
Alley, Captain, storekeeper at Silver Lake: 153
Ambulance: 39, 44, 186, 267, 283, 314; Dougherty ambulance, 283
American Fork, Utah: 258, 261
Anderson, Bill, teamster: 47–48, 58, 70
Anderson, Dick: 308
Andrews, George: 234–35
Angel Spring, South Fork of Pawnee Fork of Arkansas River: 90
Anthony, Scott J.: 309
Apache Indians: 302; fight with, 138–39; Prairie Apache, 103, 106
Arapaho Indians: 62–63, 68, 71, 319, 321; raid by, 282
Arkansas River: 58, 81, 83, 101, 108, 130, 136, 185, 220, 298, 300–303, 315
"Arkansaw Traveler," The: 243
Armijo, Joe, guide: 197–98, 300–301
Armistead, Lewis Addison and Mrs. Armistead: 149, 153–56, 164
Army organization: xii–xxiii
Arnold, Private: 76
Artillery: Fourth U.S., 235, 250; Light Battery G, 73, 76, 79; Ninth Independent Battery, Wisconsin Light Artillery, 298
Ash Hollow, Nebraska: 45, 205, 215, 217, 221; Ash Hollow Hill, 244
Ash Point, Kansas: 226
Atchison, Kansas: 227, 279–80
Aubrey, Francis X.: 95, 164

Babbitt, Edwin Burr: 248–49, 273
Baldwin City (Prairie), Kansas: 169–70
Ball of Troop B: 77, 99, 115
Balloon Corps, Army of the Potomac: 312
Band, army: 79
Barnes, Cliff: 281
Barton County, Kansas: 82, 111, 315
Bateese, interpreter: 111
Bateese Trading Post: 256
Battese, scout: 320
Battle Creek, Utah: 258, 261
Baxter Springs, Kansas: 314
Bayard, George Dashiell: 200–201, 223
Beall, Lloyd: 133–35
Beall, William N. R.: 193–95
Bear Creek, Wyoming: 194
Bear River, Utah: 259, 267
Bear River, Wyoming: 194
Beauvais, James P., trader: 224
Beauvais' Crossing of South Platte: 186, 202
Beddow, James H.: 310–11
"Bedlam," unmarried officers' quarters: 25–26
Bee, Barnard Elliott: 244
Beery, Nick (Big Nick), wagonmaster:

Index

170, 174–76; chief wagonmaster, 185, 201, 203, 228
Bell, David: 254
Belt, George: 77
Bent, William: 95, 164, 303
Bent's Fort: 95, 301; Bent's New Fort at Big Timbers, 108; Bent's Old Fort, 136, 301
Bertram, Mrs., hotelkeeper at St. Mary's: 153
Big Bend of the Arkansas: 101
Big Blue River: 28, 42–43, 96, 226, 238, 240–41, 273
Big John Springs and Creek: 110, 112–13
Big Mit: 8–9, 11, 22–23
Big Phil (Charles Gardner), mail carrier: 211–12, 218
Big Sandy: 256, 267
Big Stranger Creek, Kansas: 178
Big Timbers (Bent's New Fort): 108
Bishop, Ben: 77; in Coon Creek fight, 82–83, 108; forage master, 242
Bisonet (Bissonnette), Joseph: 294
Black's and Ham's Forks of Green River: 231, 256, 258, 267; Black's Fork, 267
Blockhouses at Fort Leavenworth: 24, 26
Blue River, Kansas: 27, 29, 43–44; Battle of the, 38–39
Boonville, Missouri: 12
"Boots and Saddles": 64, 85, 131, 136
Bordeau, James, trader: 204
Borden, George Pennington: 319
Bostwick, Major, C.S.A.: 118
Boyd's ranch near Larned: 316
Box Elder (also Alder) Creek: 192, 250, 272; ranch on, 281–83, 285
Bradford & Cabbott, Salt Lake City: 265
Brannan of Salt Lake City: 265
Branning's train: 266
Brevet commissions: xv, xvi–xxiii
Bridger, James: 64–67, 69, 71–73, 216

Bridger's Pass: 219
Briggs, former Mormon: 266
Broderick, David Colbreth: 267
Brook Hall, Media, Pennsylvania: 322
Brooke, John Rutter: 257
Brown, B. Gratz: 61, 69
Brown, John: 177
Brown, Mr. (not John), in Kansas troubles: 178–80
Brown, John A.: 274
Bryan, Francis Theodore: 219
Brydon, Edward, trumpeter: 16–18, 83, 99; transferred to band, 122; in Soldiers' Home, 141
Buckner, Simon Bolivar: 84–85
"Budgen-Ken," company club: 98
Buffalo hunting: 89–93, 108–109, 222; huge herd, 102; scarce, 191, 242; buffalo shoes and mittens, 270
Buford, John: 171–72, 226, 245
Byrd, Rev. J. H.: 174
Byrnes ("Byrns"), Richard: 20–22, 139, 230–31

Cabell ("Cabel," "Cable"), William Lewis: 236, 242
Cache La Poudre (Powder River): 195–98
California Gulch, Colorado: 278
Calvert, horse dealer: 118–19
Camp Buchanan on South Platte: 201
Camp Floyd, Utah: 243, 249, 257–59, 262–63, 276
"Camp Maclin," Wyoming: 56, 62
Camp Payne ("Fort Payne"), Wyoming: 250–51, 264, 271
Camp Robinson (later Fort), Nebraska: 321
Camp Scott, Utah: 256
Camp Supply (Oklahoma): 314–16
Canby, Edward Richard Sprigg: 256–58, 263
Candy, Charles: 141
Cañon Creek, Utah: 259
Card, Benjamin Cozzens: 238–39

Carey, Daniel: 184
Carleton, James Henry: 14 n., 23
Carlin, William Passmore: 191
Carlisle Barracks, Pennsylvania: 5–11, 16, 80, 99, 125
Carlton, Caleb: 23, 14 n.
Carr, Eugene A.: 159–60, 162
Carson, Kit: 216; sister, 305; nephew, 205
Cater, George, expressman: 222
Cavalry: xiv; see First Cavalry, Second, Third, Seventh (U.S.), Second Colorado, Ninth Kansas; see also Dragoons, Mounted Riflemen
Cavayard: 240, 243, 245
Cecil, wagoner: 217
Cecil, K. B.: 154, 228
Central City, Colorado: 278
Central Park, Colorado: 278
Chaffee ("Chaffe"), Jerome Napoleon (Jo): 282
Chancellorsville, Battle of: 312
Chapman's Creek, Kansas: 289
Charters, John A., hospital steward: 146
Cherry Creek, Wyoming: 192
Cheyenne Bottoms, Kansas: 297
Cheyenne Expedition: 185–228; capture of scouting party, 206–10; fight, 220
Cheyenne Indians: 33–34, 62–64, 68, 71, 319, 321; Cheyenne Expedition, 185–228
Childs' ox trains: 215
Chimney Rock, Nebraska: 45, 246
Chilton, Robert Hall: 29–33, 36, 60–61, 66–68, 73, 78, 89, 93–94, 102–103, 110–12, 115, 121; confers with Satanta, 104–106; character of, 105; arrested by Colonel Fauntleroy, 128; released and transferred, 139, 141–43; pride in Company B, 143; retired Confederate general, 316–19
Cholera at Fort Riley: 145–62
Chrisman, George: 251
Cimarron Crossing of the Arkansas: 83, 95, 108, 130, 302

Cimarron River: 138, 142, 304
Clark, a Kaw Indian: 112
Clark, a Mormon of Provo: 262–64
Clark, a quartermaster sergeant: 195
Clark, a settler at Camp Payne: 271–72
Clark, Hartford T.: 100
Clarke ("Clark"), Henry Francis: 219–20
Clarkson, Chaplain Daniel and Mrs. Clarkson: 146, 149–50, 153–54, 161
Clay County, Missouri: 159, 219, 282–83
Clayton, George W.: 277–81, 283, 299
Clayton, William M.: 279–81
Clayton, Lowe & Co.: 277–81
Claytonville, Kansas: 227
Colburn, Albert V.: 199–200
Cold Springs, Wyoming: 255
Columbia, Missouri: 12
Columbus, Georgia: 316–19
Comanche Indians: 58, 81, 83, 88–89, 103, 104, 106, 131, 298
Committee of Safety in Kansas: 284–85
Concord buggy: 280
Confederate guerrillas: 302, 305–306
Contractors trains: No. 62, 252; No. 23, 255; No. 15, No. 21, No. 22, No. 24, 256; No. 20, No. 24, No. 25, No. 48, No. 51, No. 54, 456; No. 60, 259; No. 34, 268
Cook, Corporal: 30–31, 36; sergeant, 59, 76–78, 90, 93–94, 102–103; fights Osages, 109; discharged, 116–17; with Steptoe, 117; with Walker in Nicaragua, 118; death, 118
Cooke, Philip St. George: 5–6, 45, 139, 142, 166, 174–76, 225–26, 245; biographical footnotes, 5–6, 225; quoted, 27
Coon Creek, Pawnee County, Kansas: 82–83, 90, 102, 108, 130, 218, 300
Cooper, Samuel: 61–62, 73
Corley, James Lawrence: 162
Cottonwood Grove on the Platte: 203
Cottonwood River: 272
Cottonwood Springs, Colorado: 280

Index

Council Grove, Kansas: 27, 37, 81, 85, 95, 110, 127, 319
Court House Rock: 45
Courts martial: 97–98
Covey, Dr. Edward N.: 219, 222
Cow Creek, Rice County, Kansas: 81, 101–102
Cox, Bradley: 229
Craig, William: 133–37, 307
Crosman ("Crossman"), George Hampton: 262–63
Crow Creek: 195
Crow Indians: 52
Cuddy, John: 78–79, 83–84, 86–87, 109, 113, 117–18
Cumming ("Cummings"), Alfred, (governor of Utah): 265
Curran, Bill, teamster: 175

Dakota Indians: 322; *see also* Sioux
"Dan Tucker": 243
Daniels, Indian commissioner: 320
Daniels, William (Billy), assistant wagonmaster: 205, 208, 213, 226, 239, 262, 270–71, 273
Daugherty, soldier drowned: 200, 203
Daugherty Island: 203
Delaware Indians: 13, 17, 96, 174–75; scouts, 185, 199, 223
Delaware (Grasshopper) River: 27, 28, 59
Denver, Colorado: 185, 277–80, 282–83, 285, 300, 308
Deringer (Derringer) pistol: 115
Desertion: 36, 80, 101, 121–22; during cholera, 158; two deserters return to duty, 229–31
Devil's Gate bridge: 271; station, 269
Devine, Pat, driver: 286, 289–90, 292
Diamond Springs, Morris County, Kansas: 109, 142
Dickerson ("Dixon"), John H.: 219
Discipline: 31–32, 80–81, 124–27
Dodge, James H.: 298–302, 306, 308
Dodge City, Kansas: 83, 130, 298

Dodson, agent for Hockaday mail: 265
Dorsey, Green, wagonmaster: 233
Dougherty, Major, post trader: 43
Dragoons: xiii–xiv; *see* First Dragoons; Second Dragoons
Drill: xiii, 6–7, 32, 76
Dripps, or Drips, Andrew, fur trader: 56, 204
Drummond, William P.: 78, 116–17, 310
Dry (Coon) Creek: 300
Duerinck ("Deurinck") Father John Baptist: 96, 152
Duffy, "Little": 23
Dunnigan, Barney: 38–39, 41
Dyer, Alexander Brydie: 28–29
Dyer, of Dyer's Bridge: 156
Dyer & Co., hay contractors: 159
Dyer's Bridge, Kansas: 156

Easton, Kansas: 27, 170, 228
Easton, Langdon Cheves: 285, 291 n., 312
Echo Cañon, Utah: 259, 266
Edwards County, Kansas: 128
Eight Mile Point near Fort Kearny, Nebraska: 241
Ellsworth, Kansas: 296
Emigration Cañon, Utah: 265
Emory, William Helmsley: 237
Erwin, J. C. & Co.: 314
Eskridge, wagonmaster: 187, 222
Espenscheidt wagon: 25
Espy, Sergeant and Mrs. Espy: 140–41

Fall Leaf, Delaware guide: 199
Falmouth, Virginia: 312
Farmer, Henry: 291
Farrell, William: 316–17
Faulkner, John K.: 285
Fauntleroy, Thomas Turner: 59, 79, 83–84, 124, 128, 134–36, 141
Ferguson, Corporal: 70, 113–14; sergeant, 90, 116–17, 139; murdered, 117
Fiddle tunes: 242–43, 245

Field ("Fields"), Charles William: 9, 11, 14–15, 21–22
Fields, Elie, a colored man: 314–16
Fifth Infantry: 220–21, 319
First Cavalry (later Fourth): Kansas War, 167; Cheyenne Expedition, 185; Utah Expedition, 221, 236; Companies A, B, E, G, 227; deserters from G, 229–31
First Dragoons (later First Cavalry): 5; Company B, 10–11, 16, 20, 24, 28–36, 38, 42, 58–59, 68, 73, 76–77, 98, 106, 121–22, 124, 128, 130–31, 134, 136–37, 143, 242, 310; Company D, 122, 124, 128, 130–31, 134, 137; Company F, 10, 20; Company K, 10–11, 16, 18, 20, 23; Company I, 18–20, 138–39; Headquarters, staff, and band, 122, 124–30, 139, 141
Fisher, Morton, of Denver: 278
Fitzhugh, Norman, sutler at Fort Laramie: 272
Fitzpatrick, Thomas: 44–45, 69, 103, 106–107, 216
Five Mile Creek, Missouri: 18
Fleming, Ordnance sergeant: 24
Flood, Mike, wagoner: 248
Foote, Rensselaer W.: 191, 220–22
Forrest, Private: 77
Forsyth, James W.: 165
Fort Arbuckle: 314
Fort Atkinson ("Adkinson"): 58–60, 62, 83–85, 95, 101–103; pow wow at, 103–107; abandoned, 107–108
Fort Bridger: 63–64, 250, 256–58, 263, 267
Fort Dodge, Kansas: 314–16
Fort Gibson: 12, 314
Fort Halleck: 313
Fort Harker: 296–97, 314–15
Fort Hays: 314
Fort Kearny, Nebraska: 10, 28–29, 33, 35, 38, 44, 58, 90, 185–86, 220–23, 240–41, 273, 281
Fort Laramie: xviii, 28, 38, 45, 56, 59, 62, 186, 190–91, 201–203, 218, 221–22, 224, 247, 249, 272, 274, 321–22
Fort Laramie Peace Council: 58, 62–73
Fort Larned: 289–90, 298, 300, 314
Fort Leavenworth: 10–11, 16, 27–29, 36–38, 56, 62, 73, 79, 95, 108, 115, 124, 142, 167, 170, 174, 203, 218, 221–23, 227, 230, 232, 238, 240–42, 247, 273–75, 277, 285, 291, 298, 302, 310–14, 319, 323; described, 24–26
Fort Lyon: 286, 299, 302–303, 307, 309
Fort Payne: *see* Camp Payne
Fort Riley: 96, 142–66, 171–72, 220, 229–31, 286, 289, 291, 307, 309, 319; established, 142–44; cholera at, 145–62
Fort St. Vrain: 185, 195–97
Fort Scott, Kansas: 10, 12, 20, 312–13
Fort Sill: 314
Fort Snelling: 123
Fort Stanton: 139
Fort Union, New Mexico: 124, 135, 139, 141, 286–87, 296–98, 302, 307–308, 310, 314, 319
Fourth Artillery: 235, 250; Light Battery G, 73, 76, 79
Fox, Private: 20–21
Franklin, Kansas: 167, 170
Fredericksburg, Battle of: 312
Frémont, John Charles: 45; Frémont's ("Freemont's") Slough, 221–22; Frémont's ("Freemont's") Spring, 191, 221
Fulton, Missouri: 11–12

Gardner, Charles (Big Phil): 211–12, 218
Garland, Robert R.: 236
Gartin, Andrew, beef contractor: 219; father-in-law of Lowe, 283
Gartin, John: 297, 300
Gartin, Margaret E. (Mrs. Lowe): 283
Gerrish, merchant of Salt Lake City: 265; Gilbert & Gerrish, 265
Getty, George Washington: 271–72

Index

Gilbert, wagonmaster: 266–67
Gilbert & Gerrish, Salt Lake City: 265
Gilpin, William, governor of Colorado: 283
Glennon, Jim: 23, 77
Globe Hotel, Salt Lake City: 265
Golden City, Colorado: 282
Golden Gate, Utah: 265
Golding, G. W. H., gunsmith: 178–80
Goodale, Tim, trapper: 44–45, 216–17
Gordon, chief engineer, Missouri Pacific, murdered: 101
Goshen's Hole (Goche's Hole), Wyoming: 192, 194
Grant, bugler: 36
Grasshopper Creek (Delaware River), Kansas: 27, 59
Great Bend, Barton County, Kansas: 82, 315
Great Salt Lake: 265; *see also* Salt Lake City
Green River: 231, 256, 267
Gregory, Colorado mining camp: 278
Grimsley saddle: 62
Grinters Ferry, Kaw River: 12–13
Grouard ("Gruard"), Frank, scout: 320
Grover, Cuvier: 73–75, 247
Guard duty: 85, 107; guard mounting, 86–87; vedettes, 87, 93–94, 103, 130

Haff, Corporal: 30
Haidee, steamboat on Missouri: 11
Hall, Sergeant: 305
Hall, John W., wagonmaster: 256
Hamilton, assistant wagonmaster: 239, 247, 250, 255
Hambrights, Missouri: 12
Hancock, Winfield Scott: 237–38
Hand, Private: 133
Harker, Fort: 296–97; 314–15
Harney, William Selby: 190, 203, 221, 230, 237
Harper's Ferry, Virginia (later West Virginia): 177
Harrisburg, Pennsylvania: 11

Hastings, David H.: xviii, 6, 37–38, 64–65, 78, 81–82, 85–86, 89, 93, 96, 99, 102, 107–10, 121, 128, 131–34, 136, 138–40
Hayes, a German of Leavenworth: 190
Hays, Kansas: 314; Hays, Fort, 314
Hays & Co., grain dealers: 110
"Headquarters in the Saddle" incident: 318–19
Heath, John, sutler: 222
Heath, Lieutenant: 107
Hefferlin, Mr. and Mrs. Martin: 171
Hickory Point, Kansas: 153
Higgins, Silas Parsons: 186
Hill, Private: 23
Hobbs & Street's wagon train: 266
Hockaday, John M.: 265
Hoffaker, teacher, Kaw Agency: 111
Hole in the Prairie, Colorado: 136, 303–304
Hole in the Rock, Colorado: 136, 303
Holmes, Theophilus: 36
Hooker, Joseph: 312
Hooper, Sergeant: 59, 66, 78; bandmaster, 141; dancing master, 141
Hopkins, chief clerk: 147–48, 154, 158, 161
Horse Creek: 67–68, 194, 204
Horses, care of: 61–62, 75; feeding, 120–21; fast ride, 321–22; "finest horsemen in the world" (Kiowas and Comanches), 89; horse-string management, 288–89; long drive, 310; picketing, 130–31; selection of cavalry horses, 118–19, 137–38; stampedes, 131–35; *see also* wagon trains
Howard, E. A., Indian agent: 320
Howard, James (Robert V. W.): 264–65, 272
Huckins, Alonzo: 313–16
Humphrey, Lyman, governor of Kansas: 322
Hunt, Franklin Eyre: 76

Iliff, John Wesley: 279

Independence, Missouri: 12, 27, 255, 284
Indian Mary: 18–19
Infantry: *see* Fifth Infantry, Sixth, Seventh, Tenth
Inspections: 22, 76

Jackson, murderer: 115–17
Jackson, bandmaster: 146
Jackson, foreman, Santa Fe Railway grading: 315–16
Jackson, Peter B.: 239–40, 255
Jefferson County, Kansas: 190
Jeffries, interpreter: 32–33, 35
Jimmerson, teamster: 204
Johns, Dr. Edward W.: 248
Johnson, Edward: 216
Johnston, Albert Sidney: 224–25, 232, 262–63n.; Col. J. S., probably should be A. S., 240
Johnston ("Johnson"), Robert: 169
Jones, lance sergeant: 20–22
Jordan River, Utah: 262, 264

Kansas Pacific Railroad: 313
Kansas Stage Company: 289
Kansas War: 167–84
Kaw Indians: 37, 109–15
Kaw River: 17, 27–28, 37, 81, 95, 161, 168, 180, 217, 313; steamboat on, 153
Kearny, Stephen Watts: xv, 27
Kennekuk, Chief: 28; Kennekuk, Kansas, 28
Kerr, Chaplain James Couper: 24
Ketchum, Chief of Delawares: 13
Ketchum, William Scott: 46, 48, 55, 67, 69, 191, 220, 224, 226
Kershaw, Jerry: 277, 279
Kickapoo Indians: 17, 28–29
Kimball, Warren: 23, 77, 310
Kinnikinnick ("killikinnick"): 88, 213
Kinsley, Kansas: 128, 299, 315
Kiowa Indians: 58, 81, 83, 88–89, 103–104, 106, 128, 134, 298

Kirkendall, Hugh, wagonmaster: 282–83
Kirmayer, Joe: 314
Knapp, George: 60–61

La Bonte Creek: 272
"Lakes, The," near Chimney Rock: 246
Lanter, assistant wagonmaster: 174
Laramie Peak: 64, 196
Laramie River: 45, 190, 273
Larimer, William H. H.: 279
Larned, Kansas: 298, 316
Laughnahan, Patrick, death and burial: 245–47
Lawrence, Kansas: 170, 174–80, 182, 284, 313; ferry at, 174–77
Lawrence Fork of North Platte: 273
Leavenworth, Jesse Henry: 286, 302n., 305–306
Leavenworth, Kansas: 179–80, 277, 279–83, 285, 290, 316, 322
Leavenworth County, Kansas: 20, 28, 180, 228, 322
Lecompton, Kansas: 169–70, 172, 174, 178–81
Lee, Charles Cochrane: 274n.
Lee, Robert E.: 318
Lee, Stephen Dill: 274
Le Framboy, Potawatomi chief: 74
Lehi, Utah: 258, 261
Lewis, E. P.: 280
Lexington, Missouri: 12, 77
Library, company: 98–99
Little Blue River: 30, 32–33, 73, 224–26, 239, 241, 273–74; fight at, 30
Little Mountain, Utah: 265
Little Stranger Creek, Kansas: 178
Little Thunder, Chief: 246–47
Livingstone & Kincaid, Salt Lake City: 265
Lodgepole (Pole) Creek: 194, 207, 209, 212–14
Lomax, Lunsford Lindsay: 200, 220
Lone Wolf, Kiowa chief: 300
Loomis, Gustavus: 28

Index

Loup Fork: 32
Love, Professor James and Mrs.: 323
Lovel, Captain: 90
Lowe, foragemaster: 157
Lowe, killed in Quantrill's Lawrence raid: 313
Lowe, Billy, of Cincinnati: 192–93
Lowe, Ellen (Mrs. S. H. Wilson): 323
Lowe, Jane E. (Mrs. L. S. McCormick): 323
Lowe, Oscar (brother): ix
Lowe, Pembroke C. S. (brother): ix, 283, 285
Lowe, Percival G.: biographical sketch, ix–xi; enlistment and first assignment, 3–24; at Fort Leavenworth, 24–26; serves in Company B, First Dragoons, 24–141; first two years, 27–77; campaigns of 1852–53, 78–123; march to Fort Union, 124–42; leaves army, 139–41; quartermaster employee, 141–276; at Fort Riley, 143–66; Kansas War, 167–84; Cheyenne expedition, 185–228; Utah expedition, 229–76; private business and government service, 277–311; visit to eastern front in Civil War, 312–13; freighter and contractor, 312–22; later life, 322–23
Lowe, Mrs. Percival G. (Margaret E. Gartin): 283, 285, 323
Lowe, Percival G., Jr.: 322–23
Lowe, Thaddeus Sobieski Constantine: ix, 312
Lowe, Wilson G. S. (son): 322–23
Lowe & Huckins: 314; Lowe, Newman & Co., 314
Lowemont, Kansas: 28
Lowe's Route avoiding Ash Hollow Hill: 205, 217

McDonald, Charles: 38–40, 42, 46–47, 55, 70, 75, 94, 118
McGilvra, John, wagonmaster: 239–42, 244, 250
McIntyre, James B.: 236
McKenzie, Private: 20–21
McLane ("McLain"), George Washington: 157–58
Maclin ("Macklin"), Sackville: 38–43, 46–47, 55–58, 79
McPherson County, Kansas: 95, 301
Magraw, William M. F. ("M. F. W."): 215–17
Magruder, William Thomas: 141
Majors, Alexander: 276
Majors & Russell: 211, 215; see also Russell, Majors & Waddell
Malaria: 241–42
Man-Afraid-of-His-Horse: 206, 215
Manhattan, Kansas: 153
Manuel (Manuel Vigil), interpreter: 206–208, 211–14
Marcy, Randolph Barnes: 231–32, 247
Marmaduke, John Sappington: 222–23
Martin, Sergeant, killed in fight with Pawnees: 30–31, 35
Martin, timekeeper: 147–48, 153–56, 161
Marysville, Kansas: 28, 42, 226, 238, 240, 274
Masonic lodge: 13, 156
Masten ("Mastin"), Frederick H.: 128–29, 136
Matthews, teamster: 93, 108–109
Maxwell, Lucian B.: 95, 164, 306; Maxwell's Ranch, 138, 304, 306
May, Charles Augustus: 236, 242
Maynadier ("Menadier"), Henry Eveleth: 247
Medical Service: 34–35
Mendenhall, John, married Sophie Mix: 274–75
Mestos, Malquis, spy against Cheyennes: 212
Miller, Dr.: 240, 275
Miller, Private: 21, 23
Miller, Jim, head wagonmaster: 221, 263

Miller, "Old Jimmy," secretary Masonic lodge: 122
Miller, Josiah, editor, *Kansas Free State*, Lawrence: 178
Miller, Russell, & Cole, Salt Lake City: 265
Millersburg, Missouri: 12
Mills, D. O., financier: 219–20
Missouri Republican, newspaper: 60–61, 69
Mitchell, David Dawson: 60, 66–69, 73
Mix, John, foragemaster: 275
Monroe: *see* Munroe
Moore, Colonel, post trader, Fort Union: 307
Moore, Crawford: 178
Moore's Summit, Kansas: 178
Morehead & Allen: 314
Morgan, Negro interpreter: 28
Mormon Road: 258
Mormon War: 243; Utah Expedition, 229–76
Morris County, Kansas: 109
Morrison, Pitcairn: 235
Morrow, Jack: 280–81
Mount Muncie Cemetery: 17
Mount Pleasant, Kansas: 240, 275
Mounted Riflemen, Regiment of (later Third Cavalry): 38, 46, 67–68, 73, 111
Mud Creek, Utah: 267; Mud Creek, Wyoming, 194
Mules: in corral, 215; endurance, 245, 310; management, 163–64, 278; with bell horse, 215, 295; four-mule team, 287; organizing pack train, 201–202; shoeing, 251–52; in stampede, 131–35; trailing, 48–55; train attacked, 82; weather perils, and protection, 256, 266
Muncie (Munsee) Indians: 17
Mundy, Isaac, and Mrs. Mundy: 13
Munroe ("Monroe"), John: 235–36, 248
Murphy, Dick and Joe: 77
Murphy wagon: 255
Musketoon: 87, 93, 107

Muster roll: 99

Nebraska City: 245, 268
Nemaha River, Kansas: 28, 226
Neosho River: 111
Nevada Gulch, Colorado: 278
Newman & Powers: 314
Nine Mile Camp: 168
Nine Mile Tree: 217, 221
Ninth Independent Battery of Missouri Light Artillery: 298
Ninth Kansas Cavalry: 291, 298–99, 308
Norris, Charles E.: 253–54
North Platte River: 45, 48–49, 55, 67, 213–14, 217, 244, 250–51, 271–73, 321; ferry, 48–49, 55

Oak Creek, Nebraska: 274
Ocate, New Mexico: 307
Odometer: 308
O'Fallon's Bluffs, Nebraska: 221–22, 244
Ogden, Edmund Augustus: 28–29, 95–96, 143–48, 155, 160; death of, 148; monument, 164–66
O'Meara, Edward: 38–40, 46–48, 55, 57, 75, 94, 106, 118
O'Neil, Private: 114
Oregon Trail: 27
Orton, wagonmaster: 147–48, 159
Osage Indians: 103, 108–109; attack wagon train, 103
O'Shea, Private: 7–8, 10–12, 21, 23
Overland (Pikes Peak) Coach: 277
Ox Train No. 60: 259
Ozakee, Kansas: 27

Pacific Creek: 267
Pacific Springs Creek: 256, 268
Pack saddles, pack train: 201–202
Page, Francis Nelson: 235, 263
Palermo, Kansas: 227
Palmer, John M.: 84
Palmer, killed in Quantrill raid: 313
Papan's (Pappan's) Ferry, Kaw River: 27, 37, 81, 86

Index

Paperwork, army: 99, 139
Patrick, wagoner: 217, 226
Pawnee Fork of Arkansas River: 90, 95, 102, 298
Pawnee Indians: 30, 32–35, 63, 73; fights with, 30–31, 90; scouts with Sumner, 186, 192; fight Sioux, 241
Pawnee Rock, Kansas: 82, 298
Pay, army: 21, 38, 99, 122
Peck, Robert Morris: 217, 228
Peel, Langford M.: 30–31, 83, 87, 89–94, 99, 107–108, 113–15, 121–22, 137, 140–41
Peel, Mrs. Langford M.: 140–41
Peel, Percival Lowe: 141
Perkins, Delavan Duane: 225–26n.
Perkins, John N.: 225–26
Perry, Charles A., of Weston: 77; C. A., sutler, 10th Infantry, 265
Phillips, Fielder, rancher: 321–22
Phillips, Dr. Samuel: 160, 241, 310
Picketwire River: *see* Purgatoire River
Pikes Peak Gold Rush: 249, 278
Pilot Knob, Kansas: 17
Pittsburg (Pittsburgh), Pennsylvania: 11, 243
Platte Bridge (Camp Payne): 250–51, 264, 271
Platte City: 19
Platte County, Missouri: 13, 184, 228–29, 277, 282
Platte River: 28, 30, 34, 197, 205, 222, 242, 245, 273
Plum Buttes (Sand Buttes): 101–102
Plum Creek: 273
Plumb, daguerreotypist of Boston: 3
"Poison Springs Country": 251
Pole (Lodgepole) Creek: 194, 207, 209, 212–14
Pope, John, "Headquarters in the Saddle" order: 318–19
Porter, Fitzjohn: 224–25, 263
Portland, Missouri: 11, 15
Potawatomi (Pottawatomie) Indians: 73, 74, 96

Powers, Otero, Lowe & Co.: 314
Prairie Apaches: 103, 106
Prairie chickens: 222–23
Prince, Henry: 259
Prison, military: 26
Prisoners, army: 79
Provo Cañon, Utah: 258, 261
Provo City, Utah: 261
Provo River: 258, 261
Provost sergeant: 79
Pueblo, Colorado: 185
Purgatoire ("Purgetwa") River, called Picketwire: 136, 303–304
Pyle, interpreter: 105–106

Quantrill ("Quantrell"), William C. raids Lawrence: 313
Quartermaster's Department: xiv–xv; Lowe serves in, 142–276
Quicksand crossings: 40, 44–45, 187–90, 198, 244
Quintin, E. L., teamster: 240; death, 275

Ransom, Robert: 168–69
Rations, army: 19, 32, 74–75
Raton Pass route: 138, 302, 305, 319
Rattlesnakes, hunted by Sioux squaws for food: 205; bite fatal to Kit Carson's nephew, 305
Rayado ("Riado"), New Mexico: 19, 21, 95; camp at, 138; garrison, 139, 141
Read ("Reed"), Horatio N. F.: 298–300
Red Cloud Agency, Nebraska: 319–21
"Red Legs" (Red Legged) Scouts: 284, 290
Red River: 138
Reed, paymaster clerk: 39, 42, 57
Reed, wagonmaster: 291–92
Republican River: 32–33, 95, 147, 150, 156, 161
Reynolds, Indian trader: 204
Rhett, Thomas Grimke: 56, 67
Rhett, Mrs. Thomas Grimke: 56–59
Rialto Ferry, Missouri River: 233

Rice, J. S., wagonmaster: 140; freighting partner, 313
Rice County, Kansas: 81, 101
Rich, Hiram, sutler: 24
Riddick, Richard H.: 187, 190, 195, 199–200, 202–209, 211–12, 215, 221–23, 227
Riecke, William: 282
Ringo, Lot W.: 13
River crossing: 199–201; in quicksand, 40, 44–45, 187–90, 198, 244
Roberts, carpenter: 178–81
Roberts, Joseph ("Jo Bobs"): 250–51, 271
Robertson, Beverly: 6–7
Robinson, Charles, governor of Kansas: 182–84
Robinson, Jack, trading post: 256
Robinson, teamster and cook: 264
"Rocky Mountain Rangers" (Second Colorado): 302
Rocky Ridge Road: 255, 268
Rogers, Private: 23
Roll call at retreat: 99, 110; at tattoo, 81, 115
Roosevelt, Theodore: 127
Rough Riders (First U.S. Volunteer Cavalry): 126–27
Routh, Simeon ("Sim"), teamster: 196, 198, 203, 223, 228
Rush Valley: 262
Russell, John ("Sallie"): 38–40, 43, 46–48, 55, 57, 75, 118
Russell, William H.: 276
Russell, Majors & Waddell: 241, 245, 256, 266, 282; Majors & Russell, 211, 215
Rustlers of cattle: 315–16

Sacket, Captain, in Kansas War: 178
Saddles and pack saddles: 62, 201
St. Johnsberg, Pennsylvania: 11
St. Joseph, Missouri: 28
St. Louis, Missouri: 11, 15, 255
St. Mary's Mission, Kansas: 96, 152
Salina, Kansas: 289–91, 297

Saline River: 309
Salt Creek Valley, Kansas: 17, 96, 115, 144, 163, 184, 232, 234
Salt Lake, Salt Lake City, Utah: 218, 231, 257–58, 264
Salt Lake Mail: 267
Santa Fe Railway: 83, 315
Santa Fe Trail: 27–28, 83, 96, 164, 185, 297, 301, 308
Sarcoxie, Delaware guide: 223
Sarpie (Sarpa), Indian trader: 32
Satanta (Sawtanta), Kiowa chief: 87–88, 104–106, 300
Sawtelle, Charles Greene: 235
Sawyer, Philip, teamster: 240, 275
Sawyer & McIlvain (McIlwain), of Cincinnati, contractors at Fort Riley: 144, 146–50, 152, 155–56, 164–65
Scott, Captain, acting quartermaster, Fort Riley: 286–87
Scotts Bluffs ("Scotch Bluffs"), Nebraska: 45, 56, 196
Second Cavalry: 294; see also Second Dragoons
Second Colorado: 283, 309; Company F, 299, 306–307
Second Dragoons: 5, 166, 186, 190, 225–26, 245, 254; Companies E and H, 86, 190
Sedgwick, John: 185–86, 195, 199–201, 222–24, 226, 231, 312
Semino's Cut-off: 255, 268
Seneca, Kansas: 28, 226
Seventh Cavalry: 323
Seventh Infantry: 37, 223, 236
Sharp, in charge of horse train: 306
Shawnee Indians: 17
Shehan, wagonmaster: 291
Shoemaker, William R.: 307
Shoemaker, Miller & Co.: 313
Shoshone (Snake) Indians: 63–68, 71–72
Sibley, Ebenezer Sprote: 170
Sibley, Henry Hopkins: 3–4, 253–54
Sibley tent: 254, 263
Sidney, Nebraska: 319

Index

Silver Creek, Utah: 259–60
Silver Lake, Kansas: 73–74, 96, 153, 291
Simmons, James, surgeon: 146, 161
Simpson, James Hervey: 258
Sioux Indians: 33, 50–54, 62–68, 71–72, 203, 205; visit to Sioux camp, 50–54; fight with Pawnees, 241; beef contract, 319, 321
Sixth Infantry: 37, 39, 186, 235; Company B, 38, 218; Company C, 191, 218, 221; Company D, 58, 84, 102, 191, 218, 221; Company G, 46, 68–69, 191, 218, 221; Band, 146
Smart, First Sergeant: 9
Smith, a butcher: 194
Smith, Dan, of Denver: 278
Smith, John, Indian trader: 44–45
Smith, L. T., partner in horses and mules: 313
Smith, William Duncan: 186
Smith's Fork of the Green: 212, 256
Smoky Hill River: 95, 161, 289, 296
Snake (Shoshone) Indians: 63–68, 71–72
Snake Root Creek: 226
Soldier's Creek, Kansas: 27, 96
Soldiers' Home, at Fort Leavenworth: 18; in Washington, 122
Solomon ("Soloman"), Owen Fort: 274
Solomon's Fork of the Kaw, Sumner's fight at: 220
South Fork of Pawnee Fork of the Arkansas (Angel Spring): 90
South Fork Peaks: 196
South Pass, Wyoming: 256, 268
South Platte River: 44–45, 185–86, 195, 198, 206–209, 212, 221, 244, 273
Speck-in-the-Eye, chief of Pawnee Scouts: 186
Split Rock: 252
Spotted Tail: 319–20
Spotted Tail Agency: 319–20
Spring Creek, Kansas: 226, 292–93, 295
Stampede: 131–35, 194, 199
Stanbury, Howard: 35
Stanley, assistant wagonmaster: 217, 222

Stanton, Edwin M.: 312
Steptoe, Edward Jenner: 117–18
Stewart of Salt Lake City: 265
Stockton, Philip: 226–27
Story, Nelson: 248
Stranger Creek, Kansas: 27, 170; Big Stranger, 178; Little Stranger, 178
Stuart, James Ewell Brown: 167–68, 184–85, 187, 189, 220–21, 230–31, 318–19
Sturgis, Samuel Davis: 226–27
Sublette, fur trader: 216
Sulphur Springs, Utah: 259
Summers, Dr. John Edward: 222, 242, 273
Sumner, Edwin Vose: 16–18, 29–30, 167–68, 185–87, 190, 197–98, 200–201, 204, 206, 208, 212–14, 217–18, 220–22, 227–28, 236
Sweetwater (Sweet Water), New Mexico: 307–308; Wyoming, 251–53, 268
Swift, Dr. Ebenezer: 248–49, 273

Talbot, Private: 20–21
Tallmadge ("Talmadge"), Grier: 264–65, 269–72
Tarry All, Colorado mining camp: 278
Tattoo, bugle call: 77, 81, 115
Ten Mile Rock, Utah: 259
Tenth Infantry: 218–19
Terry, L. G.: 289
Theater, army amateur: 23, 77
Thespian Society, army: 23, 77
Third Cavalry: 38, 67; *see also* Mounted Riflemen, Regiment of
Thirty-two Mile Creek, head of Big Blue: 241, 273, 282
Thomas, Dr. M. S.: 135
Timpanogos Cañon, Utah: 258–59, 261
Timpas, Colorado: 136, 303–304
Tompkins, Daniel D.: 276
Tonganoxie, Delaware chief: 178–79
Topeka, Kansas: 27, 73, 170
Trinidad, Colorado: 136, 305
Turkey hunting: 137–38, 309–10

Turnley, Parmenas Taylor: 237, 257–58
Two Mile Creek: 232

Underwood, wagonmaster: 291
Uniform, in field: 83
Union Pacific Railroad, Eastern Division (Kansas Pacific): 313
Uniontown, Potawatomi village: 73–75
Utah Expedition (Mormon War): 229–76

Van Vliet, Stewart: 217–18, 234, 247
Van Vliet, William A.: 286–87, 307
Vedettes: 87, 93–94, 103, 130
Vermijo, New Mexico: 306
Vigil, Manuel, interpreter: 206–208, 211–14
Villepigue ("Vilipigne"), John Bordenave: 186

Waddell, William Bradford: 276
Wagner, Private: 7–12, 23
Wagon train, corral for defense: 204, 206, 209–10, 215, 242, 292–95; Espenscheidt wagon, 255; organization and management, 162–64, 238–40, 250; inspection, 240; pay, 291; personnel, 238–40; river crossing, 189–90, 199–201; troubles, 243–44, 255, 260; Utah expedition, 238–40, 276; Wilson wagon, 243, 255; Young wagon, 255
Walker, Captain Sam: 172–73
Walker, William, filibuster: 118
Wallingford, Perry: 77, 122
Wallis ("Wallace"), Captain John: 173–74
Walnut Creek, Kansas: 40–42, 81–82, 101–102, 111–12, 220, 298, 301
Ward, Seth Edward, sutler: 191
Warm Spring (Springs): 255, 268
Water Holes, Colorado: 136
Weis, William: 299–300, 302, 306, 307–308

Wharton, Henry W.: 28–29, 44, 186
Weber River, Utah: 259–60, 266
Weston, Missouri: 77, 79, 118, 121–22, 157, 233
Westport, Missouri: 12, 167, 169
Wheaton, Frank: 202, 223, 227
Whisky drinking: 20, 79–80, 97
Whitehorn, Dr. Samuel: 156, 160
Whittier, California: 228
Wiggins, Private, drowned: 59
Wilderness, Battle of: 21
Williams, Robert: 129
Willow Creek: 194
Wilson, Attorney General of Utah and Mrs. Wilson: 267–68
Wilson, John, wagonmaster: 239–42, 244, 249, 252, 255, 291
Wilson, Levi, general superintendent of teams: 142, 163, 208, 275, 277; his father Dr. Wilson, 208, 232
Wilson, Robert, sutler: 150
Wilson wagon: 243, 255
Winchester, Kansas: 27
Wisconsin battery (9th): 298
Wood, Corporal: 14–15
Wood, Brevet Major: 148, 164; Mrs. Wood and two children die of cholera, 154–56
Wood, Leonard: 127
Wood River: 32, 34
Worrel, Private: 20
Worrel (Worrell), Sergeant, deserter and murderer: 100–101, 140
Wyandotte County, Kansas: 13
Wyandotte Hills, Missouri: 16
Wyandotte Indians: 17

Young, Brigham: 265
Young, Merrit L.: 77
Young wagon: 255

Zimmerman, in Kansas War: 178–80